WHOSE WELFARE?

WHOSE WELFARE
Private Care Or Public Services?

Peter Beresford and Suzy Croft

68 Grand Parade, Brighton.
Telephone: (0273) 673416.

First published in 1986 by
The Lewis Cohen Urban Studies at Brighton Polytechnic
68 Grand Parade, Brighton, BN2 2JY, East Sussex.

British Library Cataloguing In Publication Data

Beresford, Peter
  Whose welfare: private care or public services?
  1. Public welfare — Great Britain
  2. Social service — Great Britain
  I. Title   11. Croft, Suzy   III. Social Services and the Community Action-Research Project
  361.941   HV245
  ISBN 0-948992-00-X

Design by Fiona Keating

Typeset in 9/11pt Palatino Med by Lasso Co-operative

Printed and bound by Russell Press

CONTENTS

Acknowledgements   vi
Hanover Patch Map   viii
Foreword *by Tim Cook*   xi
Introduction — Seeing Welfare Through Different Eyes   xiii

Part 1: Learning From Local Experience
1. Patch Based Social Services   3
2. Hanover Patch   12
3. An Empowering Approach To Research   20

Part 2: A New Approach To Social Services?
4. People And Social Services   29
5. People And The Patch Reorganisation   49
6. People And Community   78
7. People, Care And Support   102
8. Social Services, Patch And People's Needs   158
9. Social Services, Patch And Accountability   198

Part 3: Involving People In Change
10. Putting Patch Into Perspective   261
11. Our Welfare: A Framework For Citizen Involvement   288

    Appendices
1. Research Method   336
2. The Interview Schedule   344
Notes and References   349
Further Reading   381

ACKNOWLEDGEMENTS

This book arose out of our longstanding commitment to explore and improve people's say and involvement in services. In 1980, one of us (PB) was awarded a two year research fellowship created by the Frederick Soddy Trust and based at the University of Sussex. The initial brief was to examine the relationship locally between statutory and voluntary welfare services — in the wake of the Wolfenden Report on the future of voluntary organisations. The major reorganisation of social services in East Sussex to a "community-orientated, patch-based" way of working became the focus of the study. Subsequently the project has been based at the Lewis Cohen Urban Studies Centre at Brighton Polytechnic, where for one year, one of us was employed part-time under an MSC Community Programme. Since then the project has been unfunded.

With the help of the General Secretary of the Brighton Council for Voluntary Service, East Sussex Social Services were approached for their co-operation in carrying out the local Hanover study that is the subject of this book. A detailed proposal was developed. The Area Manager, Team Manager and patch team expressed their support and the local Hanover Community Association also offered their cooperation. Sadly at this point the Director of Social Services decided he could not extend the project his Department's cooperation or support, and it is on this basis that it has subsequently been carried out.

Our own lack of resources means that we have particularly many thanks to offer. Because the project was unfunded and we wanted to publish this first study from it locally and independently, we decided to do this by public subscription, subscribers receiving a copy of the book and being kept in touch with other developments from the project. This approach also coincided with the participatory philosophy underpinning the project.

We want to thank the hundreds of individuals and organisations who responded and through their subscriptions, loans and gifts have made publication possible. Writing this book and carrying forward the project without funding has been a difficult and stressful task for us both. The positive response we have had has been enormously encouraging. Support has been wide-ranging, both local and from further afield, and including service workers, managers, members of voluntary organisations, community and user groups, local people, trainers, students, councillors and friends.

It has been heartening to find so many people who share our commitment to participation in services and who have given their support. Just as important are the many others who have supported this project without sharing our philosophy or perspective, but who nevertheless have been concerned to help this book become part of public debate.

We also want to thank other individuals and agencies for their help: the Frederick Soddy Trust and University of Sussex; Hanover Community Association and QueenSpark; Brighton Council for Voluntary Service, particularly John Bishop, Helen Kahn and Alan Farleigh; Selma Montford, Director of the Lewis Cohen Urban Studies Centre for her support and kindness, as well as all the Centre workers who have helped, particularly Monica Willis and Marion Devoy; Mrs Winnie Wheeler, Mrs Rosie Sullivan and the late Mrs Edie Haynes for permission to include part of their discussion about "the good old days" of Hanover; Dave Wadcock for giving substance to the idea of public subscription by his early and invaluable aid, Zena Brabazon for her help, Tim Cook for his longstanding encouragement and David Bartlett for the many insights he has given us.

There are two people we want to single out for special mention, without whose help we don't think this book would ever have been finished. First Maggie Hilton, for the understanding and support she has given us which have helped to keep us going, and second Alan Stanton, who has really shown what collaborative working means by all his efforts in editing our text, and encouraging us to develop and improve what we have written.

Finally, we would like to dedicate this book to the people primarily concerned; the Hanover patch team and associated workers, and the service users and local residents they serve, particularly the 100 people whose comments form the basis of this study.

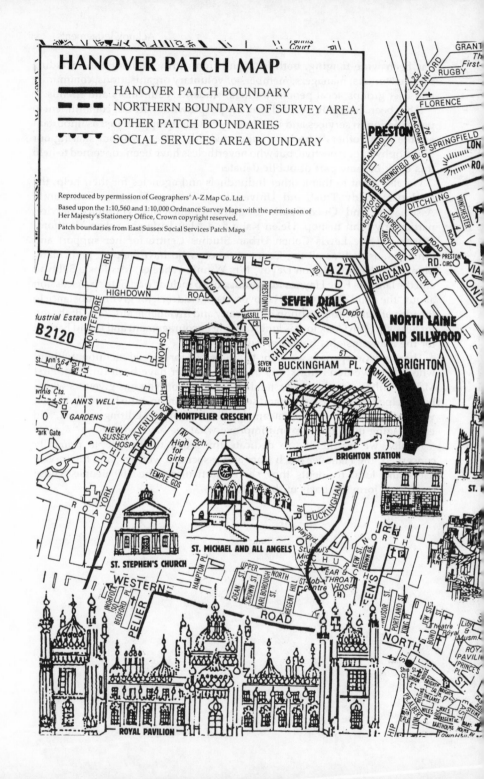

HANOVER PATCH MAP

▬▬▬▬ HANOVER PATCH BOUNDARY
▬ ▬ ▬ NORTHERN BOUNDARY OF SURVEY AREA
▬▬ ▬▬ OTHER PATCH BOUNDARIES
▪▪▪▪ SOCIAL SERVICES AREA BOUNDARY

Reproduced by permission of Geographers' A-Z Map Co. Ltd.

Based upon the 1:10,560 and 1:10,000 Ordnance Survey Maps with the permission of Her Majesty's Stationery Office, Crown copyright reserved.

Patch boundaries from East Sussex Social Services Patch Maps

In Loving Memory of my Dear Dad
JOHN CROFT
1925-1985
and our good friend
BRIAN THOMPSON
1938-1978

FOREWORD

Tim Cook

There has not yet developed in this country a strong tradition of or commitment to talking with the recipients of major public services, collectively or individually, about what is planned for them, is happening or has happened to them. The barristers argue about the silent defendant in the dock, the medical students mutter over the hospital bed and the child-care case conference decides the future of a family in the absence of that family. We all can too easily talk down, around or about service users as if they were not there even if they are. Talking to them is more demanding, unsettling and more complicated.

The authors' have an unrivalled history of working out their deep-rooted belief in the absolute necessity of engaging with service users at all points of service development because of the conviction (which a lot of evidence supports) that public welfare services cannot be effective and efficient without true user participation. That such a position also has a respectable political underpinning can be seen as causal or coincidental. The fact remains that these vital and expensive public services strive to respond to each new wave of criticism but have, as Croft and Beresford would argue — and in this book amply demonstrate, repeatedly ignored one essential ingredient: top-down services too rarely allow for bottom-up influences.

The 'patch' growth industry of the last few years has produced more than its fair share of rhetoric, and attractive rhetoric is has been too. Perhaps its very attractiveness has inhibited the more detailed examination of the reality behind it. That gap has now been addressed by this detailed, perceptive and consistently questioning study. Starting with and building on the public's view of social services — in all their facets — the study shows how remiss the patch adherents have been in following through the logic of their own impassioned arguments. But more than that — as this is a study which is not in the business of scoring points — it shows in my view how we have all missed a golden opportunity to develop a real and effective partnership between the professional and the non-political lay elements.

To take one example, it seems clear that the patch boundaries may by no means coincide with how the public perceive their communities, and different boundaries might conceivably result in more effective services and closer public involvement in them. This and many other issues raised in the study would undoubtedly mean at one level more difficulties or at least complications for service planners. But then who are the services actually for, and is not a long-term perspective what public services have too often lacked?

From a sample of 100 the authors have raised a host of important issues central to a better understanding of public welfare. To those whom I can already hear saying the sample was too small or unrepresentative I can only respond by reflecting on how too often services have developed on the back of an anecdote, a single case, or one person's passionate but untested belief. This study is a salutary rejoinder to much that has hitherto gone largely unquestioned. For that reason I am sure, sadly, that not everyone will welcome it. But it is vitally necessary that the findings become part of the debate about the public welfare services we want.

Tim Cook was a member of the Barclay Committee on the role and tasks of social workers, Chaired the NCVO working party on clients' rights in the voluntary sector, and is now Clerk to the City Parochial Foundation.

INTRODUCTION

Seeing Welfare Through Different Eyes

"It seems that there may be another story waiting to be told..."[1]

It's a windy autumn day in Brighton. Mrs Davies slowly makes her way home up Albion Hill in Hanover. She's 82 and holding a half-filled carrier bag. She stops frequently, leaning on ledges, putting down her shopping and resting in doorways. She lives alone on supplementary pension. It's just over half a mile to the seafront where she paddled as a girl, but more than five years since she's been there. It's the other side of the seaside postcard.

She and her generation, surviving into their eighties and nineties in unprecedented numbers, are now being seen as the biggest problem facing social services. They lived through two world wars and the hardships of the 1920s and '30s. The creation of the "welfare state" was owed to their suffering and determination. Yet now that they are old and particularly in need of its services, these have been called into question and cut.

In a period of fundamental economic, political and social change, welfare has once more been thrown into the melting pot. "Public choice" and the role of the state have again come to prominence as central questions of concern. New solutions and initiatives are being offered for them in both economic and social policy. It is one such in personal social services, "patch" or "community social work" — the terms are used interchangeably to describe overlapping ideas — that we discuss in this book.

Patch has been hailed as a major new development in social services. With its commitment to localisation and public involvement, it raises in microcosm many of the broader issues now confronting citizens and public policies. These include new approaches to management and organisation, changed social relations, reduced and restructured employment, the redistribution of power, and an altered equilibrium between state and market. The particular patch reorganisation we have studied is one of the largest and most comprehensive so far. This account is rooted in a locality, but for that reason has a much wider relevance.

Its starting point was talking with people like Mrs Davies who live in one part of Brighton. Studies of welfare are often disconnected from the lives and struggles of the people involved. There is a "hierarchy of credibility" which attaches more weight to official, professional and academic accounts of events and experiences than to those of people on the receiving end, whether as local residents, service users or lower status workers.[2] A basic aim of this book and the project it is part of was to challenge this. There are strong practical and philosophical arguments for giving priority to the views of ordinary people in discussions and developments which concern their needs and the services ostensibly intended to meet them. This is particularly so in the case of an initiative like patch, which itself places special stress on "community involvement", "accessibility" and "participation".

Patch raises a wide range of issues where such grassroots perspectives are at a premium. Centrally, it confronts the nature of "community", the sources and implications of people's support and the wants they have. The relationship of patch to cuts in social and other state services also needs to be discussed, especially since concepts like "self-help", "neighbouring" and "voluntarism" have become far more overtly political.

This study has several focuses. One is the views and experience of a hundred people living in one neighbourhood; another the county-wide reorganisation of social services that affects them. A third are the debates and developments at academic and political levels that are the context of both.

The book is therefore a synthesis of local study, political analysis, academic review and practical guide. It brings together a number of subjects and concerns that are often dealt with separately although they are closely inter-related. These include biography, the politics, history and ideology of welfare — ranging from feminist to right-wing interpretations, and the practicalities involved in changing policy and practice.

We also develop discussion on a number of specific topics to which patch and community social work draw us. Among these are:

- Decentralisation in social and other services
- People's own definitions of key concepts in patch and social policy
- The nature of people's needs and the relation of social and other services to them
- The move from public services to private care — by both commercial provision and women's unpaid labour
- The limitations of traditional research methods and methodology and the need for alternatives
- Key issues of work, including: women, work and caring; the implications of shifts from paid to unpaid work; and collaborative working, both within an agency and between it and the wider world
- Public accountability and democratisation: the say and involvement people have and want in services
- Services and social relations: issues of gender, race and disability; discrimination, dependence and independence.

Trying to make the connections posed by patch means that we have had to attempt an ambitious task. As well as being a platform for the comments of the people we spoke to, this study draws on our participation in training and wider discussions about patch and public services and our experience and involvement over a period of years with other people and groups in community organisations and community action.

We should also say what this study is not. It does not pretend to be a definitive statement of service users' and local people's views or needs in the way that "needs surveys" sometimes purport to be. Instead what we hope to do is engage with the philosophy of patch and community social work at its most ambitious; as it seeks a partnership between the service providers and users and other local people.

This book then, is offered as a means of raising ideas and issues for broader discussion and action, and of engaging vital but neglected perspectives. Because of the commitment of patch and community social work to participation and dialogue, we hope that the comments and views we report will be accepted as part of such a process.

The book's structure is straightforward. It falls into three parts. In the first chapter, we discuss the development and principles of patch and describe East Sussex's patch reorganisation. Next we offer a pen portrait of the case study area and its people and the local patch social services. In chapter three we discuss briefly the research method we have used.

The second and main part of the book is concerned with what the local people we surveyed had to say about social services, patch and themselves. Chapters four and five focus on their knowledge, experience and attitudes first to social services and second to the patch reorganisation and some key patch principles. Next we report on the meanings for them of two key patch concepts; "community" and "care", looking particularly at what caring and voluntary action mean in their lives and what they see them meaning for women, and relating this to feminist critiques of patch and caring. In chapter eight we discuss their definitions of their wants and needs and the relationship between them, patch based social services and broader policies and issues. Finally in this section, we explore people's perceptions of decision-making and accountability in social services, looking at what services they would like to see, what say they see people having and what they would prefer, comparing this with their experience in voluntary organisations.

The last section contains two exploratory chapters. In chapter 10 we take some of the issues raised by what people said and consider the implications much more broadly for patch, social services and public policy generally. The final chapter is intended to be a practical resource. It sketches a framework for citizen involvement which should be useful for people both within and outside agencies seeking to increase public say and involvement in services.

A word about the book's format. We have tried to make it accessible to a wide audience, avoiding unnecessary technical terms and simplifying numerical material. To avoid distracting readers with extensive footnotes, detailed notes and references are provided at the back of the book for those who are interested. Two appendices present our interview schedule and more detail about out research method. Finally we offer a short but wide-ranging guide to further reading.

We have given priority in this book to people's own words, so that as far as possible they can speak for themselves. Our aim has not only been to draw people like Mrs Davies into the picture, but also to enable them to play a part in changing it.

1.
LEARNING FROM
LOCAL EXPERIENCE

CHAPTER ONE

Patch Based Social Services

THE BACKGROUND TO PATCH

Patch was already being talked about in the British Journal of Social Work in 1974.[1] In 1979 Hadley and McGrath described five social work teams which "were adopting small sub-teams operating on a patch or neighbourhood basis, and aiming to give a high priority to collaboration with other local agencies and all forms of voluntary action in the development of a more preventative approach".[2]

In fact Hadley and McGrath's work has not only had an important research and recording function, but acted as catalyst for the widespread development of patch. In 1980 in two Patch Bulletins, they reported on over 40 patch based teams.[3] In the same year, they edited the influential "Going Local", an account of seven patch schemes,[4] and subsequently Hadley became a key member of the Barclay Committee reviewing social work. Evidence to this Committee included research which identified 218 area teams said to be organised on patch lines.[5] In its 1982 report, the Committee duly endorsed patch systems as one of "the methods of applying its recommendations for the development of 'community social work'".[6] Patch is the most discussed and developed form of community social work. By 1984 Hadley and Cooper were able to talk of a "prolific growth in types and overall number" of patch teams over the previous three and a half years.[7] Their third Patch Bulletin now reported more than 250 such schemes.[8]

Patch based social services need to be seen in the context of broader discussions about welfare and the role of the state. They must also be set within personal social services generally; their origins, role and nature, and the needs to which they are intended to respond.

Unprecedented government cuts in social spending have triggered off the greatest debate on "the welfare state" in Britain since its creation. Other influences, however, have also been at work. Arguments for "welfare pluralism" or a "mixed economy of welfare" have burgeoned under monetarist economics, but they have also captured a broader imagination. On the political left there has been longstanding ambivalence about public welfare — whether to see it as an outcome of popular struggle or method of social control. To this has been added an increasing consciousness of its failure to respond to people's needs and wants without radical reappraisal and reform. At the same time there have been major debates within the personal social services, particularly in social work, over the competing claims of "specialism" and "genericism";[9] "community social work" and "social casework".[10]

Patch can be seen as the expression in social services of two important developments. First there has been a rekindling of concern for public participation and second, a rethinking of how needs are met collectively. Patch is part of the new welfare pluralist tradition which emphasises a *plurality* of sources for welfare: statutory, voluntary, informal — and less often mentioned commercial. Its advocates emphasise the impracticality of state welfare meeting all needs, especially at a time when not only are drastic cuts being made to public services and workforce, but the very idea of welfare state services is being questioned by central government.

Proponents of the patch approach, echoing welfare pluralist themes, argue that it questions the emphasis in traditional social services department organisation on bureaucratic and professional conceptions of service delivery and present centralised hierarchic organisations that have been created to apply them. In rationales offered for patch, emphasis is placed on concepts of decentralisation, participation, mutual aid and voluntary action.

PRINCIPLES OF PATCH

Within these broad ideas, the advocates of patch have spelled out remarkably clearly how they hope it will work and what it can achieve. While we would not expect unanimity in the conception and definition of a major new development, there seems to have been a surprising degree of consensus over the detailed framework put forward, probably because a relatively small number of academics and managers have played a key part in its development. It is extremely valuable, therefore, to look at this more closely as a way of appreciating the background to the East Sussex scheme.

1. Localisation

The essence of patch is locality. This has two practical aspects; locally based teams and focus on a limited geographical area. The minority Barclay Report endorsing neighbourhood based social work preferred "a base within the area" or for staff to work from "a sub-office on their patch". Failing that it suggested that staff "may have the use of rooms on the patch where people can call in to see them".[11] On size, Hadley and McGrath have consistently advocated a population of 5-10,000 as ideal, although recently they have talked in terms of a "wider population range".[12] This compares with the Seebohm Report's 50,000-100,000 or the 25-50,000 of a conventionally organised social services area.[13] Hadley and McGrath relate team size to its task within the area: "The team should have the capacity to obtain detailed information about the patch".[14] They have also been clear about the underlying philosophy that would govern the patch team's relation with its department, arguing for:

> The abandonment of existing assumptions about the automatic superiority of the large scale bureaucracy as the principle mode of organisation, and the readiness to explore the potential of more decentralised, flexible structures.[15]

2. Greater Autonomy for Local Teams

Following on from Hadley and McGrath's comment, we find them advocating "participatory forms of management in patch and area teams" and "the exercise of a substantial degree of autonomy by patch and area teams" as an essential feature.[16]

3. Integration of Patch Workers

The minority Barclay Report pressed for wider roles for all staff, and proposed patch teams where field social workers were joined by home helps, street wardens and social work assistants, with closer integration of residential, day care and field services on a local basis.[17] Hadley and McGrath have advocated "the integration of all field and domiciliary workers within patch teams" and "a broader, more open definition of professionalism which has room to recognise the full potential of lay workers within the services".[18] Cooper made the point even more forcibly about the Normanton experiment, emphasising how a patch system raised the status of social work assistants and home helps who were "seen as capable, caring and intelligent people rather than skivvies".[19] Hadley and Cooper now also stress the need for the use of "integrated social work methods" and role flexibility within teams.[20]

4. A Community Orientation

As well as closer links and coordination between social services departments, other statutory agencies and voluntary organisations in an area, a major theme of patch is that "informal helping networks" should be used and supported. There is "acknowledgement of the present contribution and future potential of the community to provide a whole range of services for itself".[21] Jennifer Joslin, writing about a patch scheme in the London borough of Islington, stressed how crucial informal networks become — as "the national situation grows more difficult so the pressures in a community like ours will grow". For the patch strategy, "Our long term aim is to enable people to deal more effectively with their own and their neighbour's problems".[22] The objective here is to optimise the mix between statutory and voluntary organisations and the informal support that people extend to each other.[23] This approach is presented as a "community" rather than "client" centred orientation for social services departments.

5. Participation

There have been a number of positive statements about the potential for patch to bring "opportunities…for people to participate directly in formulating the help they need".[24] As Hadley and Cooper have pointed out, not all schemes "look beyond to the more formal decentralisation of power and the growth of neighbourhood democracy".[25] Yet such advocates of patch still stress that acceptability to the patch population is essential and urge "the right of local communities to share in decision-making about service priorities."[26]

PATCH IN EAST SUSSEX

> East Sussex Social Services Department is grasping the nettle for a partnership with the community.*
> *Director of Social Services, East Sussex, 1982.*[27]

East Sussex's patch reorganisation officially "became operational" on November 2nd 1981. Roger Hadley, who acted as consultant to the reorganisation, heralded it as:

> A carefully planned system of local teams covering the whole authority and integrating field, domiciliary, day and residential services in teams serving patches averaging populations of about 16,000.[28]

Four years earlier, East Sussex County Council had adopted a new social services policy which was firmly committed to "community care". It also aimed to invest more resources in prevention "to avert or postpone the need for more comprehensive and costly services"; to reduce administrative costs and improve central control of the service through more direct chains of accountability.[29] No reference was made in it to patch, but patch was the method which the Department and its new Director adopted to implement it.

---

* All quotations, except where otherwise stated, are from the Hanover residents we interviewed.

East Sussex covers an area of almost 1,125 square miles and has a population of about 641,000, over 80 per cent of whom live in urban areas, largely in the five major coastal towns of Eastbourne, Bexhill, Hastings, Brighton and Hove. East Sussex is a well known retirement area. Indeed it reputedly has the highest concentration of old people in Europe.[30] 28.4 per cent of the population are above retirement age compared with the national average of 17.7 per cent. Even more important for Social Services, almost 40 per cent of people over retirement age are aged 75 or more, accounting for 11 per cent of the County's overall population.

Two basic aims have underlain East Sussex Social Services' reorganisation; localising services and cutting costs. As the Department's Director and consultant have written, "the most radical feature of this scheme was the integration of virtually all field, domiciliary, day and residential services in small patch teams".[31] The County was divided into 45 patches initially, each to have a locally based team, with populations ranging from under 4,000 to over 25,000 people. Patches were grouped into 11 areas, reduced to nine by 1982 budget cuts, and two divisions, East and West. Except in the case of Brighton, these areas coincide with those of district councils. Each area has its own area manager, with two area managers (health) responsible for liaising with the three health districts covering East Sussex. New posts of team manager, one to each patch team, were created by combining the roles of social services manager and team leader. Team managers are responsible for local field work, domiciliary, residential and day care services.

The official intention is for "a gradual move towards 48 locally based and hospital based social services teams each covering a small area of the county", and "a centralised administration". According to the Department:

In practical terms, the structure produces a more effective, more streamlined administration — one which is able to take the department confidently through the 1980's and one which makes a positive contribution to the quality of services we provide to people in need of our help[32]

Describing the reorganisation in "Community Care", Whitehouse wrote:

The function of senior management (the director, deputy, and three assistant directors) was to provide development and support, determine overall policies and resource planning for the department as a whole, and to monitor and evaluate performance.

The day to day management was clearly to be the responsibility of the teams themselves, the 9 area officers' role being to co-ordinate team activities and to liaise across boundaries.[33]

While the formal emphasis in patch generally and in East Sussex specifically is on "community orientation", "accessibility" and local involvement — indeed the Department uses the terms patch and community social work interchangeably — the East Sussex reorganisation has followed a conventional line management model of organisation, with strengthened management and centralised control. It was officially recognised in planning and reorganisation that a three division restructuring would "better recognise the influence of our main centres of population (Brighton, Eastbourne and Hastings)", ensure "the centres of control in the eastern part of the County would be closer to the provision of services"; and "represent a slightly less traumatic change" for staff, but this was rejected, partly on grounds of cost.[34] The limits of local workers' autonomy seem to be clearly set. The Director of Social Services wrote:

> The action taken in East Sussex is to expect management at local level to make decisions within agreed policy. This is backed up by a clear detailed scheme of delegation to basic grade social work practitioners; allowing them clear decision-making ability, within organisationally approved areas of practice.[35]

We might ask whether "the agreed policy" will in any way develop from the grassroots or whether it will still come from middle and senior management and the Council. While East Sussex may have altered the shape of its hierarchy, it has certainly not done away with it. The unequal distribution of power is in the nature of hierarchies, if not their raison d'etre. This raises the second of the twin tensions in patch which account for much of its ambiguity; tensions between improving the meeting of need and cutting expenditure, and between hierarchical structure and local independence. The basis of East Sussex's move to patch has been of a wholesale reorganisation initiated and implemented from above, unlike the slower, evolutionary and more locally rooted reorganisations to community social work there have been, for example, in the London boroughs of Islington and Hammersmith and Fulham. East Sussex has not been alone in this. The third Patch Bulletin reports a "dramatic increase in the number of schemes initiated from the top".[36] This raises the question of whether this will mean the persistence in East Sussex and other such schemes of a "top-down", rather than the "bottom-up" approach to policy and decision-making that patch's advocates attribute to it.

PUTTING PATCH INTO PRACTICE

There have also been three other important developments in East Sussex's patch reorganisation. The Department has switched from seconding social workers to Certificate of Qualification in Social Work (CQSW) courses:

into a much broader based "in-house" development programme for all staff linked to a solid commitment to Certificate of Social Service training, linking trainees and front line managers on the same salary level to reinforce the department's commitment to people development.[37]

The "area development programme" it initiated was described by the Director as "a particularly significant part of the Department's training…following reorganisation" and reported in its own account of the reorganisation as "a model for change".[38]

The Department has also introduced computerised information systems for "monitoring and controlling performance" and established a media unit, later to become East Sussex Consultancy and Training Agency (ESCATA), with:

two study centres each located in a higher education establishment, each with access to production of media resources (up to twelve full length video productions per annum) and the services of a full time professional producer and graphics staff.[39]

While the Director of Social Services has written of East Sussex's new organisation becoming "fully operational" in November 1981,[40] it is probably more realistic and helpful to see patch reorganisation as a continuing process. Only a small number of teams had actually gone local at that time. Eighteen months later, less than half had. "Operational Guidelines" on "Patch Based Working", primarily intended for team managers were only published a month after the appointed day. Three years later, about three quarters of teams were in their patch, either having moved out or in existing offices. The Brighton teams were not all decentralised until the middle of 1985. By July 1985, the Department was reporting that the task of setting up patch offices throughout the County was "nearing completion".[41] But by the end of the year, more than four years after the appointed day, five teams had still to move and the operation did not look like being completed until 1987. Furthermore while it was originally decided that 16 teams could be satisfactorily located in existing offices, by 1985 pressure was growing from some of these teams coupled with others outside their own patch, to move to premises in the neighbourhood they served. An additional stage of decentralisation had also emerged, with call offices — sub-offices staffed at certain times in local facilities — beginning to be set up.

While the Director envisaged the decentralisation as a three years process, it is probably better seen as one with at least a five year time span.[42] Tying it to a particular date, however, should not blind us to the considerable undertaking that the reorganisation of services and redeployment of staff has been — especially at a time of expenditure cuts. As is readily acknowledged in East Sussex, "the development of a patch based approach is inevitably a slow process".[43]

Economy, however, continues to be offered as a reason for the localisation of teams, as for the restructuring generally, with the Council estimating "a saving of £780,000 on buildings and services over the next ten years".[44]

East Sussex's decentralisation has received considerable attention. Only Normanton's and Walsall's have gained more. Along with them, East Sussex Social Services have become part of the itinerary for local authorities planning or "going local".

Reactions to the reorganisation from within the Department have been mixed.

> So called "cynics" see it as a management exercise to get them to do more for less. Others (the so-called idealists) view it as a positive development, albeit with its problems (boundaries, resources etc...) and are prepared to work with it.[45]

The Director has stressed the gains for staff:

> Residential, day care and domiciliary staff feel much more part of the organisation than mere appendages. Professional decision-making is shared with a wider range of people, and thereby enriched. We are working from a much broader base.[46]

One Brighton social worker, reflecting an attitude common at the time of the reorganisation, wrote:

> One of the main changes is to do with the control that is exerted over us — the way that we work — and attempts to control the way that we organise as workers. Certainly in this recent reorganisation within Social Services, one of the main aims was really to try to control workers much more, and this was a direct result of workers expressing dissatisfaction with policies publicly: organising in Cuts Campaigns etc.
>
> It's couched in terms of reorganising the Department to provide a more efficient community-oriented patch based service, i.e. reorganising teams from a central base in the town out to small areas, one team covering a small area. Whereas before, Brighton was split into North and South, and people worked over the whole area, now teams are both smaller (made up of two to three social workers) and cover a smaller area. That's the way it's been presented. But it's also involved a massive shift around in managerial staff. The philosophy has been to undermine the power which field-workers have traditionally had. It's because field-workers have been the best organised and most vocal group that there is this kind of devaluing of our skills, and an attempt to crack down on meetings which involve workers across their little boundaries.[47]

Clearly there are differences of view about patch within the Department and many issues remain to be resolved. However, patch as implemented in East Sussex seems to accord with the model offered in the Barclay Report.[48] It is different from many other attempts to go local because of its scale, comprehensiveness and because the initiative and plan clearly came from the top. The question has been posed whether patch teams can "be successfully developed from on top".[49] Whatever the answer, the key criteria identified for patch; localisation, integration, wider staff roles and greater autonomy for local teams, could all be said to be present. Thus while East Sussex's reorganisation and the model of patch adopted cannot be taken to be typical or representative of others, they do offer a basis for a more general consideration of patch.

CHAPTER TWO
Hanover Patch

"There should be more accommodation for people in Brighton. We've got a pretty face, but our backstreets are an eye sore."

THE TOWN

Brighton's two faces are a recurring theme in accounts of the town. On the one side are the elaborate flower displays and the regency seafront with its elegant squares and crescent that the visitor sees. On the other, a degree of urban deprivation comparable with some of the most disadvantaged inner city areas and northern towns.[1]

Brighton's housing conditions put it among the top 10% of local authorities for overcrowding and lack of basic amenities.[2] A continuing characteristic of life in Brighton, largely resulting from its economic base as a service economy and resort/commuter town has been relatively low wages and high living costs. Its average wage rates are among the lowest in the country and it has a lower rate of employment expansion than the national average.

The 1981 Census showed that the constituency in which the Hanover patch was situated ranked in the top third of constituencies in Great Britain for male unemployment.[3] The problems facing women are even greater. Brighton was one of the first areas where women with children were required to prove alternative childcare arrangements to register as unemployed and available for work. According to the 1981 Census, the old Pier Ward in which the southern third of the Hanover patch is located, had an unemployment rate of 23.7%, more than twice the national average, and higher, for example, than that for Armagh or Ballymena in Northern Ireland.[4] Since then the number of people registered as unemployed in Brighton has increased by an average of about 1,000 each year.[5]

When we made our survey, East Sussex County Council and Brighton Borough Council had long been Conservative controlled. Since then their political complexion has radically changed. The Conservative group lost its overall majority in the Borough Council, and in the 1986 local elections, Labour became the largest single party. Since the 1985 County Council elections, East Sussex has had a hung Council.

THE PATCH

The Hanover patch area is close to the centre of town, only a short walk from the Royal Pavilion, antique shops, conference centre and seafront that make up the picture postcard view of Brighton.

We chose it for our survey for several reasons. First a detailed study of the needs of young people in that area had recently been undertaken which both complemented it and offered a basis to build on.[6]

Hanover is also not a part of Brighton normally identified as particularly deprived or disadvantaged, like, for example, Moulescoomb or Whitehawk, both of which have already had more than their fair share of research and publicity, as well as receiving particular attention in the patch reorganisation.[7] On the other hand, it does not reflect the affluence and advantage true of some districts of the town. The fact that it falls into neither extreme of poverty or plenty, social cohesion or dislocation, is likely to make it of the widest value and interest as a casestudy.

Furthermore, the patch includes a well established community association and community centre. When the patch reorganisation was planned, Hanover was an area that social workers were keen to move to because of the belief that there was a "strong community" locally and that "if patch would work anywhere, it would work there". Thus it seemed to offer a sympathetic environment for patch, with its emphasis on community and local networks.

Hanover patch is effectively divided into three by busy main roads and redevelopment. It is a predominantly residential area, without its own internal shopping centre. Housing density is very high, with little open space and few amenities for young people. It is built on steep hills which create particular problems for old people and people with disabilities, especially in the winter. Characteristic images of Hanover are women with small children hauling heavy shopping up the hills and old people carefully picking their way down them.

To the north, the patch is bisected by the main Lewes Road. Here it is a mixture of crescents, small streets, small and large houses, some grand, some neglected by their landlords. Hanover is mainly a mixture of private rented and owner-occupied housing.

The central area, which the Community Association serves, is that most closely identified with "Hanover". It is largely made up of small, attractive terraced houses in pleasant narrow streets, with a number of well-liked local pubs and a sprinkling of corner shops. It is part of the traditional Brighton working class residential area. Until the 1920s, most of Brighton's population was centrally located. In the 1930s, the Corporation embarked on policies of "slum clearance" and suburbanisation to outlying estates and areas. After the war, these accelerated, first under the wider powers of the 1947 Town and Country Planning Act and then with the large scale redevelopment of the 1960s and early 1970s. It is a pattern that has been repeated in many towns and cities with far-reaching consequences for neighbourhoods and networks.

The southern part of Hanover patch is an area that has borne the brunt of such policies. The result is a less pleasant, more mixed built environment, with a concentration of council housing; mainly houses built in the 1930s, and low and high rise flats from the sixties and early seventies. But while Hanover has not escaped the tower blocks and estates associated with inner city areas, generally these are not the grim, isolated and deteriorated blocks we have come to expect of them. Instead there are often flowers on the landings and less sense of a monolithic policy at work. The exception has been the Kingswood Milner flats. At the time of our survey, these inter-war walk-up blocks were stigmatic and unpopular. They have however recently been improved.

THE PEOPLE

Hanover is a mixed area. It is also an area in transition. It has a high proportion of working class old people, concentrated particularly in the central part of the patch. But in addition to its ageing working class population, the nature and price of its private housing has made it particularly popular with young, professional middle class first time house buyers, who have moved in in large numbers. A wide range of backgrounds and occupations are now represented locally. Manual and clerical workers have been joined by self-employed business people, lower middle managers, civil servants, and professionals in teaching, the media and social work, while commuters have joined the ranks of local workers. The first sign of the gentrification that has been taking place are the growing ranks of "for sale" signs. As Tomlinson has observed:

> The window pot-plants and the absence of downstairs net-curtains; the colour of the paintwork and the door; the lighting and the decor of openly visible lounge — all these are the cultural symbols of the invading middle-classes.[8]

This process of population change through gentrification, as well as earlier dispersal of the local population also reflects broader trends in a number of inner city areas. These are being reinforced by current government inner city policy of encouraging so-called "population mix" and private housing and investment, which actually reduces the stock of good quality housing available to people on lower incomes. This gives Hanover particular relevance for our understanding of the "inner city" more generally. It is also of importance to patch because of the ramifications of such social and demographic change to ideas and assumptions about networks, "community" and mutual aid.

PATCH AND OLD PEOPLE

Brighton has historically been a retirement area. It has the fifteenth highest percentage of pensioners living alone among local authorities, while *all* East Sussex authorities come within the top 10%.[9] The majority of old people are women, generally on low incomes. Housing and social services resources have been particularly concentrated on this elderly population. It has also meant that compared to other local authorities, rates have been consistently lower for education and higher for social services.[10]

The biggest single issue seen to face social services for the future is the rising demand envisaged from Britain's ageing population, with an increasing number of very old people in both absolute and relative terms. This concern comes from all sides of the political spectrum, both from those opposed to state welfare expenditure and its advocates. Patch and community social work are seen as offering at least part of the solution to the problem.

Hanover's high proportion of old people further adds to the insights it offers as a casestudy of patch. Old people and people with disabilities are likely to be seen as the major candidates for patch's emphasis on informal and voluntary aid. They already receive disproportionately little qualified social work support. Therefore it is particularly important to see what the ramifications of a move to patch may be for them.

PATCH, RACE AND RACISM

2.5 per cent of Brighton's population is black according to census data, although that is probably an under-estimate. There are also members of other ethnic minorities, for example, Jews, Bahais and Chinese people. Their relatively small numbers meant that the particular issues and problems black people and members of other ethnic minorities face in relation to patch and social and other services, could not be adequately explored in this study. Our sample, for example, included one Asian women and one woman of Italian origin.* However, these issues remain of paramount importance and as Brighton's Community Information Bulletin has argued, while areas like the south coast may be "very white", "white people have a knack of rendering black people invisible".[11] Furthermore racism is certainly a problem in Brighton, with actively racist political organisations as well as the more day to day oppression and prejudice typical of predominantly white areas. Race and racism are also issues for patch and social services, and while we could not develop them at neighbourhood level, we shall certainly focus on them in our wider discussions.

---

* See Appendix 1 for a more detailed statistical breakdown of the Hanover patch population.

THE PATCH SOCIAL SERVICES

> In East Sussex there is a recognition that you can't go patch simply by drawing new lines on a map. Being local is the *consequence* of a wholly different model of social services delivery.
> *Staff Officer, East Sussex Social Services Department*[12]

In the reorganisation, Brighton was divided into three social services areas, each with five patch teams. This was subsequently reduced to twelve teams through amalgamations. These were made partly because the teams involved were seen by the Department as too small and partly to save money by transferring resources from team manager posts to make up the full complement of home help organisers, one to each team.

Since then, Brighton's three areas have also been reduced to two; east and west, with two new area team structures. This reduces the total number of areas in East Sussex to eight. There is some speculation that the intention ultimately is for there to be only one social services area in the town.

All the Brighton teams are now in local offices. Hanover was the last to be decentralised, not moving to its new office until May 1985. It was a major problem for the Hanover team that it was not based in its patch during the crucial first three years. Even now its office is not actually on the patch, but instead separated from it by the wide and busy lanes of the main London road, and shared with another team. Its patch office may actually be *less* accessible for some Hanover residents than its previous home in the original centralised offices. Entry to the terraced building is by a flight of steps which clearly inhibit access. After the move, there was actually a drop in referrals, although in the months since, the numbers seem to have returned to their previous level. But there has not been the great increase in use reported by many teams in departments that have gone local.

While Hanover shares premises with another team, they have been reallocated from the old Central Area to *different* Areas, responsible to different area officers; Hanover to East and North Laine to West Area. It is not clear why this has been done, especially as there is the possiblity of later amalgamation along the lines we have already seen with several other small teams.

Another issue that has arisen as the office is now the only one in the town centre is that it has become the busiest in Brighton for callers. It is near to police, housing department, social security and other agencies, and people drop in unaware that the system has been localised. People's uncertainty and confusion about where to go, is an unexpected consequence of patch and one that needs to be understood and resolved. Here we can also see a possible tension between the aims of general decentralisation schemes to be localised and to offer people one central place where they can go.

Hanover team's move from the existing divisional offices was not given high priority in the reorganisation because they were considered close to the patch. Another reason for delay in "going local" was the inability of the Department to dispose of existing office space as quickly as expected, as the means to "balance the books" the Director envisaged.[13] As the Department's consultant has commented:

> You can operate for a limited period of time a locally focused team from a central base but you can't keep that going for too long. After a time people are going to get worn out driving backwards and forwards. Then you are into a real estate issue. The East Sussex patch system involved a £2m property deal, selling central offices and buying or building local offices.[14]

Patch Boundaries

Several, sometimes conflicting criteria, have been identified by the Department in the setting of patch boundaries. These include perceived local definitions of community, the nature of existing electoral boundaries, the number of referrals, social services establishments and caseloads in an area, as well as a desire "for the span of control of team managers not to exceed seven or eight people at the level below".[15] The Hanover patch boundaries do not appear to be based on or relate closely to other administrative, political or locally perceived boundaries. They do not, for example, accord with the ward boundaries operating either before or since the boundary reorganisation of May 1983. They have already been changed once, reducing the size of the patch, and further changes have been under consideration during the course of this study. The population of the patch, according to the 1981 census was more than 13,000,[16] making it considerably larger than the 5-10,000 optimum originally suggested by Hadley.[17] Hanover is the largest patch in terms of population in central Brighton, but as we have seen, about average in East Sussex, where some patches are as large as 24-25,000 people. Patch boundaries may still change, especially as they were fixed before most patch offices were located and may need to be altered in the light of their disposition.

Patch Working, Demands And Resources

For most of its life, to serve its patch, Hanover team has had three full time social workers, one unqualified "social services officer" (SSO), a home help organiser (until recently also responsible for two other patches), a team manager and two and a half team clerks. Also attached to the team were a social worker for under-fives who was an area resource and a court liaison social worker, with Brighton-wide responsibilities. The team's clerical staff also had to serve them. In line with practice in other areas of the County, the fostering and adoption team of Central Area, within which Hanover fell, was disbanded, and the team given an extra half-time childminding and fostering worker of their own. This reflected a move away from specialist teams and functions in East Sussex's reorganised social services. In contrast however, the court liaison social worker left the team in 1985 to be managed by the intermediate treatment section. Hanover has generally been a stable team, remaining largely unchanged since before the reorganisation, apart from these changes affecting workers with wider responsibilities. Early in 1985, it was joined by a half-time occupational therapist — the only one so far appointed in Brighton to work in one patch.

A major stated aim of the patch reorganisation was to integrate field, domiciliary, day care and residential services at team level. Some patches include a variety of residential and day care establishments, from day centres for people with mental illnesses to group homes. The only such resource in Hanover patch is the Morley Street Day Nursery, which is a Brighton-wide rather than local amenity. Indeed it is the only social services day nursery in the town. The team manager also took over responsibility for a family consultation (child guidance) centre in the patch, which was formerly managed by other teams. While Hanover has the largest number of old people in any central Brighton patch and the third largest in all Brighton, it does not have an old people's home within the patch or direct access to an old people's home, as for example neighbouring Queens Park does. While clearly each team is unlikely to have a full range of residential or day care services on its patch, the emphasis is still on team managers finding "local solutions to local problems".[18]

Although according to the Department, the size and composition of patch teams is meant "to reflect the varying demands made" upon them "by the community served",[19] Hanover, for example, for a long time had the same sized staff as Queens Park, although its population is over 3,000 greater. It also had the second highest number of children in care in the Central Brighton Area — previously the highest number — and the second highest total of receptions and discharges from care. This is higher than one of the council estate based patches which is associated with the most serious problems of child care and deprivation.[20] The largest number of referrals to the team are for old people. Second highest are those for children. The team's social workers still work mainly with children and their families, while the social services officer concentrates on old people. However, at the end of 1985, an additional half-time post was created for a social worker to work with old people and develop services for them, in recognition of the patch's particular needs.

Until summer 1984, the Hanover team operated a joint duty system with the adjoining Queens Park patch. They now run their own, which they prefer, although they have carried out reception jointly with North Laine since moving to their new office. The duty system operates from nine until eleven in the mornings, with an emergency service out of hours.

The patch has meetings once a week for all team members. They used to spend a day or half day discussing what they were doing every six weeks, but more recently this has taken place at three monthly intervals. The team manager is responsible for the supervision of the team social workers. Hanover, like other patch teams — apart from three in a pilot project — has not had its own local budget. It does have its own allocation of section one money and its own budget for home help hours which give it a sense of some control. A sum of about £40 for community groups, is also available for each team from the Area group work budget. Each team manager also has access to a small discretionary fund from the voluntary organisation budget, which is administered by the area managers. Team managers can compete for up to £300 from a total of £3000, reduced from the original £5000, for all Brighton, without going through Committee. Hanover has used this money to help a group of childminders form a group and towards setting up a Brighton Play Association.

One intention was to divide the team into three sub-teams, one for each of the three natural areas that make up the patch; each with a social worker, and also involving the homehelp organiser, social services officer and clerical staff. This was seen as a way of getting to know the patch better and of forging closer working relationships with people within it, but so far this has not materialised. Another idea which has developed, was to create an informal sub-team working with old people, made up of the home help organiser, social services officer and occupational therapist — to whom will now be added the new half-time social worker with special responsibility for old people.

One of the problems facing the team is that their large statutory caseload has limited the time they could spend in the patch and the extent to which they could develop different ways of working. So long as their staffing levels remained the same, and without being locally based in a patch office, their difficulty was seeing how they could function fully as a patch team and avoid being forced back into a traditional service delivery role. While the circumstances of the Hanover team which we have described may change, the overall context in which they can expect to operate continues to be one of spending cuts and constraints at both county and national level.

A picture emerges of a small team, with limited resources and limited control over them, with significant statutory obligations and particular difficulties because of delays in its decentralisation. What must be stressed is that generalisations cannot be made from it to all patches in East Sussex or even in Brighton. There is likely to be considerable variation, between town and country, in terms of available resources, traditions and histories and between individual approaches and styles in different teams. What does make more general discussion possible, however, is that one overall philosophy has been applied in East Sussex and that so far there has been a remarkable consistency in patch thinking more generally.

CHAPTER THREE

An Empowering Approach to Research

"No I don't want to give my time. You ask the questions, but I don't see what benefit it will be to me. I don't think interviews are of any use. No one ever takes a blind bit of notice. It doesn't matter what my opinions are, from street lighting to social services. Whatever they are, no one takes any notice."

A PHILOSOPHY OF CITIZEN-INVOLVEMENT

The underlying aim of the research project of which this study is part, has been to develop a dialogue about patch, social services and social need, between the social services department and the key people involved: users, fieldworkers and local inhabitants. While we have particular hopes that this dialogue will develop in East Sussex, the home of this patch initiative and of participants of our study, we are also anxious that the issues it raises and what people have had to say will feed into and encourage similar discussions elsewhere.

This aim has shaped the method we have used. We have adopted a "participatory approach" to research; that is one where as far as possible, people involved in the project can have a say in both its process and what comes out of it. This method also places a high priority on engaging people and increasing popular knowledge about the issues under consideration as a basis for collaboration for change — in this case to improve the match between public services and people's needs. The idea is for people to be *partners* in rather than the objects of research. We believe this makes it a particularly appropriate approach to researching patch, with its similar emphasis on partnership and participation.[1]

Our research methodology rests on a belief in the importance of grassroots views in understanding and developing policy and practice. Feminist critiques of research, to which we acknowledge our debt, have been part of the larger search for a form of working with people that empowers, rather than prolongs the status quo. As Spender has written of women's studies; "It is in the process of redefining knowledge, knowledge gathering and making".[2]

While there are signs that the views of users of social services are beginning to be recognised as having a significance of their own, there also seems to be a tendency for them to be hived off as a separate area of academic and professional study as "client studies".[3] Thus the emphasis remains on

20

discussing and interpreting them rather than on letting them speak for themselves. While such client studies may hopefully focus on service users, they may also distance and objectify them.[4] While it might seem sensible to say, as one social services' researcher has said to us: "I would have thought it was difficult to say anything useful about anything without some degree of distance and objectivity",[5] what these terms actually tend to disguise are inequalities of power and the dominance of the researcher's values and judgements.

As Oakley has argued, a feminist methodology of social science requires that:

> the mythology of 'hygienic' research with its accompanying mystification of the researcher and the researched as objective instruments of data production be replaced by the recognition that the personal involvement is more than dangerous bias — it is the condition under which people come to know each other and to admit others to their lives.[6]

While we lay particular stress on the importance and neglect of user views in patch and wider social policy, we certainly don't sanctify them as the only ones that have validity. That is why we have not focussed our attention solely on them. To do that, we believe, could be unhelpful and divisive. Instead we have been concerned with what we see as the *three* central and overlapping perspectives and roles involved: of users, workers and local people — while recognising the particular vulnerability of people using services.

We have also tried to avoid reifying the role of "users" as if it were a perennial status. In this research project, our discussions have never been with people solely as users of social services. We have never taken that as their defining characteristic. Enclosing people in this narrow role could exclude other aspects of their lives and selves. In the event, as we shall see, the result of our research approach was to include in their own right a number of people who had or were using social services in various ways.

There is also a tendency to think of social services users as a fixed group and "use" as a constant condition. One consequence can be to create a group of almost professionalised "user" spokespersons who unintentionally or otherwise may then serve the purpose of accepting, embracing and indeed propagandising for their agency's particular point of view. Again we have sought to avoid both these possibilities in the way in which we have carried out our research.

OUR METHODS OF SOCIAL RESEARCH

We have tried to keep this discussion of our research method as brief and clear as we could so that as few readers as possible would feel obliged to flick past it, having had unhappy expectations of research writing confirmed. For those who are interested we have also provided more detailed information and tables in an appendix at the end of the book.

The random sample survey of 100 people in Hanover patch on which this study was based complements and offers comparative information for our Brighton-wide study of people's perceptions of social services, needs and patch reorganisation, based on group discussions. This has been carried out by meetings with a wide range of people and groups, some coming together for the project, others having an existence of their own. They include social services workers, users and local people. The aim was to reflect the diversity of experience, orientations, problems and circumstances that confront us as human beings and which theoretically or in practice are the province of social services. They include many different interests and perspectives; from looking after children, having a disability, being involved in collective action, women's groups and organisations, to caring for elderly relations, being young and unemployed, and being homeless.

However detailed, rounded, subtle and convincing accounts may be that emerge from such "qualitative" approaches, they are always open to the accusation of being "unrepresentative".[7] It is a convenient criticism in a field dominated by political and policy-making considerations. The same is true of methods as innovatory, sensitive and self-regulated as, for example, those long used by Mass-Observation, like diaries, letters and notes forthcoming from regular contributors, including a very wide spectrum of opinion.[8] It is still not clear or easily evidenced what relationship they have with broad patterns and trends of opinion.

MAKING OUR SURVEY

There seems to be a gap between qualitative studies whose reliability and validity are uncertain and open to challenge, and quantitative methods that tend to be crude and superficial. Surveys are undeniably a blunt instrument, compared, for example, with Mass-Observations's "detailed self-portrait",[9] and this expectation of them is increasingly reinforced by the growing and simplistic use of opinion surveys for electoral purposes. However they remain the only method involving direct contact with people that can make some claim to being representative as that is understood by numerical criteria.

Jameson making our point about the importance of participatory approaches has argued effectively that while opinion polls are:

Touted as representing public opinion, they in fact represent only private or mass opinion: opinion taken in the dark of the doorway rather than in the open light of the forum; opinion that chokes off the opportunity to hear out arguments pro and con, to consult a neighbour, to read up, to ask a question, to answer back; opinion so half-hearted it is hard to take seriously.[10]

While it may not be guilty of all these failings, it should be recognised that a sample survey method of research has some major limitations. Essentially what it offers are the statements made to a stranger by people under unusual circumstances. The survey maker sets the agenda and plays a dominant role in an individualistic process which cannot be seen as a two-way one in anything like the sense that can for example be the case with group discussions, where participants can interact with each other as well as with the researcher.

We would hope however that there are some compensating characteristics in this study that help limit these shortcomings. First, as we have said it is linked to a qualitative study and ultimately it should be possible for the two to be seen in relation to each other. We also felt it was especially important to seek as unselected a public view of social services, patch and need as possible, both because of the paucity of attempts to do so, so far, and the priority of such hidden and neglected perspectives in this field. This could not be said to be provided by the group discussions method where a process of selection unavoidably took place.

Finally we also sought as far as possible to extend the participatory philosophy underlying our group discussions to the survey itself. We tried to do this not only by feeding back to people what they said, but also in the way in which the interviews were undertaken. We wanted to make it as equal and two-sided a process as possible and avoid the deficiencies and dehumanising effects of "masculine models" of interviewing that Oakley has identified.[11]

All the interviews were carried out by one of us, Suzy Croft:

> In all but one case people invited me in, often offering cups of tea and other hospitality. As well as answering their questions about me, the project, what sort of things other people were saying and what I was finding out, I could explain more to them about social services and suggest to a number who asked where they could go to get help they wanted. People clearly saw it as a social and not just a "fact-finding" occasion, showing me photographs of their children and grandchildren. One woman in her eighties showed me the plait of hair she'd had cut off as a girl. A few elderly people were deferential, but they were the exception. Although I had a questionnaire, the atmosphere was informal and people's answers frequently developed into conversations.

We would not press a claim for this study as offering statistical data from which wide extrapolations can be made. After all, it is based on a small scale survey, tied to a particular time, liable to all the limitations we have discussed. Instead it is intended as an attempt to hear from people usually not consulted about the crucial issues involved, by seeking the opinions, ideas and experience of one such group in one social services patch. One thing we can say is that what people had to say then shows great similarities to what participants in the group discussion project have said between 1982 and 1984.

We sought to make the survey as sensitive as possible. The questionnaire we used was not piloted in the usual way, but rather grew out of the schedule that developed from and formed the basis for group discussions, and was thus significantly affected by issues and concerns emerging from these. All the interviewing was done by one experienced interviewer, making possible a high degree of consistency. Not only were a high proportion of the questions open-ended, but all additional comments people made — of which there were many — were recorded verbatim as far as possible, to give people as much opportunity as possible to raise their own issues and not be constrained by the survey's own agenda. At the same time we recognise our own mediating role, inevitable in such a survey method of research. We have been very conscious of it and tried to make it explicit and to limit it as far as possible, for example, by distinguishing between people's comments and interpretations and any of our own. A copy of the questionnaire is included in Appendix Two.

We did not draw the sample from the whole of the Hanover patch area, because at that time and indeed since, there was some discussion about changing the patch boundaries. Our sampling area included two of the three natural areas that go to make up the patch; the central area covered by the Community Association where there is a high proportion of old people, and the area to the south of it where there is a high proportion of council housing. This included a population of more than 9,000 people. Data from the 1981 census shows that the characteristics of the surveyed population matched extremely closely those of the overall patch population.

The population from which the random sample was obtained was taken from the 1982 electoral roll.[12] The major limitation this imposed was to exclude young people under the age of eighteen from the sample. This is an important omission since children and young people constitute a significant proportion of the clientele of social services. However young people's views are represented in the group discussion part of the project and their needs in the area have also been discussed in another recent study.[13]

In order to make comparisons within the sample, we asked people, for example, about their occupational status and housing tenure, but to avoid being unduly intrusive, we did not ask questions about their age or social class. Instead we categorised people according to the interviewer's own estimate, except where respondents volunteered their age. While age categories only represent an estimate and must be treated with caution accordingly, there should be a high degree of consistency since only one interviewer was involved. People were subsequently placed in three socio-economic categories. Class A approximated to middle class profession-als and class C to working class. Class B represented an intermediate group, including, for example, a shopkeeper, publican and assistant manageress.

Most people fell into categories A and C. The composition of our sample reflected the make up of the patch population closely according to a wide range of characteristics: tenure, economic position, proportion of single parents, of women in employment with dependant children, and so on. Most significantly there was a slight over-representation of women, and an under-representation of old people — which followed from the pattern of refusals.

GETTING INVOLVED

We carried out the survey between 5th August and 5th October 1982 — that is between nine months and nearly a year after the reorganisation was officially initiated. Including all those eligible for interview (190), the overall response rate was 53%.[14]. This included a refusal rate of 33% which we felt was high.[15] Among the main reasons for refusals, seemed.to be people's understandably low expectations of the effectiveness of such surveys and — mostly from middle aged and older people — a reluctance to get involved, or not feeling involved in such issues. For example:

"No I don't follow anything local I'm afraid."

"No, I don't do nothing like that. I have nothing to do with them. I don't like elections even. I don't like being asked my opinion."

"I'm alright. I've no problem really. I don't want to do it."

"I'm not interested really. I haven't got any problems. My husband's got a job and that's it."

This kind of inward-looking approach and sense of disassociation from the issues involved in the study, of local needs and social services, was a theme that recurred in the survey itself. It may also have figured more generally in the responses of those who said they were not interested or too busy to take part in the survey. A few people who did take part explained why they had and significantly the reasons they gave were exactly the opposite to these. For example:

"You've got to take an interest in what's going on around you, otherwise you've no right to moan about it."

"This area is very unfriendly and people don't get to know each other.at all. North Laines is more friendly."

"I'm interested in trying to improve things..."

Such a refusal rate, as well as telling us something about the limitations of this method in exploring issues of need and services,[16] may also offer some insights into the nature of local social relations and the involvement people feel and have with their locality and in each others wants and needs within it. The issue of people's insularity in this area, for example, was also raised several times in the survey itself, as we shall see. These are key issues for patch. It may be as one of the people we interviewed suggested:

> *"Your survey is going to be over-representative of those people who are interested as opposed to those who just shut their doors and don't want to know."*

Whether or not this is the case, it does seem likely that people's reactions to such a survey may to some extent at least reflect their more general attitudes to and perceptions of local ties and local involvement.

2.
A NEW APPROACH
TO SOCIAL SERVICES?

CHAPTER FOUR

People and Social Services

"Social services is just a name to me."

PEOPLE'S VIEWS OF SOCIAL SERVICES

This chapter looks at people's experience and knowledge of social services, and their attitudes towards them. Although we interviewed people after the introduction of patch, we didn't attempt to draw two pictures — "before" and "after". Nor do we assume that people's views are somehow fixed and static, so that our survey becomes "the" view. This would be to interpret the reorganisation in East Sussex as no more than an administrative matter, with local people and users unable to be more than passive objects of change. We have seen that patch looks beyond this towards a partnership with users and a dialogue with the local community. Indeed, "acceptability to the patch population"[1] is taken as a key feature.

We therefore asked questions about people's knowledge and views of local social services, but included an attempt to explore their experience and ideas about the *process* by which their needs and views and experience have been or might be engaged by the Department and patch team. We discuss this in the next chapter. It will be clear that for patch to succeed it must begin to carry local people along with it. From this it follows that what people don't know, and their misconceptions, are as important as their knowledge. At the same time, we would not want people's lack of knowledge or feelings that they were not consulted to be read as a "failure" of Hanover patch to engage them, so much as to suggest what could and should still be done.

What might we expect people to know about social services? We should begin with a warning. Social services receive little attention compared with other spheres of public welfare and are not even considered by many major studies and discussions of social policy[2]. While the least change in mortgage tax allowances, for example, commands immediate headlines, only scandals and catastrophes bring social services departments to such prominence. Almost as much is spent on them as on "law and order", but much less is said about them.[3] In this way they are as hidden from public attention as the poor law before them, and perhaps for many of the same reasons of fear, shame and disrepute.

From their workers' point of view it is plain that they are involved in issues at the heart of our lives. For many individuals and families their contact with the social services department will come at a time of tragedy or crisis. It is worth spelling this out in some detail. Social service workers have an underlying context to their work which involves death and bereavement, infirmity, and adjustment to disability in ourselves and others. They are concerned with breakdowns in the widest sense — from broken relationships to homelessness. The most important and intimate relationships are opened up to them, between men and women, partners, parents and children, old people and their families. Tangled in personal issues are those of sexuality, race and social change, as well as crucial issues of human rights; parents' access to children, old people's entitlement to live independently, and compulsory detention in institutions.

The content of social services work is not the only minefield. The personal social services are a major area of local authority spending, and as such in the frontline of political arguments about public spending cuts. In 1981/2 local authority revenue and capital expenditure on social services totalled £2,3000 million — more than seven percent of all local authority spending.[4] From accounting for only eight percent of expenditure in East Sussex in 1965, they grew to fourteen percent in 1979 and a cost of £22 million, making up one sixth (17%) of the rise in County Council spending over the whole period.[5]

Moving to a more individual level, a local patch might be expected to contain a number of people with knowledge of the Department and its work. This might either be from direct personal experience or indirectly, for example, through other people's contact. In our sample, we found such a proportion of users and their neighbours, relatives and friends. There were also workers in the service and their close contacts, and other people with some connection with social services, for example, staff in related work such as medical care and teaching. Added to this personal knowledge will, of course, be what people have learned from the Department's own publicity — about its services generally, and about the change to patch.

PEOPLE'S EXPERIENCE OF SOCIAL SERVICES

In our survey, people were asked if they had any experience of and had ever used the Social Services Department. The difference between it and social security and voluntary organisations was made clear to minimise any confusion. Its address at the time, Princes Street, was also mentioned, since local people were as likely to know and talk of it as "Princes Street" or "the welfare" as social services. Only 16 of the sample said they had any such involvement with the social services department, although in the course of conversation, another eight mentioned experiences they had had, making a total of 24. It is not clear why there was this discrepancy; whether, for example, it was due to an initial failure to connect social services with the particular experience or service received, or an overall uncertainty about what social services were.[6]

For six of the 24, contact with social services came from working for it, either now or previously, for example, as a home help, administrator, craft instructor and in a children's home. Two people worked in related occupations, a woman as a staff nurse, a man as an ambulance driver. Another man was a foster parent and one elderly woman was social secretary of a pensioners club and had also got a bath aid for herself from social services. The dealings of five more people with social services had concerned someone else — a relative or neighbour.

"...I've been up about trouble with my (young) brothers. I think a social worker came up."

"With my mother. They got her into a council home. They did it very quickly."

"They dealt with my husband's elderly parents and my mother and now my stepfather who is senile. He goes to a day centre now and they gave us home help in the past."

Only six people were currently in contact with the Social Services Department, one of them the ambulance driver, through his work, the other the foster parent. In all ten people had themselves been clients of social services. So clients made up less than half of those who mentioned having some experience of social services.

"Just recently I was in hospital and so I have a home help — only once a week. The social worker got me into a day centre." (woman in her late 60s)

"We have dealt with them. I was divorced and they helped me get custody." (man in his late 30s)

"Yes, to try and get out of here." (Milner Flats, run-down council walk-up block; young woman with four small children.)

"They got me that thing to pull on my stockings and they put a seat in my bath and a handle on the wall and I have a home help." (woman in her late 70s)

While people's contact with social services covered a variety of needs and issues, most concerned problems of physical disability and old age, and the residential, day care and domiciliary provision made for these.

Those who had been on the receiving end of social services, either for themselves, or for someone else (excluding the foster parent) were not typical of the overall sample according to several key criteria. They fitted the view of users of social services as unrepresentative and disadvantaged. 11 of the 15 were reliant on poverty level state benefits; 13 were categorised as working class; eight were of retirement age and above, and eight lived in council housing. This was even more striking with the 10 clients, all of whom were working class, six being council tenants.

CONTACT WITH WELFARE STATE SERVICES

In addition to the 24 people who had some contact with social services, our sample included another 23 who either had indirect contact with the Department or involvement with other welfare state services. These ranged from several teachers and a man whose sister was a home help, to a clerk in the NHS, a midwife and a man whose wife had been brought up in care. It is not surprising that almost half the sample had some kind of connection with welfare in this way. The same is likely to be the case for any group. The welfare state has become a deeply rooted and far-reaching part of our lives and society. We might also expect such proximity to welfare among these people to have increased their awareness and understanding of social services.

PEOPLE'S KNOWLEDGE OF SOCIAL SERVICES

Yet in spite of 47 people in our sample having some such experience of or link with social services or the wider welfare world; despite the Department's own publicity, and social services being a major item of public expenditure dealing with fundamental issues that can affect us all, its importance was not matched by people's responses. Our survey suggested three key ways in which this was the case. Throughout the interviews, people frequently gave the impression that this was the first time the issue of social services had been raised with them. They had not formulated or articulated their thoughts and attitudes about them before. Second, the survey suggested that social services are perceived as marginal to most people. This is linked to the third feature, one of the most striking findings to emerge. When we asked them what they knew about what local authority social services did, 64 people said they knew very little or nothing. Only seven thought they knew a reasonable amount, none that they were well informed.[7] Comments made clear how little information people had and that it was frequently inaccurate.

> "Is it like clubs and that? Don't know anything about it."

> "Not a lot. They help old people don't they?"

> "...The housing, that sort of thing? I don't have anything to do with them."

Another 29 people tried to describe what social services did. Of these 19 showed only a very general or limited knowledge and four others were inaccurate or mistaken in what they said. For example:

"I suppose they give lists of playgroups and childminders etc."

"They help the distressed and poorly paid."

"I have help with the rates."

"They provide home helps, child guidance, presumably district nurses, health visitors — things like that."

"They're supposed to help people who've no money or are out of work. Help young girls get furniture for their homes."

"Everything from meals on wheels to unemployment benefit. I suppose right from children to old people, all their needs whether physical or financial."

Taken together those who said they knew very little or nothing, and those who suggested it by their descriptions of social services, a total of 87 people had little or no knowledge of what the Social Services Department did.

The 47 people who had some contact with social and other welfare services were more likely to know more about social services, although most still knew little or nothing. Nine of the 13 people who had a reasonable degree of knowledge either worked for social services or in a related occupation, or they had friends or family who worked there. Indeed, occupational contact seemed to give a greater knowledge than use of social services. Only three of these 13 people had themselves been clients, while 12 of the 16 who had used social services knew little or nothing about them.

Older people are one group who might be expected to have a greater familiarity with social services. This is partly because such a high proportion of social services resources are provided for them, and also since these — from meals on wheels and home helps, to lunch clubs and day centres — are more widely used and everyday services with less stigma. However people over 60 in our sample knew no more about social services than other people. In fact 19 out of 20 people aged 60 or over indicated they knew little or nothing about them.

The question of stigma is important in considering whether some people might be reluctant to mention social services or disclose information about them. There is no reason to believe this to be so in this case. People both in this survey and the larger research project of which it was part, seemed to be forthcoming about any dealings they had with social services, even if they might sometimes not wish to discuss the particular nature or details of them. Furthermore, a 1981 national survey of public attitudes towards social workers showed a similar level of contact. 10% of those surveyed had come into contact with a local authority social worker. About 14% had been clients of hospital, local authority or other social workers and a further 6% had met one who was visiting friends, relatives or acquaintances. Only 8% had ever discussed a problem with a social worker.[8]

WHAT SOCIAL SERVICES MEAN FOR PEOPLE

We asked people several questions about how they saw social services. Following from their feeling of having little knowledge, many peopls were either "don't knows" or mentioned their lack of experience to qualify their answers. "Very difficult to say, I've had so little contact", was a typical comment.

> *"I don't know much about them, but I'm sure a lot of people in Brighton don't get what they're entitled to. But I should imagine the service is a very good one if you take the effort to go ."*

> *"I don't have any direct experience. It seems that there probably aren't enough resources for a town this size. They are very much overworked. I know they are cutting back on the home help service."*

People's misunderstandings and lack of knowledge ran through their responses, emphasising the extent of their unfamiliarity with social services.

> *"Is there a social services now?"*

> *"Don't know. I'm not qualified to answer."*

> *"Are they the ones that do the dole money?"*

> *"Until we retire, we don't know anything about social services. We might do then." (middle aged woman)*

> *"I've had nothing to do with them. Until I need them, I wouldn't be able to say."*

> *"I don't know anything about what they do. I didn't know there was one!"*

Despite the low level of information, people nevertheless had opinions about social services. This raises the question of how people develop their views and on what they base their accounts of social services. Some, as we have seen, gained them from occupational or social contact or direct or indirect use. For others, the media, word of mouth and particular incidents that came to their attention or in which they were involved seemed to be the main opinion formers. The possible effects of other more subtle influences like folk memories, the legacy of the poor law and class and cultural stereotypes, remain unclear. People also offered their own insights into the factors and problems involved in the social construction of information and opinions about social services.

> "*My friend has just been promoted to Area Manager. There is generally little information. There are two kinds you hear. First, social services mistakes, for example, Maria Colwell. Second what pressures they are under, how little resources they have, especially under a Tory Government.*"

> "*I haven't got a very good opinion really. I've heard of a case last week where a man died in Whichelo place (a few streets away in the same patch), an old man and the welfare should have called but she didn't come 'till Monday and he was dead.*"

> "*I haven't come into contact with them so I could (only) speak through what I've read in the press.*"

> "*I think people are given a false impression. You only hear about the bad cases in the paper. I suppose they are doing a good job.*"

> "*I suppose in theory they are a good thing, but whether they are in practice, it's difficult to say when you've had no experience of them.*"

Only one person referred to the Social Services Department *itself* as a source of information, and that was someone professionally involved as a teacher.

> "*I know you can be contacted in case of children being at risk. I've seen circulars about children in school. There was a conference to inform children of the service. Parents in need can go to social services for clothing grants for children.*"

As we have said, people's information was incomplete and sometimes inaccurate. Undeniably there was speculation and supposition in their opinions. This must be considered by a patch initiative which seeks to involve them in a dialogue and understand their responses. Of course we interviewed people during the continuing process of patch's development, and our contact itself raised — and was intended to raise — questions which would feed into this process. People also "thought aloud" to us during the interviews. Asking people their opinions about such issues itself generates fresh thinking about what they want and how they feel about them. In the parallel research with groups of users, workers and local people, discussion, recording and subsequent revisits have been part of the process.

What then can be said about the comments and views of social services we heard during the course of these interviews? To take the most negative point of view, we might wonder whether, confronted with a researcher, questionnaire in hand, people wouldn't say something about anything, ignorance being no bar.[9] There were high rates of "don't knows" to some questions about social services, but in general, as we have said, people's lack of information did not stop them having opinions about them. The average rate of "don't knows" for questions about social services was 25%, in contrast to the much higher proportion of people identified as knowing little or nothing about them.

Less harshly, our approach could be criticised for placing too much emphasis on getting the views of people who couldn't be aware of the practical constraints operating on social services.

Again, such criticisms would misunderstand the purpose behind our survey, which at this point was not to test some inferred "objective validity" of people's knowledge and views of social services. The context of this study after all was a patch initiative which seeks to involve people in a dialogue about services, and to understand their responses. The fact of inadequate or inaccurate information is itself important, as are the opinions people hold. In a crucial sense, our survey may be helpful precisely because it touches the local grapevine. People's attitudes, positive or negative, are an important point of departure for patch.

We also believe that survey material in this book will show that people were more realistic in their assessment of constraints on social services, at both local and national level, than might be assumed. But there is a more important point here. Social services *themselves* are also often limited by their lack of knowledge about the worlds and circumstances of their users and local people. Often they provide what they see as needed rather than what is actually wanted. This has been a key patch argument. It again points to the importance of dialogue. Our aim here has been to try and redress the balance, so that social services may begin to gain further insights from local people and develop the dialogue that will make for better understanding of each other by both services and citizens.

ATTITUDES TO SOCIAL SERVICES

Bearing these issues in mind, let's now look at people's comments and views about social services. As well as their responses to particular questions, people made numerous comments during the course of interviews which help to build up a subtle and complex picture of their attitudes. When we specifically asked people what they thought of social services, apart from 35 who either said they didn't know, or couldn't answer through lack of knowledge or contact, 17 people felt able to offer unreservedly positive opinions about them.

"It's a good idea. They do a needed job."

"They help us in a lot of ways."

"I think they are a good thing and if it was necessary we would go to them for help."

"They do a good job."

But negative, equivocal or mixed opinions accounted for 40% of responses. People's views about social services were mixed, although negative comments slightly outnumbered positive ones. Taking together all responses made in the interviews, 36 people made negative comments and 28 positive ones. Those who made negative comments about the Social Services Department were similar to the rest of the sample according to sex, proportion who had had contact with social services and estimated age and social class, although their stay in the area tended to be slightly shorter. Positive comments about social services came from people who while similar to the rest of the sample according to sex, were estimated to be older, more likely to have had experience of social services and to have lived longer in the area. There was also an over-representation of people classified as working class and under-representation of those classified as middle class.

People's negative comments covered a wide range of concerns, many of which might be expected; of insufficient and inappropriate provision and services, inexperienced staff, not getting help when it was needed, stigmatic and degrading treatment, and the Social Services Department's remoteness, lack of concern and understanding, errors, interference, failure to inform, and its lack of knowledge of certain problems.

Some remarks were fairly sweeping:

"I think it's all paperwork and resolutions."

"I think they're pretty poor in Brighton."

"I think that certainly in the area in which I work — which is children — social services often take actions without consulting teachers who see the children regularly — but in other areas I'm not knowledgeable enough to say." (teacher)

Many comments, of course, were equivocal:

"They're alright I suppose."

"They might be helpful."

"I suppose they provide a service for people who need it."

"Home helps are very good. I know of them. I don't think a lot of the meals they have. I wouldn't eat them."

People's opinions about social services did not seem to be related to the level of their knowledge about them. 18 of the 22 who expressed positive views when asked and 19 of the 23 giving negative opinions, said that they knew little or nothing, or indicated a limited or inaccurate knowledge of social services — a pattern which reflected that of the rest of the sample. The high proportion of people who expressed positive views without apparently knowing much about social services, suggests a pool of good will towards them, available to be built on.

The attitudes to social services of people who had actually used or had some experience of them are of particular interest. Five of the 16 users did not feel they had been helpful and one offered an important qualification to his praise:

> "The services are good when you get them, but you have to push and push to get anywhere."

Eleven of the 24 who had used or had contact with social services made positive comments, and this was a higher proportion than in the rest of the sample. On the other hand, as we have said, users did not feel or suggest that they knew more about social services than other people interviewed. If we include comments from the 47 people who had some experience of or link with social and welfare services, a wide range of critical comments begins to build up.

> "If you'd asked me last year, I'd have liked to get out of here, but then I saw the day centre and that put me off. I thought I'd like an old people's home but now I don't think I'd like it." (retired man)

> "The social services are often too remote. Especially for the old lady I knew. Coupled with the fact that as an 80 year old, she wasn't able to ask for help in the 'right' way."

> "I've come up against a lot of mistakes that have been made by social services due to lack of communication." (staff nurse)

> "I've only had that one experience, (in) which I didn't get anywhere."

> "There should be some awareness of the vast problems of alcoholism by social services .... We tried to make social services aware and they're not interested. Social services haven't got a ruddy clue. Anyway they don't deal with it."

> "Social services haven't helped me that much. They got the twins into a play school but only for three days a week. They won't take them five days because they said I won't then spend enough time with them. I've nowhere for them to play here at all." (Young mother of four, living in bad housing conditions)

> "I think they're stigmatic aren't they? It's a shock if you're not used to having to use them and you end up using them, like my father (who) had a stroke."

> "I can't afford the home help. It's not fair at over eighty to be expected to pay for it. Same with the meals on wheels. You have no choice. They bring you two days at a time and you have to heat it up. The old lady up the road, she's dead now, she said some days she just chucked it in the bin." (83 year old woman living on a state pension and supplementary benefit. An additional payment is not made to people on supplementary benefit/pension to cover the cost of a home help.)

"I don't think they could care less."

"They stick their noses in everything."

"You get more understanding from an everyday person."

When we asked people whether they thought the Social Services Department had any understanding of, or interest or concern in the kind of issues and problems that concerned them, 48 answered no, only 29 yes. The pattern was the same whether or not people had used social services.

"They don't know what's going on."

"To a certain extent, but only to a certain extent."

"None at all. They're not concerned about working class people at all. If it was £10,000 for a Rolls Royce for the Mayor, it would be a different matter. Even the lighting in this street is no good."

"I think they would have if I went down there."

"I'm sure they do what they can."

"No, not me. Are they interested or is it a job? Like I'm a painter and I don't care what house I paint. Have they the same attitude?"

"Yes, but their rules and regulations are such that they can't always get the emphasis right."

"They don't get down to the basis of a problem."

"Yes, but they look at things from afar."

"They don't ask me any questions. They don't ask if you're in need of anything."

"I think social services are like any like body. They are bound up in their own problems, so it probably tends to be out of touch with what is going on."

"The major problems, yes, but your everyday problems, I shouldn't think so. You can complain, but they won't necessarily take any notice."

It is interesting that men's attitudes to social services did not seem to be significantly different to women's. Men are often shadowy figures in social work and social services. Most clients and users (and indeed most workers) are women, and both the positive and negative experiences of social services are mainly had by women as mothers, carers and when old themselves.

Assumptions that government attacks on welfare state services have popular support were not borne out but rather challenged by this study. While people had much to say that was critical of social services, this was certainly not synonymous with anti-welfare or anti-social services' users' attitudes.

Nor did it accord with Taylor-Gooby's conclusion that:

"Fluctuations in (public) support for the poor (since the second world war) pale into insignificance when set against the enduring distinction between the constant high levels of support for favoured groups and low levels of support for the unfavoured".[10]

Yet social services, like social security, are strongly associated with the unfavoured groups he was talking about. Perhaps this says something about his reliance on conventional public opinion survey data, with all its limitations.

Only ten members of our sample made what might best — and at most be called reactionary comments, either against social services (2) or their users (8) — and some of these were ambiguous and have only been included to avoid any criticism of understating the strength of this opinion.

"We are so heavily taxed. Social services — do you really want to pay more hangers-on?"

"Well my honest opinion is they give too much to the lay-abouts. I agree they should cut down on their expenditure."

"They do good for people who need them, but some get things that are unnecessary."

"If (people) can look after themselves they wouldn't need social services, but I have a vague feeling people are too dependant on the state."

"I've no patience with those who can't manage. But then of course we don't go out much or smoke, drink or go bingoing. By not doing any of that we manage." (old woman)

The anti-scrounger comments, however, also revealed complexities and contradictions that have more often been ignored, usually for reasons of political expedience and ideology, than analysed and explored. One man in his sixties, for example, said:

"I think there's too much done for some people like the unemployed. I was brought up 'if you don't work, you don't get paid'."

Later though, he qualified his remarks saying that more help should be given "the genuine unemployed and OAPs who are struggling". It was clear he was finding it difficult to reconcile his traditional beliefs with the fact that his son , a skilled worker, had been made redundant and could not get regular work, despite making every kind of attempt.

One woman had herself been in care from the age of ten to sixteen as her father had left, and her mother with a large family to bring up, couldn't manage. All the children went to the same home and then eventually back to their mother. But she was concerned about "scroungers on the dole", feeling "people could get jobs if they wanted to", and extolling the virtues of private medicine. At the same time she said:

> "I think it was good social services helped my mother and looked after me. It's also good that the old lady next door gets help from them and can go to the day centre."

People expressed much more concern about inadequate resources and cuts in social services. 18 members of the sample raised such issues.

> "Judging by what I've heard they've (social services) been depleted a lot over the last few years."

> "I think they do a reasonable job seeing as they don't have much money. Their money is always under threat, put it that way."

> "Pensioners should get home helps free. They can't pay for them. My husband and I have been very ill this year and we thought of getting a home help, but we couldn't really afford it". (woman aged 70-75)

> "I don't think they should be cutting the services like they are. They should be giving them more freedom and more money."

> "I know my sister (who is a home help) does far more work than she is paid for. She works hours she's not supposed to work, but she can't get through to them what the position is."

> "A lot more money could be spent on them. More social workers are needed for the old and mentally ill. The mentally ill are neglected."

> "It seems that there probably aren't enough resources for a town this size. They are very much overworked. I know they are cutting back on the home-help service."

People's perceptions and preconceptions about social services raise important questions about them. As we have seen, those surveyed were often under quite basic misapprehensions. In spite of our efforts to limit misunderstanding, some still confused social services with social security, health and other services. They were also less likely to distinguish between different departments in the way that social policy analysts would take for granted. Sometimes they were unclear or mistaken about where services they had received had come from, or who a particular worker was they had seen. As a result it was not always clear to us, although in collating responses we followed what people said unless something else they said clearly contradicted it.

"They were very good to me when my husband died. I don't know who he was, but I saw a man, he helped us a lot." (she was unsure where she saw this man)

"There's an old lady next door with terminal cancer, it's taken 5 weeks for a welfare visitor to come. I took her to the specialist at the hospital who told her straight she had cancer and he said he'd get her a welfare visitor." (It emerged that she meant a community nurse)

WHO ARE SOCIAL SERVICES FOR?

But other ideas and assumptions about social services held by members of the sample raise much more complicated issues. Some clearly saw social services as provided for particular groups, or people with particular problems.

"You always think of social services helping the old and the poor, but not the average person, I suppose."

"They are some sort of use, I suppose up the rougher areas of Brighton where you have families breaking up."

"I think really it is mostly the older people who do need social services. I may need them as I get older as well."

"I understand they are to provide a service of support and assistance for those who can't help themselves for a variety of reasons."

As well as the 14 who made such explicit comments there were a few more ambiguous observations along the lines of "Presumably they're good for the people who need them", where it was not clear whether people had in mind a particular *kind* or *class* of people for whom social services were intended, or circumstances or problems that might befall anyone.

A much larger number of people (34) overlapping these, expressed the same attitude in a different way, saying or implying they did not see social services as being for people like them (19) or themselves as having any needs for social services (17). Again the two overlapped.

"I have no needs relating to social services."

"It doesn't affect me."

"My idea of social services in my own life is nil."

"I haven't any problems they'd want to cope with." (unemployed young teacher).

"I don't need help from social services.... I've never needed it or wanted it." (young man who had been unemployed for 18 months and in trouble with the police)

"I'd have thought they have enough without worrying about what problems I've got." (young woman expecting a baby)

"Only that it's stupid that people in our age group (66) — we've had a tough life — don't get help. I suppose they do their best for those who require it."

"It couldn't offer me very much as I'm not really the sort of person who needs social services, not at the moment anyway." (teacher in his 30's)

The woman part-time teacher was an exception who said "I think of social services to be called on in moments of need". What people seemed to be saying was "I'm not the sort of person", or "I haven't the kind of problem or need for social services to deal with" or perhaps, "that I would take to them". What was not always clear though was whether they meant they did not *at present* have needs to take to social services, but might one day, or that they could never envisage such a course of action for themselves. A couple suggested that it was something they might think about again or find out more about, when they were older. People's low expectations — their reluctance to burden social services — seemed to underlie some comments. In some cases the implication also seemed to be that people wanted or expected to keep clear of social services. Six people made explicit their desire to keep away from them, although their comments might also have meant that they were anxious to avoid the *reasons* for coming to social services' attention and not just social services themselves.

"I'm glad they're there, but I don't want to have to use them."

"Any experience of them? No, not if I can help it."

"I don't need them, thank God."

One woman, however, at the end of her interview expressed a feeling about welfare that many people have shared from the poor law to the present:

"I'm sorry I don't know much about social services. I like to get on with my life.... I don't like people telling me what to do. I suppose some people do need them though."

The number (42) who seemed to see social services as for others and not for themselves was matched closely by the 41 who when asked, said they would not like to have closer contact with social services. They were also more likely to be included in this category than the rest of the sample. People categorised as working class were under-represented and those categorised as middle class were also over-represented among them.

While some of the people surveyed seemed to want to keep social services at arms length, others as we have seen, appeared to think that social services were not intended, or didn't offer services for the kinds of needs they had. Some of those who said that they didn't think social services had any understanding or interest in the kind of issues and problems that concerned them, didn't seem to expect them to, saying, for example, "there's no need for them to", "I don't expect that", and "It doesn't really apply". What is also not clear is whether people's disassociation of social services from their own needs sprang from their own choice or self-perceptions, or as many of the responses when people were asked whether they thought social services had any understanding or interest in their needs, suggested, because of their perceptions of social services' orientation and nature. Elsewhere in her interview, one woman said:

> "In my circumstances, I don't think I'd ever get any help from social services as I've no children and I tend to associate them with families. My marriage has broken up and I've been through a very traumatic period, but I don't think they would have helped."

The question for us is whether this woman *should* have expected social services to be concerned with the kind of problems she had faced, or those facing the unemployed young teacher, or the young man who had got into trouble with the police when he was out of work. Were people like these mistaken in thinking that social services were not for them? Were others right to see them as for certain stigmatised or disadvantaged groups rather than "for people like me"?

THE MARGINALITY OF SOCIAL SERVICES

There are serious implications here for the development of patch and community social work, which for many of its proponents entails an explicit move away from this marginal and stigmatising role.[11] It aims to counter both the notion of client as passive receiver of services, and social services being concerned for "those-other-people". This is especially important in any attempt to relate to "informal helping networks" which are assumed to be far less stigmatising and more commonplace.

We can see this clearly in the way that the Social Services Department in Brighton has presented itself. The team manager of the patch surveyed, for example, stated at the beginning of a series of local radio programmes about the reorganisation of social services in Brighton:

> It's very difficult to define all the things that a social services department are involved with, but basically it comes down to caring about the physical and emotional well-being of people in the community.[12]

And the situation in Brighton is not unique. It is not unusual for publicity about a social services department to stress the wide availability of its services, although this is invariably qualified by the small print.[13]

Of course, the problem here is not one of patch's making. There is a longstanding discrepancy between the formal and substantive aims and nature of social services. The personal social services provided by Seebohm's community based family service[14], were no less intended to be a universalistic service than local authority education, housing, recreation, and the health service. They are still presented as such. Social services, however, have never effectively offered a universal service.

As one local authority social worker said recently in a national magazine, "society employs us to deal with what it sees as its dross, the dregs, the losers". But what was interesting was that essentially he seemed to accept this definition of their role, going on to say: "Most of us came into social work with more idealistic aims. We want to improve their lot, not leave them at the bottom of the heap."[15]

One of the striking features reported in the aftermath of the 1985 Bradford City football fire disaster was that:

For the first time, social workers are dealing with a different class of society. At St Luke's, normally half the burns patients are already known to social workers. They are either elderly, handicapped or alcoholics. But of the fire victims, only one was already known to social services. Most of them come from a middle class background.[16]

There is no doubt that it is oppressed and disadvantaged people and groups who have most contact with social services, notably working class people without recognised occupational skills, women, black people and members of other ethnic minorities, single parents, old and disabled people. Not only have social services tended to give low priority to the needs of particular people, like those with mental handicaps or who are single and homeless, but they have also clearly not become part of everyday life for a significant proportion of people in the way, for example, that libraries, parks, baths, evening classes and other local services have. The trend has been in the opposite direction. Cuts in social services spending have meant that they have tended to concentrate even more on the areas of so-called "statutory obligation"; non-accidental injury to children and the reception of children into care, the processing of juvenile offenders, institutionalisation of old people and the hospitalisation of people identified as mentally ill.

What is being done is to define social needs as problems rather than as natural parts of our day-to-day life. It is as if there were a covert message at least that we shouldn't really be using social services. As one of the people interviewed put it:

"The social services are like the Samaritans — you've got something wrong with you. I feel that about the majority of social workers. The social services are wrongly conducted. They see you as having something wrong with you."

Not only does it seem that the social services department is essentially directed at the deprived and stigmatised, but it also looks and feels like that. Thus we heard in the local radio programme about Brighton Social Services:

Presenter:	It may take a little time before you see anyone — and the waiting room in the meantime, with its graffiti on the walls and metal chairs is hardly a consolation.
Hanover Patch Social Worker:	I'm afraid that's right, yes it's not something that we all agree with having, but they're the only facilities we have at the moment, I'm afraid.... We have private interview rooms... again its bare, the carpet isn't clean, the chairs are marginally more comfortable than in the waiting room but I'm afraid it isn't particularly comfortable.[17]

Certainly in terms of use, social services appear from our survey to have a residual role. Nor can this role and apparent low level of use — in terms of the local population generally — be explained by recent expenditure cuts, policies of retrenchment and reduction of services in this and other authorities. People were asked if they had *ever* used or had experience of social services and this would include the expansionist days of the late 1960's and early 1970's as well as social services' present straitened circumstances.

The people we surveyed may not have had a clear idea of the formal aims and nature of the social services department, but in terms of who social services were actually for and what they did, the stereotypes and feelings of a significant number of the sample seemed to be borne out by the reality. It was not the case in our survey as was reported of the first national survey of public attitudes to social workers that "plainly social services departments have established themselves fairly strongly in people's minds in the nine years that they have been in existence".[18] A few people seemed to see their lack of information as their own fault and when asked what they knew about social services made comments like:

"I'm sorry I don't know much about social services."

"I'd like to know something about it, but perhaps I should find out. We do pay for it, so it would be nice to know."

This feeling some people had that they should know something or more about social services — and it was their fault that they didn't — was also frequently expressed in the larger linked research study of grassroots views of social services. Many more people in the survey (34) pointed to the failure of social services to inform local people.

"I think a lot of people don't know to ask.... There should be more advertisements." (midwife)

"There should be more places to go to. Where can you get help? We don't know where to go. It should be known more."

"I would like to know more. I would like to know what our entitlements are. Like people don't know what benefits they are entitled to."

"They obviously don't make themselves well known."

One woman recounted how social services hadn't seemed to know what help was available when she asked:

"I'd have like to have known how to get a welfare visitor for the old lady next door. I went to Princes Street as the doctor didn't help — I went to Social Services and she said, 'well I'm not sure how you get a welfare visitor. I don't think it's our department dear'. I couldn't believe it. If they don't know, who does? So I came home and rang the doctor and in the end he sent a nurse. I even asked the caretaker and he said 'buggered if I know!'."

Judging from such responses, it would appear that the Social Services Department was failing to communicate to people what it did. Another woman said:

"I think perhaps they don't give out enough information about the services they do have. I don't know anything about social services. We got a leaflet through the door about £2 million in unclaimed benefit and I think it's the same in social services. You don't know what's available."

There have been successful supplementary benefits take-up campaigns in Brighton and other towns and cities. There is no reason why there could not be similar campaigns initiated by social services to inform and alert people to the services which are available and to which they are entitled.[19]

THE NEED TO KNOW

While such an exercise is necessary and important, on its own it would not be enough. The issue is not just one of a lack of information. This would not explain why more than 30 years after the creation of the welfare state and over a decade after the reorganisation of personal social services into generic social services departments, one finding from this survey is how little most people know about them. The issue is also one of the *nature* of social services.

The three aspects of social services we have just been exploring — people's knowledge and experience of and attitudes towards them — are in close and complex interrelation. As we have seen, people would frequently give their lack of contact with them as a reason for not knowing much about social services. Similarly, their lack of or erroneous information about them appeared to be a factor in whether or not they used them. Their attitudes towards social services, not surprisingly, seemed to influence and be influenced by their experience and knowledge, or the lack of them. It seems unlikely that it would be just the failure of social services to inform that explains people's limited knowledge of them. We would expect a much higher level of knowledge, for example, about education or health services, because their use is much more commonplace. So we find in a survey of a non-statutory community project that the high proportion of local people who knew about it and what it did, corresponded with a high level of use and involvement in it.[20] Significantly in East Sussex there has been a major campaign against education cuts, but there has not been the same campaign against cuts in social services. While people have been no less affected by these, they do not represent the same cross-section of the population that parents of students in state schools do.

As we have already observed, our survey suggests that people's stereotype of social services as provision for particular disadvantaged and stigmatised groups, rather than the general population, does not seem to be far from the truth. Indeed, they are inadequate even to meet these particular needs. People's low level of knowledge about social services, like their attitudes to and use of them, seem to be related to their residual nature.

One interpretation that could be placed on our finding is that people didn't want or expect social services to have other than a residual role. They did not see them for themselves, but for a group of deserving people they were prepared to pay for; and, some of them — less perhaps than the right wing media might suggest — for a group of undeserving people they did not want to support. But this is to assume that what people saw as the reality was what they actually wanted. It ignores the fact that social services — rhetoric apart — have not presented themselves for popular consumption. Unless they give people a reason for seeing them differently, they are unlikely to escape being seen as marginal. It is also difficult to see how they can become less marginal to most people so long as they have the limited and increasingly restricted resources allotted them, and their present narrow role and orientation to certain institutionalised needs. This is where patch comes in.

CHAPTER FIVE

PEOPLE AND THE PATCH REORGANISATION

"I believe that what these changes are designed to achieve in terms of more appropriate services to the consumer mark a major departure in behaviour for a local government or civil service department. It is at one and the same time threatening and exhilarating."

Director of Social Services, East Sussex, 1982.[1]

THE PROMISE OF PATCH

Patch has been advanced by its advocates as a means of overcoming most if not all the problems raised in the last chapter — social services' marginality for most people, people's lack of contact with and knowledge of them — as well as a number of others of equal importance. The question must be whether patch really offers the prospect of doing so. According to the Hanover patch team manager:

> What basically going patch means is getting a small team of social workers and home helps and home help organiser out into the small communities. Although it's been around for several years in small areas of the country, East Sussex has taken the initiative in introducing this system of working.[2]

East Sussex's Director of Social Services said that the patch reorganisation represented:

> The establishment of a genuine attempt by the local authority to devolve its main force of practitioners into the community. It is a very strong commitment, both political and from senior management to be nearer the consumer so we understand the situation as he (sic) lives. (Also) to be closer to networks, other organisations and individuals with a contribution to make, to be a closer point of access. (And) to apply and attempt to get the service we provide to the lowest possible level.[3]

A Social Services Department patch handbook for voluntary and community organisations said that the intention was to:
"provide a more accessible and responsive social service to the public throughout East Sussex"

and to

> "strengthen at a *local* level the collaborative working arrangements with the other key services such as primary health care staff, schools, GPs, voluntary groups and so on."[4]

However, we do need to treat such hopes and claims with caution. The national debate on patch and community social work has been a rather one-sided one so far. As we have said, the discussion has been led from above and largely dominated by patch's supporters. Apart from conservative critics like Pinker and Leighton,[5] there have been very few discussions from a different point of view, and even less from people on the receiving end as day-to-day carers, service users or local residents. In 1983 Hadley was writing:

> Yet while patch systems have become recognised as a distinct method of service delivery, welcomed by some and seen as a dangerous threat to professional standards by others, it remains the case that we know remarkably little about just how many patch teams there are in the country, how they are structured and managed, and how well they operate.[6]

Just over a year later, though, he was able to point to a prolific growth in patch and provide detailed information on individual schemes.[7] Yet there has been no appreciable shift in involvement to the grassroots in the dominant discussion over this period, as far as we can judge. Certainly we have not encountered it in the contacts we have had with service users, workers, local people and groups in different parts of the country.

PEOPLE'S KNOWLEDGE OF THE PATCH REORGANISATION

Patch had been officially in existence for at least nine months when we asked people about it and had been in process of development for a period of years before that. There had been articles in the local press, the local Community Association newsletter, items on local radio — including the series of six programmes focusing on the Hanover area we have cited — public meetings and other public information. Nevertheless we found that only 18 members of the sample — less than one fifth — knew of the reorganisation. Why this was we don't know, although one possibility worth exploring is that it is another consequence — and indeed cause — of people seeing social services as marginal.[8]

The people who knew about the reorganisation were not representative of the overall sample. It was those who were *less* likely to use social services who were more likely to know about it. People categorised as middle class were over-represented (7/18 compared with 26/100 in the sample) as were those who had some occupational or social contact with social services. Three people knew from working in the Social Services Department, four from friends or relations working in it, and one from being in a related occupation. One learnt of it through being a foster parent, another from a social worker or aide visiting them and a third from a visiting nurse. Radio Brighton, the Community Association newsletter and local press had informed five people. Again the level of knowledge among users of social services was low. Only two of the ten clients and four of the other users were aware of the reorganisation. Almost all who knew about it (16/18) came from the 47 people who had direct or indirect contact or involvement with the Social Services Department or other welfare agencies.

We asked people when they had heard of the patch reorganisation. Four of the 18 didn't know, including one man who said, "I thought they were still in the process of doing it", reflecting the confusion over a reorganisation announced long before it was actually implemented in full. Most had only heard of it a few weeks or months earlier. Only four knew of it before the appointed day. These were two teachers, one past and one present social services worker — the latter having learned of it two years before. Thus only one person in a sample of 100 knew about the reorganisation when it was at the planning stage, and she was a worker in the Department.

Seventeen of the 18 people who knew of the reorganisation said they knew little or nothing about it, (9), or showed inaccurate (3) or scant (5) knowledge of it in their comments.

"It's more a neighbourhood team. There's a team in each neighbourhood."

"Not an awful lot. There are certain social workers responsible for forging closer links with children's homes and schools. It is obviously better. One person will know the problems."

"They've reorganized into six different patches and there's one social worker to each different patch."

"My sister (a home help) went to a meeting in Hanover where she works and she told me how they're dividing it into patches."

"There are some new areas. I don't know why they were called Patch."

Only one person, again a Social Services Department worker, was able to offer a detailed explanation while the comments of two others raised questions about the reorganisation:

"Well it seems that the intention is to decentralise rather than specialists working centrally. I know its been put across in a bit of publicity. I think it's supposedly to get the teams into the community, but I suggest its a cost-saving exercise."

"I know they were closing children's homes and moving offices out to them."

PUBLIC CONSULTATION OVER PATCH REORGANISATION

We asked people if they had ever been consulted or their views sought about the reorganisation. None said they had.

"I haven't known of anybody who has."

"I've seen a social worker though, telling me what to do and what to eat."

However, when we asked people if they would like to have been consulted over the reorganisation, 59 said they would have done.

"Yes, because we had a lot of our people (old people) taken away from us. It upset quite a few old people as well." (former home help)

"Anything that affects you and you're helping to pay for, you have the right to be consulted."

"It's democratic isn't it?"

"Of course this is half the trouble. There are lots of things like people not claiming what they could claim. They could give out more information. They should let you know and you have a say in it."

"Yes, as a resident of the town. Anything that affects people in the town should be put to them. Planning permissions are advertised in the papers and that's not good enough."

"It's hard to say. There's not much I could do. I'd like to have been asked, but I think it would have been futile."

Thirty people said they would not like to have been consulted, but of these nine did so because they did not associate social services with themselves and two because they did not feel adequately informed.

"It hasn't concerned me so far. If I were involved, like a one parent family, I would want to be (consulted)."

"I don't know anything about it. How can I contribute?"

Thus the picture that emerged of the patch reorganisation from people was very similar to that of social services generally. The process of reorganisation does not seem to have represented a qualitative change in the Department's way of working. People generally did not know about it and were not involved in it. No one had been consulted and very few knew what it meant. The situation seemed to be the same in 1984 when we revisited the people with whom we had had group discussions. Most still seemed to know little about the patch reorganisation. Furthermore, as we have seen from some of the comments of the people we interviewed who did not want to be consulted over reorganisation, the marginality of social services to many people continued to be a factor in their attitudes towards it.

This lack of local awareness of, and involvement and adequate consultation in the reorganisation would appear to be the antithesis of what patch is claimed to represent. This is particularly disappointing when we recall that one of the major principles identified for patch was "the right of local communities to share in decision making about services priorities"[9], and that an essential feature proposed for this "community-centred strategy" is that it is "readily accessible and acceptable" to local people.[10] The minority Barclay Report endorsing neighbourhood-based social work quite specifically envisaged "greater participation from the community... as partners in formulating policies on services development and also in criticising and re-evaluating existing services".[11]

What we were hoping to see was East Sussex starting its adoption of a patch system as it meant to go on. In other words, using the planning and consultation phase of the new scheme as an opportunity — in the words of its Director of Social Services — "to move closer to the consumer and seek more consistent methods of testing consumer reaction".[12] The importance of consultation and public participation beginning at the earliest possible stage has long been recognised.[13] The problem so far has been the general failure to ensure this across the board of public policies, from planning and housing to health and personal social services. From what people told us, patch did not appear to have escaped this longstanding deficiency. It is one that makes true partnership between people and policy-makers very difficult to develop.

It would be wrong, however, to see the apparent failure of this patch reorganisation to involve or consult local people as peculiar to East Sussex. In none of the seven case studies of patch included in "Going Local" were local people or service users consulted over the reorganisation. The initiative for the move came instead predominantly from upper and middle management and academics involved in linked research.[14] The trend is for patch increasingly to be adopted "from the top down".[15] Thus the failure to involve people in the process of reorganisation our survey identified in Brighton would seem to be typical of a more general picture in patch reorganisation — and indeed of decentralisation more generally.[16] The best known initiative in decentralising local authority services is that in Walsall, and this was undertaken with "a singular lack of tenant or community control and participation".[17]

This raises some other issues which it is worth considering briefly before we turn to what people themselves had to say about patch. Patch has been cast by its proponents as a "pro-active" approach to meeting need — going out and being in the community — which they have contrasted with the "reactive" role of conventional centralised social services which respond to emergencies and issues coming to them.[18] However it is difficult to see how patch can be seen as active in this way, unless it takes the initial steps of going out to consult with people and find out what they want. Emphasis has also been laid on its capacity to gather detailed information about the local situation, "informal networks and systems of care, and the pattern and potential of local voluntary organisations".[19] Again, how can this be achieved without early and close consultation with local people?

PEOPLE AND PATCH

We wanted to find out what people thought about some of the key ideas and principles associated with patch. To do this, we asked them their views on the localisation of social services, social services' increased reliance on voluntary organisations, volunteers and people's own "informal helping networks" and of them working in closer partnership with voluntary and community organisations.

It might be argued that people would not know much about these issues, especially in the light of their generally low level of information about social services and the reorganisation. They would not be familiar with research findings which could cast light on the.problems and benefits involved. What one might do is merely give weight to people's preconceptions, prejudices and stereotypes. Even if this were the case, we would suggest that such attitudes were significant and could not be ignored, since the outcome of the reorganisation would ultimately be dependent upon them. But we would argue that people's views were important and material for more positive reasons.

The patch approach to social services has been advocated as enabling the improvement of services for the benefit of, and to involve the community. The views of "the community", as a matter of principle, can hardly be excluded from the debate. These are the people who make up the voluntary and community organisations on whom greater reliance is to be placed; from whom volunteers will be drawn and who will be the recipients of their services, and whose "informal helping networks" are being looked to. Their attitudes and expectations are of immense importance if social services are going to build upon "the community" — as has been the emphatic watchword of patch — rather than operate in isolation from it — the criticism patch advocates have made of traditional social services. Local people have particular insights to offer and their own experience and specialised knowledge. It is these we wanted to explore.

LOCALITY

First we asked people what they felt about having social services teams based in local offices. We explained that the intention was to have one in each of the 15 patches (since reduced to 12) into which Brighton had been divided. In cases where people found it helpful, they were shown the size and boundaries of the patch on a map. More than three quarters of the sample (77) expressed some support for or agreement with the idea.

Table 1: Responses to Question 12a: "What do you feel about having Social Services teams based in local offices?"

Response	Number
Supported the idea	77
*Unqualified support	44
Support with qualification	15
Equivocal support	7
Thought it "sounded a good idea"	11
Opposed to the idea	5
Mixed feelings	3
Unable to comment through lack of information	7
Other	3
Don't know	5
Total	100

*Included comments like "a good idea", "very good idea", "very sensible", "excellent".

The main advantages people saw were that social services would get to know the area and its people better and be more accessible. Support, however, was not unreserved. What we see in people's responses is that while many basically favourable comments were made, these were often hedged with all kinds of reservations and equivocations. Less than half the sample and only just over half those with experience of social services were unreservedly in favour of localisation. This contrasts with the unqualified acceptance by many of patch's advocates of its principles and practice as good in themselves and synonymous with additional improvements to the existing system.

> "I think it's a good idea if they're willing to do what people want."

> "It's a good idea as long as there's not too much turnover in the staff themselves."

> "If they were able to provide a good service or a better service, it would be better."

Similar reservations and uncertainties about what localisation would actually mean and what it would really be like also came from those who expressed mixed feelings or said they didn't know.

> *"Two things really, actually contradictory. It will make social services more accessible if they're physically located on the area, but some people might not like the authority, the welfare on their doorstep."*

> *"I don't know what they're replacing. I don't know if it's better or worse, especially not if it's designed by bureaucrats — then it will be for their benefit."*

VOLUNTARY AND COMMUNITY ORGANISATONS AND VOLUNTEERS

We asked two questions about voluntary organisations. First what people felt about the increased emphasis and reliance on voluntary organisations and volunteers associated with patch. 59 people expressed some measure of support, while 19 were opposed to it. Only just over a third were unreservedly in favour of it.

> *"It's quite a good idea because a lot of older people who were fit and able would be pleased to think they are able to help."*

> *"Volunteers are good. They're called 'do-gooders', but that's unfair."*

> *"I'm very much for voluntary organisations."*

> *"I'd like to be a volunteer in something like that. If you can get your hand in, you know what's going on."*

Table 2: Responses to Question 12b: "What do you feel about an increased emphasis and reliance on voluntary organisations and volunteers?"

Response	Number	
Supported the idea		59
*Unqualified support	36	
Support with qualification	19	
Equivocal support	3	
Thought it "sounded" a good idea	1	
Opposed to the idea		19
Mixed feeling		10
Other		2
Unable to answer through lack of information		1
Don't know		9
Total		100

* as in Table 1

We went on to ask about the idea of social services working more closely with voluntary, community and self-help groups. This drew the strongest support from the sample. Apart from the three people who had assumed they already worked closely with them — "I'd have thought they did that anyway" — more than three quarters (77) of those surveyed offered some support for the idea. Almost two-thirds (63) were unreservedly in favour of it. Only four were opposed to it. Perhaps we shouldn't be surprised at such a positive response to this question and such a small number of dissenters. At face value it is particularly uncontroversial, and people had strong arguments to offer in support of it.

"It would make it easier on (people). Old people would get more care taken."

"That's what they should do anyway. Nobody works together."

"The self-help groups and volunteers need the help I think."

"That's a lot of the trouble with that little Maria Colwell. One person didn't know what the other was doing."

"I'd like to see that as it would cut red tape. I think voluntary groups know where the need is more than official groups."

What emerged from both questions, and indeed elsewhere in the interviews, was that many people were well aware of the issues involved in using volunteers. 28 people raised practical objections to social services *relying* on volunteers, and a further 11 opposed their increased use as a matter of principle. Only seven people made positive comments about them. People asked whether volunteers would actually be forthcoming (13); commented on their unreliability (4); worried about their lack of skill and need for training (4), and the need to be selective (1).

"I think generally you don't get enough volunteers for anything. You generally get a negative response so voluntary organisations fail for this reason."

"It's good providing you can get volunteers. The actual service would probably suffer if you just relied on volunteers."

"I hate the word "professional", but I don't think they should rely on volunteers for an essential service, especially with all the unemployment about."

"I think if people had time, it's a good idea. People would help I think. I was involved in setting up the Westhill Community Association and that worked very well. But I think it's wrong to rely on volunteers when it should come out of the public purse. We are supposed to be a caring society."

Three of those who favoured an increased reliance on voluntarism seemed to do so because they couldn't see any alternative.

"They'd have to as the Council wouldn't pay for it, or Mrs. Thatcher."

"In our society the jobs are not going to come back so people will have to do voluntary work."

Two others saw mass unemployment as a reason for it, rather than an objection:

"There's such a lot of people unemployed. I think that system would work."

"A lot of people out of work might like to do that kind of work."

Several others posed the kind of quandary which has helped give weight to arguments for increased voluntarism at a time of government cuts.

"I'm not sure what I think about voluntary organisations anyway. It seems wrong that welfare should depend on volunteers, but in a caring society, you'd hope people wouldn't have to be paid to look after each other."

On the other hand, those opposed to an increased reliance on volunteers, argued the need for more resources and against cuts in paid workers and the use of voluntarism by government as a means of cost-cutting and evading its own responsibilities.

"Don't know about increased reliance. Certainly those willing to assist need support and help too."

"A Conservative trick to cut expenditure."

"I think voluntary work is a good thing, but if it's a short cut to have fewer social workers, then it's bad."

"That's a difficult question. Some people like to do things and work voluntarily, but it's a get-out for them (the local authority) to do it without being paid. I think people should be paid."

Perhaps we can draw some more general inferences here which certainly require further consideration locally. Many more people gave unqualified support to the idea of a partnership with voluntary groups than that of reliance upon them. The reservations and questions they raised are neither unrealistic nor far removed from the issues being debated by academics and policy makers in this area. It was also clear that people tended to speak more of volunteering — where they might have personal knowledge — rather than voluntary agencies.

"I don't think they'd have much luck getting volunteers."

However, this wasn't always so by any means.

"Well I think certainly if people are prepared to do it, but I think the WRVS and Red Cross are strained. There's a lot of old people in Brighton."

A final point here is that favourable and positive views about voluntary organisations were hardly ever posed as alternatives to state provision in the way that many advocates of the former have proposed.[20] If in a sense we were inviting people by our questions to endorse an increased emphasis on voluntarism, they declined to do so.

"I suppose that's the ultimate aim of a do-it-yourself basis."

"Well that in itself I don't think is bad, but I don't agree with a reliance on voluntary work."

"I'm all for cooperation, but I'd like the emphasis on state paid work."

"That sounds good, but I reserve judgement... If it supplements the Council's services, it could be better, but not replace them."

"INFORMAL CARE"

We move now to discussing what people thought of relying more on "informal helping networks". This is a term used by advocates of patch and other "community care" approaches to describe the idea that a substantial part of the help provided for people comes from family, friends and neighbours.[21] The distinguishing feature of such "informal care" is that it is based on unpaid labour. Appeals for a greater emphasis on informal caring associated with patch based social services have been adversely criticised for harking back to a lost and often idealised past.[22] Such nostalgia was explicit in comments from two of the people we surveyed.

"Oh yes, I'm a believer in that — people looking after each other like it used to be."

"Yes... it's all kind of community spirit that has been lost over the years."

On the other hand, our discussion of voluntarism suggests that people's responses become harder-headed on questions concerning themselves rather than agencies "out there". So it is not surprising that such idealised comments were very much the exception and people's views about reliance on informal networks were far more sceptical.

Table3: Responses to Question 12c: "What do you feel about an increased emphasis on 'informal helping networks'?"

Response	Number
Supported the idea	55
*Unqualified support	37
Support with qualification	17
Thought it "sounded" a good idea	1
Opposed to the idea	30
Mixed feelings	8
Other	3
Unable to comment through lack of information	1
Don't know	3
Total	100

* as in Table 1

In all just over half the sample expressed some degree of support for the idea of an increased emphasis on "informal helping networks" — or people looking after themselves. But only 37 supported it unreservedly and nearly a third disagreed with the idea.

Nine people commented specifically on the virtues of self-help.

"If it helps them to help themselves, all good and well."

"Oh yes, everyone should help themselves."

Other people, however, cast doubt on the practicability of such an approach under modern conditions.

"It's a reasonable idea. People if they know somebody needs something specific done, they will do it. It possibly may work, but people are becoming more self-contained and you often don't have much contact with people in the street — like up here — because of the increase in people working full-time. Unless you have children of the same age you don't have much contact."

"I suppose neighbours could do it. I don't know. I don't mix too much. Some people are neighbourly."

"I agree it's a good idea, but I don't think it works. People don't get involved in each other lives. It's better to go to an organized help system."

"Must be kidding dear! That wouldn't work. Mind you there's some nice women round here, but I don't think people even know the next door neighbour. I think people should be more neighbourly. I do think the old comrade spirit has gone."

"We all like to think we're good neighbours, but we don't always do it when it gets down to it. The community centre does things voluntarily, but it's always

the hardcore few who end up doing the foot work."

"That's alright so long as it works. People's time is tied up so much these days."

A number of people (6) again made the general point that it would be difficult to recruit volunteers. Five people saw the value of an increased emphasis on informal helping networks as helping people maintain their prized independence.

"That should happen to elderly people. They should be helped to be independent."

"That's good. I know from my sister (a home help) many elderly people want to live alone and be by themselves and be independent, but with help."

But the belief that people should be able to be independent, may have been confused here with an assumption that informal care was necessarily capable of making it possible. Other people pointed out that such an approach and indeed the maintenance of people's independence, required government resources and effective support from the Department.

"Anything that helps people look after themselves is better than relying on the state, but people have to have money and moral support."

"I think that would be quite a good idea as I think a lot of old people certainly could look after themselves with a lot more back up. I work in a hospital and I see a lot of it. They need a lot more back up than what they are getting."

"I think to remain independent is better, like sheltered accommodation."

"I think for instance if somebody, like me is keeping an eye on someone like the old lady next door, the welfare should make a point of seeing me and asking me how she is. I suppose if she met me, she'd just think I was a nosey old bitch, but she's got no one to help her. She's not got much money. This Social Security is no good at all."

But the argument was also offered that some people might be no more likely to welcome the intervention of social services activities and guided informal helping networks, than any more formal welfare involvement — perhaps even less so.

"I think that happens a lot anyway. Some people are neighbourly. But it would be good to know if there was a qualified nurse or doctor in the street. But a lot of old people might not want people to interfere. They might feel put upon."

"For older people I suppose. I'd hate to feel that everybody in the street knew what I was doing. I think it's trying to get everybody involved in the community

and I don't think younger people like that. I know I don't. I don't like knowing my neighbours as I feel they're peeping out of windows."

As one woman said, any change in emphasis to an informal care approach should first have people's approval. Its very informality could also pose additional problems:

"That's a good idea as long as the people themselves are happy with it. If a voluntary worker decides not to do it one day, then someone will have to do it."

An even more fundamental criticism made of increased reliance on informal helping networks, concerned the limits of its usefulness. People were concerned about the cases where people couldn't look after each other and more help was needed.

"There must be times when people can't look after themselves."

"Which people would be involved? Would it mean short-term sick or chronically disabled or blind people or the elderly?"

Others made the point that "self-help" and self-reliance were already the rule for most people, without any increased official dependence on informal helping networks. They also gave some idea of the strains and shortcomings that could be the reality of such arrangements.

"I thought we all looked after ourselves! No one else does."

"That's a catch question regarding old people. Old people have to look after themselves, because there's no facilities to look after them. It's cheaper."

"Not keen. I'm going on older people. I look after an old lady. If it weren't for me, she wouldn't see anybody."

"I've got an elderly couple of relations. She is 81 and has angina and he is 83. They've got no one else and now he has cancer. At Christmas I was trying to visit them both in different hospitals."

Private Care Instead Of Public Responsibility?

Some people felt that the Council was already abnegating its responsibilities.

"I don't think they worry about old people enough."

"I don't know if I agree with that as I don't think the Council takes that much interest in people anyway."

"If people were able to (look after each other), all well and good, but I see people

round here who need help and obviously don't get it."

For some of them and a number of others, the increased emphasis on informal care embodied in patch could be a way for the Council to reduce its responsibilities and resources even further.

"...it sounds like window dressing and an evasion of responsibility."

"Well I think it's a good idea in that most elderly people would prefer to be at home, but if it's just used as a measure to save money, then it's short-sighted."

"Seems to me to be a doubled-edged sword. It's just words. My friend (in social services) mentioned this. I think she was relieved there was a system that would take pressure off social services."

"It's wrong. It's part of the general attack on people's needs and rights."

"Probably not a good idea as people who go to social services need help anyway."

What they and others wanted to see was the government itself providing the services and resources that people needed.

"A good idea if people rely on themselves, but I thought social services departments were there for people who can't rely on themselves."

"Again I would say it's very unfair to expect people who may not have time, ability, health or facilities to do it. It is the duty of the state to help."

PATCH IN OVERALL PERSPECTIVE

Having asked people's views about particular aspects of patch, we followed this up with a question about their feelings on patch generally. 41 of the sample gave unqualified support to patch in general, and 40 had reservations, gave qualified support, had mixed feelings or were opposed to it. The patch principle that was picked out for approval most often (by 16 people) was localisation, and the gains seen to come from it. Not one person singled out greater reliance on informal care for the same kind of praise. This question enabled us to cross-check people's earlier responses, and more interestingly, to hear comments which had not emerged before, particularly from workers and users of social services.

"It's alright providing they'd given us more notice. It's all happened so quick. We only had a couple of days notice." (home help)

"It's ok providing it doesn't create more bureaucracy. In my job I deal with the Brighton Area Health Authority and the amount of bureaucracy is just beyond words."

"It depends where the offices are and whether anybody will be on duty. It's shocking trying to get help at weekends. Everything is too far out and goes through too many people."

A blind and disabled woman also expressed her basic and important concern:

"As long as I get some walks it would be alright. Would they (social services) know someone who could do my hair? I shall miss Philip (a social worker(?) who had visited her) terribly."

Reviewing the replies to our questions about patch we also tried to find out whether there were any differences in attitudes towards patch between different groups in the sample. There were no appreciable differences in responses according to either sex or estimated social class. On the other hand, clients of social services appeared more likely to favour the reorganisation than the rest of the sample. This might have been because they hoped for some improvement to social services as they had known them, or alternatively because of benefits they had experienced from the reorganisation. The former seems a more likely explanation, both because of the low level of information about reorganisation and because only three clients were currently in contact with social services.

Perhaps the most interesting responses were those of the twelve people who said they were involved in voluntary and community organisations. Significantly, seven of the 12 were opposed to increased reliance and emphasis on "informal helping networks", compared with less than a third of the overall sample. Only four unreservedly favoured an increased emphasis on voluntary organisations and volunteers compared with over a third of the total sample. Their feelings about patch generally however were similar to those of the rest of the sample. Their strong reservations about greater reliance on voluntary organisations, volunteers and informal care, are particularly important in view of their first hand knowledge, experience and involvement in voluntarism.

With the exception of the issue of closer working with voluntary and community organisations, in general at least half the sample expressed reservations about patch and the principles associated with it. The issues of increasing emphasis and reliance on formal voluntarism and informal care drew most opposition and the lowest levels of unqualified support, with just over one third of people favouring them. This echoes the finding of the New Society/National Institute for Social Work survey of public attitudes to social workers, in which:

only 22 percent (of the sample) agreed that they (social workers) should fulfil the role that Jenkin (the then Secretary of State for Health and Social

Services) sees for them — that is encouraging "local people to find ways of helping their neighbours in need by voluntary action".[23]

People's uncertainty about what patch would actually mean was expressed in a number of ways. These included the relatively large number of comments (26) in response to our questions like "it sounds a good idea" or "on the face of it, quite good", where people signalled their difficulty in judging. Also there were many hedging comments like:

"If they are willing to do what people want."

"In theory it should offer a better response."

Sometimes people equated patch principles with the benefits attributed to them, without distinguishing between the two.

"Well I think it's a good idea rather than have one main building. It's good as the social workers will get to know the people better — more close-knit really."

Others did not take such gains for granted, or see changes like localisation as necessarily a virtue in themselves. This questioning attitude has not generally been apparent in professional and academic discussions of patch. But such questions do need to be raised. Will social workers' response to local needs necessarily be better because they are locally based — particularly given other constraints operating on them? Will social services really feel more personal and will they actually be more accessible as some people expected when they expressed support for patch? At another level is it always an improvement for social workers to know local people "better" when their role is as much a regulatory as a welfare one? Large question marks still hang over all these issues, and they still have to be adequately addressed by patch and its advocates.

We have seen that a large proportion of those surveyed were cautious and critical of patch and unwilling to take it on trust. Nor did people respond to patch or accept it as a package. As has been seen, some of its idess were more populat than others. Only 10 people supported unreservedly all four aspects of patch about which they were asked. Eighteen supported them all with only one qualification or reservation. Only 30 people gave some measure of support to all four proposals and 59 to three or more of them.

Looked at differently, we can say that a large pool of positive feelings towards patch existed among our sample. If this was qualified by people's concerns about what patch might entail, this only parallels critiques made elsewhere.[24]

"It seems to me that it probably involves a financial cut-back and that's probably why it has occurred."

What also emerged from the sample was a widespread lack of knowledge about, and uncertainty how to judge, whether the patch reorganisation was feasible and what it would actually mean in practice — and considerable doubts on both issues.

Partnership — A Missed Opportunity

Local people were not even consulted by the Department on the basic issue of the setting of local patch boundaries.[25] Yet as we have seen, they had important and pertinent things to say. For the people we surveyed, their relatives and friends, it appeared that a valuable opportunity had been lost to engage them in the early stages of the scheme. This applied particularly to the 47 people with some kind of connection with social services and other welfare agencies. Almost all the people we interviewed who knew about the reorganisation (16/18) came from among their number. They also included most of those who made unreservedly positive comments about the Social Services Department (13/17). Thus a valuable and accessible source of experience, knowledge, goodwill and actual or potential interest in the Department was neither consulted or involved in the reorganisation. Yet clearly in patch terms they represented a fertile resource to be tapped and built on. A few of the people we surveyed even had the impression that the reorganisation had yet to happen, and many others took a wait-and-see attitude.

> "A good idea if the community participates, which I can't see happening. The whole method meant people did know each other. Now we've got to start from scratch. Time will tell."

Again, a major point that emerges is that people who supported the notion of a partnership between the so-called statutory and voluntary sectors, were warier when this was posed as a *reliance* on the latter. This gave rise to a degree of scepticism when informal caring networks were considered for use by state services. Indeed the difference is one that advocates of patch have hardly begun to consider. There is an issue here of the gross imbalance of power between the statutory and voluntary sectors, with the economic and political dependence of most of the latter on the former growing more marked.[26]

It is difficult to see how in such a partnership the problem of voluntary and community organisations being overshadowed by the intentions of statutory services, or of them becoming a reflection of their aims, interests and priorities, can be avoided. It is not clear how patch can make possible closer working with voluntary and community organisations that is at the same time less unequal, without the creation of new structures and safeguards and ways of funding the voluntary sector that put its independence on a much more secure footing. We shall shortly see some of the problems posed by and for such partnerships as they have emerged in the Hanover patch.

PATCH: PRINCIPLES INTO PRACTICE

In this philosophy, the user is not only a client, but a partner in the planning and provision of services.
Roger Hadley and Morag McGrath, "When Services Are Local", 1984. [27]

*In theory this kind of thing is very good, but will it work in practice?"
Middle aged man interviewed*

THE NEIGHBOURHOOD CARE SCHEME

On the 5th June 1982 a meeting was called by the Hanover Social Services team at the Hanover Community Centre. The team manager explained that while still centrally based, "we'd rather be out here". He referred to one project bringing the team into the patch — a patch surgery or advice session planned for every other Wednesday morning at the Community Centre. This had just been held for the first time the previous week. However, the main purpose of the meeting was to discuss another initiative. As the manager put it: "to invite all the people we thought might have an interest in the social problems of the area ... to get some ideas from you how we could offer a more positive service in the Hanover district."

The (then) senior social worker[28] told the 40 or so people from related services and voluntary organisations who had been invited that while nearly half the team's referrals concerned old people, they made up only 10-15 percent of allocated cases. There was a concern to find out what was happening to the rest.

The team manager explained that it had become apparent there was a problem when they had learnt of old people waiting outside their front doors during the winter's snow for someone else's home help to go by, to get them food from the corner shop, as they couldn't get there themselves. He went on to say that they wanted "to float the idea of a neighbourhood care scheme with you before we go to the residents". The team didn't want "to impose the idea without getting your views.... Our idea is to have a meeting for interested residents". This was the first time that the idea of a neighbourhood care scheme had surfaced locally in a more open meeting.

As we shall see, the idea of a neighbourhood care scheme was already being pursued by the team. Several other ideas were raised by people at the meeting, like telephones or intercoms for old people or a street warden scheme.

However, before the end, the team manager announced: "We shall be launching within the next few months a neighbourhood care scheme... and calling a meeting with residents and publicising what we're doing".

People from other agencies did not respond to the team's idea of having meetings like the present one on a regular basis. Nor did anyone take up the offer of joining the team in a working party to discuss the idea of a neighbourhood care scheme.

A public meeting called subsequently about the scheme brought little response. As a result, the first real public forum was the AGM of the Hanover Community Association held on the 21st July. By then the patch surgery no longer existed. In her report, the Hanover Community Association Chairperson summed this up as "Social Services came and went". According to the senior social worker it stopped because "it just didn't work". There had been only three or four sessions and nobody had come to two of them, so it had been decided to discontinue them. They have not been restarted since.

At the same meeting, the Hanover senior social worker stated that "we've decided on a neighbourhood care scheme for the old and handicapped in the Tarner area" of the Hanover patch. The scheme which was originally scheduled to start in October 1982 began in November. It was initially funded from the Social Services Department's voluntary agencies budget and an urban aid application submitted to fund it and two other similar schemes over the Hanover patch area from April 1983.

We asked the people we surveyed whether they knew that the Social Services Department was planning to set up a neighbourhood care scheme. Our survey was carried out between August and October. Yet only six people said they knew of the intention to set up a scheme and only one of those lived in the area it was intended to cover, or its immediate vicinity.

"I think I read it somewhere."

"I read about it in the (Community Association) Newsletter."

"I heard vaguely about it."

The neighbourhood care scheme and local surgery show major discrepancies between theory and practice as patch was applied in Hanover. In neither case does it appear that local people were effectively consulted or involved. Judging from our survey, most were unlikely to know about the plans for a neighbourhood care scheme, although eight of the people we told thought it might be a good idea. This may also be the reason for the lack of response to the patch surgery sessions. Neither idea came directly from local people, service users, local community or voluntary organisations. Instead both were initiated by the Social Services Department; in the case of the neighbourhood care scheme, in partnership with the Brighton Council for Voluntary Service.

A report of the first six months of the Tarner scheme, now renamed the

"Hanover Neighbourhood Care Scheme", makes clear the origins of the project and helps explain why so few people seemed to know about it.

In April 1982 discussions began between Social Services and Brighton Council for Voluntary Service. Brighton CVS was asked if it could support a neighbourhood care scheme for one area of Brighton. The scheme was an expression of partnership between a voluntary organisation and Social Services, drawing on the expertise and personnel of the CVS and the resources of Social Services. As the first scheme of its kind in Brighton, it was seen as an important initiative, giving substance to the new "patch" system of social services.

The CVS saw the scheme as an opportunity to design an innovative project, supporting a neighbourhood style of work as well as a centrally based service. The proposed scheme drew a great deal of interest from team managers in Social Services who saw it as a model which, if successful, could be used in other areas.[29]

The report described discussions with voluntary and statutory agencies in the summer of 1982, including the June meeting at the Hanover Community Centre, in terms of ensuring: "that lines of communication were kept open and that both existing voluntary resources and potential referral agencies were kept informed of developments".[30]

The nature, location and funding of the project were all decided by the Social Services patch team and Brighton Council for Voluntary Service. It was not a response to local demand, so could it be said to be what was wanted locally? According to a leaflet about it:

The aim is to assist the housebound by offering help in a different way. This might mean visiting to keep a friendly eye on neighbours, making sure that they're alright, escorting disabled people on shopping expeditions or perhaps doing a bit of shopping for people when you do your own. Some people may need minor repairs in their homes. For example, they may need a new plug fitted or a light bulb put in or their lawn mowing occasionally. All these things would be greatly appreciated by housebound and infirm people.[31]

As for enabling local groups or people to have a future involvement or say in the scheme, as part of the discussions, a meeting was held in July 1982 at Social Services:

drawing together major voluntary organisations and statutory bodies to inform them of the scheme and to consider whether a neighbourhood forum might be developed to support the care organiser. A local forum did not seem feasible, but an interviewing panel was agreed, consisting of

Social Services, Age Concern and the CVS.[32]

In October "the scheme became public, with a leaflet drop around Hanover, articles in the press and radio interviews".[33] So far, however, the scheme has not been locally controlled. Instead it has had a steering group made up of its organiser, together with a development worker and volunteer organiser from the CVS, and the patch team manager and social services officer — who are responsible to their agencies.

All this does beg the question of whose needs the neighbourhood care scheme was primarily meeting; those of people in the area, particularly those who are old and housebound, or those of the Social Services Department and the Council for Voluntary Service. This is the perennial problem with ready-made proposals from outside. Before we go on to examine this issue in the wider context of East Sussex Social Services' policies for old people and the Department's approach to patch working, we want to address some of the difficulties and dilemmas facing the Hanover patch team.

What we have seen in the example of the neighbourhood care scheme is an apparent process of consultation revealed as essentially an information exercise. This is a common characteristic and shortcoming of such participatory projects. However, as we have also seen, the patch team had very limited resources, limited control over them and also considerable and continuing conventional social services responsibilities. In advancing the idea of a neighbourhood care scheme, they would have been able to draw on their own knowledge of the area and their experience of and contact with local people over a period of years. However, as we have seen, community social work and patch imply a different approach based much more on direct community involvement and participation. Neither the patch team, nor the CVS had the resources or facilities to undertake adequately the kind of consultative process that identifying and setting up a local initiative like the care scheme would have required. Even to carry out a comprehensive information exercise would have been a major undertaking which may have been beyond their resources.[34] At no time was the patch team able to devote even one of its members to the scheme full-time, in spite of its scale and the importance attached to it.

We would not want our discussion of the neighbourhood care scheme to be seen as critical of the Hanover patch team. They have clearly had a considerable commitment to it, reflected both in their efforts to inform and involve people through meetings, leaflets and publicity, and in their continuing support for the project. What they have lacked has been the necessary resources. Our own preliminary survey of people's views in Hanover, for example, has taken us hundreds of hours of work. This kind of opportunity was not available to the team. It would be wrong to expect them to be able to take on the massive task that effective community consultation and involvement demand. We would suggest that the scale of the task has consistently been under-estimated by advocates of community social work and patch. Indeed we would see the problem of resources for the patch team as a theme running through our discussion of developments in Hanover.

THE RELATIONSHIP WITH DEPARTMENTAL POLICY

We now want to discuss two broad areas of policy that have an important bearing on developments in the Hanover patch. First is social services' policy for old people, which is subtle and complex, and second, the part project work plays in the Department's approach to patch.

East Sussex Social Services' policy for old people has been based on a reassessment of what is called "the balance of care". This has not only meant a greater stress on the contribution and coordination of other departments, like housing and health, [35] but also re-examination of its own domiciliary and residential services and an increased emphasis on commercial and voluntary residential provision and on "neighbourhood care". [36] This policy has been associated with an increasing reliance on joint funding and a reduction in social services spending in real terms. It has been comprehensively criticised by the National Union of Public Employees. NUPE argued that East Sussex County Council provision for old people ranked 33 out of 39 non-metropolitan counties despite the County having the highest proportion of elderly people in the country. Its residential care provision for old people was below the DHSS guidelines and declining further. Only three local authorities appeared to provide a more restricted home help service than East Sussex.[37] This was confirmed in 1985 when East Sussex again emerged as one of the authorities at the bottom of a "league table" of home help provision, failing to meet minimal guidelines laid down by the DHSS.[38] NUPE argued that the County did not give adequate recognition to the cost implications of its proposals, either for other departments or for the effective implementation of a policy of community care. Instead there seemed to be a reduction in real terms of the provision of care for old people, despite the increase in their numbers, particularly in the over 85 age group which attract the highest level of service, both in East Sussex and nationally.[39]

Development projects have been a major way in which the Department has sought to move from a case work to a community social work way of working in the patch. [40] Increased involvement in project work has also been a feature of moving to patch in other authorities.[41] The area development programme initiated by the Department's training sections and senior management was based on a series of such projects. They have been seen as a means of realising the aspiration for team managers "to find local solutions to local problems."[42] According to the Director:

A wide range of targets was chosen for the projects from establishing a linking system for local voluntary groups and assessing the needs of elderly clients, to setting up foster parent groups at patch level and helping to form a self-help group for isolated families on a local authority housing estate.[43]

As this suggests, they have been used crucially to develop "community involvement" and community care. Thus they are closely linked with the Department's policy for old people as one of the ways of implementing its commitment to neighbourhood care, although East Sussex places no less an emphasis on such schemes for other client groups, for instance children in care and young people with mental handicaps.[44] The Hanover neighbourhood care scheme represents such a project, although it was not initiated as part of the area development programme. That is why it is important to consider it in the broader setting of social services' policy for old people and increased emphasis on "informal care". We can begin to see it making sense in terms of the priorities and preferences of the Department, if not those of local people.

The introduction of the Hanover neighbourhood care scheme coincided with cuts in the home help service. Hanover suffered a 25 percent reduction in their home help hours. The recorded demand for home helps is also likely to understate the actual need. For example, as we have seen, some people are reluctant to accept the service because of the minimum charge levied, which is not covered by an additional social security payment. Reductions in the home help service have also been exacerbated by the increased demands placed on it through East Sussex's closure of old people's homes as part of its policy of community care,[45] and reductions in hospital beds for old people.

Just over a week before the local paper ran a feature article on the neighbourhood care scheme, "The lifeline team with a kindly touch",[46] it reported a total of almost £1 million cuts planned for social services.[47] The article about the care scheme concluded:

with increasing numbers of old people living longer the Tarner project could be one answer to the problems of dwindling resources trying to cope with growing demands.[48]

According to the Project's six months report:

Hanover was chosen (as the place to base the project) because of the high imput of home help hours in the area. It was clear that Social Services would not be able to meet the demands being made of them. It was also clear that these demands were often outside the statutory workers' brief.[49]

Every effort seems to have been made to try and reduce the cost of the scheme. Not only was it originally funded from the voluntary agencies budget, but the urban aid funding sought would mean that only a quarter of the cost would have to be borne by the local authority. Applications for the position of neighbourhood care organiser were sought from:

> Those who can offer a permanent commitment and have a mature approach to those in the community.[50]

However instead of employing someone full or part-time, "an honorarium of £400 pa (was) offered with an expenses allowance."[51] In the event the project never got the urban aid funding for the three schemes and coordinators originally envisaged. It was agreed instead that the original single scheme should continue to be funded by the local authority from the voluntary organisations budget, while extending the area it covered.[52] It now covers two thirds of the Hanover patch, and another similar scheme has been started in the adjoining Queens Park patch. We can see from this that voluntary care schemes, no less than statutory services, have resource implications, and can be just as vulnerable to difficulties in getting adequate resources.

There may be no direct link between cuts in the home help service and the introduction of a neighbourhood care scheme. The latter's stated aims were different to those of the home helps, and stress laid on it being "a complementary service to their's".[53] However the question arises not only of whether neighbourhood care can accomplish the task originally identified for it, but of whether needs which can no longer be met by home helps may not come the way of such a voluntary scheme by default. Most referrals to the scheme come from the Social Services Department, and given the shortage of home help hours, there is undoubted pressure on the patch team to consider using volunteers instead. The Brighton CVS acknowledged in its report that:

> There were some problems relating to other statutory workers in Hanover. Home helps felt their services were being undercut by volunteers and it was important to make clear that their tasks were not being done by volunteers.[54]

From the point of view of social services, the scheme has been useful in diverting referrals seen as inappropriate, in a context of declining home help hours. Where there are cuts though, there will unavoidably be rationing. At the same time there is likely to be some overlap between the role of home helps and such a voluntary scheme which undertakes "minor household repairs, sorting out problems with the DHSS, shopping and visiting." [55]

By late February 1983, the project had recruited a "hard core" of about a dozen volunteers, although volunteers had been welcomed from all over Brighton.[56] By July 1983, still with 12 volunteers, the project had a caseload of 40 individuals.[57] Two and a half years later, the situation was very much the same, although volunteers now tended to be more local. Referrals, however, have had to be restricted to avoid outstripping the number of volunteers.[58]

The value of the scheme and the desperate need for old people to have a means of raising help if they get into difficulty were highlighted in November 1985. One volunteer made local headlines as "the caring Samaritan" when he came to the rescue of an elderly man who had collapsed in his home after a heart attack. "It was just lucky I called in that day", he said.[59]

If needs that were the responsibility of the home help service, but could no longer be met by it, were to come its way, it seems very unlikely that such a voluntary scheme could meet them. In one of the BBC Radio Brighton programmes on local social services, the Hanover home help organiser said of home helps:

> I look upon them as the front line workers... I think to go in day after day to somewhere that (is) sometimes not very pleasant, all sorts of situations, and they go in and battle on and take on paying bills. They go in their own time and take washing home. I think they are an amazing group of women.[60]

Not only should we ask ourselves whether all this should be expected of home helps, but it certainly could hardly be expected of a neighbourhood care scheme like that established in Hanover. Neighbourhood care also raises wider issues for the home help service. Not only are there understandable fears among home helps of being left with the domestic and more demanding tasks while interesting inter-personal work is taken over by volunteers.[61] NUPE has also criticised East Sussex Social Services' policy more generally as undermining and narrowing the role of home helps. It expressed its concern about the possible privatisation of domestic work previously undertaken by home helps and its adverse effects both for users of the service and for the service itself.[62] There has been growing pressure in this direction, highlighted by government proposals in 1985 for Northern Ireland,which have been seen as a blueprint for the mainland, to abolish the existing home help service and replace it with individual grants to service users to make their own private arrangements and a small vestigial service for "more vulnerable clients".[63] Yet this comes at a time when there are growing arguments for *extending* the role of the home help as a central figure in services for old people and other groups,[64] and when the importance of home helps as key workers "crossing the difficult boundary between formal and informal care", is increasingly evident.[65]

PATCH POLICY AND THE NEEDS OF OLD PEOPLE

It is important to look at the needs of old people in the area from a broader policy perspective. It is possible to do this in this case because a long term development group exercise on "Growing Old in Brighton" was carried out by the Department of Health and Social Security and East Sussex Social Services

Department from 1977 to 1979. [66] It is unlikely that the needs of the old people in the area will have changed in any fundamental way since then, other than to have increased with local and national population trends. The then Director of Social Services emphasised the problems facing the Department, with one in ten of the East Sussex population aged over seventy five, double the national average, (the figure for Hanover patch is nine percent[67]) and "in the light of the increasing numbers and "increasing frailty" of local old people.[68]

In 1977 working groups made up of people from all sections of the Social Services Department, workers from voluntary and other statutory agencies and from the DHSS, met regularly over a period of three months and identified a series of policy issues for work with old people. These included prioritising work with old people, giving further consideration to the people themselves taking part in the planning and provision of day care services, wider use of home helps, provision of day centres, extra vehicles and drivers for day care use, improved assessment and admission to residential care, more training and support for residential staff, more use of volunteers and the appointment of a volunteers organiser. In the following year, it was still felt that old people received insufficient attention from qualified social workers, that there was a need for more and smaller day care centres and that transport was still inadequate. At the final meeting of the project in 1979, home helps still felt that domiciliary care had not received enough priority and that it should be the focus of future developments, and transport for day care was still inadequate.[69]

Few of the issues raised by this broadbased and long term exercise actually seem to be addressed by the patch reorganisation. Most of them involved additional expense. A number have still not been implemented, indeed with cuts the situation has worsened conspicuously with reductions in residential provision and in staffing in real terms, in both residential and domiciliary services. It may be that social services will be able to address these issues more effectively in time, but not we would suggest because of the localisation and increased emphasis on informal aid and voluntary action that represent the main basis for patch's claims for improving services. Patch seems to emerge as a parallel development rather than a response to the needs and issues identified.

EMERGING CONTRADICTIONS

Returning now to the two patch initiatives in Hanover, the social work surgery and neighbourhood care scheme, both seem to add weight to the uncertainties, objections and suspicions expressed by many of the people we surveyed. People seem to have been largely uninvolved in and unconsulted about either of them. Both appear to have been carried out in much the same way as the reorganisation itself, without prior information or consultation.

Insofar as this was the case, both they and the reorganisation were indistinguishable from traditional social services as perceived by many of the people we interviewed — distant and divorced from their lives — the antithesis of what patch is supposed to represent. They clearly did not correspond with the "underlying principles" of patch described by Hadley and Hatch, of:

> "working locally with the community in defining and providing a service instead of imposing a predetermined system from a headquarters remote from the people affected."[70]

On the other hand though, the Hanover neighbourhood care scheme is understandably regarded by its initiators as an important example of partnership between voluntary and statutory agencies. While it has remained small, it has increased in coherence. Monthly meetings and weekly surgeries have started for volunteers, and new volunteers now receive some training.[71] In accordance with Departmental policy, Hanover patch team has extended this approach with the introduction of a Cope scheme for developing "family groups" based at the local day nursery.[72] Significantly, however, the neighbourhood care scheme was developed in association with a Brighton-wide rather than local voluntary organisation and volunteers are still largely drawn from outside the patch. This contrasts with the arguments offered for example in the Barclay minority report for neighbourhood based social services as a means of supporting *local networks.*[73]

Summing up, the principles and practice of patch appear to have been contradictory in the experience of most of the people we surveyed. So far, in Hanover at least, the patch reorganisation does not seem to have made possible improved communication or consultation with local people. East Sussex, as we have said, was the first large authority to go patch. This is no small event and yet the reorganisation was implemented without local consultation or awareness[74] — a process which we have seen repeated in microcosm in Hanover. For a patch-based system to be "community orientated" as envisaged, it is to be expected that local involvement and understanding would be encouraged from the earliest possible time. Our survey suggests that this has not always happened in East Sussex. Any attempt to make it happen later may be too late. Our research also points to a different process of policy development, where people may be kept in touch with what is happening, but do not themselves share in decision-making in the way patch proponents have advocated.

It is surely crucial for a policy as dependent on community involvement as patch to have an informed and supportive public. Yet we found no consensus in favour of patch among our sample, but instead major reservations, particularly about voluntarism. This is especially important for a policy in which community orientation is held to be a key factor. It not only points to the need for effective consultation if appropriate policies are to be developed, but it also offers a strong warning that patch may not get the practical or political support from people that it depends on.

So far we have tried to explore the relationship between the theory and practice of patch by reference to both the views and experience of local people and local developments in Hanover. What we want to go on to do next is to explore a range of other major issues relating to social services and of importance to patch which we examined in our survey, and in so doing look at the additional insights they offer into both the ideas and practice of patch. The first of these issues is "community".

CHAPTER SIX

People and Community

*"I'm all in favour of that (community), providing it's not organised
into it. Either it is, or it isn't."*

QUESTIONING "COMMUNITY"

We can appreciate the temptation for readers to hurry through a discussion of
"community". The term has come to seem devalued and over-used: either
"the warmly persuasive word to describe an existing set of relationships, or
the warmly persuasive word to describe an alternative set of relationships".[1] It
is a remarkable concept. However much dismissed and despised, it flourishes
undiminished. From "community architecture" and "community farm" to
"community press" and "community enterprise", this term, devoid of almost
all meaning, is placed at the head of a widening range of projects and activities
to endorse and legitimate them. In "community relations" it is still offered as a
euphemism to gloss over issues of race and racism. But to neglect it in our
discussion would be to miss several important questions. Community is a key
concept in patch, however much its advocates blur this by using words like
"neighbourhood" and patch itself as synonyms. Why have they found it
necessary to rely on vague and unspecific concepts of "community", which
have given ready ammunition to their critics? They speak of "a community
orientated strategy",[2] "a community based alternative"[3] and "a community
centred model of organisation".[4] They have given the term a fresh lease of life.[5]
    However, as Baldock argues:

"Every community worker knows that 'the community' does not exist".[6]

Criticism is sharper still when "community" appears to be conflated with
locality. While the majority report of the Barclay Committee on social work
included in its conception of community, "communities of interest" which
might be spread over a large area,[7] the minority report saw locality as crucial to
its model of neighbourhood-based social work.[8] Indeed as Finch and Groves
observed:

It is difficult to see how "community" can avoid a geographical connotation when it is used in the context of community care: if it is a question of bathing an elderly person or doing shopping for the housebound, a degree of proximity does seem rather necessary.[9]

Arguing that a number of different "actual and potential networks and structured relationships" *do* exist, Baldock goes on to attack patch enthusiasts.

The locality does play a role in social life. But it is a restricted one. It is most important for those who are least mobile — the elderly and young children and their mothers. People belong to networks that are not in the least locality-bound. This is especially true of the groups of people that generate much of the workload of social services department social workers.[10]

A third argument against patch notions of "community" is that with one rhetorical bound a problem is transformed into its solution. On the one hand, the minority Barclay Report appears to accept that an area's potential for collective action will be a key factor affecting the likely existence of informal helping networks.

We recognise that many areas and estates seem to have very little community spirit or identity; we also realise that a community can be very hostile to individuals or groups within it and that areas which seem to have the greatest social needs often seem to have the weakest informal networks. Our view of neighbourhood is, in short, far from a rosy or sentimental one.[11]

On the other hand, the Report premises its argument for "a focus based on the support of (local) systems of informal care"[12] by stating the following.

What we are emphasising is the fact that most dependent people whose needs come within the remit of the personal social services (the frail elderly, the mentally or physically ill and handicapped living in the community, families with children at risk and others) are tied because of frailty, illness, fear, handicap, low income or habit to their local area, whether or not it has any sense of community."[13]

In other words it sidesteps the problem by treating "neighbourhood-based social work" as if that didn't also imply a pattern of relationships conducive to community care.

As Finch and Groves put it, "contemporary writing about community care does appear to presume the existence of locally based 'communities' which already provide helping services",[14] even though recent research has increasingly called the assumption into question.[15]

The most radical criticism of all comes from feminists. Far from being woolly or imprecise, they argue that "community" is a euphemism for something very specific. For Wilson,

The "community" is an ideological portmanteau word for a reactionary conservative ideology that oppresses women by silently confining them to the private sphere without so much as even mentioning them.[16]

Women are now also pointing out that whereas traditionally the territory of men has been their place of work — although mass unemployment is changing this — the home locality is very much the province of women. The "community" is women's space just as "caring" is women's work. Women are the "community" patch social services' advocates are talking about when they speak of "informal networks and care". The "community" has been women's domain and now male led social services are planning to enter and alter it.[17] Finch pursues this argument to raise the fundamental question of whether non-sexist policies of community care will ever be possible without fundamental change in society.[18]

There are a number of questions here which we wanted to explore with the people interviewed. Some of the issues raised by feminist critiques of caring will be looked at in the next chapter. Here we take as our starting point the concepts of patch itself, and the fact that "community" and "neighbourhood" continue to be presented to users and other local people as part of the patch "partnership". They are used to imply both a place and a focus of relationships.

WHAT "COMMUNITY" MEANS FOR PEOPLE

What do local people make of this? We asked our sample what "community" and "neighbourhood" meant for them and what they thought when other people used these terms. Then we asked whether the area was a "community" for them and what they felt about living there. For a small number of people community was something they didn't want to get involved in (3), an idea tied to traditional village life (2), or something that meant nothing or had negative meanings for them (11).

"I think a person who talks about community is a liberal sort of person who doesn't know what a community is."

"I think of it as a trite twentieth century word."

"Nothing really! It's a myth."

One woman raised the dilemma that villages have taken for granted for generations, but patch social policy makers have so inadequately addressed:

> *"It sends a shiver up my spine — everyone knowing each other and gossiping. I suppose when you need help, it's nice to live in an area where people do know you."*

For 17 people "community" meant a particular building or facility, quite often for others to attend, not themselves.

> *"Where I can go, like the lunch club."*

> *"I take it to be like the Hanover Community (Centre) up the road. I've never been there. Where they have different activities."*

> *"Everybody getting together, like having a hall for meetings and jumble sales. Get togethers."*

> *"I suppose to me it means a place where there are things for children, but I don't think it's that successful."*

While there was no consensus about the concept and some interpretations were unorthodox and unexpected, the majority of the sample (59 people) discussed community in the abstract in very similar language to patch's advocates, in terms of locality and relationships.

> *"Where people come together, interact with one another and work for the good of that area."*

> *"Everybody helping each other out."*

Some people matched or even went beyond what patch proponents hope from "community" as a solution to particular problems.

> *"Where people know each other. They know when someone hasn't been seen for a while. They know what's going on."*

> *"People knowing each other and getting together and discussing what's happening. The kids glue sniff in the park opposite and if this was a good community, this could be sorted out."*

> *"A community is where the individual is not lonely and isolated and where the family is more than just nuclear and there is an element of trust in relationships with neighbours."*

We can sum up these responses by drawing out certain recurring themes and ideas from people's comments. *Involvement* describes ideas of getting together and joining in; people being an interdependent part of each other's lives. *Mutual Aid* covers notions of people taking responsibility for each other; helping and doing things for each other. *Mutual Action* means people working together and dealing with issues collectively. A further strand was *Local and Mutual Knowledge* about what goes on locally, and each other's needs and problems. And, finally, there was simply *Friendship and Enjoyment*.

Of course it is possible to see all this as nothing more than a dream or myth of community — especially when we compare it later with the more hard-headed picture people have of their reality. However, the point should also be made that in many people's minds there may be a large measure of agreement with the ideals of community social work and patch.

It is also clear that people's ideas went beyond the emphasis in patch discussions on informal support for individualised problems, to cooperation and collectivity to deal with local problems as such rather than in isolation. In policy terms, it could for example represent the difference in orientation from setting up a voluntary scheme to get someone's shopping, to seeking funding for a mobile or community shop, accessible to people to be able to get their own.

People were quite able to contrast their idealised picture with what they saw as the reality.

> *"It means a group of people that should be interdependent. The community is the people you should be able to help. But these days it doesn't work. Even if help is needed, it's 'mind your own business' and 'blow you Jack'."*

LIVING IN HANOVER

Before we move to how people experienced the area and "community" in practice, readers might find it helpful to refer to the tables in Appendix I showing the age and social class breakdown of our sample and the patch population.

When we asked people what they thought about living in the area, 70 made positive comments, just seven qualifying them. Only 14 expressed bad feelings about living in Hanover. There was no significant difference according to length of stay, sex or estimated age. Apart from a third of people who said they liked the area without specifying why, the main reason given by 22 people was its centrality and convenience; its nearness to shops, facilities, the town centre and work.

> *"I quite like the area as it's near the town. It's good to be near with the bus fares being what they are."*

> *"I like the district. It's very nice and quiet and central, easy to get to the Downs, sea, shops."*

"It's handy for the shops. If you want anything on a Sunday they're open. Good grocers, a pub and a butcher's."

"It's convenient. It's hellishly noisy. Street dust is appalling, but it has the advantage of direct access to the town by bus and living on a main road means that in bad weather the road is gritty. The small roads are hairy in winter."

Hanover is hilly and three people singled that out as a problem.

"It's alright apart from the hills. That's why he's got a car." (Her disabled husband had a battery car)

"I'd like to be off the hill a bit as I've got a crippled foot."

The relevance of accessible shops and inaccessible hills becomes apparent when we recall the concern of the Hanover patch team about elderly people unable to buy food.[19] Four other people made the crucial if often overlooked point that whatever an area may be like, to live in inadequate and unpleasant housing is likely to be of more immediate and over-riding importance.

"The environment is OK, but the conditions are cramped living in a flat with a child."

"Terrible — the flats." (Tenant of run-down council block)

"I hate it here. I liked it in Devonshire Place (just outside the Hanover patch). We had to move from there as the family wanted it back. The room was charming, everything where you wanted it." (Tenant of run-down council block)

Eighteen people made positive comments about the area connected with community and neighbourhood. Although people's attitudes to the area generally showed no significant difference according to estimated social class, a difference did emerge here, mirrored in the breakdown of age and length of stay. Although the numbers are small, it was the middle class people involved who had the kind of positive things to say about "community" that would seem to support the case for patch based social services.

"I do quite enjoy it. I know quite a lot of people here. It's easy to get into the community."

"We chose the house because we like the area and the house and the neighbours are like us politically, they think like us. It's quiet here and quite neighbourly."

"There is a community spirit, but it's a bit of a deprived area and there are hooligans. We're near the (council) flats."

Only one was critical:

"A bit claustrophobic. You hear too many family arguments, noises etc."

In contrast, the other eight people, all but one of whom had lived much longer in the area than those who were middle class, offered a view of "community" locally that was much less cohesive and supportive, which was also linked to its changing population.

"I quite like it. It has gone downhill a lot in the last five or six years. There's a lot of "immigrants" — people who haven't previously lived in Brighton, so there isn't the same close knit community."

"I'm out all day so I can't say really. I don't know any of my neighbours intimately."

"It used to be very nice, but half don't want to know now. It's not so friendly. They're all new people. The old ones have died or moved out."

"I had a business (here) for 18 years and I didn't do what so many do, milk the district and then get a bungalow. I stayed with my own people — people I understand. People move out now. They don't live over their shops. It's a twilight area. It upsets me now. I was 30 when I came out of the army and my wife and I pushed a barrow for four years."

Not only did they have quite different views of the state of "community" in the area, but they also revealed that the presence of one group affected the "community" of the other.

"It's changed a lot since I was younger. There used to be a lot of older people. Now it's all young couples moving in and first-time buyers."

Another old woman made a similar point earlier in her interview when talking about her own isolation.

"All along here at this side, it's young couples and they all go to work. They have to get the mortgage. They don't talk to you. The lady next door goes to work at Marks and Spencers. All my neighbours have either died or moved."

One man put the area into a political perspective:

"I'm moving at the end of the year to get away from here. I've lived in Brighton since I was seven and I've just seen it decline in every respect; facilities, housing — all aspects — travel, buses, especially with the Conservative Council. Brighton seems to have the most car parks per square mile in the country. Every spare bit is for cars."

IS IT A COMMUNITY?

We next asked people: "Do you feel it is a community round here?" The sample was divided. 49 people thought there was and 43 that there wasn't, with eight "don't knows". People identified obstacles and aids to community and being part of one.

"Not this road. It's too busy (Queens Park Road). The side roads have more. The volume of traffic has increased so much, you only know your immediate neighbours."

Being in full-time paid employment, especially outside the area, and particularly in the case of women, on whom prevailing social policy notions of "community" largely seem to depend, has an important bearing on the issue. One woman who had lived locally for 21 years and was in her sixties said that while she still knew a lot of people in the council flats where she lived who had moved in when she did and who were all friendly together:

"There are a lot of new people in now who are out at work all day and so I don't know them."

Having young children also seemed to affect whether people felt they lived in a community.

"People are becoming more self-contained and you don't have much contact with people in the street like up here, because of the increase in people working full-time. Unless you have children of the same age you don't have that much contact."

"It is (a community) if you've got young children."

The 34 members of the sample who had under-fives or children of school age living at home with them — and who closely reflected the social class composition of the overall sample — were more likely to feel it was a community locally (22/34).

While some people felt strongly that the area was a community:

"Definitely. Go to the corner shop and you can spend hours waiting to buy a pint of milk!"

Others put a different interpretation on it.

"No (it's not), but I think some people would like to feel it is so."

"… not really. I think you tend to make one or two friends, but I wouldn't say there is a community spirit."

Thinking that a community existed, did not mean that someone wanted to be part of it — a few people didn't. Others acknowledged it existed but felt excluded themselves.

"I think there is some degree of community, but I don't feel part of it."

What many comments did refer to were networks of people based on particular interests, ages and social class. One man drew a distinction between individual and collective experiences of "community".

"I think there is a community in the sense one can meet people and communicate in that way, but not in the sense there are community activities, but that's the fault of the people in it."

What then of the Hanover Community Centre, the formal structure ostensibly aimed at collectively linking these together? Some people referred to it in this context. While some saw it as encouraging "community", others didn't, and few of those who mentioned it, seemed to use it.

"I only see my neighbours once a week in their cars. I don't speak to anyone else in the street. I've never been to the Hanover Community Centre. I'd not recognise anyone else in the street." (elderly man)

"There is (a community), sort of. We get a Hanover newsletter."

"Since that Hanover thing has been here, yes. It's done this area a lot of good. People seemed to be closed off from one another before that."

"... I don't know anybody who goes to that Community Centre."

"It probably is (a community) because of the Hanover group. I didn't know much about it. I know people go to their meetings and things. It might be run by Social Services for all I know."

"Nothing now. We've got a community centre round the corner now. They do dinners there but it's 40p and there's no choice, because it's done by welfare people. My friend went there and it turned her up. I look after myself anyway. I cook proper food." (woman in her eighties)

As one man remarked later in his interview:

"... I feel that your average local person isn't involved in the Community Centre really. But then to be fair, they probably wouldn't want to be involved in it anyway, so I don't know what the answer is."

COMMUNITY AND CLASS

From what we've said about the area and from people's comments, we could not discuss "community" without focussing more precisely on social class and — very much an interconnected issue in Hanover — length of stay in the area. As one working class resident said:

> "I do think round here that there is a working class community and a middle class young community and I think that's felt at the Community Centre. It's seen as a "leftie" stronghold. There were two playgroups there, one middle class and one working class and the two didn't mix at all. Working class people do use it, but separately, if you see what I mean.

Hanover Community Association and Centre have also been discussed by Tomlinson. His valuable study, based on participant observation and interviews, brought together the issues of gentrification and social class differences. He concluded that "the illusion of communality that is characteristic of the community association in the gentrified area is shattered by the durability of class-bound cultural experiences and forms. In the end, working class activists and middle class activists are not working towards the same goals". The Community Association became the site of "confrontation or at least tension between different class cultures". It was another expression of gentrification, rather than something that transcended it.[20] The issues that Tomlinson identified in relation to the Community Association were strongly reflected in our findings about people's perceptions more generally of "community" and their impact on it. This was first expressed when we asked them how long they had lived in the area.

Table One: Responses to Question 1: "How long have you lived around here?"

length of stay	number
One year or less	16
Two to three years	12
Four to five years	9
Six to nine years	16
Ten to nineteen years	17
Twenty years or more	30
Total	100

This revealed some polarity in our sample, with almost half having lived there ten years or more, in many cases much longer, while more than a quarter had lived in the area three years or less. A contrast in mobility also emerged. While, for example, thirteen people had lived locally all their life or for more

more than 30 years, 16 people had lived there a year or less.[21]

These differences in length of stay in the area were closely associated with differences in estimated social class.

Table Two: Length of stay in the area by estimated social class

| Length of stay | class category | | | |
	A	B	C	TOTAL
Three years or less	15	4	9	28
Four to five years	6	2	1	9
Six to nine years	4	3	9	16
Ten years or more	1	7	39	47
TOTAL	26	16	58	100

While more than two-thirds of people categorised as working class had lived in the area for 10 or more years and only a sixth for three years or less, more than half those categorised as middle class had lived locally three years or less and only one for 10 years or more. 24 working class people had been local residents 20 years or more — eight all their life — while seven of those who were middle class had lived there one year or less. In this sense working class people we interviewed were more likely to be "locals" and middle class people "newcomers". This gives a measure of the gentrification which Tomlinson described as the most significant process at work in the area; "the conversion of long-established indigenous working class territory into up-marketed fashionable middle class residential areas".[22]

Further evidence of a more mobile group of younger, middle class professionals joining and replacing the traditional working class population can be seen in the relationship between estimated age and social class in our sample.

Table Three: Age distribution of the sample by estimated social class

| Age | class category | | | |
	A	B	C	overall sample
Up to 29	14	3	14	31
30-39	9	4	9	22
40-49	3	3	10	16
50-59	—	5	6	11
60-70	—	1	15	16
Over 70	—	—	4	4
TOTAL	26	16	58	100

Nearly two thirds of working class people were aged 40 or over, while most middle class people were under 40 and none was 50 or over. There was also a strong correlation between class and length of stay among younger people. Those who were working class were much more likely to have lived locally for a long time than those who were middle class.[23]

This brings us to the key finding that emerged from the question of whether or not people felt the area was a "community". Opinions mainly varied according to their length of stay and estimated social class.

Table Four: Breakdown of responses by length of stay to Question 18: "Do you feel it is a community round here?"

	Length of Stay		
Response	5 years or less	10 years or more	All sample
Yes	23	19	49
No	9	25	43
Don't know	5	3	8
Total	37	47	100

Paradoxically, the longer people had lived in the area, the *less* likely they were to see it as a community. This however was largely related to the correlation between length of stay and social class. It didn't for instance seem to reflect a naive enthusiasm among newcomers. For example, of those who had lived in the area three years or less, middle class people were still more likely than others to think it was a community. The important difference in attitude to the existence of community locally was based on social class. There was no difference between men and women, nor any appreciable difference according to people's feelings about the area. Significantly feeling there was not a community was not a strong enough reason for not liking living there. [24].

Table Five: Breakdown of responses by estimated social class to Question 18: "Do you feel it is a community round here?"

	class category			
Response	A	B	C	Total Sample
YES	16	9	24	49
NO	6	6	31	43
Don't Know	4	1	3	8
Total	26	16	58	100

Although the small numbers involved mean that the results should be treated with some caution, nonetheless some inferences can be drawn. Middle class residents were more likely to think that the area was a community and working class people considerably more likely to think that it was *not*. Reasons for this emerged from their comments echoing what they had said when asked what they felt about living in the area.

"It was (a community) but gradually it's disintegrating. People come and go a lot — first time buyers and then they sell up and move on."

"There are some nice people round here, but though I've lived in this street almost 23 years, I only know a handful of people." (woman in her late seventies)

"... There's a lot of new people and young people in flats. I nod to people, but they don't always take any notice."

The relationship that emerged between estimated class, age and length of stay also revealed two contrasting sub-groups in the sample. These were working class people aged 40 or more who had lived ten years or longer in the area, and middle class people aged less than 40 who had lived there five years or less. The former accounted for nearly half (25/58) of those categorised as working class; the latter, more than threequarters (20/26) of the middle class people. The first group were much more likely to think there was *not* a community locally than the second (14/25 compared with 4/20). They in turn were more likely to think there *was* a community (12/20 compared with 9/25).

Our findings challenge any assumption of grassroots consensus about "community". Instead they paint a picture of antagonisms and tensions. Tomlinson's analysis of the Hanover Community Centre adds weight to this view as well as offering additional insights. As he put it, "the early days of Utopian togetherness" in getting the Centre off the ground "were soon felt to be an illusion of community". What his account unfolded were the quite different and conflicting meanings which community had for the two groups of traditional working class residents and middle class newcomers.

When such groupings get together, any sense of community that is developed may well rest on different sets of assumptions.... As soon as the illusion of community was revealed for the cluster of contradictions that it was, then it was unsurprising that the (Hanover) neighbourhood would become the base for the political ascendency of the Social Democratic Party (in Brighton).[25]

Tomlinson was talking of "the contested cultures and rival views of the world" that operated in Hanover because of gentrification.[26] But we can expect similar issues of contested values to apply when indigenous populations are brought into relation with incoming community activists, community workers, and most significantly here, patch based social services, under the banner of "community".

THE "BREAK-UP OF COMMUNITY"

"We live in a more stratified society than is recognised. There are working class and middle class "ghettoes". I think Brighton is pushing people it doesn't want out into the estates on the outskirts."

Similar findings to ours were reported by Mackenzie in her Brighton-wide study of gender and environment. Many older residents of Hanover she interviewed, for example,

commented on the "community breaking up" both as a result of slum clearance to the south of the area, the concentration of "problem families" in the Kingswood Milner flats, and as a result of an influx of "new people", mainly young families, many of whom had higher incomes than long term residents and "gentrified" their homes.

At the same time, she found that women in Hanover and adjoining Queens Park had the most complex set of formal and informal networks and the smallest geographical range of the three areas she studied.

Long term residents throughout the area had strong and complex family and community ties. Of the 13 women I spoke to in Hanover, seven had lived there all their lives and had family in the immediate area. All of these relied heavily on family and neighbours for support and exchange of services.[27]

Such traditional networks do still exist in spite of the perceived "break-up of the community". But important changes are taking place in Hanover as elsewhere, and not just leading to a changed population "mix" according to class. As well as middle class people taking over the remaining terraces, poor people and members of ethnic minorities are confined to the least desirable housing, and old people are segregated in separate flats and sheltered accommodation. At a time of such social and demographic changes, questions are raised about the future of the networks we have known and the effect on such a dwindling resource of social services' intervention.

Tomlinson also contrasted the impetus for community action and involvement of working class participants "whose lives have become increasingly self-contained within a life-time" with middle class participants "who are perhaps looking for a collective form of action that they have never had".[28] Mackenzie's findings illustrated this. A number of women noted to her that:

women while actually engaged in performing household duties were more likely to be alone, less likely to engage in informal collective work where neighbours helped with preserving, cooking a celebration meal or caring for a sick child.... Women helped one another with shopping, child care, advice on pregnancies or on jobs. More recent arrivals tended to be involved in more formal community networks, community associations or the childbirth and child care networks...[29]

This decline in some forms of traditional informal collective action, and women's involvement with different kinds of networks according to class are also likely to have important implications for patch working and its "community orientation", which we shall be discussing later in the chapter.

THE SIZE AND SHAPE OF COMMUNITY

We ended by asking people "What sort of area makes up your "community" or "neighbourhood" for you?". Intended to explore the issues of size of locality and networks, it also produced further definitions of community and alternatives to it that were not necessarily tied or solely related to place.[30] These included knowing people, public relationships, places associated with work, church, pubs, neighbours, community associations and proximity to family and friends. They further emphasise the diversity of people's ideas of and about "community" and social ties.

"To me it's that I can walk up this street and people speak to me and know me..."

"I feel one needs the local church and from that stems everything — the Mothers Union, youth clubs, groups, etc..."

"The pubs round here and the people you meet in the street."

"Those people just below the bracket — not the higher class — the middle, if you know what I mean."

Table Six: Breakdown of responses to Question 19; "What sort of area makes up your "community" or "neighbourhood" for you?"

Response	Number
There is no community	35
Small area	22
Medium area	3
Large area	7
Alternative definition or conception	19
Other	5
Don't know	9
Total	100

Most of those who saw their community in terms of an area (22/32) saw it as a very small one, from a few streets to just part of a street or a few houses. For example:

"These two streets and a small area up St. Johns — the shops where everyone goes."

"This road. Everybody knows each other and the old people are looked after. But there's not many young couples here who don't work in the area."

"This street. It's pretty good neighbours here. From here to eight houses up."

"A bit of this street. Mostly they keep themselves to themselves".

A few saw it as a larger area, made up of the streets running off a larger road or a triangle formed by two streets and a school. Only seven people saw it as anything larger than this. Mostly they identified the area served by the Hanover Community Association. This has not only established an identity locally, but it is also a coherent area of small streets bounded by larger, in some cases, main roads. However, only one of the people who identified "community" with the Community Association in this way was working class.

Not only did some of the areas identified by people extend beyond the patch boundaries, but the largest was only a third of the size of the Hanover patch. This suggests that where people see community in terms of locality, it is likely to be very small. This has important ramifications for patch, both in East Sussex and more generally. East Sussex patch teams cover populations ranging from about 4,000 to 25,000 people. Hanover patch is near the average of 14,000 inhabitants.[31] A population of 5-10,000 has been the optimum regularly cited by patch proponents. In Normanton, the best known and most thoroughly researched example of patch, patches described as small cover populations of between 5-8,000. Patch warden schemes in the town have been further localised within these patches to cover a neighbourhood of between 1,200 and 1,300 people.[32] "Going Local" reported that a majority of patch schemes operated with patches with a population of 10,000 or less. [33] However as we mentioned earlier, a "wider population range" for patches is now being suggested.[34] Judging, for example, from East Sussex and Humberside, patch sizes in practice also seem to be getting larger rather than smaller.

Our findings suggest that even the smaller population numbers originally urged may still be much larger than makes sense in terms of people's own ideas and sense of community where that is framed in terms of locality.[35] Some patch proponents are beginning to talk of dividing patches into sub-areas with sub-offices. However, any substantial reduction in the effective size of patches is likely to result in a considerable increase in cost because of the additional staff, premises and resources needed.

COMMUNITY AND LOCAL VARIATION

"Nobody likes to be interfered with in this town"

As we have seen there has been some recognition among advocates of patch that the potential for their "informal helping networks" may be conditional on locality. This has been associated with characteristics like redevelopment, rehousing, and economic decline.[36] Some of the people we surveyed, however, pointed to another potentially important constraint on "informal care". While a few members of the sample — mainly middle class newcomers — commented on the friendliness of the area, others referred to the reserve both of the town and the county in which it is situated.

> *"Some people help one another, but not many. There's not much of that in Sussex. Sussex people do tend not to involve themselves in things. Sussex people aren't that friendly...They keep to themselves." (young Sussex woman)*

> *"It's not friendly. There's funny neighbours — they wouldn't help you.... It's not neighbourly. We come from the north — Rochdale — and everyone helped each other there. It was much different. We've got a good neighbour next door, and the pub next door, but she's from the north — Blackpool — as well, so that's why she helps."*

> *"They try to do the Hanover Community Association thing, but that's flogging a dead horse. They're individuals round here. There's no camaraderie like South Wales where I come from.... They don't mean it, but they can't help it. In Wales Mrs Jones knew Mrs Thomas and everyone knew everyone else."*

> *"People here don't want to know. If I didn't do for the old lady across the road, no one else would.... I come from Walthamstow and I wish I'd never left. It's friendlier there and people are closer to each other."*

Whether or not these comments, which came from Brighton as well as non-Brighton born people, were valid, they raise a more general issue for patch and "informal care". There are likely to be such variations in social relations, expectations and attitudes according to national, ethnic, local and regional traditions, cultures and mores, relevant both to concepts and patterns of "community" and "informal helping networks". Proposals and policies for patch need to recognise and take account of them.

COMMUNITY: PAST AND PRESENT

One of the most fundamental criticisms made of notions of "community" and "networks" adopted by patch, is that they rest on nostalgic and romanticised views of the past. Patch is only the latest in a long line of social policies to use them — from community work in the 1960s, to community policing in the 1980s. Patch proponents do not disagree that time has brought major changes in local life and relationships. We have seen, for example, the far-reaching effects gentrification has had in Hanover. But what are the implications of such changes in "community" for community social work, patch and the networks on which they have laid such stress. Mackenzie's study points to some of them:

> Older women speaking of their early married life, and young women remembering their childhood saw a decline in informal communal child care arrangements where "we all lived in each other's houses" and in sharing and borrowing networks. These networks all assume that most women are at home or at least in the immediate community and are available to one another for most of the day.[37]

"THE GOOD OLD DAYS. NOT REALLY"

We can get a much fuller picture from the comments of former residents themselves. Three women in their late sixties met for tea at the Lewis Cohen Urban Studies Centre in Spring 1984 to talk about life in the Carlton Hill area, in the southern part of the Hanover patch, before it was redeveloped between the two world wars. [38] We touched on this policy in Chapter Two. In 1933, Brighton Corporation, as part of the government's slum clearance programme demolished what it considered to be its worst slums. Many of the people from Carlton Hill were moved to new housing estates such as Whitehawk and Manor Farm. But what was it like before then?

'There was all shops round here.

You didn't have to go to the town to get anything.

There was a sweet shop. Pip used to keep that.

And Burbury's had the butchers didn't they?

And I lived opposite the butchers. And from there, there was a butchers, a green-grocers, and then there was one house, and then there was Miss Watford...

The oil shop.

Round the corner of that was Miss Christmas what kept a little bakers.

My mum used to stand — we had an area, a basement area — now my mum used to stand indoors. She never went shopping and she used to say "go over there and get me that bit of beef that you can see in that window". And we used to have to stand outside the window and keep pointing to the bit of beef.

So she did it all from home?

Yeah. All from the window, my mum.

And the children all did the shopping?

We didn't have to go anywhere hardly see.

We used to go to Edward Street and James Street.

We never went up Albion Hill.

More like here to James Street, yes, that was our area.

———————

...Oh yeah, but they did have to work hard didn't they?

Cause we were poor.

My mum, my mum was always standing at tubs washing.

Yeah, they were poor days, they were really. What about my mum then?
Yeah, your mum was a washer, wasn't she? Mine was an ironer.

My mum used to have to do all the washing for the creche. (The Tarner Land
Nursery School)

They did have a hard life didn't they?

No washing machines.

I mean all they washed with really was two pounds of soda and a bar of
Sunlight soap.

We never had no soap powder.

You used to have to wash and all in that.

And she'd stand there all day, a big, like sack type apron, and they'd stay there
all day long.

And me and my sister used to have to do the housework Sunday morning. Big
wringer out the back.

Cause she used to have to go to work all week, and she used to say "are you
ready for this broom" and she used to chuck it down the stairs to me.

But they never had wringers. They had mangles, the old wooden mangles.

And I used to have to stand and turn that handle!

...Your mothers tended to stay home most of the time then?

Yeah.

My mum never went out to work.

Well my mum did.

Did she never go out for anything? Never had a walk? Or fresh air, or...?

No, no, they were stuck.... We had a yard, a big yard out the back and she used to go out in that yard, backwards and forwards, scrubbing down...

We lived there all those years and never had to lock the door. Nobody ever locked their doors.

We never shut windows.

On our front door upstairs, we never even had a handle.

You may have heard the old saying, "lift up the latch and walk in", and that was a hole in the door with a bit of leather strap on it and you used to pull that, and as you pulled that, the latch came up.

Nobody ever moved out. Houses never became empty, so nobody moved in... We knew everybody.

Most people married other people in the area.

We did have strangers from the lodging house (in the area), but that's all, and some of them were there years.

When the women had babies, everyone looked after everyone else. We used to have to run along Wellington Road for the midwife and bring back her bag. We always thought the baby was in the bag!

If anyone was bad, you could go knock their door — go and tell Mrs. so and so I'm not very well. They'd come in to you, but how could you do that now?

You could walk around here anytime of the day or night, even as kids and you were quite safe.

The neighbours always sat on the doorsteps on summer nights, talking to each other.

When it was twelve o clock at night, if it was a very hot night, we went down the beach for a paddle — midnight bathing! But you couldn't go there now midnight bathing. You'd be frightened to come home.

Most of them people stayed in that place until it was pulled down. I moved to Hollingdean — beautiful house. My husband bought it. But it wasn't home. I wanted to come back. To me this area is home.

That is why I think people didn't want to move — because the community was there. If you took them away, in my opinion, they didn't last long. It's like taking a baby from its mother.

The people who did move out to the estates... Lots of them who are old now have moved back into this area... into flats!

Because my dad had some bad times — because he was on the building — and we really had terrible times, we had to have the parish up. They used to come in, "Sell that. You don't need that, sell that", and my mum had a machine there that my gran used to earn her living on — "sell that". But anyway, my dad got hold of him one day and slung him out.

I didn't know my father. He was blown to pieces in the 1914 war. My mum went to work all her life. Used to do laundry — worked in the laundry and then come home to take it in, and she had ten children.

Up Southover Street, we used to go up there (the soup kitchen). We used to get a bowl of soup and taters boiled in their skin and big whatsername of rice with jam in and we used to call that romuck... Oh it was terrible — up Southover Street — what's the community place (the Hanover Community Centre) now, that's where it was.

We were poor, but we were clean.

Yeah, we were happy as children.

We used to play for hours in the street — marbles and buttons.

When you look back though, really they say about the *good* old days. Not really. I know we used to have some laughs and some good times, but not really.'

Taken together, these comments and those of the people we interviewed suggest two almost completely contrasting social structures; the past, static and locally based, the present, highly mobile and wide-ranging. The old community the three women recalled had little movement; of population, of women outside the home — some women barely ever leaving the house — and of people outside their neighbourhood. It was self-contained for shopping, social life and support. Now instead, population is constantly changing, women are much more likely to be in outside employment, and inhabitants to be away all day. Only six of the 55 women that Mackenzie spoke to in her study, for example, shopped inside their local area, and all of these had limited mobility. Four were old and two mothers with young children.[39] What is striking is that patch based social services make most sense in relation to the remembered model of community from the *past* rather than the present. Not surprisingly it is with that kind of model of community that they have been associated, and on which they seem to have been based.

We should add a further word of caution. As we have begun to discover ourselves, the more carefully you look at "community", the more complex and fugitive it becomes. If it is to be a premise of policy, then it must be subjected to much more careful thought and discussion than patch proponents so far seem to have given it. Our perceptions of community not only vary with the reality, but also according to our own position. We have seen this in relation to social class. It may equally apply to other factors, like different times in our life. Through our life-cycle we are likely to have different access, involvement and interest in neighbourhood and local networks — as children, adolescents, parents of young children, middle-aged and elderly people — and want different things from them. For example, the community recollected by the three women in their discussion was conditioned by the fact that they were then children and young people. Their view of it now might be very different. We need to be aware of such issues when trying to develop "community-based" services.

PATCH AND "COMMUNITY": SOME UNRESOLVED ISSUES

We have argued that patch rests on certain assumptions about "community" and "neighbourhood". Our survey suggests that these may not fit very well with people's own experience and perceptions. It points to the variety of meanings, often unexpected and negative which community had for people. Less than half those surveyed in an area often associated with community spirit, and with a well established community centre, felt there was a community locally.

Where people did have a sense of community based on locality, the area involved was mostly much smaller than seems to have been adopted in the development of patch. So while the reality of local community often appeared limited and tenuous the study also suggests that popular ideas of "community" may be different and sometimes broader than those underpinning patch. This implies that patch schemes need to consider both the ideas and actuality of "community" on which they are dependent. The risk from not doing so may be to base policy on the former, while workers and users have to face the reality of the latter.

How far, in fact, are local community or neighbourhood networks a prerequisite of patch? There is some ambiguity about this. It has been argued that patch based social services are not simply going to place greater reliance on informal care, but will also be concerned with *"supporting"* it. This largely seems to mean trying to encourage and harness "informal helping networks" by setting up voluntary schemes and groups, recruiting volunteers, supervising, administering, and working through them. In this way institutionalised "community care" seeks to compensate for any limitations to the informal care on which it is ultimately based.

We saw this in the example of the Tarner Neighbourhood Care Scheme. There the Brighton Council for Voluntary Service worker involved in setting up the scheme was quoted as saying that it was "an area lacking something of the community spirit to be found elsewhere in Hanover".[40] The means adopted to overcome this lack was to try and organise informal care. In this way patch based social services are quite literally concerned with "community" development. But where local community ties are insufficient to ensure adequate care and support for people — as generally seems to be the case — then patch schemes based on voluntary care are equally unlikely to be adequate. The essence of such schemes is to transform social relations, but they cannot transcend the social forces that affect them. They too will be rooted in the nature and limitations of local community — unless people from one area, social class, or indeed race are recruited to serve the needs of another.

Our survey, as we have seen, raises major questions about this. It suggested that "community" itself as well as perceptions of it, were significantly affected by social class differences. Patch proponents have recognised that informal networks are likely to be weakest and least effective in areas of deprivation. An area of mixed population like Hanover is likely to be seen as offering more promising conditions. Our sample, however, not only showed that the perceptions of "community" of middle class and working class people were different and that the presence of one group affected the "community" of the other. It also pointed to practical and other issues, like people being away at work all day, that may contradict patch assumptions of the better-off serving as a major source of support for local old, disabled and isolated people.

Social class divisions raise another fundamental issue which we can see in Hanover in a particularly clear form. What emerged from the sample was evidence of two broad configurations; middle class people who were likely to have lived and to stay in the area for a short time, who had a sense of local community, and working class residents who were older and had lived locally longer, who did not. The people ostensibly in a position to offer local support were the middle class. Those particularly likely to need it were elderly working class people. Would this work and what are the implications for patch of such a divided or heterogeneous "community"? We have seen the difficulties the patch team has experienced in recruiting working class volunteers from within the area for the neighbourhood care scheme. Recruits to the new Cope scheme have so far tended to be middle class. We have also seen the class-based problems Tomlinson identified in the Hanover Community Association, with working and middle class people wanting different things; the latter an extension of activism, the former leisure opportunities. But the questions raised are not simply about whether one group or class would be able or willing to respond to the needs of another. Referring back to the ideals of patch, we need to ask whether it is possible for this to happen without problems of colonialisation and paternalism. Tomlinson found that the greater power of middle class interests won the day. Would the outcome be any different with patch? These are questions we can only raise here, but they have far-reaching implications. Tomlinson has commented on the failure of much of the mainstream literature on voluntary action to consider its cultural meanings and to put it in its broader context of "period, place, politics and people".[41] The class, race and gender issues voluntary action associated with patch raises make this especially important.

The next chapter takes up these issues of "community care" and links them with people's experience of care and support. The question we need to explore is not just whether social services can engineer "informal helping networks", but whether this is actually what people want.

"It's good to create a community feeling, but only if the people want it. You can't make people join in. A lot don't want to."

CHAPTER SEVEN
People, Care and Support

"I get the kind of care and support I want from friends — definitely,
but from the state, definitely not!"

THE MEANING OF CARE AND SUPPORT

A crucial welfare question facing politicians and policy-makers is how to deal with the growing numbers of very old people as public expenditure declines in real terms.[1] A new concept seems to hold the key — "informal care". As the 1960s saw the "rediscovery of poverty", so in the Thatcher years, the rundown of public services has coincided with an official realisation that most of the caring in our society is done "informally" by family and friends. There has been a flurry of research and projects to measure and maximise "informal helping networks", "neighbourhood support" and mutual aid.

Of all the warm, cosy and essentially ill-defined terms used in social work and social services, "care" and "support" are most open to criticism. Are they as the new right tauntingly suggests nothing more than a manipulating and mystifying "care speak"?[2] Patch takes these concepts and makes them central to its strategy, emphasising informal care, informal networks, voluntary action and their relationship with formal social services. The meanings attached to them, however, have generally not been made clear.

While the Barclay Report offered definitions for terms like client, community, counselling and social care planning, none was given for care or support. Davies in "The Essential Social Worker" offered some insights into prevailing social work thinking about such concepts. The global and professional definitions of care he provided sit uncomfortably together. They are indicative more of a continuing vagueness and confusion in social work than of any consistency or clarity of purpose.

> The social worker fulfils a predominantly service function... Caring in any society demands both an immediate response to felt need — an attempt to assuage the pain of today; and a sensitivity to the way in which policies might be changed in order to bring about better conditions overall — an effort at reducing the incidence of pain tomorrow.... To care for someone

implies also a willingness to fight for him or her — the soft and the hard roles are interdependent.

The notion of caring cannot be so easily distinguished from other tasks.... The caring functions demand the same high standard as decision-making, surveillance should be as responsible a function as assessment; and, in any case, in day care and residential settings, the idea that one can clearly distinguish between maintenance and development is wholly false; both functions are equally a part of social work, neither should be regarded as more professional than the other.[3]

Davies defined "support" less fully, but with "care" it seemed to be part of a notion of maintenance, which was his essential social work concept.

The essence of social work is maintenance: maintaining a stable, though not static, society, and maintaining the rights of and providing opportunities for those who in an unplanned, uncontrolled community would go to the wall.[4]

There is a very real problem here, not simply of finding "acceptable" definitions, but of obscuring important differences. Illich, for example, adopted the term "vernacular" to describe informal and reciprocal links between people, and specifically to distinguish them "from sustenance that comes from exchange or from vertical distribution"; that is from the market place or institutionalised services.[5]

But again it is from a feminist perspective that the most helpful discussion of "caring" has come, "highlighting both the complexity of its dimensions and the considerable degree of sensitivity required to formulate alternative policies which are both adequate and acceptable to all concerned".[6] Graham, for example, in her exploration of the concept has emphasised the affection as well as labour involved,[7] while Ungerson has looked at the clear sexual division of labour associated with the provision of physical care through the perspective of the gender and sexually based taboos that seem to be involved.[8]

One of the great values of the feminist approach is that it pays most attention to carers and people being cared for. Later in this chapter we look at this in more detail. But if social work and social services appear to have taken certain meanings of care and support for granted, how helpful is it to adopt a new terminology, as patch has, without first considering people's own experience, preferences and conceptions? So far, this has hardly been done at all.

We asked people in our sample what care and support meant for them. This is not a question we would expect many to have been asked before or an issue many may have thought much about. However very few people said they didn't know (6) or that it meant nothing to them (3). Most people gave some thought to the question before answering. What was most striking was the heterogeneity of people's answers. A wide range of meanings were given. Not everyone offered definitions for both terms. Some saw them as synonymous. Others drew distinctions between them. The clearest and most common distinction (23 people) was with some kind of *financial* assistance. Another five people saw either care or support as having something to do with the provision of material aid or amenities.

> *"Support could be financial and care is someone who comes up to see if you're ill."*

> *"Support is financial support and care is looking after the physical and mental well-being of the individual."*

> *"...Support is for those who haven't got what they want and need in the home."*

People drew a variety of other distinctions between care and support, again emphasising the range and idiosyncrasy of meanings attached to them.

> *"I think if somebody cares for someone, then they are concerned for them and support is actual help and helping them to be secure and happy."*

> *"I presume care means a longer term, intensive commitment to looking after someone. Support is more having someone available to turn to or talk to."*

> *"Support has got to do with being in the background and being prepared to use, if needed, a safety net of friendship. Care has got to do with love, I think, in a non-syrupy way. It's to do with the way one behaves to other human beings."*

> *"...Care is when they (social services) know of an old person or sick person, mentally or physically, or of a young mother whose husband is out of work. They go and see and care for them, and support comes from other departments. They help with the bills — cash or kind."*

> *"Care is looking after the deprived and support is looking after people who are temporarily in need for whatever reasons."*

Significantly, 24 people saw the provision of care and support either partly or entirely in terms of formal services.

> *"Care is when social workers know you're down and out of work and depressed and they come round to see you, and social security is the money you get."*

> *"If someone were housebound — home help service — that kind of thing."*

> *"Support means social services are there to provide necessary financial needs and material things — things some people can't buy or get, and there if you need someone to talk to."*

> *"I would say hospital care and that sort of thing and if I was out of work I could go*

and claim money for food."

"Care for me means that people are well looked after and if they are ill they have doctors and nurses they need or their rent paid."

Some people stressed the importance of care and support being available as of right, responding to the individual's wants and not being or feeling like charity.

"Care is treating citizens with dignity and respect which they are entitled to and support is that they should have the basic amenities for a fuller life."

"Care and support means seeing the old and disabled are looked after properly. They don't have to beg or plead or go cap in hand."

"The fact that you are an individual and have individual needs. The support is that you should be allowed to have those needs and keep your identity and helped to retain your individuality within a framework of loving and needing..."

"I'd say there is not enough emphasis on the state providing help. I don't think everyone is aware of what they are entitled to."

"I think of basic financial support — enough money to feed, clothe and keep warm. Care is health — hospital care, sickness benefit. It should be a fundamental right."

The meaning most often attached to care and support, and offered by one third of the sample was helping or looking after other people, being helped or looked after, or mutual aid.

"Taking an interest in people around you, seeing to their welfare, helping if you can — even if it's just to spend the time of day. Support is the same."

"If people have problems, telling them where to get help and advice. Making their lives a bit more comfortable."

"A practical and altruistic outlook on life."

"Much what I said before about what a community is — taking responsibility for other people when they need help."

"Care means helping other people when they need it at important times."

"Care and support are trying to help each other, caring for each other. I'd try to help people as a Salvationist. It's my Christian duty."

Seventeen other people related care and support to particular groups whom they saw as vulnerable, like poor, young, disabled, housebound, sick, deprived, and particularly, old people. Six confined them to family and friends. Only four linked care and support with neighbours, neighbourhood or community.

"I don't have anybody in. I have good neighbours."

"I always think of loving care as far as my family is concerned. They all come first no matter what."

"Care is attending to the immediate needs of one's family, then to other relatives and close neighbours and support means participating and helping in community activities and policy decisions that help bring members of the community together."

"That would mean neighbours helping each other presumably. The role of the social worker should mean people feel secure in their community and have help to fall back on."

This is particularly interesting in view of the emphasis in patch based social services on "informal caring networks" and the much larger number of people who linked care and support to state intervention and services.

To summarise then, the responses of the people we interviewed suggest a complexity and diversity within these taken-for-granted concepts. Care and support were seen to involve individual rights and state responsibilities, and be based on love and friendship, kinship and neighbourhood ties, and voluntary and statutory obligations. They might involve material, emotional and social assistance and include advocacy, advice-giving or just being available. People spoke of improving the quality of life, meeting temporary needs, or redressing disadvantage and deprivation. Care and support could be an integral part of day to day life or a last safety net; something that applies to us all, or a residual role for those pushed on to the margins.

"Care and support really means if you are desperate you've got someone at the end of the telephone and someone to talk over your problem when you get to breaking point."

"Care and support means helping people to look after themselves in their own homes."

"Care and support is care for the people that need helping out financially and physically. It's one and the same word really, helping them put their point across."

"It's difficult to define. I can't really put it into other terms, helping others — that sounds pretty feeble."

IN PEOPLE'S OWN LIVES

As we saw, when offering their interpretation of the terms, nearly a quarter of the sample saw the provision of care and support either partly or entirely in formal terms. However, when asked from where they got *their* care and support, almost all referred to personal relationships. The reason for this inconsistency is not clear. Perhaps it says something about people distancing welfare from their own lives or not seeing it as central to them. It might also reflect the lack or inadequacy of state care and support in practice, or simply that they perceived the concept differently in different contexts.

Almost two thirds of the sources of care and support people mentioned were partners or relatives. Friends made up the second largest source of support. Only one person mentioned neighbours; and seven, formal or professional services, of whom only one referred to social services.

34 people, surprisingly woman more often than men (perhaps because of their greater awareness of and candour about such issues), referred to a partner as a source of care and support; in 15 cases the sole source they mentioned. This emphasises the importance of such a close, confiding sexual relationship in providing social support. Yet this is an aspect of informal care and support that has not so far received much consideration or analysis from advocates of "informal helping networks" and patch based social services. It is difficult to see how patch could "encourage", "support" or provide substitutes for such relationships. On the other hand, the break up of such relationships has major, often profound, effects on people's networks of support. It may result in moves to another area, the break up of friendships and family relationships; even attenuated parental relationships. One man, for example, said he got his care and support from his "wife and colleagues at work", yet he was in the process of divorce and shortly moving from the area.

This raises the question, not yet convincingly answered by advocates of patch, of what happens to people and areas where there are neither strong social networks, as they have envisaged them, nor much potential for developing them. Population movement, arbitrary and isolating redevelopment, the nature of the housing market, economic decline, and other political, socio-economic and cultural factors have all had profound, often destructive effects on traditional local networks and on the likelihood of sustaining new ones. These features characterise inner city areas where the role of the social services department is at a particular premium.[9]

Most people (60) identified only one source of care and support, about a quarter (27) two, the rest no more than three (7) or four (1). The most common combination as we might expect, was family and friends. Five people said they had no care or support. All were on a low income, and all but one were aged 65 or more.

Table 1: Breakdown of responses according to sources of care and support to Question 47: "In your own life, speaking for yourself, where do you get care and support from?"

Source	Number
Partner/relations	93
family	37
husband	21
wife	13
relatives	2
mother	2
parents	6
adult children	4
sister	2
daughter	2
non-adult children	2
living-together partner (male)	1
aunt	1
Friends	22
friends	17
friends lived with	1
girl friend (of man)	1
woman friend(s)	1
work mates	1
No one/nowhere	5
Don't need any	1
Self	12
Professional support	3
State services	3
Social services	1
The Church	3
God/a higher power	2
Money/earnings	2
Neighbours	1
Other	2
TOTAL*	150

* Some people offered more than one source of care and support.

"Only when I was working and going to work, otherwise no. No family, no friends. I haven't any. I don't mix."

"I've got nothing. I've got no support."

"No one, nowhere."

Twelve people said they got their care and support from *themselves* — four of them citing no other source:

"I'm a bit of a loner..."

"Me, nobody else."

Seven members of the sample, mostly older married women said they didn't mix much with other people.

"I live in my own little world — don't join in."

"I keep myself to myself."

This finding of how few people members of our sample relied on for care and support is not only interesting in itself. It also contrasts strongly with present arithmetical approaches to networks which emphasise the *number* of sources of support people have. Wenger, for example, in her major study of support for old people living at home, arguing against the stereotype of the "ailing, lonely, forlorn old person living on a subsistence income in poor housing", concluded that most elderly people had support networks with five or more members. However, it remains unclear what such networks actually mean; what reliance people feel able to place on them, and how they relate to the key concerns and traumas of old people.[10]

PEOPLE'S PREFERENCES FOR CARE AND SUPPORT

We next asked people if they got the kind of care and support they wanted. Their comments cast light on what that meant for them as well as some of the problems they perceived.

"I think so. I don't feel neglected."

"I think so, non-institutionalised."

"Not quite because of relatives living away."

"I think I do pretty well and my employer is very supportive of me and my wife."

"I think so. I'd like it a bit different, but..."

"Yes, but I don't get it from my family. I do regret that."

"We're covered with our pensions."

"Not always from the state."

"I think so. If there's no family there, you've got to have someone close you can turn to."

"Not entirely. I think in general I've often been in need of better care in terms of physical wellbeing."

"You never do, do you? You're lucky if you do."

"I don't get as much as I want, but I feel as much as I can expect considering they've (family) got their own lives to lead as well as mine."

Those who said they were not getting the care and support they wanted (20 people) were similar to the overall sample according to class, sex, age and whether in employment, but they were more likely (7/20) to be dependent on poverty level state benefits and to be single (9/20-36/100). A few people said they did not get *enough* care. To find out more about this we asked the last 35 people we interviewed an additional question. Nine of them felt they were not getting as much care and support as they would like, and again they were more likely to be single (6/9). Being single can clearly put people at a disadvantage in a nuclear family orientated society where conventionally informal support largely comes and is culturally expected from within the family.

To develop these issues further, we asked people if they saw any obstacles in the way of caring or being cared for as they preferred, either for themselves or for people more generally. It was a question a number of people found difficult to understand and where they needed to be prompted. They were much more likely to see obstacles in the way of care and support for other people (71) than for themselves (31). They also had more to say about them than themselves. This may, for example, have been because they had in mind groups with particular problems, like old people, or because they were more prepared to talk about difficulties affecting other people, since in our society problems like isolation, loneliness and lack of support may be felt to reflect badly on the individual. This may also have a bearing on the relatively low number of people who said that they did not get the care and support they wanted. It is certainly an issue for further examination.

There was no significant difference between those who reported obstacles in the way of care and support for themselves and the rest of the sample, except that they were more likely to be middle class (13/31). Obstacles identified were more likely to be material, social or related to state services, than personal. The man who said "It's just me I think", was unusual. People referred to distance, lack of money and material resources; to problems from getting older and old age; inadequate state services, including social services; unemployment, problems inherent in the family and marriage, as well as from being alone. Social attitudes and the disintegration of community were mentioned as well.

"I've been alone all my life. I've never married. That's been an obstacle."

"I find it difficult to get hold of a certain person in social services to explain. You can't get through to them. If you could deal with one certain person all the time, it wouldn't be so bad."

"In any family life there are always obstacles."

"A difficult husband."

"I think because employment prospects for many people are so limited they feel unable to care and support themselves and their family."

"People not knowing what your needs are, and it being a strange society where we can't voice these needs because of pride."

"Yes definitely, especially in privatisation of health care."

"Yes like getting a well paid job is very difficult, also getting nice flats."

"The only obstacles are the fact that one Department doesn't work with another so if you did need someone, you wouldn't know where to go for it which is very bad."

"I've got a brother who has gone to London. He went with a lot of money which he had saved over the years. He's now at a loss and I'd like to see social services help him. There's probably thousands like him who have nobody. I can't help him as he's so far away. He can't get a job. When he does it doesn't last long. So there's obviously something wrong. I live sixty miles away and my parents two hundred, so we can't always go to look for him, especially when he doesn't want to be found."

People seemed to see obstacles in the way of caring and being cared for, for people more generally, in similar terms.

"I suppose it's to do with the amount of people in the (social) services. If you haven't got enough people to go round, then people will be lonely."

"I suppose I'm lucky because my husband is aware of what's going on and caters for our needs. I suppose social services should give out more readily available information."

"Sometimes you think people aren't getting the care they want moneywise."

"I think with children, we often don't give them the care and support they need, but the help we want to give them. We misinterpret their needs and look at them in terms of what we want to do and not what they need."

"Some people haven't got a family life like I've got."

"The breaking up of the extended family and unemployment. At least in the '30s you had lots of relatives."

"People don't have the same values anymore."

"There's a cynical attitude to life on the part of modern people - especially urban communities."

Several people singled out particular problems facing old people.

"There's not enough places for them. There should be more sheltered accommodation for old people."

"This goes back to old people. There's not enough things being done to help them. There's no finance or transport for them."

"Old people are left alone too much."

"I think the trend will continue where you'll get left on a shelf as you get old."

PEOPLE'S FEARS OF INTRUSION

Although only one person talked in terms of "any obstacle" being "purely personal", 10 people raised a related issue.

"People sometimes put the obstacles there themselves through their own independence."

"I don't think a lot of people let it be known they need care. A lot of the older people won't accept it."

"It's true for ninety percent of people. They don't let themselves be cared for."

It was particularly associated with old people.

"I tried to help the next door neighbour. But people keep themselves to themselves."

"I know from my sister (a home help) that there are many elderly people who are too proud to ask for help..."

"People resent not looking after themselves."

"Volunteers would come up against awkward old people who'd shut the door and not want to know."

The people making such comments here, didn't ask why it might be that old and other people fought shy of formal or informal care and what their attitudes might say about *these* as well as about themselves. As one woman said, "a lot of people are afraid to come forward with problems". As we have seen elsewhere in the interviews, people were aware how "caring" behaviour and services have a continuing association with intrusion, dependency, stigma and paternalism. This also poses major questions for patch, since such attitudes seem to be as much a reaction to *informal* as formal intervention. It cannot be assumed that people will respond more readily to informal or voluntary "care" than to statutory or non-statutory welfare agencies. Indeed the kind of fears of people "knowing your business" or "living in your pocket" raised by some of our respondents may mean the opposite is true.

Other research has also raised this point. For example, a study of 50 users of Family Service Units showed that their "fear of being the victims of gossip led to the claimed minimising of contact with neighbours, thereby reinforcing the isolation of many of the estates". The researcher concluded:

> ...neighbours are not an "option" that F.S.U. users consider.... For the majority, especially those living on post-war housing estates or in high rise blocks, there is virtually no neighbourly "relations", to judge from descriptions I received. To talk in these circumstances of informal resources not being exploited is to cast the issue in misleading terms, for very often people simply did not know those living next door to them.... It is not stretching a point to say that neighbours arouse great suspicion due to the strong feelings of anxiety that gossip provokes. Neighbours are perceived as vulture-like, always on the look-out for gossip to retail.[11]

Patch based social services have the potential to be far more intrusive than their traditionally organised counterparts. While they have been criticised from some quarters for representing a substitution of voluntary for statutory action, in another sense they can be seen as an *extension* of the state, closer into people's lives. Their capacity to have increased access to local information has been one of the important advantages claimed for them. It is one thing though to know that a supportive eye is being kept on a housebound old person — although they may not actually welcome it — but quite another to use the knowledge of local people to supervise and even regulate the behaviour of a single parent or young person seen as "at risk". The area officer of Normanton in West Yorkshire commented:

> I'm not afraid to use the big stick and to remind parents and relatives what their obligations are.... We have got the resources in the community to help and monitor most family problems. [12].

In Southsea in Portsmouth, one of the case studies of patch described in "Going Local", increased local knowledge seemed to mean being able to identify "haunts of habitual truants and in liaison with the education welfare officers stopping these being used", rather than investigating the need for their use.[13] It may be unintentional, but there is also something ominous in the view of the minority Barclay Report for neighbourhood-based social work and social services that "Clearly a knowledge of local cultures, problems, thought patterns and structures is important". Otherwise the social worker is likely to be "seen as an outsider, coming from the 'welfare'".[14] But that is just what they are likely to be.

A couple of the people we interviewed made the comparison between patch and community policing. While this was apparently prompted by their similar rationales of being community based and orientated, patch also seems to share community policing's commitment to surveillance and the stockpiling of data, again with more rhetoric about public participation than effective public accountability.[15] Gordon has argued that community policing comple ments "fire brigade" policing rather than offers an alternative to it.[16] The same question is raised about the relationship of patch to the "crisis intervention" approach of conventional social services.[17]

In his "alternative view" to the Barclay Report, Pinker attacked community and patch based social work's indiscriminate collection of information and the threat it posed to privacy. As he remarked:

> At a time when profound public disquiet is being expressed about the indiscriminate and often unreported collection of information about ordinary citizens by public and private bodies, we are now invited to endorse the creation of a proliferation of local data banks based largely on hearsay, gossip and well-meaning, but uninvited prying.[18]

Lambert has described the way in which these can be used by the social services department.

> It is not difficult to see how monitoring, with the aid of extensive local knowledge helps the local organisers of a "preventative" service to "use the big stick".... The "pattern" of policy and control relies upon monitoring through the collection of information about people in their relationships. This information is co-ordinated by qualified workers who represent statutory agencies. The information is being fed through an increasingly adept and single-minded planning system, which seems to pay little significant regard to those about whom the plans will be made.[19]

It is easy to see how such an intrusive, colonising approach to welfare, reminiscent of the locally based poor law relieving officer,[20] would act as an even stronger incentive for people to keep to themselves and out of the way of social services for fear of being interfered with or subjected to its control. As Pinker has argued:

> The desire to locate and provide for unexpressed needs is not a defensible reason for jeopardising people's right to be left alone.... Those with unreported needs would be properly protected if social services were more efficiently publicised.[21]

And we would add, if they more closely matched what people wanted.

CARE AND SUPPORT — OR SOMETHING ELSE?

People's expectations, fear and resentment of interference from a "helping relationship" do not necessarily mean that they wanted to live according to some model or idea of individualised independence. Rather, it seems that their apprehension was perhaps of unequal and dependent relationships with others over which they would not have a fair share of control. So is it the kind of support implied by patch that might be wanted — someone, for example, carrying out tasks for people, looking in to see they were alright or offering them "befriending"? Or would they prefer the wherewithal to look after themselves and maintain their own social life, whether through material resources and conditions or through forms of support based on an equality and mutuality of relationships that would be taken for granted in the ordinary run of people's lives? These are large questions for patch and social services. They offer another reminder of the need to make few assumptions about the meaning of care and support and to avoid defining them narrowly. Hopefully some insights will be offered when we come to consider people's own perceptions of their needs and situation and their relation with broader issues, in the next chapter.

To summarise then, people identified a wide range of social, cultural, demographic and material issues affecting informal as well as statutory care and support. Our survey indicated some ambiguity in people's preferences for care and support. Speaking for themselves, it appeared that most preferred them to be based on informal, personal relationships. But whatever people's preferences, there could be obstacles in the way of them, no less with informal than with formal arrangements. Thus while the encouragement of informal care has been seen as a means of overcoming the problems of reduced resources facing statutory provision, it is no less affected itself by a variety of constraints. People's ideals are mediated by the realities affecting them. Patch based social services have been concerned with reinforcing or institutionalising informal care. What may also be needed are ways of making it possible for formal services to be more like informal care in terms of desired features like flexibility, informality, proximity, meaning, mutuality and the nature of relationships involved, while still being wage based and collectively organised. This is an important theme and one we shall return to later in the book.

PATCH, CARING AND WOMEN

Caring raises profound issues for the rights and equality of opportunity of women. Because of their commitment to informal care, these become key concerns for patch and community social work. They also have important implications for all shades of political opinion, for left wing as well as right and centre local authorities have espoused ideas of community care, even if they have placed different interpretations on them. We have already referred to feminist writings on community care and community social work. They offer one of the most important critiques of patch, although, so far neither patch nor community social work has addressed them adequately. Caring is a focal point for such feminist critiques. Here we want to consider our survey findings in relation to them and the competing claims of patch advocates. This will require a fuller discussion of feminist inspired arguments and evidence. It will also draw us to consideration of women and paid employment as well as their role as carers, because of the inextricable interrelation of the two.

Most caring is carried out by women. The evidence suggests that this is true across the range of caring situations, whether we are talking of caring for old people or children with disabilities. [22] Many women are carers for much of their lives, first for their young children, then for their ageing parents and finally as elderly women themselves, for their elderly husbands. An Equal Opportunities Commission survey found that three times as many women as men were looking after elderly or disabled relatives.[23] There are estimated to be at least one and a quarter million unpaid carers, usually mothers, daughters or sisters of elderly, physically or mentally disabled people. [24] One survey showed that such carers devoted between two and 10 hours a day to caring activities.[25] Another found that mothers of young children spent an average of 50 hours a week looking after them.[26]

It was within this broad context that we sought to explore people's views about women's role as carers. We asked the people we interviewed whether they felt women were expected to do most of the caring and supporting in our society. Almost all felt they were.

Table 2: Breakdown of responses to Question 50: "Do you feel women are expected to do most of the caring and supporting in our society?"

Response	Women	Men	All
YES	53	34	87
NO	5	7	12
DON'T KNOW	1	0	1
TOTAL	59	41	100

Men were over-represented among those who answered."no" to this question, but three of them seemed to be saying this *shouldn't* be expected of women, with comments like "it should be shared equally". 46 people made additional comments expressing their feelings about the issue. Six said they felt caring should be equally shared and two others said it was between them and their partners. Four thought the status quo accorded with women's particular skills and aptitudes, taking these as innate rather than related to socialisation.

"Definitely. Women are tougher." (man)

"They are more motherly figures." (woman)

"I think women are more approachable." (man)

"I think women understand you more." (woman)

Others identified trends and expectations maintaining women as the main providers of care and support.

"The emphasis on the woman is more so these days. Regarding the old people, the emphasis has gone back more on women." (man)

"Men look to women and expect more from us." (woman)

"They are expected to." (man)

"It's a woman's job, I suppose. A man thinks it's beneath him." (man)

"The women do look after the elderly." (man)

A number challenged the prevailing caring roles imposed on women, some describing what they actually meant for them.

"More than they should, women have to. You're expected to go out to work and still maintain the role you've always had." (woman)

"Women themselves expect to do it, but obviously they can't if they haven't got a living wage." (man)

"There are three people I know in the block who go to the day centre and they have husbands in the wheelchair and it's shocking for them at night-time and that, so there's a lot that could be done." (woman)

"Women are more capable and better at it. But I know through my sister two or three very efficient and dedicated men home helps and male nurses." (man)

"If they can, I think some men should. They get their pension these men and then they just sit around." (woman)

"I do take that for granted as I've been conditioned that way and they (women) do tend to be orientated towards caring, but I suppose men could care just as well." (man)

It is not just that women are expected to be and actually are the main carers. Inextricable from this are patterns of male socialisation which mean that men may be less able to look after themselves and for there to be cultural expectations for this to be so. Women are then drawn in to provide support where this might not be expected to happen in the case of a man. One retired man we interviewed saw as his particular problem:

"As regards a man, it's cooking. If you don't cook you let yourself go and you land up in hospital like I did, needing a blood transfusion."

We also wanted to find out what people's feelings and expectations were about the relationship of social services to prevailing definitions of women as carers.

Table 3: Breakdown of responses by sex to Question 51: "Do you think views like that (women being expected to do most of the caring and supporting) are built into the Social Services Department?"

Response	Men	Women	Total*
YES	14(13)	20(19)	32
NO	14(14)	13(13)	27
DON'T KNOW	16(13)	28(28)	41
TOTAL	44**	61**	100

* this is the total for the sample.
** In five cases, members of the sample wanted to be interviewed with somebody else, for example, a husband or wife. In these cases, the sex of both has been included in the breakdown. This accounts for the discrepancy between the total of men and women and of sample members. The numbers in brackets represent the numbers of actual sample members.

There was a high rate of "don't knows", related to people's low level of experience and knowledge of social services. However more than half the rest said they thought that assumptions of women doing most of the caring were built into social services. This proportion — about a third — was the same for people who had experience of social services or some connection or involvement with welfare state services more generally and those who had not. Men were over-represented among those who thought social services were not discriminatory in this way. Only three people made comments in support of such an orientation.

"Women have got a different approach and outlook, haven't they? You can't expect a man to think of little things like women do." (woman)

"It is a woman's job." (woman)

"Women should be in the social services to help elderly people. A lot of elderly women want to talk to women." (woman)

Others referred to the way that social services placed particular reliance on women as carers both in the structure of their work force and in their expectations of informal care.

"Most people employed in social services and health services are women." (man)

"A lot of men make the decisions (in social services), but a lot of women carry out the decisions." (man)

"It's going more that way." (woman)

"I think so. It's your "duty" if you are a daughter." (woman)

"But I think that is a wrong attitude to women and it's a misinterpretation of men's roles as well." (man)

"They automatically think that women cope better. Most of them are women too." (woman)

"They shouldn't be (expected to do most of the caring),though that's a government policy, tied up with politics." (woman)

"I think they should employ more men home helps and male nurses..." (man)

"...there's no reason why a man can't do it." (man)

THE EXTENT OF INFORMAL CARING

For patch's proponents, the issues raised so far in this chapter may be seen as the challenge they are addressing rather than impediments in the way of their arguments. After all, one aim of patch restructuring is said to be supporting informal networks and removing obstacles in their way. Advocates of patch based social services have emphasised the degree to which many people "are already involved in informal networks of care",[27] and the potential of these for social services.

> There is a real debate over how large the reservoir of informal caring networks are. We do not know, but are convinced that social services departments as currently structured and organised are neither in a good position to discover, nor tap them. The practical approach we describe offers the prospect, as its pioneers have shown, of more effective use of existing resources, a closer working relationship between the citizen and social worker in which both have more significant and responsible roles to play...[28]

They have rejected feminist arguments that such "community care" policies appear to be discriminatory.

> Nor is the practitioner of community-centred methods likely to accept the view that his (sic) approach is bound to reinforce the traditional role of women as carers and make it more difficult to develop more equitable sharing of such work between the sexes. The practitioners argued that it is a principal concern to optimise the use of resources in a manner which is more equitable than the existing system. One of the effects of introducing community-orientated methods, they claim, is to generate more resources

and better knowledge of the informal carers who need them, both of which facilitate the introduction of more equitable policies.[29]

There is, however, already strong and growing evidence to suggest that the contribution local residents can make to informal care and support is severely limited. The authors of the Dinnington neighbourhood services project which sought to integrate local services and informal care more sensitively, found that while such "informal networks were extensive" in this tradational mining community, they were also "variable and often vulnerable and volatile". They also questioned the extent to which such roles were interchangeable.[30] Abrams and others in their study of neighbourhood care projects concluded that the part local residents could play while positive was also severely restricted.[31] The researchers in the National Institute for Social Work's "Networks Project" found that:

> In London at least, the elderly living alone may now be able to rely less on relatives than the studies of the fifties or sixties would suggest. As they become frail, their contacts with friends are reduced and their needs exceed those which neighbours, for all their importance, can be expected to meet.[32]

Our survey offers some indication of the nature and extent of informal care and support undertaken and experienced by our sample as well as raising a variety of broader issues about them in the context of patch.

Eleven women in our sample had children aged under five. Another nine women had children of school age living with them. Those with under-fives had little outside help. It is also to be expected that most of them, reflecting the general population, had the main parental responsibility for child care. 42 women had husbands or male partners. Again, if they reflect prevailing patterns in the division of domestic labour, many, if not most of them, are likely to be undertaking a caring and domestic role for their partner. One other woman, although she was married and said she got her care and support from her husband and children, also said:

> "I would say I'm single. We go our different ways. If I want to go out, I do. If he does, he does."

We also asked people if they looked after other relatives at home or elsewhere. Four said they did, at home.

"My sister when she comes to stay." (woman)

"My husband." (woman)

"My wife who is an invalid." (man)

"My stepfather who is senile." (woman)

Thirteen said they looked after relatives elsewhere.

"My mother-in-law is pretty fit, but we look after her when she is ill." (woman)

"My mum and auntie in their homes." (woman)

"I occasionally have my Down's Syndrome sister to stay or I go to my parents' house to look after her." (woman)

"I look after my niece during the day when my sister goes to work and I look after my little old lady." (woman)

"I keep an eye on mother in Brighton." (woman)

"I go up to check on my nan at the Queens Park area." (woman)

"My grandmother in her home every day." (woman)

"I babysit for my sister's children." (man)

"I've just started looking after my son's godparents who are eighty." (woman)

"I look after my elderly cousins." (woman)

During the course of interview, a number of people made other references to looking after or providing support for relatives, friends and neighbours. Because these arose incidentally, if anything they are likely to under-represent the scale of such informal care rather than reveal its full extent. In this way, five more people mentioned aid and support they gave to relatives while eight referred to informal support they offered neighbours.

"...I look after Winnie (old woman) next door." (man)

"I look after an old lady. If it weren't for me she wouldn't see anybody." (woman)

"...housewife and general helper to my dad — he's an OAP." (woman)

"I don't think there's enough social workers. My neighbour next door, if ever she's in any bother, she'll always come here. She can't get it from her family." (woman)

"Like I do for the old lady over the road. I like that as I work over the geriatric hospital at the weekend." (woman)

Another man stressed the reciprocity of the arrangement:

"Communities are where people live together and socialise with each other. Like it means here, I look after this man's cat and dogs when he's on holiday and he looks after my garden. It's there if people are allowed to live properly."

A woman who ran a sweets and tobacconist shop also stressed the mutuality of care and support.

> *"My mother and father live with me, but I don't really feel I actually "look after them"... I get my social life looking after my parents."*

In addition, seven people referred to care and support they had previously offered to relatives or neighbours.

> *"My children are grown up now. I had my mother with me for a number of years." (woman)*

> *"When my husband was ill, I was having to look after him — up and down half the night." (woman)*

> *"I helped the woman next door with terminal cancer." (woman)*

People also referred to care and support they themselves received from neighbours, friends or relations; six currently and two on previous occasions.

> *"I've got a family, so it makes a difference, but people without a family..."*

> *"We've got a good neighbour next door and the young fellow over the way is helpful, and the girls next door." (elderly couple, the husband with a disability)*

> *"When I was in hospital my husband was left on his own. A few friends helped from Hanover Street, but it was a struggle."*

Twelve other members of the sample, mostly but not all young, received material support, generally from relatives and mainly from parents, in the form of living in their home or housing they owned or rented. This is an aspect of informal support that should not be overlooked, especially in view of the worsening housing position of young people and the government's ideological commitment to increased parental responsibility for young people.[33] The increased cost of and reduced access to housing and the worsening economic situation of young people through mass unemployment and reduced welfare benefits are likely to increase this particular reliance on family or friends' informal support, with growing numbers of hidden households and hidden homeless people.

MAPPING PATTERNS OF CARE

Although our sample is small, it nevertheless offers some interesting insights into the characteristics of informal care. In particular it raises a central question for patch and community social work in their aim of "tapping into" such networks — over the issue we have repeatedly met — the effects on women.

Of the 59 women in the sample, 47 mentioned providing care and support for neighbours and relatives, or had children or partners to look after. Another three had previously looked after relatives or neighbours. Of the 47 current carers, 14 were in full-time and seven in part-time employment. This compares with 30 of the 41 men in the sample who were in full-time paid work.

Once we move away from the close relationships with partners and children, the picture that emerges is of a substantial number of people providing current care or support to relatives or neighbours. There were 29 of these. Out of this total, eight were men and 21 women. It is worth looking at this group in more detail. They were as likely to have children as the overall sample and the women were more likely to have partners (16/21). Thus the women were more likely to have significant responsibilities for care and support of close family. What also emerged was that people in this group were more likely than the rest of the sample to have financial difficulties (22/29), to be reliant on poverty level state benefits (7/29) and to describe their income as inadequate or difficult (13/29). Their age range was different from that of the overall sample. There were fewer young people and more who were older. Seven of the 29 were aged between sixty and seventy, so the idea of informal care being an avenue of support for older people was here contradicted by evidence that older people themselves were a major source of support. This reflects more general findings showing that 58 per cent of carers of elderly people are themselves aged over 65 and many suffer from ill-health.[34] People were also more likely to have lived a long time in the area. 18 had lived there 10 or more years, only two, three years or less. In all 20 people referred to support they offered relatives and this was frequently linked to living locally. As we might expect, longer stay residents were much more likely to have relatives living near or relatively near by them than more recent arrivals. For example:

"Both our parents live locally within quarter of a mile and are elderly, so it's an easy way to look after them."

"My daughter lives in Falmer (near Brighton) and she'll come down."

"I came here in my twenties with my parents from London and I always regretted it really. My mother always thought I'd go back, but I didn't like to leave them as I was the youngest." (woman in her late thirties)

Such blood care relationships are unlikely among more mobile newcomers. It is probably also a declining pattern both in the case study area and more generally as social, economic and demographic trends exert pressures against the continued geographic proximity of extended families. Family may still provide members with care and support, but they will find it harder to do so on a day to day drop-in basis.

Significantly this group of carers was as likely to be in full or part-time employment as the overall sample. Thus for them informal care and support were not an alternative occupation to paid work, but an additional one. What emerged was a picture of a group of people many of whom had a paid job and also child care responsibilities. The typical carer was a woman, often older, with financial difficulties, often with children and probably also with a male partner to look after.

THE REALITY OF CARING

What did informal care actually mean as far as those members of our sample caring for and supporting relatives and neighbours were concerned? It needs stressing that for some it meant more than one commitment. For example, one woman provided support for elderly parents and an old woman neighbour; others for a mother and an aunt; elderly in-laws, then an elderly mother and then a stepfather. Thus it could involve several, perhaps changing responsibilities over a considerable period of time, at the same time when children would be likely to be young and income and resources at their most stretched.

Several of those providing care and support for others also faced particular difficulties themselves. The late middle-aged woman looking after a neighbour with terminal cancer had a sick husband. An old woman who had to look after her husband when he was ill was herself severely disabled. The husbands of two other women carers were unemployed - one for two years. An elderly woman looking after two relatives in their eighties had herself been waiting two years for surgery to her feet.

Informal care might mean dropping in to see a parent, providing some baby-sitting or running a few errands. It could also mean a very great deal more.

"I was left to manage."
"My next door neighbour had a nervous breakdown and tried to kill her ten year old son. It went on for a year - a year of terrible strain for me. I took the son in. I realise that social services are very stretched anyway and do try and help with old people, but I think because they saw someone like me around, they didn't stretch themselves. I'd phone them up when there was a real emergency and they'd say someone would be down in a few minutes and no one would come - no one would come. They got her sectioned in the end. But when it ran out she discharged herself from the hospital - she just left in her dressing gown and slippers. I got home from shopping to find her sitting on my doorstep. I had to have her in her house and knock and see if she was alright, if anything needed doing and have the son with me. She wasn't any better. Because the section was ended they didn't want her back in the hospital because she'd been there long enough as far as they were concerned. So it was a situation of her living in the house on her own, me seeing if she was alright, yet trying not to see her too much because I

had her son with me - trying to keep him away. But it got too much. My own daughter was only six then and she saw all this happening. I kept phoning social services and I was left to manage. The strain was terrible. In the end, social services found a foster home for the son for a few months. The son needed to be away from the mother and the mother needed not to see the son. Now everything's alright. It's all over now. They live together again, but it was a terrible year.

I've also got my stepfather to look after. He's senile now. He gets up at two in the morning to go back to Canada. I can't leave him alone in the house. I have to get up in the night. I don't get any sleep. He goes to the day centre now. The occupational therapist says he can't really concentrate. So I suppose he nods off and then doesn't sleep at night. It's terribly wearing. I've had no understanding. I think you are really just a number. The volume is too great for the people who care. Like when I had a crisis in June and July, the psychiatric nurse came and said "Oh there's far worse than you are". I know that, but it doesn't help, especially when you've had no sleep."

"They don't care."

"It was frightening. I'd had problems. One of my sons had died suddenly. My doctor had helped me and I had my family. It was because I started to help the old woman next door who had cancer — she has a lump on her head which has to have treatment — and she's got cancer in her body. It came home to me with great force, what a desperate job you can be in, in our society when you've no relations in spite of all these services. She'd had three weeks out-patient radium treatment and been taken to hospital everyday by ambulance and then she was told that she should just come to outpatients in three weeks time and she asked if she'd get a lift and they said "you'll have to make your own way here" — as if it wasn't the thing to ask. Making her own way there for that woman who is seriously ill, meant either getting a taxi, which she can't afford — she couldn't possibly walk, plus the fact she's in terrible pain. She'd either have to go up to the sixth floor of the block of flats and phone from the public phone for a taxi which would cost her a terrible lot of pain — getting up in the lift or up the stairs — doing that, or she would have to go out and get a bus, which is just inconceivable — she couldn't possibly do it. Luckily I've got a car, so I've been able to take her. But they don't know anything about me, anything about how she is on her own, whether she gets any food or drink. But they don't care. I wanted to get a home nurse for her. The doctor didn't do anything, the specialist didn't do anything. So I went to social services and asked them, and she just shrugged and said she didn't know what to do. In the end I phoned the doctor again and he finally, after five weeks, got her a home visits nurse.

There's another old lady, right, upstairs there. Three weeks she's alone until someone realised they hadn't seen her. They break the door down and find her at death's door."

Both of these were examples not only of inordinate caring responsibilities placed upon women, but also of their perception of the failure of state services to carry out their responsibilities. Research has shown that the presence of carers, particularly a woman, prejudiced the likelihood of receiving scarce statutory services. [35] One aim of patch is to increase reliance on informal care. But in this area, the shortage of statutory services and provision meant that the existence of informal care on a significant scale was already assumed and relied on by the different agencies involved.

In several cases people linked the need for informal support to the failure to make adequate state provision, which they saw as a preferable alternative.

> "We used to go in every day (to old woman next door). Now she's being helped by Social Services...and it's much better."

> "My sister (a homehelp) goes in her own time to look after an old lady and that shouldn't be necessary."

> "I looked after my mother for about six years with no help."

> (There should be) "more help for senile old people, more help for their families and those living at home. I've got experience of that as there is an old lady along the road who is deranged at times and they don't seem to get a lot of help. Her husband and son go to work and that's when she's at her worst."

> "...it's the same for mentally handicapped people, and people left to look after them without adequate facilities — and they need more."

We can see, particularly from the example given by the last woman, not only the failure of statutory services to meet major local needs, but the inadequacy of relying on "informal care" to ensure the conditions and support to maintain people in any kind of reasonable life. This was also reflected in a number of the descriptions people gave of informal care arrangements in which they were involved where a picture emerged of isolation, dependency and vulnerability.

> "All she had was her home help twice a week and me going in to see her every morning with a cup of tea. We went away one Christmas and she saw no one all that time."

> "I look after an old lady. If it weren't for me, she wouldn't see anybody."

> "I've got an elderly couple of relatives.... They've got no one else.... It's getting very difficult to cope."

> "If I didn't do for the old lady across the road, no one else would. She would die for all they care."

One woman painted a graphic picture of what informal care in the family had meant in the past.

"My mother had 13 children. When I came home from school I had to look after all the babies as I was the oldest. That's why I only had two myself. What a struggle it was for my mother. Washday was hell. On wet days you had to dry everything inside so for a week you'd have steaming clothes blocking you from the fire, making your eyes run. All the women had big families. They didn't have much money. There was no help. Life was a big struggle."

THE COST FOR CARERS

Some of the experiences people related to us, like the woman who had been the sole support of a next door neighbour with terminal cancer, show starkly the unacceptable pressures and demands that inadequate services or services orientated to voluntary aid can actually place on people, particularly women.

The harsh picture of the high costs of caring for carers emerging from our survey cannot be dismissed as either unusual or anecdotal. It is consistent with a growing body of evidence highlighting the physical, emotional and social strains of caring. For many carers this means arduous work, lifting and carrying, being on call all the time, never having a moment to themselves, being tied to the home and becoming isolated from outside friends and contacts. Frequently such caring has to be carried out in unsuitable, unmodified housing, on low income and generally without social recognition. The resulting anxiety, loneliness, loss of sleep, guilts, resentments and exhaustion, are reflected in high rates of physical and mental illness.[36]

PATCH AND ITS FEMINIST CRITICS

We want to pause here and consider an issue behind the discussion so far. We have noted that proponents of patch and community social work have so far taken little account of either feminist criticisms or research informed by this perspective. The results of this omission are, unfortunately, cumulative. By this we mean that there have been four stages or levels at which dialogue with feminist informed arguments would have brought an extra clarity and sharpness to patch arguments. In the first place, the earlier writing about patch and community social work tended to treat the position of women as unproblematic. Sometimes even the gender of "volunteers and good neighbours" was not thought worth mentioning.[37] However when a strengthening feminist critique emerged, a second opportunity arose to engage these issues, and, as we have said, by and large the debate was not taken up. But the next stage did not just entail sets of conflicting social policy analyses or recommendations. Following the Barclay Report community social work and patch's advocates were involved with a rapidly increasing number of actual schemes and reorganisations. The lack of a dialogue in the academic and policy making worlds implied far wider consequences for people affected by social services outside. Crucially the contribution of a feminist informed perspective now appears to be missing where practice remeets theory — in other words where monitoring and evaluation of patch is underway.[38]

As before, we hope that the material presented here will contribute to such a programme of exchange and debate. However, there is a particular difficulty in trying to contribute to and locate this within such a debate, when the particular issues have not been addressed by patch. The need then becomes not only to present the experience and views of some of the "informal carers" in our sample, but to explore the context of this much more widely. For patch and community social work can hardly be evaluated and monitored to any purpose unless the sharpest critical questions are asked.

We shall try in the rest of this chapter to explore the areas within which this essential dialogue needs to take place. We do this first by looking at both recent Brighton-based research and then the more general feminist informed writings on women as carers and paid workers. Then we want to consider patch's position in relation to this evidence and argument. Finally we shall look at some of the other relationships social services and patch may have with voluntary action and informal care.

WOMEN AS PAID AND UNPAID WORKERS

While we have talked of a feminist informed perspective, it is important to say that this has not just been a matter of opinion or even of interpretation. A principal feature of feminist writing and research has been its strong factual foundation. Because questions have been asked about women as carers, employees and in their other roles, they can no longer be taken for granted as part of an overall statistic. Women researchers who have focussed on the position of other women have shown us just how far predominantly male sociologists had obscured women's experience — when it wasn't left out altogether.[39] Male dominated social policy and social policy research have tended to be gender blind.[40]

The second and crucial feature of this feminist informed work is its stress on the inter-relationships between the different aspects of women's lives and how outside forces affect them. It is not simply that some women "happen" to find themselves looking after elderly or disabled relatives, thereby joining a distinct group of "carers", or that others "happen" to lose their jobs. As we have seen in our own survey, the pattern of paid and unpaid work neither lends itself to description in terms of separate groups, nor can it be divorced from the changes and social forces outside. A pertinent example is that the social services department is an employer as well as a service provider.

In Chapter Six we took pains to avoid the suggestion that there was a concerted running down of the home help service and a simultaneous recruitment of volunteers in East Sussex. But the absence of such an intentional shift is not the issue. A feminist perspective would require patch's advocates to evaluate it in its broader context, including gender. Otherwise there is the danger that we are invited to judge a range of "projects" and initiatives presented essentially in isolation.[41]

For women in Brighton, as elsewhere, it is difficult to ignore these wider issues. Further insights into the questions raised by our survey are provided by four recent Brighton studies. Willis comparing the position of men and women, followed up people made redundant from a Brighton cash register factory.[42] Mackenzie, as we have already seen, was concerned with the inter-relation of changes in gender roles and the urban environment associated with the extension of women's dual roles in the household and labour force.[43] Henwood studied employment, unemployment and housework by interviewing women and men in and out of paid work.[44] Finally, Swirsky examined the effects of unemployment on a group of local women.[45]

Each of these studies adds weight to our findings about women and caring. More important, both our survey and this other research is consistent with wider studies. The picture is of women as the main providers of informal care and support, conspicuously less likely to be in paid employment, but instead economically dependent on partner's incomes or inadequate and discriminatory state benefits.

> The caring cycle forces women out of the work cycle which offers promotion, work benefits, pensions. They have to take time off work, or look for work, usually part-time, near home.[46]

Such women become trapped in a cycle of low paid, insecure, often part-time employment, with little prospect of improvement.[47] Women carers are significantly more restricted in their life choices than men.

Modern trends in women's employment challenge expectations of their continuing availability as carers. Most women are in paid work. They make up more than 40 percent of the labour force. Women, especially married women have participated in paid employment increasingly since the 1950s. One quarter of the labour force are now married women. Women are also spending more time in the labour market. More than half with children under sixteen go out to work. The vast majority of women return to work after having children. They are also returning to work more quickly than they used to and more are working between births. Women in full-time unpaid domestic work throughout their adult life should now be regarded as the exception rather than the norm.[48] Without women's earnings, four times as many families would be in poverty as there are now. Changes in the structure of family life mean that women are now the chief breadwinners for one family in seven.[49]

Brighton has a higher than average number of women in paid employment. As Mackenzie discovered in her study, "wage work by married and independent women has long been a feature of Brighton's economy, at least for the working class, partly due to its history of relatively low wages and high living costs and to its high proportion of 'female' service jobs".[50]

The four Brighton based studies point to the importance of paid work for women and the hardship caused by its loss. In her empirical study of employment, unemployment and housework, Henwood found that paid work was as important for women as for men, "despite their socialisation (which has tended to cause some ambivalence towards paid work for most women)".[51] As Mackenzie observed:

> For most of the women I spoke to, and for all of those who came to maturity since the war, wage work was simply a natural and unexamined extension of being a wife and mother, part of the mother's responsibility for ensuring by whatever means available the health and social security of her family.[52]

Perhaps the key word here is "extension" because as feminists have convincingly demonstrated, women's engagement in paid employment has not resulted in a lessening of their domestic responsibilities. Instead they are largely left with a triple shift of housework, caring and paid work. In her redundancy study, Willis found that through their life, women did most of the domestic work, including caring.[53] Most of the women Mackenzie spoke to in Brighton with childcare responsibilities were also in paid employment.[54]

Women's continuing role as the primary houseworkers is not only the main block on their involvement in the labour market. It also gravely disadvantages them in employment. They largely work in segregated occupations, in work defined as unskilled, for less pay than men, and with fewer opportunities for training. They are concentrated in lower paid industries and occupations. All this perpetuates the narrow economic argument that they should give up work or change jobs when caring responsibilities arise.[55]

One of the principle reasons for the expansion of women's employment in the decades before the current recession was the increase in work for payment which women had previously undertaken for no wage in the home — service work, cleaning, and the caring occupations.[56] The trend of government social and economic policies has been to reverse this. As Coussins and Coote have argued:

> As the welfare state has been pruned back further and further, so the "family" has been called upon to step in and fill the gaps. What does this

mean in practice? Mum, the centre of the family, will replace,in her unpaid capacity, the social worker, health visitor, the geriatric nurse, the nursery teacher and a range of other paid professionals. Patrick Jenkin (as Secretary of State for Social Services) was quite explicit about the welfare state:

"The family must be the front line defence when Gran needs help... All experience shows that trying to help people outside the family context can bring poor results with heavy costs. Involve the family and there is a very much greater chance of success."[57]

In other words, as women become unemployed through cuts in jobs as home helps, aides, care workers, catering staff and so on, the expectation is that they will return to the home to continue caring unpaid. The leaked Cabinet Family Policy Group papers showed this to be part of a clear ideological commitment to welfare based on family, private and voluntary sectors. The Policy Group's proposals included: encouraging mothers to stay at home; "responsible self-reliant behaviour by parents"; re-examination of the role of the Equal Opportunities Commission; and more family involvement in looking after young unemployed and elderly people, and people with disabilities. [58] The Government's review of local authority social services departments appears to have been underpinned by the same commitment to unpaid caring by women.[59]

Women's employment is still regarded as secondary to men's. Women have been hit more heavily than men by recession and mass unemployment. Women's unemployment has risen at three times the rate for men. Women have also suffered disproportionately because they work in industries and occupations where job losses have been most severe.[60] A Brighton based study of employment changes associated with office policy, reflecting broader trends, showed that women were concentrated in the clerical and secretarial posts where most job losses due to new technology are taking place.[61] Women also form the majority of part-time workers, and part-time jobs have been particularly vulnerable in the recession.[62] They are also less likely to have the protection of unionisation and are more likely to be selected for redundancy on a "first in, first out" basis because of interruptions for childbirth.[63] In her Brighton study, Willis found that women made redundant found it harder and took longer to get new jobs and were less satisfied with them than men.[64]

Women have borne the brunt of cuts in welfare state services. They are more reliant on social services than men both as employees and users.[65] Cuts have exacerbated the problems facing them as carers and paid workers. They have reduced the amount of employment available to them, since women's jobs have been most affected, as well as their access to employment, for example, by reducing child care provision. Even when more welfare jobs were available, many women were debarred from them by the lack of child care facilities. Mackenzie cited the problems encountered in Brighton by health, education and social services in recruiting women staff in the 1970s for this reason.[66] Cuts have further discriminated against women, as Mackenzie found from her interviews in Brighton, by placing "a greater burden of domestic and caring work" on them.[67] There is increasing pressure on women to take over such caring responsibilities from declining health and social services.[68] The study by Black and others of three social services teams, confirmed reports of another way in which cuts in home help hours are resulting in more unpaid work for women.

> For some clients hours had been cut, for others the service withdrawn altogether. Organisers considered that this placed unfair burdens on home helps, who often carried on doing the work for clients in their own time. Many clients interviewed verified this by mentioning the unpaid tasks their home helps often did for them.[69]

RESTRUCTURING WOMEN'S WORK

If the triple shift and low pay are the main difficulties facing women workers, unemployment is no solution for them. One value of feminist informed research is to show the complexities involved here. Women rarely have easy choices. The other Brighton studies we have looked at suggest that for most women the loss of paid employment resulted in interlinked problems of social isolation, lack of money and loss of independence.[70] The same problems have been identified elsewhere.[71] Both Swirsky in her study of the effects of unemployment on women and Willis in her exploration of redundancy, emphasised the importance of workplace relationships for women.[72] Not only did they offer companionship, but as Willis reported, after redundancy, "there had developed an informal network of communication that would be used if anyone knew of any possibilities of employment".[73] This is another important, if vulnerable, kind of informal helping network, though one largely overlooked by patch proponents. It contrasts strongly with the pattern of local relationships Willis encountered among the same women.

> Neighbours were the people with whom there was the most striking lack of relationships.... People had little social life outside of work; and, with unemployment, it had decreased further. People said that, with going out to work, there had been little time for either the neighbours or a social life.... After redundancy friends and neighbours continued to assume a marginal importance in people's lives.[74]

It is also very different to traditional patterns of neighbouring that patch still often seems to assume. In the mass unemployment of the 1930s, unemployed people in Brighton, for example, appear to have relied on such relationships of mutual dependence.

"Times were very hard in those days. To have any meat on Sunday we had to queue up for three hours on a Saturday night for sixpenny worth of giblets from the butchers behind the Town Hall. Family, friends and neighbours meant everything to us. Neighbours thought nothing of looking after the children or the old people when they were ill. If people had a penny they would give you a halfpenny. Neighbours would always pop in with a few coppers and some food."[75]

One of the key issues that feminists have addreased is the tension for women between caring and being paid workers. The price many women now have to pay is inadequate childcare services and part-time employment with markedly inferior conditions. The strains of the dual responsibilities of paid employment and unpaid caring not only impose enormous burdens on women, but also perpetuate their social and economic inequality. The position of single parents is particularly difficult. Some of the highest costs have also been shown to be borne by women caring for elderly relations and adults and children with disabilities.

Black and other ethnic minority women face particular hardship and discrimination in the labour market and as carers. Services for members of ethnic minorities are especially inadequate and inappropriate, placing even more responsibilities on women.[76] Whether as carers or people receiving care, they face many additional problems, including the triple discrimination of ageism, racism and sexism and the perpetuation of white myths like, for example, that all black people have extended family networks to fall back on.[77]

Neither the political right's facile solution that women should withdraw from the labour market, nor equally simplistic arguments against them having caring roles, offers a way forward. The feminist conclusion and what many women are now conspicuously demanding is that women should have the same choices as men; either to be in paid work and not be expected to be the main carer, or alternatively, if they want to provide care, to have the necessary material resources and support.[78]

Feminists have argued for a restructuring of the division of paid labour between men and women, accompanied by a redistribution of unpaid work, with men taking equal responsibility for domestic labour and childcare. They have called for caring policies, services and benefits that equalise access to and involvement in the labour market for women and counter prevailing expectations of women as primary carers. Finch and Groves have argued that "the challenge is to devise community care policies which do not disadvantage women".[79]

PATCH AND WOMEN'S RIGHTS

How does patch accord with this aspiration for the equalisation of women's opportunities, and with the attitudes and experience of the people we interviewed? Patch proponents have argued that their "participatory alternative" to centralised welfare "does not assume... that it is desirable or feasible to persuade women back into the home to bolster the caring services".[80] However, it coincides with and is reliant on government policies and plans which are doing this. For example, as Henwood has argued, the 1981 White Paper "Growing Older" which "still stands as the manifesto for the frail elderly, emphasised reduced reliance on statutory services and the growing importance of 'the community'. In particular,it was stressed that 'care *in* the community must increasingly mean care *by* the community'".[81] Research has shown that statutory residential and domiciliary services are *simultaneously* declining, instead of the latter replacing the former.[82]

There is no doubt that economy has been a key reason for the political right's interest in women's unpaid caring. The former Secretary Of State For Social Services, Patrick Jenkin, saw such informal care as a justification for cuts.

When one is comparing where one can make savings one protects the Health Service because there is no alternative, whereas in the personal social services there is a substantial possibility and, indeed, probability of continuing growth in the amount of voluntary care, of neighbourhood care, of self help.[83]

The Audit Commission, a body set up by the Conservative Government in 1983 "to increase efficiency in local government", published its first major study of social services provision in 1985. This report, "Managing Social Services for the Elderly More Effectively", described how social services departments could achieve savings by encouraging people to care for their elderly relations.[84]

Patch and community social work, however, have offered a different rationale for informal care. As the Barclay Report argued:

We cannot emphasise too strongly that a community approach is not cheap, although we believe it will give good value for money. But it will only give value if it is well enough resourced. To underfund a community approach is to run the risk of discrediting the entire notion of shared care.[85]

Nonetheless, a key premise of the patch and community social work approach is that most caring is carried out informally. But as Finch and others have argued, it would be wrong to assume that women want or choose to care for their relatives because that is what they are doing.[86] We have already seen some of the cultural, economic and social pressures pushing them in that direction. Patch may be confusing choice with necessity. It is also inadequate to suggest that caring tasks are performed predominantly by women because they happen to be more usually available since they are less likely to be in full-time employment.[87]

As Price observed in her discussion of women, employment and unemployment in the recession, unemployment data seriously underestimates unemployment, particularly for women.

> Evaluation by gender is crucial especially where a segregated labour market exists. The danger is that (existing) data will be interpreted to show that unemployment is less of a problem for women who have "chosen" to go back into the home. Policies may then be developed that will capitalise on this lack of choice, such as women taking over more of the roles formerly provided by the social and health services. This then may be the real employment "prospect" for large numbers of women in the 1980s, when what is needed are policies designed to give women more equality of opportunity in employment rather than less.[88]

We have seen the link between women's exclusion from and marginalisation in the labour market and the caring obligations heaped upon them, and also that women in full-time employment are still more likely to have the triple responsibility of domestic and caring work. In addition new studies are beginning to suggest that large scale male unemployment is not leading to any substantial transfer of domestic work to men.[89]

Patch and community social work so far seem to have taken the gender-biased distribution of caring for granted. While women continue to bear the brunt of the responsibility, the policy makers and prime movers are still largely men. Much more attention needs to be paid to the nature of the labour market, women's position in it and its ramifications for any policies of community care. For example, as Land pointed out in her analysis of the effects of women's and men's work at home on their paid employment, grandmothers are still expected to take on major responsibilities for child care.[90] They come second to husbands in looking after children of working women.[91] But will they be available similarly in the future? Will they want to give up work? Middle-aged women are more likely than younger women to care for elderly and chronically sick relations. They are also more likely to be in the labour market.[92] Social policies like patch and community social work may take their full-time involvement in caring for granted. But this increasingly conflicts with the part they play and expect to play in the labour market.[93] Very little account seems to have been taken of such women's needs, far less their wishes, to have paid employment outside the home and do some but not all the work of caring.[94] The social and economic consequences — as well as those for women's equality of opportunity — of the continued substitution of paid by unpaid work, must be addressed. As one woman we interviewed said, speaking for many others:

"I have to work because I need the money. My husband's not very well paid."

Feminists argue that the only way that women can participate on an equal basis with men in paid employment is with a reduced responsibility for child care and domestic labour. But the community orientated policies of community social work and patch are not only based on women's existing domestic and caring responsibilities. They are also likely to *add* to them. Women will not only have to look after their children without adequate support, but also increasingly *other* people needing care and support.

It is also important to remember that a switch in emphasis by social services departments away from state care is likely to mean a two-fold increase in the responsibilities placed on informal and voluntary care. These will not only have to take on those tasks previously undertaken by paid social services workers. But as other services seek to reduce their expenditure, the work load on such informal and non statutory care is likely to be increased as patients are discharged earlier from general and psychiatric hospitals, more people need support because they cannot move from unsuitable and inadequate housing, and so on.

The general failure of domiciliary and day care services to keep pace with the needs of a growing population of very old people because of cuts in public expenditure, and the substitution of council residential provision by "community care" are *increasing* the amount of informal care required. All the evidence indicates that the additional recruits required for the institutional ised schemes for harnessing and extending "informal care" and "helping networks" will largely be unpaid or low paid women.[95] Patch's advocates argue that it is concerned with an increased emphasis on the support of informal carers. However, such schemes are often concerned with providing advice and education rather than practical aid.[96] In addition, the kind of child care schemes associated with patch's orientation, for example, mother and toddler schemes and playgroups, are not the sort to enable women to be in full-time employment, but rather ones which offer part-time shared care.

Paradoxically its expansion of low and non-paid women's work runs counter to one of the most attractive starting points of patch — its attempt to offer a flexible, non-bureaucratic alternative to the traditional social services hierarchies. If as feminist commentators have argued, the subordination of women is at the heart of hierarchical centralised organisation, [97] then patch advocates have undermined their own programme by leaving gender off the agenda. As Walton commented shortly after the formation of social services departments:

> The future of social work in this country, as part of social care services, now seems to be well and truly in the hands of a male elite.[98]

We would argue that the advocates of patch cannot be consistent with their own principles and remain neutral on this issue. It is clear that women's situation in social services departments reflects their subordinate position in the overall labour market. They are concentrated in non-professional, non-managerial, manual and clerical occupations.[99] Not, of course, that the issue is getting a few more women into management.

Patch based social services, if anything, seem to reinforce this occupational inequality of women. Not only are they encouraging more unpaid or pittance paid roles for women. They are also creating new categories of low paid workers to carry out and organise daily care, who are predominantly women. This emerged in Hugman's study of social services' organisational structure and occupational ideology. He identified gender as one of three dimensions of dominance in social services departments. Interestingly, he saw in patch the "continuing segregation of general caring and virtuoso roles", based on "gender bias" with the relations between social workers and the new ancillary women workers "one of increasing hierarchical separation".[100] What patch "flexibility of roles" actually seems to mean, for example, in the case of home helps, is more responsibilities being heaped upon them without any improvement in pay, status or say.[101]

Such an intensified hierarchy is disappointing if we had hoped for the realisation of another of patch's aims — the integration of workers, with less professional distance and a recognition of the value of lay workers. Writing of the Normanton patch system, Cooper and others described the ideal patch worker as:

> Usually middle aged and married, with some experience of life, very often with a knowledge of voluntary work before she started and with relatives in the area, it is very unlikely that she will move or have particular ambitions.[102]

Or as Finch saw it:

> In other words, the ideal patch worker is a married woman looking for work locally, who is competent to take on quite a responsible job, but who has no aspirations to geographical or social mobility, and whose lack of qualifications justify her low status and pay.[103]

The caring envisaged in all such "community care schemes", she concluded, "whether it is done by volunteers, paid workers or relatives — implies not just domestic work but a qualitative relationship with the dependent person, of a type characteristically assigned to women in our culture".[104]

PATCH, WOMEN'S WORK AND THE PEOPLE WE SURVEYED

The comments of the people we spoke to cast additional light on this discussion. They confirm the feminist informed critique. The choices facing most women were either being overburdened with paid work and caring, or caring and not being employed, with all the attendant social and economic problems. How do patch and community social work relate to their experience?

When we asked people where they got their care and support from, almost all referred to personal relationships, although nearly half saw the provision of care either in terms of financial assistance or formal services. But while people largely got their care and support informally and generally preferred it that way, they saw many obstacles in the way of it being satisfactory, including the inadequacy of formal services. Most also saw it mainly meaning responsibilities for women, and in several cases, as we have seen, people linked the need for informal care for people with particular needs, to the inadequacy of formal provision, which they saw as a preferable alternative.

This is consistent with the findings of a recent survey of public preferences for the "care of dependency groups". This suggested that most people would prefer a structure of public and paid services which would support such individuals to remain in their own homes wherever possible, and would not want to attach the major responsibility for care to relatives. [105] Similar findings have emerged from a 1984 national survey. When asked which alternative they thought best for old people who did not need to be in a hospital but were not entirely able to look after themselves, 65% of the sample selected "to live in sheltered accommodation in their own flat, but with someone to look after them". 71% of pensioners gave the same answer. Only 20% of the sample and 14% of pensioners wanted "to live with their families with younger people around", and 13% of both the sample and pensioners to live in a residential home. [106]

Thus people's preference seems to be for care *in* the community rather than the care *by* the community which patch and community social work largely seem to entail. This also suggests that while it is important to equalise the responsibility for caring between men and women, both in informal and paid settings, just redistributing the burden in informal caring, without making sufficient equal opportunity formal provision available, is unlikely to accord with what people want, or do more than shift responsibility from one overstretched group to another. It is also likely to create additional problems for both women and men, just as the existing gender bias in caring does. Graham, for example, in her study of women, health and the family, pointed out ways in which because women are socially defined as the carers, families are affected through the complementary roles forced on men.

They may, for instance, be compelled to work long hours of overtime to make up the family income, thus not only seeing less of their children, but also leaving responsibility for their health care to women. She also found that if a couple decided to reverse roles, a man was still likely to encounter prejudice as the caring parent, for example, in health clinics. [107]

"COMMUNITY CARE" — COMMERCIAL "CARE"

Our Objectives: A Strategy Of Care In The Community...
East Sussex Social Services [108]

So far in this chapter we have focussed on "community care's" reliance on women's unpaid labour. But it has been based on *twin* policies of privatisation, both of which are likely to be damaging to carers and the people they care for. As well as demanding an increased unpaid contribution from women, "community care" has been associated with a massive growth in commercial provision. Private residential places have grown by almost 300 per cent over the last five years.[109] The two policies are underpinned by the same ideological and cost cutting commitments. According to the government White Paper:

The Care in the Community Programme introduced in 1983 has encouraged a reduction in the numbers of people inappropriately placed in long stay hospitals. The Programme enables funds to be transferred from health authorities to pay for alternative more appropriate forms of care.[110]

The House of Commons Social Services Committee, however, suggested something else.

It may be — we have no evidence to prove it — that health and local authorities are deliberately directing the elderly in need of residential care into the private sector....[111]

Certainly while the 1978 DHSS document "A Happier Old Age" insisted that "there should be a commitment to keeping people in their own homes",[112] the reality seems to have been very different. According to the author of one study "the evidence is that people are going into private homes who would not have gone into local authority homes".[113] Through the NHS and social security system, money has been provided to keep old people and people with special needs in commercial accommodation, but not to provide statutory support services "in the community". East Sussex's Director of Social Services has himself argued the importance of a formal assessment system before people are placed in public, commercial or voluntary homes.[114] Pointing to the human cost of "privatisation" the journal Community Care has argued that:

often subsidised through supplementary benefit payments, the homes have a vested interest in taking in residents when the interests of the elderly person, or someone with special needs, could be to have support in their own homes.[115]

The imposition of upper limits on social security payments for private residential care, however, means that even this often inappropriate option is now being denied people , again forcing them back on their families and women carers.

Not only is there no firm data that commercial homes are more efficient or more appropriate than statutory ones,[116] there is longstanding evidence of their shortcomings. The provisions to regulate commercial provision are inadequate.[117] There is also no provision for considering the needs of individual residents. As Tibbenham concluded, looking at the boom in private sector residential homes:

> Whereas local authority homes are usually the foci for the provision of a range of other services aimed at keeping clients in the community — meals on wheels, sheltered housing, day centres, etc — private homes are not and have no incentive to provide other than traditional full residential care.[118]

While of course commercial provision varies in quality and conditions, studies do show a lack of facilities and of therapeutic care, lower levels of waking night time duty staff and appropriately trained and qualified staff.[119]

The predominantly women workforce are even worse off than their sisters in the far from ideal conditions of statutory services, with more part-time work, less job security, a low level of unionisation, low pay, poor conditions, inadequate training and frequent understaffing and over-work to keep costs down.[120]

East Sussex

> I wouldn't say that the patients were neglected. They're just deprived. Deprived of a lot of things that they should have that they don't.... Care is the one thing they're deprived of.
> *Julie Reed, Auxiliary Nurse, Private Nursing Home* [121]

Brighton and East Sussex have been in the vanguard of the expansion of commercial provision, like other resort towns and counties with large elderly populations. While patch advocates have sought to distance themselves from right-wing interpretations of "community care", there is no doubt that East Sussex's patch reorganisation has been associated with a major switch to private provision for elderly people. East Sussex has the highest proportion of private "rest homes" in the country and four times the national average of private nursing homes.[122] As Barefoot Video argued after working with Brighton and Hove health workers and a local community association to make their own independent videos of "community care" policies for old people, while "the policy is community care, the reality is private care".[123]

The problems identified nationally are no less evident in Brighton and East

Sussex, with people going into commercial homes rather than being able to stay "in the community" as they wished, for want of statutory community-based health and social services. Instead of meaning adequate home care facilities, "community care" has frequently meant alternative institutional care. Local community services have been undermined, rehabilitative hospital beds reduced, and private old people's homes subsidised. The conditions in private provision workers and local people reported on their videos were often unsuitable and far from satisfactory.[124] This stands in some contrast to the view of the Director of Social Services, who, while acknowledging the need to develop more domiciliary services, believes:

> It would be fair to say and pretty honest to say, that by and large the balance of care for the elderly in Hove is pretty good. There's a good cross-section of opportunity, both private, voluntary and public there. [125]

PEOPLE AND VOLUNTARY ACTION

As well as people's — and particularly women's — involvement in informal care, we were also interested in their participation in voluntary and community organisations. We asked members of the sample if they were involved in any. 12 said they were. Their activities reflected the range and heterogeneity of voluntary action.

"Yes C.N.D."

"I help at the Hanover Community Association."

"Yes, I'm involved in an organisation that looks after young mentally handicapped adults, and also an able-bodied and physically handicapped youth club."

"I do charity work once a year. It's held once a year."

"British Red Cross Society."

"Through the church, I belong to a group called 'Euphoria'. It's a youth club. You just oversee the young people."

"An old age pensioners club run from St. Joseph's Church. They're very good to the old people. There's a commiteee and I'm elected on it." (woman aged seventy six)

Two others of the 12 said they were involved in clubs for old people as users — although it is questionable whether a simple distinction can be made between users and "voluntary helpers" in such voluntary organisations, not only because old people themselves represent their main resource, but also because they may be involved in their decision-making and day to day running. Those defined as "helpers" as in the two cases here, may also themselves be older or elderly. People's involvement in community and voluntary organisations was more likely to be as a volunteer than a user where this distinction could be made, but it is often likely to be blurred, with roles overlapping. For example:

> "We use the local Community Association and I have done teaching there in the past."

Four other people answered "no" to this question, but were actively involved in their church.

> "I belong to the Salvation Army though, and do the mother and toddler group."

> "Not at the moment, only working within the Church. That takes up a lot of time. I'm on the Church Council."

People also mentioned several other voluntary organisations and activities they were involved in.

> "I help down the school."

> "I visit the John Howard home for people with multiple sclerosis."

> "No, but I run a football club and I'm a member of a trade union so I get involved in their discussion to a certain extent."

> "No local ones, just the Royal Society for the Protection of Birds and the Camping Club. I pay about a hundred pounds a year."

Three other people, both in answer to this question and elsewhere in their interview, mentioned past involvement in voluntary action and organisations. For example:

> "Not now. I have been in the past, but I've retired through family commitments."

In addition six people referred to past attempts or present intentions to do voluntary work.

> "I'm a Roman Catholic and I offered my services to the youth club over there — boxing and that — but they never contacted me. I'd like to do youth work."

> "I'd like to in the future when I decide to give up work."

> "There's quite a few people in this block and we did think of getting an empty store room and making a club room. One room is for the Council and one is for the welfare. It would be nice. There's nothing for old people round here. We could

make an evening of it.... I reckon if there was an empty building round here, we could see the agent and rent it..."

"I joined the Lions Club, but it was too cliquey."

"I haven't got the time. When I pack up work, I'd like to."

One of the questions we asked people about social services was whether they would like to have closer contact with them. Ten people answered in terms of their preparedness to give voluntary help — in addition to those already involved.

"If I could help and do good by it."

"Only in things I thought I could help out with."

"I wouldn't mind being a helper."

"A good idea. There are times when it would do me good to go and see someone and help them out..." (woman recently widowed)

As has been seen, the people offering informal care and support to neighbours and relatives were significantly different to the overall sample according to a number of characteristics. While the numbers are low, the same would also seem to be true of the 20 people involved in voluntary and community agencies and activities. The distribution of men and women was similar to that of the overall sample, as was the proportion of women with partners, but women were less likely to have children at home (3/13). Money was more likely to be a problem for the twenty (15/20), and they were more likely to be dependent on state benefits (6/20) . They were slightly less likely to be in paid employment (9/20). They were also slightly older than the overall sample (8/20) aged 50 and over, and short stay residents were over-represented among them (8/20) had lived locally three years or less. They were much more likely to identify unemployment as a problem for themselves than the overall sample. (10/20).

Patch and community social work tend to consider these two groups together as the "voluntary and informal sectors". If we add together all those people involved in some form of voluntary action; acting as a foster parent, or providing informal care and support for neighbours and relations — other than partners or their own children — we arrive at a total of 46. If we also include those who had previously been engaged in these activities the total is 50 — half the sample. However, the striking thing about these 50 is that the overlap between those involved in offering informal support, and those involved in voluntary and community organisations was only four people.

Thus a tentative conclusion to be drawn from our survey, reinforced by the differences between the two groups, is that informal carers and volunteers may be drawn from different people rather than the same pool of participants.

This may be important for patch and conventional "community care" policies, where there is emphasis on reinforcing or compensating for informal care with organised schemes that are volunteers based. People prepared to be involved in one activity, may not be interested in the other. We have also already seen two groups emerge from our sample and other local research; long stay working class residents, including many old people, and younger, middle class newcomers, more involved in organised "community activity" and networks and identifying more strongly with "community". Recent research on volunteers has pointed to a distinction between formal "employment-like" volunteering and more informal neighbourhood based activities and suggested these are sustained by quite different expectations and assumptions.[126]

As we have already mentioned, when we asked people about patch and informal care, some felt it would be difficult to recruit volunteers. There is a lack of comparative data to indicate whether or not such fears are justified. What does seem to be clear though, is that people's responses to requests to volunteer depend very much on how carefully these are planned, and particularly on what they are for.[127] While "volunteer" and "voluntarism" are key words in the vocabulary of contracted-out welfare, people, it seems, are more likely to see themselves specifically as blood-donors, visitors, fundraisers and so on, than as "volunteers".

The attitudes to patch of people involved in informal care and other voluntary action were interesting. Their views on patch reorganisation and the idea of an increased reliance on voluntary organisations and volunteers were similar to those of the overall sample. They expressed a similar level of practical and philosophical objections to increased reliance on volunteers (17/46). The 29 people currently offering informal support to relatives and neighbours revealed a similar degree of support for an increased emphasis on "informal helping networks" as the overall sample. But those involved in voluntary work and organisations were more likely to be opposed to the idea (9/17). Taken together they were slightly less in favour and more opposed to an increased emphasis on informal care. Thus our survey suggested that people already involved as informal carers or volunteers may not necessarily be particularly strong supporters of patch and related patch principles and indeed the opposite may be true of some. It also showed that they were no more positive in their attitudes to social services than other people.

The 46 carers and volunteers had approximately the same social class distribution, length of stay in the area, proportion in paid employment (25/46 compared with 59/100) and age distribution as the overall sample, although this meant, for example, that a quarter of them were aged 60 or over. Men were under-represented (15/46 compared with 41/100), while the women involved were more likely to have children at home than all women in the sample. The 46 were more likely to mention having money problems (36/46 compared with 66/100), more likely to be reliant on poverty level state benefits (12/46 compared with 17/100) and more likely to single out unemployment as an actual or feared problem for themselves. Thus in a number of ways the people taking on these tasks seem to have faced *more* responsibilities and *more* problems than the overall sample. The people who were giving unpaid help, were, it might be thought, among those who had more need of it themselves than some others.

Our survey identified a high proportion of people providing informal care and involved in voluntary and community organisations and activities. It should be repeated that this figure if anything is likely to understate the scale of involvement. As we have said, participants were not asked a specific question about the informal care they offered to neighbours, friends or others, but only about that to relatives,so much could have remained concealed. It must also be stressed that this high level of involvement was identified *before* patch reorganisation had resulted in any major increase in reliance on informal care by local social services. As we observed earlier, patch advocates have emphasised patch's role in further "tapping" "informal care". The central question which we believe needs to be addressed, is how much more tapping is either feasible or justifiable in view of the enormous amount currently undertaken, often by those with the least resources and most responsibilities and problems. And this question arises before we consider the many social, cultural, economic and demographic obstacles and counter-forces in its way.

In all 12 people in our sample, mostly, as we have seen, when asked whether they would like to have closer contact with social services, expressed an interest in voluntary work. It is debatable whether these, for example, can be seen as the potential pool of voluntary carers envisaged by patch proponents. We say this partly because of the considerable fall-off between initial interest in voluntary action and the amount that actually materialises and relates to existing needs, and because of comments people made to us. Seven of the 12 were in paid employment and qualified their interest.

"If I had the time, if I didn't go to work, I'd love to."

"I wouldn't mind helping but I do work and do tupperware, and with children — but in the future..."

"I'm doing a summer job which is hard work, but when it ends, I'd like to do voluntary work, looking after people."

"I haven't got the time. When I pack up work, I'd like to."

Again eight of the 12 were women and six were already offering informal care and support to neighbours and relations. They appear an already overstretched workforce on which to base a whole new policy of increased reliance on informal care and voluntarism. They also illustrate one of the many conflicts between paid employment and conventionally defined community care. The only way in which the latter is likely to become a practical alternative is by the continued replacement of paid by unpaid work.[128] While patch advocates say this is not their intention, it clearly seems to be that of right wing proponents of "community care".

Despite the indications from our survey of a high level of participation in informal caring and voluntary action, local needs were not being met. This was clear from the people we spoke to as well as from the Social Services Department itself.[129] The level of support available, particularly for vulnerable groups like old and disabled people, single parents and those badly housed and on low income was inadequate. What was also clear from our survey was what a limited impact all this informal aid and voluntary action could have on the wants and needs people identified for themselves and others.

The right wing argument that the state provision of social services encourages and is symptomatic of a decline in people's self-reliance and sense of responsibility, is not borne out by our study. Nor is there any support here for the view that informal aid has broken down.

The picture emerging from our small scale local survey is also confirmed by the findings of a recent national survey of voluntary work and neighbourhood care. About one in five of the sample interviewed had done some voluntary work during the week preceding their interview; more than one in four volunteered at least once a month; and almost half had done some voluntary work during the year before the survey. A significant minority (23 percent) of the sample helped in "neighbourhood care" activities on a regular basis. Three quarters gave some help in their neighbourhood at some time or another, although mostly on an irregular basis.[130]

Our survey, however, suggests that while there might be a lot of such activity, it was not enough. Paid workers and state support were still necessary if the level of care and quality of life were to be maintained and improved.

While, as we have said, our study may have under-represented the level of informal care undertaken by our sample, as a teacher we interviewed and quoted earlier said:

"Your survey is going to be over-representative of those people who are interested as opposed to those who just shut their doors and don't want to know."

It may be true, as he suggested, that there is some correlation between those who don't want to take part in surveys concerning their area and people who have a more generally inward-looking approach. As we have seen, among the reasons people gave us for taking part in the survey was wanting to help and hoping to improve things. If his assumption was justified, then it may mean that in areas like the one we studied, a significant body of people are not involved in providing informal care, other than to their immediate family, and furthermore are unlikely to be responsive to any attempt to involve them. It is difficult to see how patch orientated social services departments will mobilise them to become part of the newly expanded labour force they require to provide unpaid care.

VOLUNTARY ACTION: INDICATIONS FROM HANOVER

We can get some idea of the actual response to appeals for unpaid caring and support in the Hanover patch from the neighbourhood care scheme that was set up. We have already seen some of the difficulties encountered in attracting large numbers of local volunteers. Most of the relatively small number of volunteers recruited initially came from outside the patch area. The low number coming from inside the project area as well as the fact that referrals were coming from outside it, were a reason given for extending the area the scheme covered.[131]

What is not clear is why local people seem to have been slow to get involved in Hanover's neighbourhood care scheme. It could simply be that they were not interested or did not have the time. On the other hand they might have been reluctant to take part in something in which they had not been involved from the start, and which did not result from an initiative or demand of their own. While Brighton Council for Voluntary Service, one of the initiators of the project, said:

> The public image of the scheme is that of a locally based voluntary project, with little reference to either Social Services or the CVS,[132]

as we have seen, the scheme quite clearly was not that. A key question is whether people want to take part in such participatory activities designed and set up without their effective involvement and over which they have little or no control.[133]

HARNESSING VOLUNTARY AND INFORMAL CARE

Our study adds to a growing body of evidence showing the vast scale of unpaid caring and the high human costs involved. It raises practical and philosophical questions about social services seeking to harness and extend what seem already overstretched resources. But there is also another equally important issue; what are the implications and possible effects of such intervention for informal care and networks?

A central argument underpinning patch based social services has been the need to look again at the purpose and organisation of social services, and to challenge assumptions of the automatic superiority of large scale bureaucracy and traditional professional roles. There has been a questioning of "the emphasis placed on bureaucratic and professional conceptions of service delivery".[134] Patch's supporters have pointed to the failure of conventional social services to pay adequate attention to the contribution of voluntary and informal care, to be properly coordinated with them, and their undervaluing of their contribution. They have stressed that their aim is to build on these and to reshape statutory services in their image.[135] The worry is though, that it is the opposite that is taking place, with informal aid restructured by social services, both in conception and practice, in *their* image.

Not only have the initiative and impetus for community social work, patch based social services and their "community orientation" come from social services rather than the "community". It is also difficult to see how there can be any equality in the relationship between the two to ensure that the aims and approach of social services can be balanced, mediated and if need be challenged by those of local grassroots interests. The "community", particularly the informal caring relationships on which so much emphasis has been placed, are by their very nature not organised to exert an influence over social services. Any such organisation immediately changes their nature and institutionalises particular interests. It would also be inappropriate to see the voluntary sector, which has many unresolved problems of public accountability of its own, as a suitable or adequate representative of local needs or interests, even if it might appropriately seek to safeguard its own.

Advocates of patch have begun to refer to the networks of unpaid caring and informal aid on which they place such emphasis as the "informal sector",[136] reifying and institutionalising these subtle and complex parts of people's lives and expressions of their relationships. Such incorporation of them, not just in terms of their use, but also of their conception, recasting them in the same social administration terms as existing provinces of welfare, like the voluntary and statutory *sectors*, rather than redefining these, symbolises the problem. It points to the very real danger of informal care and support being colonised and appropriated by social services and social policy makers — albeit unintentionally. Such dangers are beginning to be recognised from a variety of perspectives.[137] And while social services may not have the power to take over or dominate informal care and ties, their intervention may seriously weaken and threaten them. Writing from "a social worker's viewpoint", Didrichsen argued:

> Under present economic and political circumstances, neighbourhood work appears to promise solutions to many contemporary problems, particularly those relating to economic stringency, social control and the protection of local democracy. Further, I argue that this process will make the social worker's role *more* managerial and potentially *more* repressive in respect of certain client groups, whilst at the same time accepting that for other client groups it could represent an improvement.[138]

David has pointed to another way in which social services may subvert unpaid caring. In her discussion of the "teaching of motherhood", she raised the issue of the nature of relationships between paid and unpaid carers and pointed to the way in which the imposition of prevailing ideologies in social services and other welfare agencies could have divisive and damaging effects on women by perpetuating notions of motherhood based on inequality between the sexes.[139] It is possible to see similar consequences with the extension of social services' ideological assumptions to other areas of unpaid caring by women. Black women, for example, rightly argue that their networks are *their's* and that social services do not have a right to use or appropriate them.[140] Little if any attempt has so far been made in either government community care policies or patch and community social work initiatives to explore the particular caring needs and realities of black and other ethnic minority women, although such policies especially affect deprived multi-racial areas.

The irony is that while patch and welfare pluralist philosophies are framed in terms of giving a greater role to voluntary organisations and informal effort in place of statutory provision, it is the *state* which is seeking to mobilise such non-statutory and unpaid caring. Thus they can be seen as concerned not so much with a reduced role for the state, as a different kind of intervention. Instead of primarily providing services to meet our needs, the state will be involved in organising, supervising, extending and even reinterpreting our own self-help. For example, a recent study describing projects "which set out to make full use of community resources in providing services or care for groups within the local population", concluded that:

Social services departments must identify social needs, harness and deploy community resources to meet them, and if necessary pay volunteers to provide a sustained service. Traditional assumptions are challenged about the boundaries between professional and voluntary activity. It is suggested that — to ensure a full and effective partnership — volunteers must be recruited trained and deployed directly by statutory staff.[141]

Neighbourhood care becomes something to be "exploited". Just as Max Beerbohm caricatured the Webbs and their fabianism as playing toy soldiers, so the social worker is now being advanced in a similar role, but in a development that is meant to be a revulsion from such centralised "socialism". So Davies, for example, in an embarassingly naive and arrogant notion of social engineering, offered a new definition of social work in his revised verson of "The Essential Social Worker", saying:

It is now clear — clearer, indeed as each year goes by — that those who are employed in positions traditionally labelled as social work are emerging as grassroots community managers. carrying discretionary powers and welfare responsibilities that extend beyond mere *caring*. Social workers are community entrepreneurs; their job is maintenance, and they approach it by imaginatively balancing a variety of skills and roles in which the coordination of other operators in the agency and the community plays an increasingly important part.[142]

PATCH AND PARTNERSHIP

A criticism that has been made of the community social work that the Barclay Report advocated can also be raised about patch based social services.

> The community is viewed as a resource to the Social Services Department. Should it not be the other way around? How far is it legitimate for the Social Services Department to "manage" the community?[143]

There has been much talk in patch and community social work about "partnership". East Sussex's Director of Social Services has argued that one of the aims of their patch reorganisation was to create "the opportunity for local partnership to develop between community resources and statutory services".[144]

As the consultation group convened by a volunteers advisory service said:

> Partnership is a central concept in Barclay. It needs both clearer definition and more critical evaluation. Is it necessarily in the *community's* best interest, for example, for statutory and voluntary agencies to "plan a partnership which is mutually reinforcing"? (Barclay 5:41) We need to ask: Partnership with whom? For what? Who benefits? On whose terms? How is it achieved?[145]

The 1977 Wolfenden Report on the future of voluntary organisations strongly advocated a mixed economy of welfare with a much larger contribution from the voluntary sector.[146] It represented the first major call for what has since burgeoned into the so-called "welfare pluralism" that has gained enthusiastic support from all political quarters and many social administration academics and members of the voluntary sector. In 1981, three researchers reporting on the reality of the relationship between voluntary and statutory agencies in Britain wrote:

> The "David and Goliath" proportions of the voluntary-statutory relationship inevitably meant that the local authority set the terms for voluntary involvement. And these terms were limiting...

> Detailed voluntary involvement in the production of new policies and routine consultation over the effects of existing policies were virtually non-existent. When challenged councillors would put up... obstacles to such involvement...[147]

The General Secretary of the Brighton Council for Voluntary Service, writing of their study, pointed to the narrowness of this partnership.

> The reality of partnership between statutory and voluntary organisations appears to rest on collaboration over specific functions and services and between individual organisations, rather than the broader work of participation in planning involving the (voluntary) intermediary body.[148]

The Hanover neighbourhood care scheme offers another insight into partnership between voluntary and statutory agencies. As the Brighton Council for Voluntary Service saw it:

> The scheme draws together the concept of voluntarism and the resources of the statutory sector in a way that is appropriate to the area in which it is based.[149]

But whatever benefits it might have brought to the welfare agencies themselves, this partnership could not be said to have given local people or users any effective say or involvement in the development or management of the service.

INSTITUTIONALISING INFORMAL CARE

How far social services departments would be able to "manage the community" and generate increased informal care remains unclear. But there remains the question of whether their involvement in informal care would change or undermine it. We have already seen the tendency of social policy professionals to recast informal care in the image of formal welfare. Earlier we raised the issue of how many more recruits were likely to come forward as informal or voluntary helpers in response to patch requests. But how many people prepared to offer informal aid spontaneously would also be willing to under the aegis of social services? And what would be the effect of institutionalised informal care, particularly where payment is involved, on existing arrangements and people's preparedness to maintain them? The use of such small scale payments is increasingly being seen as a means of generating and maintaining networks in deprived areas where they are thought to be particularly weak and vulnerable. However, in their study of three social services teams, Black and others described as typical one social worker's comment:

> I feel that (social) services that are available here damaged a good deal of this (informal care).... You can have a family living next door to an elderly person who over the years has been caring for them day and night.... Now

they hear that someone down the road is doing exactly the same but getting paid for it, say under the Good Neighbour Scheme, and they say, why should we do it unless we get paid for it.[150]

There are also ambiguities over whose needs such organised voluntary action is actually meeting. In East Sussex, self help groups for carers, for example, are now tending to be set up through the Social Services Department or large voluntary organisations like Age Concern, rather than at the independent initiative of carers themselves. Social Services and carers may well have different needs. The Department may want a stable continuing service which is known to be regularly available and to which clients can be referred. For people involved, however, the need may be for something much more personal and ephemeral. While the Social Services Department sees itself as seeking to sustain and support informal networks,[151] more thought needs to be given to the ways in which it may subtly and perhaps unintentionally be restructuring and transforming such voluntary action.

THE ROLE OF COMMUNITY ORGANISATIONS

As a focus for and catalyst of social relations, we might expect community associations and community centres to have an important role both in developing informal networks and in encouraging informal support. This assumption seems to be implicit in the local and central government policies that have made community centres and club-rooms the main amenity provided in council estates and deprived areas. But the question remains, to what extent such provision can fulfil such a role.

We have seen how Hanover has an active community centre and association. It offers a variety of activities including an elderly residents luncheon club, writers workshop, junior youth club, mother and toddlers group, theatre company and so on. The assumption of one woman we interviewed that "the Hanover Community Association brings people together" seemed to be shared by a number of people, but very few actually seemed to use the Centre or Association. It is interesting from our study what little part both appeared to play in providing people with support, although they were quite often mentioned as criteria or manifestations of "community" in the area.

Frequent reference is made to such community organisations in patch proposals and discussions, as a key "community facility" or "resource", as well as a potential outpost for local social services workers. There had been recognition by Hanover patch social services of the significance of the Community Centre and Association as concrete expressions and institutions of the locality and "local people". As we have seen, the patch team, as they have elsewhere, had attempted to hold sessions in the Community Centre and to enlist the support of the Community Association for their activities. But could such neighbourhood organisations play a non-institutionalised and more far-reaching role in increasing and supporting informal care and networks?

The authors of a government research study of self-management in a neighbourhood community centre concluded that:

> The Social Services Department assumed that there was an untapped potential for voluntary involvement in the community and that lack of involvement resulted from a lack of opportunity and/or apathy. Our survey showed that there was indeed, a reluctance to join or hold office in most kinds of formal associations, but this was part of a general pattern of leisure not untypical of such a stable, working class area where previous findings have shown, groupings tend to be largely informal, based around the pub, social club or home. For the reasons underlying such a life style we need to look not just at the residents themselves, but the outside pressures and cultural values influencing social patterns.[152]

This is consistent with Tomlinson's analysis of the conflicting class interests at work in the Hanover Community Centre. It again raises questions about the effect on existing informal relationships and networks of the intervention of incoming agencies and interests. The part played by middle class residents in the Hanover Community Association in introducing competing interests, ideologies and objectives in a traditional working class area, may equally be played elsewhere or in other circumstances by middle class activists, paid community workers, social workers, or indeed patch workers.

This discussion of the relationship between social services and informal care raises two important points. First, a large question mark hangs over the assumption that social services will be able to involve more people in caring, when many, including most women, already seem to be doing this anyway. Second, while informal care represents the way many people might ideally like to receive care, will social services' intervention qualitatively change it: if so will the kind of organised "informal care" of social services still be what people want? Our findings suggest that for many it may not be.

INCREASING INFORMAL CARE OR SUPPORTING THE CARERS?

> At present we have a crisis and breakdown model of personal social services intervention. If five to ten per cent of those who provide informal care were to break down and request the admission of their relative to homes or hospitals, our systems would be in chaos.
> *Olive Stevenson*[153]

A prime task of the area team should be to support informal and formal voluntary action.
Roger Hadley[154]

Readers may already have sensed some ambiguity in this discussion of social services and informal care as to whether patch is primarily concerned with increased reliance on informal care or increased *support* for it. This ambiguity is important and seems to arise not only from contradictory messages coming from patch and community social work, but also tensions between their philosophies and practice.

"Helping to support the informal carers" has been expounded as a principle of patch since patch first became an important issue on social services' agendas in the late 1970s.[155] Contrasting existing social services with patch, the argument goes:

> Such informal care, however, is often provided at considerable cost and may ultimately break down because the carers can no longer cope. It is often only at this stage, when it may be too late to help the carer, that the social services department is brought in. The appropriate response, it is argued, would be to place far more emphasis on support of the informal carers, whether family, friends, or neighbours and volunteers, in order to extend the numbers helped, to try and ensure that no individual carer should have to carry intolerable burdens, and to preserve and strengthen community caring networks.[156]

At the same time, part of patch's "alternative rationale for the provision of care" is seen as "recognition that many unqualified people, whether working informally as volunteers, or as ancillaries with the social services department, have the potential to offer practical and other supportive care of a high standard". [157] Discussing the case studies in "Going Local", the editors concluded that "the use of local volunteers, on both formal and informal bases, is the most common means of interweaving the team's work with the community". Those involved in the schemes all claimed that one way they could "tap more resources" was "by developing volunteer support".[158]

Thus in patch, a commitment to supporting the carers is coupled with increased reliance on informal care. What needs further examination is the balance between the two, and what supporting carers actually means.

As we have said, patch proponents, while arguing for a pluralist approach to the provision of welfare, have denied a desire to run-down statutory services. But as we know, the increased emphasis on informal support has coincided with reductions in social and other health and welfare services. The Hanover neighbourhood care scheme, for example, has been described as a "preventive strategy".[159] But prevention doesn't just mean using volunteers or keeping an informal eye on an elderly person so that they aren't institutionalised through neglect. It can also involve, for instance, adequate community nursing so that people do not end up having to be hospitalised.

Recognition of some of the costs of caring, fears of "creating two clients instead of one by overburdening informal carers" have led to new rhetoric like "caring for the carers" and important new organisations like the Association of Carers. The Department of Health and Social Security mounted a major project in 1983-1984 into "supporting the informal carers" which laid stress on "their rights and needs".[160] It drew together 50 schemes from all over the country which provided local support to informal carers, "to be used by policy makers in planning services to support informal carers and by practitioners in devising schemes at local level".[161] But here we come to another of the major issues surrounding present approaches to providing "support for informal carers". The methods on which greatest emphasis is being placed are themselves largely based on increased informal, voluntary and low paid caring by women. Thus supporting the informal carers becomes synonymous with increasing informal and unpaid caring. What is presented as the former may actually be the latter. Of the 50 schemes described in the DHSS report, 13 were based on volunteers and neighbours; 11 on self help or support groups; and 18 on low paid workers, some on Manpower Services schemes, several employed only part-time. A number of schemes only offered temporary or "respite" support. Typical of the wages mentioned were £1.70 an hour from 8 am to 8 pm and £2.00 an hour from 8 pm to 8 am, for part-time care attendants in a family support scheme.[162]

The three main methods now being developed to provide support for carers are home attendants, taking on some or all of the responsibilities of informal carers; fostering schemes for old people and adults and children with disabilities, to provide a break for carers; and "support groups", where carers can get together. We have raised some of the problems associated with the first two. They tend to be low paid and short term. Support groups offer social services departments a particularly attractive option. They are cheap to run, needing only some staff involvement, a place to meet and perhaps alternative provision for people being cared for, which may be met by an informal or volunteer "sitting" service. They also offer the prospect of becoming independent of social services. They are seen as a means of providing the "emotional support" carers need [163] as well as information, training and advice. But can we really agree with Contact-A-Family — a network of voluntary self-help groups for parents of children with disabilities, that "a problem shared is a problem halved"? [164] Research on attitudes of parents of children with mental handicaps, for example, found that nearly half did not find contact with other such parents helpful.[165]

Involvement in support groups can actually add responsibility to carers, especially if and when social workers who have set up such schemes withdraw and the group has to be serviced, maintained and funds raised. It also raises all the issues of congregation and segregation faced by members of disadvantaged and stigmatised groupings. When,in a video, the DHSS asked carers what *they* wanted, they talked of time to themselves, to do the things they couldn't ordinarily do. [166] While such groups are undoubtedly an important source of support for some carers, it is not clear how far they are able to meet these needs. There is also the question of how much they serve as a means of sharing and trying to cope with problems which social and other services might otherwise be dealing with by making available necessary resources and provision.

Carers themselves call for *practical* support.[167] The DHSS has argued that "most carers require a 'package' of care, combining financial benefits, counselling, respite care, domiciliary services, day care, short stay residential care and other forms of support".[168] A Department of the Environment research study came to a similar conclusion, that it was "a package of care of statutory and informal help" that was needed if frail elderly people were to be enabled to stay at home.[169] As we mentioned earlier, nearly a quarter of the people we interviewed saw the provision of care and support either partly or entirely in terms of formal services. A similar number saw support in terms of financial resources, indeed that was how they distinguished it from care.

Yet as we have seen, the emphasis in policy so far has been on self-help, volunteer and low paid methods of support. All but one of the schemes concerned with the provision of support described in East Sussex's account of its patch reorganisation fall into this category. [170] So have all the initiatives that have been undertaken as yet in Hanover patch.[171]

Caring may seem to have emerged from this chapter as an onerous and unpleasant activity. But there is nothing inherently negative about it. The difficulties have to do with the lack of choice and appropriate support available to women carers. We saw earlier how one woman we interviewed regarded having her parents living with her as her social life. Many women value the role of carer, just as many others want to be cared for by women.[172] The love and affection that is often the basis for caring can readily be subverted and spoiled by the intolerable strains placed on both the carer and person cared for. Finch has argued the importance of policies which take such "emotions and affections more seriously... releasing relatives and friends to offer more personal warmth and affection" by removing "the fear of becoming entangled in pressures to provide domestic and nursing care".[173]

It is not possible to provide an adequate framework of support services for carers cheaply. Rationing is increasingly the norm because of shortages of volunteers and insufficient domiciliary and day care workers. A number of commentators, including the Equal Opportunities Commission, have offered proposals to improve the situation for carers, including the expansion of domiciliary health and social services and changes in employment legislation entitling carers to periods of leave without prejudice to their employment, on the model of maternity leave.[174] The Association of Community Workers has also outlined an alternative approach to supporting informal aid, which so far does not seem to have been explored or pursued in patch thinking.

> We believe that the way to encourage informal networks is to put more emphasis on resources that allow informal networks to flourish, eg appropriate planning and housing allocation policies, cheap transport and telephone systems — in essence an environment which encourages people to want to have contact with each other, meet informally and to develop and sustain their links, affections and care for each other.[175]

Such proposals, however, while improving the position of women carers, would not in themselves challenge or end sexual divisions in caring. As Finch and Land have said, "the same kinds of economic and ideological barriers would operate as in the case of the informal caring 'solution', so long as the relationship between men's and women's position in the labour market and in the home remains fundamentally unaltered".[176]

The present emphasis on "supporting the carers" also begs the question of whether it will always be support — even practical support — that carers want. Some, particularly women, may in fact want a real choice of whether to be primary carers at all. Most services now — except for residential provision — like laundry services, respite care, part-time and temporary care attendants, are there to prop up the carers rather than to take the brunt of responsibility from them — if that is what is wanted.

However, apart from the DHSS video we have mentioned, few attempts have been made by the advocates of community care to find out what carers *themselves* want. Little if any effort has been made in either government community care policies or patch and community social work initiatives to explore the particular caring needs and realities of black and other ethnic minority women, although such policies have particular significance for deprived multi-racial areas.[177]

Concern with "support for the carers" has also signalled a shift in priority away from people receiving care to those providing it,[178] instead of a renewed commitment to the needs of both. It is only recently that there has been a greater recognition of the rights and wants of people with disabilities and others needing support. This change in emphasis is clearly linked to cuts in formal services, increased reliance on informal carers and official anxiety about their breakdown. It is however potentially divisive. It raises issues about the different, sometimes conflicting needs of carers and people receiving care, and whether what the latter actually want is to be "cared for" or enabled to live independently through the provision of necessary support services.

In the next chapter, we shall be looking at people's own definitions of their wants and needs and their relationship with social services and decentralisation. People's experience of and attitudes on these issues have major implications for caring, support for carers and for people receiving care, which will draw us back to them.

CHAPTER EIGHT

Social Services, Patch and People's Needs

"I need more money.... Basically, everything is a struggle. You have to watch the pennies."

EXPLORING SOCIAL NEED

"Need", like "community" and "care" is a key concept of social services and social policy. We wanted to explore the relationship between "need", patch and the role of social services. We tried to do this through our sample's own perceptions and accounts of their wants and particular circumstances. We also sought to examine any relationship that they might see and that there might be between their needs and broader issues.

At first sight, to survey people's needs may seem to be a retreat from the approach we have taken in this study. Needs surveys are more usually associated with a model which takes users as the "object" of welfare provision. And they often become merely arguments over which indices justify what distribution of resources among competing professionals. Attempts to map the needs of particular client groups have also rightly been criticised for raising unrealistic expectations.

In raising the issue of need with our sample, however, our intention was not to make a needs survey, or to suggest we were offering a definitive statement of local needs. What we hope to suggest is that patch and community social work could approach the needs of a locality in a way that is both more open and productive. In other words, the agenda we propose for patch is to look at the relationships between particular issues, problems and wants of local people and the work of social services. Beginning with the accounts and perceptions of people in our random sample, we hope to contribute to this process.

Earlier, we raised the issue, emphasised by the survey, that while social services are often formally framed in broad terms as community services for all, in practice they generally do not operate in this way. Instead they are seen as — and are — much more specific. They work with certain groups and provide particular, even idiosyncratic services. As our survey suggested,

158

many people do not think they are for them.

Before embarking on a discussion of need, we must first say something more about it. Like other commonplace social services' concepts, its meaning has tended to be taken for granted — more often implied than stated. At the same time, the concept has long been the subject of academic analysis. Typologies have been constructed and detailed definitions offered.[1] Such conceptualisation of need is not neutral. It involves political and theoretical choices.[2] In practice "need" frequently seems to serve as an externally imposed measure of political and bureaucratic judgements of what people should have. Thus where people have wants, likes and desires, social policy has given them needs. We are not concerned here with developing the social administration discussion or categorisation of need. Instead, what we see as valuable are people's own conceptions and definitions of their need, as a basis for discussion and dialogue between them and agencies providing services.

Patch and community social work have not ducked the issue of need. In many ways their advocacy of changes in the structures and methods of social services came about because existing services were seen as unable to meet needs. They have also reflected a realisation that social services don't know very much about what people want, nor how they perceive what social services offer. Indeed, the disagreement within the Barclay Committee about the future of social work largely concerned this issue. In his minority report, Pinker saw the majority and neighbourhood-based social services reports as "a renewed attempt to diversify and extend the remit of social work beyond the bounds of credibility". He himself advocated "a definition of the role and tasks of social work which bears a credible relationship to the needs of cients, the capacity of ordinary social workers, the availability of resources, and the problem of accountability".[3] There have been other expressions of this desire for a more specific social work and social services from different vantage points. Advocates of intermediate treatment, for instance, have argued that:

...social work is likely to fail or have the opposite of the intended effect, unless it is very specific about whom the services it provides are for...[4]

They have emphasised their commitment to a specific objective:

...of providing a community based delinquency management project which maintains youngsters at home as an alternative to care and custody.[5]

The difficulty with this approach is that social services cannot be considered in isolation. It will seem unremarkable to say that they are inextricably bound up with the wider world and that this bears on any "specific" needs or aims practitioners try to meet. But social services do sometimes appear to treat fundamental human problems largely without reference to the bases of these problems. The relationship of social services to larger issues, from political policies, to social, economic and cultural conditions, has so far been inadequately explored, particularly by social services' own policy makers and mainstream theoreticians.

However, the issue is not whether social services should themselves set wide or narrow boundaries to their work. Patch and community social work, we believe, imply that both the shape of social services provision and its priorities would be worked out in a partnership and dialogue promised with users and local people. Whether patch can actually go beyond the individual and crisis intervention — as its advocates aspire — will, we suggest, depend on the answer to a wider question. Can it relate meeting needs to people's own perceptions of those needs and their wider social relations?

To begin, we wanted to find out more about how people see their own needs. For a number of our sample, "need" seemed to be a foreign way of framing their thoughts. Since many people may not be used to thinking about themselves in this way or being asked this kind of question, it may lead to distortion if either policy makers or analysts try to fit people's feelings into this kind of conceptual framework. We made this mistake ourselves. Fortunately, we found that people's perceptions of their wants and circumstances also emerged from other questions and from comments during the interviews. This not only gave a fuller picture of their "needs", but also let us check on answers to the specific question about them.

Table 1: Breakdown of Responses to Question 15: "How would you describe your own needs?"

Response		Number
Unmet needs (total)		58
more money	17	
health/medical care	7	
child care provision	5	
employment	3	
housing and housing related	6	
support/neighbourliness	3	
educational	2	
improved public transport	2	
improved public amenities	4	
social contact	3	
social services	3	
other unmet needs	3	
General statement of needs*		6
No or minimal needs/alright		42
Other		1
Don't Know		3
TOTAL		110**

* Two of these respondents also specified additional facilities/resources they wanted.
** These add up to more than the total of individuals since in some cases more than one need was mentioned.

Despite the question's limited usefulness, asking about need offered some interesting insights. People placed different interpretations on it. A few talked about what they saw as basic.

"My needs are primarily to hang on to the job I've got and the health to continue to do so, and the support and love of people about me. I'm lucky. I have all the basic necessities."

"I need a roof, food, clothing, in common with most other human beings, but other things also."

A few seemed to assume a narrow meaning of need in terms of social services.

"I think I'm alright. I don't need help from social services."

"If I had to go down (to social services), I would, but at the moment, I manage."

However, half the sample spoke of some unmet want or outstanding requirement they had. While these were wide-ranging, significantly a high proportion concerned the need for more money and public services. Very few concerned informal support.

The other main response to this question came from the 42 people who said they had no or minimal needs — "I haven't got any"; "I'm pretty well alright". In some cases their view of need seemed to be tied to an idea of self-reliance, contrasted with formal social policy and services which have appropriated the term — "I haven't got any needs. We can look after ourselves". Some people answered by specifying the met needs they saw as crucial for themselves.

"I haven't got any at the moment. I've just retired from the Merchant Navy. I'm 65, but I'm fit and active. I have a little job and I feel 25."

"I haven't really got any living at home. I've got a job."

"I don't think really anything springs to mind. I think if I had children my needs would be different." (young separated woman)

Elsewhere in the interviews 34 of the 42 people who had said they were alright or had no needs, mentioned what clearly constituted unmet needs. These ranged from housing and employment to money and public services. This points to the importance of careful framing of questions about need if research or discussion is not to give a misleading picture of a large proportion of people satisfactorily managing with the problems and needs that confront them. The eight people who made no reference to unmet needs, were also unrepresentative. Seven were in full-time employment and only one reliant on state benefits. None of them described money as a problem.

LOCAL AND GENERAL NEEDS AND PROBLEMS

A few people talked more generally of their local needs, and this leads to the next question we asked — about particular problems people faced living in Brighton. As well as offering some sort of check on the previous question, the aim here was to try and set people's wants and circumstances in a local context. They did not necessarily differentiate between local and national issues, and such distinctions were not always possible, for example, over issues like unemployment and public spending cuts. Problems may also be both national and local in nature as well as in origin, like for instance, heavy traffic.

Table 2: Breakdown of Responses to Question 16: "What particular problems or difficulties do you feel people like you face in Brighton?"

Response	Number
Financial problems	17
Environmental problems	13
Inadequate amenities and public services	17
Housing problems	10
Inadequate public transport	6
Unemployment	11
Inadequate informal support	2
Loneliness	2
Violence/fear of going out	6
Other	5
No particular problems	25
Don't know	6
TOTAL	120*

* The total came to more than 100 because some people identified more than one issue as a problem.

What we found was that this question was taken as another opportunity to describe general difficulties people faced — doubtless because of their importance to them — as well as those relating particularly to Brighton. Money problems, for example, from inflation and high direct taxation on low incomes were mentioned. Other financial difficulties which were directly related to Brighton were low local wages and high rents and house prices.

Again, significantly only three responses concerned inadequate informal or formal support, while most (61) were concerned with the inadequacy of local public provision, money and unemployment.

"No attention is paid to the unemployed. Brighton is regarded as an affluent society and they disregard the unemployed."

"Brighton Council needs push, push, push all the time before you get anything done."

Environmental problems included the unpleasantness of the local built environment, the area's steep hills, parking and pollution from dogs, and noisy and dangerous traffic.

"Common to all inner city environments, lack of natural beauty, a brutal environment..."

"Everyone has small back yards in this area and there's no play streets and only one park which is small and ruined by dogs..."

People referred to the inadequacy of a wide range of public services and amenities, particularly housing. The lack of social and recreational facilities, and the cost of services, troubled people, as did the shortage of facilities for all ages — young, old and middle aged.

"I think councillors make decisions without consulting people in Brighton. I used to live in Reading Road and I think the Marina had good points, but I think it was put on us. The councillors are all hotel managers and it's all vested interests. We've got a huge conference centre paid for out of the rates. The only good thing is the swimming pool. We need a sports centre."

"The shops and the buses are difficult here though. Yes, now I come to think of it, there's no bus up here at all. There's a lot of old people and no bus comes up Edward Street at all."

"Finding things to do. There's not a lot to do for older people. It's all discos and roller rinks."

Twenty five people reported no particular problems living in Brighton. Where they elaborated on this, satisfied needs and self-reliance were again mentioned.

"I have no problems or difficulties. I walk everywhere. I love my job."

"I consider myself pretty lucky. My husband and I have both got our health and strength. I go out to work and we pay our own way."

Once again, during the course of interview, 13 of these people did refer to particular local difficulties that faced them. They spoke, for example, of the severe local education cuts, general decline in Brighton services and amenities, and lack of local authority child care provision. The remaining 12, like those who reported no general unmet needs — with whom there was an overlap (4) — were also unrepresentative of the sample. 11 of the 12 were in full-time employment, with only one person reliant on state benefits. They were also more likely to have unreservedly positive feelings about living where they did (11/12). Again these are the kind of characteristics we might expect to lessen the likelihood of people experiencing local difficulties.

MAKING THE CONNECTIONS

The next two questions (41 and 42) asked about the links people saw with larger issues or trends. First, did these affect their own needs or situation? 46 said they did and 49 said "no". Five didn't know. Then, asked whether local or national policies created or worsened the problems they faced, 56 said "yes" and 38 "no". Six didn't know.

It was apparent when asking these two questions that some people found them difficult to answer — particularly the first. Some people made no immediate connection between their needs and problems and outside influences. Others were more hesitant.

> *"Nothing I can put my finger on at the moment."*

> *"Can't think of any offhand. I'd need time to think."*

During the course of interview, 11 people who initially say wno connection began to comment on broader issues or policies affecting their situation.

What we would suggest is that this type of research method and such questions in particular seem less suited to enable people to articulate these connections than, for example, the group discussions we used elsewhere in the research project. These provided people with a dynamic situation where thoughts and ideas could be developed and exchanged.

Despite the likely under-representation of the number of people making these explicit links, what the survey suggested was that most people did *not* see their needs or problems in isolation, but made political and structural connections. Taking together responses to these two questions and comments made elsewhere in the interviews, in all, three quarters of the sample referred to larger issues or policies affecting their needs or exacerbating their problems. These ranged from street violence to the threat of nuclear war. The social class of the 75 matched that of the overall sample. This is an issue of some importance, particularly in view of the frequent arguments and assumptions from the political left that people are unable to make such connections and need to be informed or educated to do so.[6]

What was also clear from people's answers was that they did not always distinguish government policy from wider trends or movements. While it is sometimes difficult to make this distinction, as for example in the case of recession, people often did not do so even when it was possible. This becomes important when we consider that current Conservative ideology is expressly concerned to reduce people's expectations of the state and disassociate it from the meeting of their needs. Nearly half the "wider" issues identified by people were directly related to local and central government policy. Not only were government policies conspicuous in people's replies, but many of the other matters they raised were also at least indirectly related to government policy.

The same key issues were raised by people in response to both questions, which were earlier raised when asked about their needs and problems — issues of unemployment, inadequate public services, inadequate income and increased costs and taxes. A feature of answers to the latter questions was that people singled out central government policies as bearing most heavily on the worst off.

> *"For people at the bottom of the pile, they're going to be well and truly jumped on. If you're down, you're going to stay down. It will be assumed you have no value as you're in that situation, although you may have a lot to give."*

> *"It's fairly obvious the government is taking it out on the least well off, plus their think tank dismantling the NHS."*

People commented on the general inadequacy of state services, service cuts and how the increasing cost of services like gas and electricity greatly added to their financial problems.

> *"Gas and electricity bills. That's become a problem. I know the government classes television as a luxury, but I think for pensioners it should be less." (woman in her 60s)*

Cuts concerned people both because they were seen to be jeopardising essential services and in some cases threatening their jobs.

> *"The greatest fear is the decline in all services. I might lose my job through cuts. If Chris did want to get a job as a teacher, it might be a difficult thing to get. As a result of cuts, the standard and progress of services won't be maintained, so they'll have no function and can be cut completely."*

The overlap in responses may suggest that people were as much expressing their general preoccupations as responding to the particular questions. On the other hand, people mainly saw larger issues affecting their needs as material and political issues. For example:

> *"I think my unemployment was to do with the government, definitely. I really tried hard for a job the first six months, but it got so bad I gave up. I was so discouraged. In the end I got a job through a friend. That's another thing, transport to my job is diabolical. The buses are really bad. I have to go 12 miles. I have to get a lift with a lorry driver and if he doesn't come in, I can't get to work till 10.30 or 11 as the first bus isn't until 9 am. I'm supposed to be to work at seven am."*

They highlighted the harsh and far-reaching effects such material factors, particularly unemployment and cuts in public services,could have on people's needs, generating fear and insecurity.

"My sister lives in West Sussex and I've seen what happened to her with cutbacks. Handicapped children have been upheaved just for the sake of money."

"The delay in the wife's hospital treatment, which is a big bind. She's been ill eight or nine years and since I've retired, her illness is in the background all the time."

Only a few people talked in different terms, for example, of changes in social relations or social behaviour, and of the social consequences of political reaction, and the effects these might have on their and other people's needs and situation.

"General social behaviour — violence."

"The greater mobility, both social and geographic."

"I think in a number of issues, for example, attitudes towards women, homosexuals, ethnic minorities, we are in for a backlash and that is disturbing."

What is not clear is whether such issues were only Infrequently mentioned because people less readily thought of them or because they saw political and material issues as having much more importance and impact on their wants and situation. Social and cultural patterns and behaviour, individual wants and needs, and material and political forces are all interrelated. Certainly the structural relations of social relations and their bearing on individual need are of great importance both for the role of social services and for the prospects for patch.

LOCAL OR NATIONAL?

It was not always clear whether people distinguished between local and national policies when asked whether these affected their problems. For example, 18 people identified public service cuts, notably in education and the health service, as creating or exacerbating problems for them. Only three specified local cuts and except for a few cases where people explicitly referred to national policy, it was often unclear how they perceived such cuts. It is quite likely in this case that a number of them had local government cuts in mind since East Sussex had long been a Conservative shire county, apparently committed to the same kind of public service cuts as Conservative central government. This is an important issue, especially for local authorities which wish to maintain services, but are constrained by central government controls. Will local people blame them for cuts in services and increases in rates, which result from central government cuts? Evidence here lends some weight to the view that people did not necessarily see such policies in parochial terms, but could make the connection between declining local services and central government policy.

"National policies. All the cutbacks affect me of course and locally the cutbacks in education will affect the children and the choice of schools for them. I can't afford to move."

"There shouldn't be so many educational cuts. Once you cut there's nothing for young people to look forward to. They are our future after all. The government is responsible for so many youngsters having nothing."

Responses to this question also included the only racist comment made in the survey.

"Immigration should be cut down. I'm not racialist, but with so much unemployment".

Three people saw trade unions as creating problems for them, as had one in the previous question about links between wider issues and their needs. Three others identified strikes and industrial disputes as an issue, two making the connection between them and government policy.

"The trade unions forced high wages and now the employer does the thing he knows — he cuts down staff straightaway. So now you have people on £150 per week and others have about £60 in full time work. It's a them and us brought about by the trade unions. I was made redundant at 60.... Wages going up means the sack for a lot. If food prices are cut, they look to see how they can improve their profits and they cut their staff. There's rich and poor in the same class now."

"I think everyone is affected by unemployment. At the moment my husband has to strike because the union says so, which I think is bad. That's not democracy if you have to strike when you don't want to."

"Nationally it comes back to the (national) health service dispute (1982). That's getting other unions involved and there's trouble ahead. I think it's partially government policy.

But again what emerges here is that many more of the people interviewed identified government policies as the problem rather than, for example, the role of organised labour, despite government and prevailing right wing media interpretations to the contrary.

THE SCALE OF NEED

"I need more money. He gets £33 pension. I get £17 (working part-time in a hospital geriatric ward). The rent is £14 per week. I work to make ends meet. How long I'll be able to work for, I don't know. I get rent and rate rebate, but the supplementary won't help. You work all these years and you get nothing back." (woman aged over 60)

We want now to explore in more detail some of the main areas raised by people when they talked about their wants and problems. The four questions we asked people about these — all of which were open-ended — revealed a range of needs and issues. We wanted to get a fuller idea of how widespread these and any others might be among the sample. To do this, as well as asking additional questions about people's particular circumstances, we also looked through each interview for other comments they made about wants and problems affecting them and other people.

First, though, we should perhaps repeat that the area from which the sample was drawn, is not known locally as an especially deprived one. It was chosen as an area that did not reflect an extreme of advantage or disadvantage. While it includes a higher than average proportion of older people, many of whom are likely to be dependent on poverty level state benefits, it also contains, as we have seen, a growing population of more affluent middle class professionals. Much higher levels of social deprivation and disadvantage would be expected in other parts of Brighton, like, for example, the large council estates of Moulsecoomb and Whitehawk. Hanover's problems are not exceptional, nor the most severe. If anything they may understate the problems facing people in such urban areas.

Table 3: Breakdown of Issues Identified by People as Affecting Them.

Issues	Number
Inadequate income/money problems	66
*Inadequate public services	35
Unemployment	27
Inadequate housing/housing problems	24
*Cuts in public services	14
Violence/vandalism	11
*Inadequate public amenities	10
Need for childcare provision	8
Loneliness/isolation	6
TOTAL NUMBER OF INDIVIDUALS	85

* Excluding social services.

Poverty

At least 17 of the sample were receiving poverty level state benefits, including family income supplement, supplementary allowance and supplementary pension. In an additional 10 cases, it was not clear whether old people were eligible for or receiving supplementary pension, or if they had another source of income as well as their state pension.[7] Adding those living on low wages below or around the poverty level, there is good reason to believe that a quarter or more of the sample were living in poverty as conventionally defined.

When asked, more than half the sample (53) said that money was a problem for them. More than a third (35) described their income as "inadequate" or "difficult to manage" on, and 13 of those who said it was "comfortable" or "adequate" qualified their answers.[8]

"Adequate when I was working." (currently on sickness benefit)

"For myself, quite adequate. I've no patience with those who can't manage. But then of course, we don't go out much or smoke, drink, go bingoing. By not doing any of that we manage. I save up and we have a holiday each year which I organise for a club."

"As long as I'm working, adequate. When I'm not, it will be tight." (woman aged 59)

In all two thirds of the sample in response to these or other questions said they had money problems or were worried about money for the future. Their comments give an idea of the appalling problems some faced.

"It's very difficult to manage. We had all this (the house) before I packed up work. My husband brings home about £57 and our mortgage is about £45. I wrote off for FIS but they say we don't qualify. We've got into so much debt, it's ridiculous. They say he can work overtime, but he only gets that once a month.

He works for British Rail and with all the strikes and that, we've no money. We'd be better off on the dole, but if he packed up work, he wouldn't get the dole for six weeks, so what would we live on? ...We're so hard up, me and my husband don't eat. We never use the central heating, gas fire or hot water." (woman with two children aged under two)

"I'm very lucky. It was hard when my children were young as my husband wasn't in regular work, but now things are smoother. I do worry about when I retire as my husband and I won't have more than a state pension and when you've been independent all your life, it's hard to call on people." (woman in her fifties)

"At the moment it's awkward as the amount of money I get from the dole, once I've paid the rent and given the missus her money, it's awkward like. We only get it once a fortnight and the following week, it's awkward. The Council gave me the money for wallpaper for this room and that's the only time I've asked for money. I like to pay my own way."

"I need the basic minimum wage on which to live, which isn't supplied by social security or unemployment benefit. I need to eat, to travel when I want, to buy new clothes, money for entertainment." (man in his middle twenties)

"If I didn't have this little job cleaning tables, I wouldn't be able to live. No one could live on a retirement pension."

"If I give up my job, we cannot manage at all. A family is out of the question for us. We have no car. We just enjoy the basics — a house and this isn't a mansion, no extra nonsense." (young couple)

"I haven't been left long (her husband died a year before). I'll find out (the problems) when I start to pay my bills. I've got a thousand pounds to find." (woman of 76)

One retired widow living on supplementary pension said, "You exist really. I get £40 a week". But what was most shocking was that this was an improvement for her on much of her experience.

"I have an income now which I can rely on. We never had that before. My husband was often out of work, and we had a job to make ends meet. Now I've got that regular coming in and I've not had that before unless I went out to work and got it."

Unemployment

Eight of the sample described themselves as unemployed, with the partners of two others also out of work. However 27 of the people we surveyed referred to unemployment as an issue of personal concern to them. If that seems a high proportion, if anything, the survey was likely to under-represent the impact of unemployment, since the sample was drawn from the Electoral Register which excludes young people under eighteen, who have one of the highest rates of unemployment. Fear of losing their jobs, as well as being out of work and the unemployment of those close to them, clearly troubled many people.

"The recession, that's affecting every job. There's always the thought you could be out of work. I've just changed firms as the one I left wasn't doing well."

"At the moment I'm unemployed. I've been out of work 17 months and everytime

I go for a job, they say I'm too old or not qualified. I've applied for a job with the Council, but they gave me one as a caretaker too far away for me to take it as my mother's got cancer. I've just come in from the Job Centre, but there's nothing there."

"Basically, as an unemployed person, to move if I want a job or accept below subsistence wages — that's my main disability."

"The government has a duty to find jobs for people. It's a tragedy. I think we're really lucky to be both working."

Housing Problems

Nearly a quarter of the sample referred to housing problems they had. These ranged from living in unsatisfactory and unsuitable housing and the high cost of housing, to inadequate access to housing. The situation is likely to have worsened since we made our survey. This is because of the continuing local process of gentrification and the deteriorating housing situation generally, with low rates of house building and cuts in resources for improvement and council repairs.

"We've got damp here. We got a petition up. It was put to the Council, but it was ignored. Nothing ever happened."

"The housing definitely. That's the main problem. They give you no choice where you can live." (tenant of run-down council block)

"I'd like a flat of my own, something I could afford." (man aged about 20, living with parents)

"You pay your rent for these (council) houses and they aren't modernised. These houses are 45 years old and not a thing done to them."

"I need more space with a young family; a larger house and a larger garden."

Public Services and Social Need

In all, excluding housing and social services, 49 people referred to inadequate public amenities or services and cuts in public services as a problem for them. Many of them mentioned more than one policy or facility. While the nature and severity of these problems naturally varied, all could be seen to diminish the quality of people's lives and to obstruct the meeting of their needs, some profoundly. Problems arising from public services included increased charges and unsuitable services. But they came mostly from the shortage and shortcomings of services. Conspicuous among the services mentioned were public transport, health care, education, and street cleaning and maintenance.

"The buses — they're unreliable and there's not many of them. When you've got bad legs, it's very difficult." (woman in her seventies)

"I think when my husband was ill and things were getting me down, I would have liked a night sitter. I was up and down half the night, but the doctor wouldn't get hold of one."

"When you look at schools now, closing down, crowded classrooms.... It's worrying to think if you have kids what it's going to be like for them."

"There's so much rubbish in the streets."

"I don't think the bus fares should be so high."

"I have wanted to go into hospital for two years to have my feet done."

"When I was at the Job Centre a couple of months ago, I mentioned that social security seem determined to make you take any job, and the woman said to me, 'well if you were paying tax, you'd want them to as well'."

The Effect of Cuts

Almost all the references made to public service cuts were to cuts in education and the national health service. The particular concern about education cuts appeared to be linked to the recent and contentious reorganisation of education in East Sussex and the relatively high proportion of the sample who were teachers. As we have said, Hanover has tended to attract professionals like teachers and social workers because of its centrality and relatively low price of housing compared with other parts of Brighton. Ten of the sample were teachers, four of them unemployed and one working part-time. In all 21 of the people we surveyed were normally employed in the public sector. This reflects its increasing significance since the run-down of manufacturing industry has so far been faster than the cutting of central and local government employment and privatisation. Thus as people's comments emphasised, government cuts represent an acute threat both to people's jobs and their services.

"As long as education is run down, then that makes my work more difficult." (teacher)

"The cutbacks in the health service are making things worse for me. We get all these problems at work (nurse at the University) as we deal with psychiatric breakdowns. It's difficult getting people into hospital."

"The local education issue is the closing down of schools in Brighton and that has a bad effect on the Brighton community." (teacher)

Social Isolation and the Lack of Amenities

The problem of amenities people mentioned mainly concerned the lack of social and recreational facilities.

> *"I'd like to see something to stimulate a social life, possibly more events where you can meet people." (man in his late thirties)*

> *"I'd like a sports centre with a creche provided. Recreational facilities are needed. I did a craft morning. We had some interest but it got too expensive. We did it at the community centre at Whitehawk. We learned a bit but it fell through. It was in the wrong area. I made a lot of friends, but just people like me!" (craft instructor)*

> *"I do feel that facilities locally like the swimming baths are too expensive. There's no notice taken of what mothers with young children need."*

> *"Socially, it's dead. Everything is expensive. Sports facilities are dreadful. Squash costs £2.50 a game. The swimming pool is extortionate."*

> *"It's more entertainment that's needed. The entertainment only happens in the summer."*

Linked to this felt lack of social amenities were the problems of loneliness and isolation that people expressed.

> *"It's agony when you sit here all bleeding day.... If I could get out, I'd jump over the pier. I'm too old now."*

> *"It's lonely at the weekends. I've got a young friend who pops in occasionally. My daughter lives in Falmer (near Brighton) and she'll come down."*

> *"Lack of social life. That's my need."*

> *"Loneliness is my problem, as I've just lost my husband three months ago. Days are long. Evenings are very long."*

> *"Nobody to come in and help. No phone and no relations."*

Just as there is likely to be a link between loneliness and a lack of social amenities, so isolation seemed to be exacerbated by the fear of violence, reflected in an overlap between those who felt isolated and those expressing a fear of going out. The latter were all women, and mostly older women, reflecting a broader trend.

> *"But the elderly won't go out at night, so it's pretty lonely. But you don't want people knocking on the door as you're afraid to open it."*

"We're frightened to go out after dark. There's too many nasty characters around here."

"I'm frightened to go out in the evening anyway. There's an old boy along the road here. The kids terrorise him, but nobody does anything about it."

Child Care Provision

Another of the key issues people identified was childcare. Again, all but one of those expressing a need for child care provision were women and mostly what they wanted were day care provision and baby-sitting. None of them described themselves as a single parent.[9] One woman who said she had a partner to look after her child with her, added:

"We're not married. We're living together and I've got a little girl of five months and the social (security) won't give me any money for her. They say you're living comfortable, but I think that's all wrong. I'm not a married woman. I should get money for her."

We asked women with children if child care was a problem for them. 11 had under fives. Three of the women asked this question said it was. Others commented:

"I enjoy my son."

"Because of our jobs — shift work — we can coordinate child care."

"I can't tell you that. I've been away and I want to get a childminder and I don't know if it's difficult or not. I shall know when I try, when I get back from holiday."

Eight of the women were working, some part-time. We asked those who were not if child care was a problem preventing them working. One said it was, as did a woman working part-time. Others' comments indicated the complexity of the issue and the way in which, as we saw in the last chapter, for women in our society having paid employment and looking after children are needs which are set against each other.

"I prefer to look after my own kids."

"I wouldn't work anyway and leave her (baby)."

"It's a vicious circle. You want children and you enjoy them, so you want money to take them out. So you need to work, but then you can't be with them and if you didn't have children, you wouldn't need to work."

In all eight women referred to their need for child care provision during the course of their interviews. Two other women made more general points.

"I do feel that if you're left on your own with children, you're in a very difficult position. For example, if you want to do an evening class to get qualified, you have to have a baby-sitter — which you can't afford. If you do have a job, then you've got to find a baby-minder. Similarly, it's difficult to get a university place and grant. It's hard with children to get off being reliant on social security and get a job if you're single."

"In this day and age when women have to go to work, the state should be more responsible for child care and people should pay more taxes. Children are important, the most important thing in the world, but everyone should pay towards it, not just parents. Children should be in a family, but there should be more help from the state." (a midwife)

Other general calls for more child care provision echoed this demand.

"That's a facility lacking round here — facilities for one-parent families — nursery schools."

"There should be creches for mothers who want to work."

"We need more for children to do in school holidays, organised and inexpensive."

PROBLEMS FOR THEMSELVES AND OTHERS

As can be seen from the case of child care, as well as referring to issues that were a problem for them, people also identified problems for others. Thus, they did not just make demands for themselves, but also raised the needs and problems of other people and groups. This gives us an idea not only of how widely such problems were experienced among the sample, but also what they saw as difficulties for other people.

It was not always possible to distinguish whether they were referring to issues affecting them directly or local people more generally. For example, when an old person remarked about the problems of loneliness, they might have been referring to their own situation, or that of other people in similar circumstances. Similarly it was not always clear whether people were concerned about public service cuts or the inadequacy of services in relation to their own needs, or those of others. We only included people in the first category when it was explicit from their responses. Only 10 of the people we surveyed did not identify at least one of these issues as a problem for them or others.

A quarter of the sample saw a lack of public amenities, mainly social and recreational facilities as a problem for people. All ages were mentioned. A number of older people referred to the particular problems for young people, just as those who were younger referred to the lack of resources for middle-aged and old people.

Table 4: Breakdown of Issues Identified by People as Affecting Them and Others

Issues	Number
Inadequate income/money problems	69
Inadequate public services	42
Unemployment	39
Inadequate housing/housing problems	31
Inadequate public amenities	25
Cuts in public services	23
Violence/vandalism/crime	14
Need for childcare provision	13
Loneliness/isolation	10
TOTAL NUMBER OF INDIVIDUALS	90

"They should do something for single people. A place where they can go and make friends."

"There's not much to do for young people between 16 and 18 who aren't supposed to go in pubs."

"Young people, especially unemployed young people need somewhere where they can do things, occupy themselves, not in an authoritarian, disciplined kind of way, but something they could enjoy and not spend a lot of money. I don't mean table tennis. I'm sure they're fed up with that, but perhaps a place to acquire skills."

"Well I think, when I think back, for the elderly people around this community, there isn't enough going on for them."

"There's not much for 40 or 50 year olds."

People's comments included a number of more general ones about issues and policies affecting them and other people. For example:

"We sail to the Falklands, but we can't deal with basic needs."

"I think the trend will continue where you'll be left on the shelf as you get older."

"Our house was broken into last year and our front door smashed. We had a lot of money stolen, even the telephone box with coins in it. A week later, I lost my purse in Hollingbury and the police said, 'What you expect to get it back from there?'. They said with the high rate of unemployment, I had no chance of getting it back."

"I'm concerned about people who are short and hard-up of money. Especially the old people. There seems to be a lot that they have to go without, especially my grandmother. She's worried about her bills."

"They're not building anything to give the married couples a chance. That should be the main priority in Brighton... There should be more accommodation and housing for people in Brighton. We've got a pretty face, but our back streets are an eye sore."

"I'd like something done about the house next door. There's no one living in it. I feel someone should be living there. If I could find some good squatters, I'd put them there."

Taken together in this way, people's comments give some quantitative idea of the problems they saw facing them and others. But they cannot adequately convey the subtlety and complexity of any individual's actual experience or feelings. We have tried to do this by reporting in fuller form what two of the people we interviewed said. These brief autobiographies are not offered as typical of the sample, but as reflecting the degree of difficulty faced by some people, as they saw it. Both were elderly women. The needs of old people and people with disabilities were identified by social services as a particular priority in Hanover, and one for which it was hoped patch and patch projects like neighbourhood care schemes could play a helpful part.

"He Said He Was Very Sorry, But There Was No Money Left"

"I had bread ten days old in the house at Christmas when the snow was on the ground, and not a soul knocked on the door to help. My sister's just died at 91 and I've no kin left. I've got a bad heart and bad veins. Some days I feel pretty queer. Now today, I'm alright, but where can you go today. I'd get blown over with the weather. I'm the last of six now. I try to be cheerful.

I could move. I did have the offer of a flat, a private flat (she's a private tenant), but I didn't know where it would be. I wouldn't know anybody if I went.

The old lady downstairs is older than me and the woman next door who I knock on the wall to has lost her husband. So I can't keep knocking to her.

I've just been to hospital because I've got a hiatus hernia. I tell you what I tried to do. I wrote to a councillor last year to ask if I could have a phone, but he wrote back and said he was very sorry but there was no money left. I offered to help pay for it. I wouldn't keep phoning people up. It was just for emergency. I was widowed 23 years ago, but I never had any children. My sister never did either. My brother's wife, she had seven, but I've lost touch. They never see me. I lost my husband's pension when he died.

I had to have this flat modernised. They did it for me as I fell down the back steps and the man came and said he couldn't repair them, they had to be replaced.

I've just buried my sister. She didn't have enough money so I had to put £55 towards it and the social security would only give me £30. I didn't know I could get assistance for nine years. I drew my pension and I didn't know.

I would like to have the phone. I lay in bed last night and thought about it. If I take it out of the bank, then there won't be enough money to bury me and I don't want to be buried as a pauper.

I used to have a home help, but they started charging, so I gave up. What I need mostly is the phone and someone to do my shopping. All my neighbours have either died or moved. All along here on this side it's young couples and they all go to work, they have to get the mortgage. They don't talk to you. They do dinners at the Community Centre, but it's 40p and there's no choice because it's done by the welfare people. I look after myself anyway. I cook proper food.

I'd like them to come and give me a visit sometimes and help me out. To think I'm 82 and I had to go out in all that snow. But I did meet a girl round the corner and she helped me, took me to the shop and brought me home.

The social services don't ask you any questions. They don't ask if you're in need of anything.

I worked 12 years on the Palace Pier in the office. Then cleaning for three or four years. Then I worked at York Place until I had a bad leg.

Now next month, I've got the telly to pay, the license, my rent and my water rate, over £100, all next month, but I save that in stamps.

I like Mr Callaghan. I don't think much of Mrs Thatcher. I don't think she knows what hardships are. I lost my mother at 63. I was 23. It broke my heart. She struggled all those years. There were six of us and my dad was often out of work. My husband wanted us to get married straightaway. He was a prisoner of war in the First World War for 18 months. He got shot in the side and it got his kidneys. That's what got him in the end. I think it was to do with the hole in his side that caused his kidneys to be diseased. My mum was ever so kind and good to people and my brother brought him home and that's how I got to know him. I've lost five of my brothers and sisters in the general hospital.

With the meals on wheels...the old lady up the road, she's dead now. She said some days she just chucked it in the bin. And the bus. We pay half fare and you have to be in by half past three or it's full fare. My husband always said I need a soapbox! And when you're 80 you get five shillings extra — and you can't buy 2lbs of sugar with that.

I tell you what I did when my sister was very ill and she lived over the road and I saw her going downhill. I had a bit of beef in the fridge and I had to take it over the road to cook it. So I decided to have her over here and I had a put-you-up here and she could have my bed. So I told the nurse, and the ambulance men carried her over. She gave up her flat and I sold her things. I only had her a fortnight and she lost her memory. She went barmy.

I got no sleep. I had a friend come over to help. She thought I was trying to poison her in the end. I went downhill. I couldn't leave her at all. She told my friend I was after her money and of course she hadn't got any. I had to bury her. And of course me having her over here, they cut her pension right down. In the end they got her into a hospital.

She was there nearly six years. They were good. For five years, I went up to the hospital to have my Christmas dinner. But last year I had it on my own. 82 and the first time on my own. I sat here and everyone was out. I've had a sad life really. My husband didn't want children as he had had an unhappy life. His father was a pig and his stepmother only wanted his pay packet. And I do regret it now."

"I Don't Know What Will Happen When We Don't See Philip Any More"

"Janet Johnson from social services was very good. She brought young Philip and did aome spring cleaning. She's the head of Age and Infirm. He works at Princes Street. Monday and Thursday he comes. He's only 24. He's very kind. He's going to college. We don't have a home help. We can't afford it. I saw him the other day and he said he was leaving. I've got so fond of him, like a grandson. Well I certainly like the social services, but I don't like the social security because they don't give us any money. There's such rows there. It's alright at Invalidity upstairs.

You must excuse me in this hairnet. I'm going thin at the front. I get so depressed. I used to have such thick hair. My husband and I are both on drugs. We have very poor health. We're so housebound. I long for someone to take me for a walk. I'd like to go on and have help for as long as possible and get someone to take me for a walk. Walking and the launderette are our main problem.

Poor Sid is such an angel. We've been married since 1975. We both had unhappy marriages years ago. We met in the hospital. We'd both had breakdowns.

It was good at Devonshire Place, where we lived. One room all compact. But the Council wouldn't give us anywhere else. The Housing won't help. I was delighted with the blind welfare man. I'd never had any help before when I met him. He used to come every Wednesday, but not anymore.

Would social services know someone who could do my hair? I shall miss Philip terribly. Philip wants us to have meals on wheels as my husband can't cook so well now as he's epileptic. It's difficult to get the shopping. One home help we had was good. She used to do our shopping and go to the launderette, but when it came to paying, we had to give her up. We couldn't afford it. Last winter it was £1.50 a day for the kettle and the electric fire. As it is, we're awfully badly off for clothing. It used to be good at WRVS, but it's really bad now, really terrible stuff, awful.

There's not much round here. It was nice when we first came. There was some young fellows here and Sid played beach ball with them. If only they'd make this (room) self-contained, but I suppose the Council can't afford it. We've got one neighbour at Flat 5 — your friend Sid — but that's all.

I hate it here (run-down Council block). I'm homesick for Devonshire Place. We got notice to leave in October (the year before). Sid went to his solicitor and he told us they couldn't get us out for a year. They wanted to get us out straightaway. We didn't know what to do. We had no furniture. The Council gave us this (shabby chest of drawers, with drawers that don't open or shut properly), and a fridge and a cooker. Course they wanted us out. They wanted to do the flat up, moneyed people you know, and so mean.

The solicitor was shocked when he saw the floor in here. He said they should have done it before we moved in. So then the Council did it. We had a broken window and they mended it. The last interview we had with the young lady at Housing was horrible. She was really. We thought we'd get a bit of priority with my blindness and Sid's ill health. It's terrible here for him. The Housing say so many people want their flats.

My doctor gave me largactyl as I never sleep. That's what brought on my nervous breakdown as I could never sleep. The doctor thought they could do something for my eyes, but the specialist said the nerves were severed. It was all brought on because I had a lobotomy in Colchester Hospital. I never got a penny compensation. It did no good. The effect wore off anyway. I was terribly bad mentally and they took all my possessions. They took all my lovely jewellery, furniture and home. I never got it back. They wouldn't give me anything back. I can stand physically suffering, but not mental suffering.

I was in hospital for 29 years. For 15 I was in bed. I nearly went mad. I longed for exercise, but they wouldn't let me go out walking. I used to get violent and bang my bed. I longed for movement. The nurses in the mental hospitals I've been in were so cruel, all the pay in the world wouldn't change their nature. When I was a girl, I saw the inmates at Springfield (Tooting), the "loony bin" as I called it. I used to think how awful to be like that. I felt sorry for the nurse.

I come from Wandsworth Common. I remember Battersea — where you live. I loved it. My grandmother had an account at Arding and Hobbs I remember the bombing in Battersea and Balham. I saw a bus in a crater in Balham High Road once. I don't know what didn't go on there. I worked as a clerical assistant till the war. I always suffered from ill-health.

I've got cancer as well as anaemia. I heard them say in the hospital because I had a breakdown. But Sid looked after me last time. H block (in the hospital) is terrible. I met Sid in a rehabilitation ward, when I got better, after all those awful years of suffering.

Sid only has one fault. That's a terrible temper. He does swear when he's in a temper, but I'm no angel am I? Who am I to judge?

But really I was quite passable when I met Sid wasn't I? I had nice hair. Now I'm terrible. I look awful; pale lips, white face, the world's worst eyes. It's not money, but health I crave. I'd like to look like Miss World! I can't read now. I don't like Braille. I can't take to it. My doctor told me to have new teeth.

We sometimes go out for a drink. Sid likes a drop of whiskey. I have a Guinness. We like to go out for a drink. I need little sewing jobs, and someone to do my hair. But I don't know what will happen when we don't see Philip any more. We're very worried about it."

The problems described by another elderly woman paint a grim picture of what "care in the community" can sometimes mean. She had not wanted to be interviewed, saying, "No, I don't want to know about anything any more. I've got a very sick husband". She then called after me (Suzy Croft) to find out what I was doing and said:

"My husband's dying. He's deaf and blind now. He can't swallow. He can't talk anymore. I have to make him a soup to drink out of meat and potatoes. The doctor told me he had six months left a year ago in June. He's dying, that is, if I don't die first. I've no one to help. I never see anyone. It's terrible. It takes two or three hours to feed him. His nails are all ingrown. It's terrible to see someone suffer like that. We don't have a nurse to help him at all. I do everything. I've never heard of social services. I don't know what they are. I've been to Age Concern twice, but they couldn't help me. I've also been to the Salvation Army to get the address of a chiropodist. My husband's feet were so painful. It's £4, but I wouldn't mind that. No one should suffer as he does. I've not been to the (sea) front this year, nor last year. I shan't get there this year. It will have to be next year. I've no fight left any more. It's all too much. The house has got filthy, absolutely filthy."[10]

Such experiences are far from unique. As the emphasis on "informal" and "community care" increases, we are beginning to hear more first hand accounts of the previously hidden hardships of caring. This is largely because of the efforts of agencies like the Association of Carers.[11] What is worrying is that as such stories become more commonplace and we become more accustomed to them, instead of acting as an impetus for improved policies and resources, they again merely raise policy makers' and politicians' levels of tolerance.

PUBLIC POLICY AND SOCIAL NEED

What emerges from this examination of the needs and problems people identified as affecting them and others, was how fundamental many of them were, like money, jobs and housing. Also conspicuous was how high the proportion was involving public policies. Where people lack resources of their own, clearly they become particularly reliant on public services. So for example, the 63 per cent of households in Hanover without a car, face particular difficulties because the area is hilly and public transport inadequate.[12] Many of the needs related to public provision that people identified, also concerned social and recreational needs; being together and doing things with other people. Not only did many of the wants and issues people reported have strong local, structural and political relations, but many people saw them in that way and made such connections. Such problems and issues were widely experienced. They were not confined to a small minority of the sample, but cut across social class, age, gender and other differences. At the same time, some people were faced with particularly extreme and severe problems.

It is helpful to look more closely at the relationship between people's wants and needs and the local and central state. We can see some of the effects on people of local Council policy from "Brighton On the Rocks" — a case study of monetarist policies at work in Brighton. The authors argued that:

> There has been a sustained drive against those public services which are geared to the needs of the ordinary people of Brighton... In short, there is no question of the Tory Council's entrepreneurship when it comes to Council activity that favours private capital, nor of their willingness to spend freely on the rates. Yet given their general commitment to minimise rates, the Council's commercial initiatives have meant an even greater clamp-down on the democratic services.[13]

They evidenced this by showing how a number of such services had remained static or declined, for example; spending on Council house repairs per house (since 1974), the bus service, street maintenance, staff-student ratios at Further Education Colleges, spending per head on parks, miles of streets cleaned, swimming pool facilities at the four traditional sites, the number of toilets and attendants, and museums (excluding the Royal Pavilion) since 1974. In addition, some services had worsened through higher charges restricting their use, for instance, the bus service and the new swimming pool. Finally some services had remained static or declined although the real cost of providing them had increased — notably, the cost of refuse collection, the cost per house of Council house administration and the level of Council house rents.

On the other hand, a number of projects or programmes which reflected the Council's interests and values had expanded, in a number of cases, despite long and strong public opposition. These included the Brighton Marina, with its £5 million interchange at its entrance; the £10 million subsidy to the Conference Centre; and a "succession of major housing schemes built by private contractors, which in spite of outlays of £27 million since 1974, added nothing to the public housing stock because of the policy of Council house selling".[14]

As we reported in Chapter Two, since we made our survey, the political situation in Brighton has changed. The longstanding Conservative control of Brighton Borough Council — which is responsible for services like housing, planning and environmental health — has ended, and even before the 1986 local elections, this had had an appreciable effect on council policy. Similarly in the May 1985 local elections, the Conservatives lost the overall control they had long had of East Sussex County Council, whose responsibilities include social services and education. While it is not yet clear what the effects of this will be on Council policy generally or on patch and social services specifically, it is likely to mean that decisions will now be hard fought. Nonetheless, the problems facing the people we interviewed and others remain. If anything they are likely to have worsened since we spoke to them, with increasing unemployment, cuts in public services and rising charges.

THE RELATION OF SOCIAL SERVICES AND SOCIAL NEED

The question is how do personal social services — the social services department — and particularly *patch* based social services, relate to the wants and needs raised by people in our study? We are not suggesting that the social services department should be dealing with them all. Clearly it couldn't and shouldn't be expected to. However, the problem is that social services departments frequently are, directly or indirectly dealing with such issues or their outcomes. Thus, old people are sometimes rehoused in social services residential provision for want of appropriate general or sheltered housing. Homelessness and inadequate housing are still factors in some children being received into care. Social services departments make grants in money and kind to people in need because of the inadequacy of their state social security benefits. There is also the greyer area of provision like day nursery places being allocated by social services on criteria that are related to material problems of inadequate accommodation, income and other resources.

While social services in practice are thus drawn into such areas of wider public policy and social need, most of the major concerns expressed by the people we surveyed are unlikely to be seen as coming within their terms of reference. It is only recently, for example, that the implications of unemployment for social services have begun to be explored. There is however now growing evidence that unemployed people dominate their work.[15] Apart from offering welfare rights advice, social services' main response to unemployment seems to have been to see unemployed people as a source of volunteers or low paid workers for them, and social services' main involvement with unemployment policy has been the increasing dependence for funding of voluntary agencies on government Manpower Services Commission unemployment schemes.[16]

This ambiguity over wider questions of policy and needs was again reflected in the fact that only a minority of people felt that social services were concerned with the kind of issues and problems that affected *them*. At present the relationship between the role of social services and such social needs remains obscure and inadequately explored. We have already commented on social services' sometimes broad rationales, yet narrow reality. But even if we accept that social services should not be concerned with the kinds of needs and problems identified in our survey — and the reality still seems to be ambiguous — it is still necessary to know how social services stand in relation to such needs. How else in a situation of changing social needs can the role of social services be understood or make sense? We need to consider that role in relation to the far-reaching changes taking place through large scale unemployment, regressive redistribution of income and the run-down of welfare state services. East Sussex's Director of Social Services has commented on the changed approach that will be needed from social services to meet the challenge posed by demographic and economic trends.[17]

All this may seem unduly theoretical when compared with the day to day business of running a local authority department. After all, don't social services distinguish needs that are their concern and those that aren't in commonsense ways? Clearly some will be seen as the responsibility of other departments, though they may overlap with and sometimes even arrive at the door of social services. Political, legal, managerial, professional and trade union requirements will all play their part. So will the availability of resources, prevailing policies, local traditions, historical accidents, the existence of capital equipment and buildings — not to mention personalities and individual preferences. But what if any is the philosophical or theoretical basis for such discrimination?

Pinker, as we have seen, saw the two community-based models of the Barclay Report as reflecting or inviting a limitless role for social work. He argued instead that:

> Social work should be explicitly selective rather than universalist in focus, reactive rather than preventive in approach and modest in objectives. Social work ought to be preventive with respect to the needs which come to its attention; it has neither the capacity, the resources nor the mandate to go looking for needs in the community at large.[18]

But as Jordan has argued:

> Pinker suggests that social workers always and necessarily do most good and least harm if given certain specific (if unpleasant) tasks which are residual to the roles of major social services. But he fails to identify how these unpleasant tasks and unfortunate clientele may increase, in number

and in desperation, as the policies of the major social services develop. If housing, education, health and social security are being cut at a time of economic recession, the number of "social casualties" and "deviants" does not remain the same, it grows. Hence even a modest reactive social-work service can find itself playing a relatively larger and larger role in a shrinking welfare state. This can lead to the development of a Poor Law level of services just as quickly as the institutional changes that Pinker criticises.[19]

Thus even Pinker's narrow, apparent absolute is relative to the role and nature of other public services and does not offer us a distinct role in relation to need for social services. The issue is not simply whether social services should have a universal or residual role. Neither local authority social work nor social services seem to have their own discrete province. Instead both seem to be arbitrary and accidental constructions, most clearly derived from the nineteenth century poor law and its replacements, which do not appear to coincide closely, for example, with what the people we surveyed saw as their major problems and needs. East Sussex Social Services have spoken of people's "social services needs" as if describing a distinct category of need.[20] But the term is tautological. It lacks any independent criteria and reflects instead existing practice and provision.

Earlier, we showed that nearly half our sample saw social services as for other people and for needs other than theirs. But this was certainly not because they didn't have any particular problems or wants, or were less likely to have them than other members of the sample. Only two of them expressed no wants or problems. The others identified the usual wide range of needs and issues, some of which, like child care, isolation, and fear of violence, could be seen to come within the remit of social services. They mostly seem to have been correct though, in assuming that social services were not for them; that is to say, that their needs would fall outside their particular, narrow terms of reference. But if traditional social services, with, for example, their residual and regulatory approach to child care, and their institutionalised social provision, seem to have little relevance to most of the needs to which the people we spoke to gave priority, what about patch-based social services?

PATCH AND SOCIAL NEED

While critics like Pinker have condemned patch for attempting to "broaden the remit of a group of workers who are already over-extended and under-resourced",[21] it has been seen by its advocates as a means of stretching resources and making social services more accessible and more acceptable to local people. Can we expect then that with patch the needs raised by many more people in our survey could be met by social services? We shall try and answer that by looking at some of the key ideas associated with patch and some of the claims made for it.

We have seen that central patch principles or ideas include: localisation, with social services teams based in patch offices; an increased emphasis and reliance on voluntary organisations and volunteers and so-called "informal helping networks"; and closer working with other agencies, voluntary, community and self-help groups. In 1980 Hadley and McGrath reported four claims related to these and other patch principles, made by all seven patch schemes described in "Going Local". First, "patch organisation enhanced their capacity to identify people needing help earlier than in conventional systems", making possible earlier referrals. Second, they were "able to tap more resources", and thus able to help more people. Third, because of earlier referrals and closer contact with clients, they "dealt with fewer emergencies". Finally, they could "support more people in the community" and therefore had to "admit fewer to residential care".[22]

More recently, similar claims were made by the area officer for the Normanton patch scheme. While acknowledging the limited nature of their evidence, Hadley and McGrath argued that their research on Normanton suggested that such claims were justified.[23]

A New Approach to Need?

Certainly some of the needs mentioned by the people we interviewed; someone to help with shopping or hairdressing, to go to the launderette, take them for a walk, for company and the like, could be met by voluntary or informal help — the "increased services tapped by social services" — assuming it was forthcoming. But these are needs that traditional social services met by means of paid schemes and paid workers, like home helps and aides, as well as reliance on voluntary organisations and volunteers. What a patch approach would represent is not so much a change in orientation or extension of social services activity, as an attempt to undertake it *differently*, with an emphasis on unpaid aid, linked to a reduction in resources. Self-help, community and support groups might also be encouraged to help people to cope with problems like unemployment, inadequate income or even poor housing. But clearly what people actually wanted were jobs, adequate income and decent housing. Thus both the validity and feasibility of such intervention can be seen to be questionable. As members of one London team reported, patch work had meant more involvement with groups and projects for them, "but our efforts at community social work continue to be with selected (and traditional) social services client groups, and not with targets defined and achieved by the community".[24] It certainly seemed that a young couple we interviewed had something different and more substantial from social services in mind than self-help or voluntary action when they said:

"Being young, we're quite insular. We have jobs. But if we were ever made redundant, we'd need social services to help us out. They've got to be there."

It is also difficult to see how the kind of community development role associated with patch could make much impact on such problems. Recently patch proponents have argued that local knowledge "can provide powerful ammunition in making the case to resist cuts and in pressing for additional resources".[25] However, the history of struggles by social services departments on behalf of clients and community is not encouraging. They remain subject to strong political and managerial constraints, despite decentralisation. These factors, together with the exposed and contradictory position of workers; and local groups' and people's perception of social services' at best ambiguous position, represent formidable obstacles in the way of patch-based social services having an effective role in responding to major issues like these.[26]

PATCH AND PREVENTION

Prevention is a theme running through the claims made for patch. If needs are identified earlier, so the argument goes, social services will face fewer emergencies. It will, for instance, support more people in "the community" instead of admitting them to "residential care". Prevention in patch thus seems to mean reaching people earlier in a predicted social services career and bringing them into the system at an earlier stage. The implicit conception of social services is rather like a pipeline along which people travel. Referral away and informal support out or instead of involvement with social services seem to be cast as preferred outcomes, while admission to residential provision is one of the least valued alternatives. Thus contrary to Pinker's fears that patch seeks to take on too much, to judge, for example, from the model emanating from Wakefield, a pioneer of patch, it may actually be concerned to discourage use of social services — as if seeing such use as undesirable. Thus:

> Patch or community social workers are those who know their neighbour-hood intimately and can call upon local helping mechanisms to prevent people from becoming clients or prevent clients from getting too far along a system.[27]

Pinker in his minority Barclay Report rejected this preventive rationale of patch and community social work, arguing:

> It would license strangers (including volunteers) to enquire into the personal circumstances of citizens who may neither have asked for help nor committed any offence.... There is already considerable disquiet about the existence of "at risk" registers in our present system.[28]

It is difficult to see what this patch idea of prevention would mean in relation to the needs and problems most often mentioned by the people in our survey. Delay in reaching the appropriate agency or service was not so much the issue concerning people as the *inadequacy* of such services, be it income maintenance, public transport, recreational amenities or housing. How much would earlier referrals of people needing help mean — emergencies apart — without sufficient resources and appropriate services at the end of them? Cuts in services mean that agencies will be less likely to offer the help that is wanted. In addition problems like unemployment, low income and bad housing can hardly be "prevented" by patch-based social services except to the very limited extent that they can influence other government departments, or act as advocates for individuals or groups against them. But even if they are more able than traditional social services to secure people's welfare rights or to make rapid and appropriate referrals, so long as people's actual entitlements are inadequate and public services overstretched, improvement is unlikely to be far-reaching.[29]

To take an example, probably the major responsibility facing social services departments are obligations involving children, particularly regarding "non-accidental injury". They have the powers and resources to remove children from their homes and families.[30] But in Brighton, as elsewhere, they largely do *not* have the resources to keep families together with adequate income and amenities — if that is what they want. Patch's advocates have tended to frame this issue as one of becoming acquainted with a situation before a crisis requires reception into care or some other major social services' intervention. But how will earlier involvement through improved information and contact mean anything more than closer surveillance, unless additional resources are made available for the family concerned? Reception and retention of children in care are known to be associated with low income, inadequate housing and lack of support. There is an over-representation of black and single parents related to the particular social and economic hardships they face, including women single parents' especially poor access to paid employment.

We have already argued that social services' capacity to resolve the material problems facing people is extremely limited. But even if we take a specific example, day care provision for under-fives, it is difficult to see how patch can play a more effective preventive role. Brighton has minimal day nursery and nursery class provision, and the improvements needed in under-fives services would demand different policies both within and beyond the Social Services Department. Given present government policies this is unlikely to happen, even though East Sussex Social Services are shifting their emphasis in child care from residential to "community provision".[31]

Self-help arrangements for child care, discounting for the moment their potentially regressive effects for women, might meet some child care needs, but they would be unlikely to meet those of working mothers or of women and men who did not want merely to exchange care of their own children for care of other people's.

Hodgkin and others, discussing the prevention of children's admission into care, argued that:

> The notion of preventative care needs to be much more carefully explored and the political and economic context in which it takes place needs to be emphasised, particularly with respect to income maintenance, housing, racism and daycare for the under fives. Within this context, SSDs need to spell out and promote their preventative strategies.

They adopted a tripartite continuum of prevention as their model. It is the latter dimensions of this that seem to make up the patch conception of prevention; "secondary prevention" — providing help when problems have already arisen, and "tertiary prevention" — avoiding the worst effects of a child having to spend long periods in substitute care. However it is patch's relation with "primary prevention" — "those services which provide general support to families and reduce the general levels of poverty, stress, insecurity, ill helath and bad housing"[32] which remains unclear. A crucial social services' contribution to this in child care policy is day care provision for under fives. Yet so far patch is no more associated with this as a universal service rather than a residual welfare one than conventional services.

Prevention For Whom?

It is also difficult to see patch resulting in fewer emergencies of the kind that most troubled people in our sample, like loss of employment, onset of illness or loss of income. The concept of prevention associated with patch seems to have less to do with the needs and problems highlighted by the people we interviewed than with the internal workings and ideology of social services.

Is it too harsh to suggest that patch's "prevention of emergency" actually means deflection of pressure away from social services? In other words, that an emergency is defined as such when it becomes one for social services.

A similar interpretation might be given to another important term — "at risk". By improving the surveillance of designated "at risk" individuals or families, patch may reduce the number of unexpected "emergencies" seen to require reception of children into care or admission of old people into residential provision. But the social services' user is not the only one "at risk". The social services worker and department also run a range of potential risks, from censure and even scandal and disgrace if something goes seriously wrong, to castigation if reception into care is seen as inappropriate, unjust or unsuccessful. This latter example is not speculative. It is clear from the literature of patch that providing a measure of informal or low paid supervision or support for an old person "at risk" is intended to "prevent" him or her coming into residential care. Cooper and Denne of Wakefield Social Services Department illustrate this patch way of thinking. Their choice of example is also significant. While there might be agreement that diversion is appropriate in the case of incarceration or institutionalisation, would the same be likely to apply of someone, for example, wanting short term residential accommodation, counselling or access to other social services provision?

> Overall success (in social work and social services) is demonstrated by reductions in the number of clients moving through the system. Thus, if a hundred children a year are going to detention centre and the main departmental aim is to be realised, some diversionary strategies are needed. Success or failure will be demonstrated by changes in detention centre sentencing by cost and by offending rates. Similarly, reductions in removals of any client from home are also balanced by measuring financial and human costs.[33]

Yet we would hardly regard success in a medical setting as measurable by reductions in the number of patients, unless other changes were also taking place reducing the need for health care. Similarly changes in numbers of children "received into care" cannot be taken as a measure of anything but changes in social services' policy and practice. Developments in child care policy are resulting in some authorities in the reduction of numbers of children admitted to care, particularly residential care. However this is taking place at a time of worsening social and economic conditions and is generally not being accompanied by an increase in primary prevention services like under fives day care provision. What this may actually mean for families and children are worsening conditions and an increased reliance on the unpaid labour of women kith and kin. Thus what may no longer be an issue for social services, is likely to continue to be one for such disadvantaged families.

"Community" Versus Communality

It is also important to question patch's assumption that maintenance "in the community" is necessarily preferable to people being in residential provision. This may say more about the nature and expectations of existing residential provision — from children's and old people's homes to hostels for mentally ill and mentally handicapped people. We need to remember that there is also a positive potential in group and collective living. Residential life, with its possibilities of mutuality and communality, might be greatly preferred by some people to the appalling isolation often experienced "in the community". As we have seen "independence" of formal services may be maintained at the cost of enduring dependence for those people, mainly women, left with the unpaid or low-paid responsibility of providing "care and support in the community".

Residential provision should not be seen as an undesirable last resort for those cases where it "can't be helped". We need to look very carefully at what supporting more people in the community actually means, and if it means the kind of straitened and disadvantaged lives led, for example, by the two women whose brief autobiographies we reproduced, then something more must be demanded and provided. Similarly residential provision should not be rejected because of the inadequacy of traditional facilities, but reconceived and improved in accordance with what people want. Judgements must be made in terms of what people themselves see as improvements in their lives, ensuring the quality and kind of life they want, rather than on the basis of crude and facile categorisations according to "living in the community" or being in "residential care". Ironically in some authorities, children's homes that have been closed in the shift from residential to "community-based" provision, have been reopened as hostels for mentally handicapped and mentally ill people as part of "community care" policies.[34]

INTEGRATING AND DECENTRALISING SERVICES

One of the "essential features" identified with patch is "close liaison with other local agencies and groups".[35] A major claim made for the localisation of social services is that they would thus be better acquainted with people's needs and better able to refer them to other agencies. We have also seen how East Sussex Social Services have laid stress on the contribution and co-ordination of other departments like health and housing. This reflects central government policies of "care in the community" and joint funding between health and social services departments.[36]

Such a blurring of distinctions between departments doesn't only make sense in terms of the changing "balance of care" between different departments, with for example an increasing emphasis on local rather than health authority provision for mentally ill and mentally handicapped people. It also accords better with people's needs. As we have seen, these now fall to many different departments and are not readily compartmentalised into any one — least of all social services.

Another approach to breaking down departmental divisions some local authorities have attempted has been amalgamation. So, for example, St. Helens, Lancashire, has combined housing and social services into a "personal services department".[37] But perhaps the most important initiative can be seen in the general decentralisation of local government services already under way in some areas. Thus in Walsall and other local authorities, neighbourhood offices are being pioneered,

For investigating and developing demands forthcoming from the local community (to provide) a complete local authority/welfare rights service...at a community/estate level.[38]

One of the explicit aims of such offices has been to:

Alter the departmentalised mentality prevalent in local authorities — removing the need to pass the buck.[39]

The intention is to provide under the one roof of the neighbourhood office a wide range of interdepartmental functions to local people. These include council housing management; housing aid; general aid — including social services' referrals; community services — including the provision of facilities for voluntary groups; and the identification of local needs and possible projects.[40] Thus a role that has been identified as one for patch-based social services is also being seen instead, perhaps with greater justification, as forthcoming from more general decentralisation and integration of services. The London Borough of Hackney's first plan for decentralisation, known as "Redprint 1" contained some of the most radical proposals for decentralisation that have emerged. While these were never adopted, they reflect the recognition of the importance of departmental structures and perspectives for any plans to decentralise. As the three outside researchers employed by Hackney to examine its decentralisation of services subsequently wrote:

The concept of the zero-based budget, which has run fairly constantly through the decentralisation debate within the Hackney Labour parties, raises the issue in a very clear way — should local government structures and practices be built upon consumer and client need or upon the system's needs? In other words, one should be careful in using existing local government structures as the vehicle for either the development of the decentralisation policy or its implementation. For if they do become the main vehicle there is a possibility they will, if quite unconsciously, tend to reproduce themselves within the "new order".[41]

...unlike any other comparable initiative in the UK the Redprint argued for a redefinition of services in a way which fundamentally cut across existing professional lines of demarcation. In other words the Redprint challenged the expectation that a decentralised office should necessarily contain a neighbourhood social work team, a neighbourhood housing team, etc.... A typical neighbourhood office would instead contain:

A Neighbourhood Co-ordination and Information Team;
a Family and Personal Support Team;
a Community Resource Team;
a Housing Support Team;
an Environmental Improvement Team;
Local Services Teams.

The Redprint was not, as some people tended to imply, attacking the notion of professional specialisation. Estate managers were not going to be doing social workers' jobs; rather the proposals advocated the concept of decentralised multi-disciplinary teams...[42]

Both the discussion and development of patch have been overtaken by that of more general decentralisation. This is being planned and implemented in a growing number of Labour local.authorities. It has mainly been associated with the political left while patch has also been associated with the political right and centre. Such broader decentralisation raises questions about the decentralisation of single departments along the lines of patch. The caring role of social services also extends the issue beyond local authority services to health.

General decentralisation has had a more explicit concern than patch with devolving power to local control as well as localising administration and service delivery. This has been reflected in a much more developed debate on the problems of democratising services, the kind of structures that might be needed and of the relationship between decentralisation and democratisation.[43] Patch and its advocates have so far barely addressed the issues raised by this more radical approach to decentralisation, although they equally concern them, and patch needs to be related to this wider debate.

THE MISMATCH BETWEEN NEEDS AND SERVICES

As we have said, some of the needs and problems people expressed in the survey could be met by patch approaches like volunteering or "harnessing informal helping networks". But apart from any practical or philosophical objections, it is questionable whether that is what most people wanted. Only in a very few cases, like the old woman who wanted someone to go for walks with her or to go to the launderette, did people see this as an answer to their needs. Most referred to the inadequacies of services, lack of jobs and the need for more amenities and clearly linked the meeting of their needs with changes and improvements in these. They did not seem to envisage being visited by volunteers, becoming volunteers themselves, joining a support group or participating in any other patch support techniques, to cope with their problems, but of having access to appropriate mainstream services and opportunities to meet their social, employment, health and other needs, ordinarily and informally, like other people. It was less the kind of "support" that patch could offer them that was wanted than the resolution of the larger material issues that were creating and exacerbating their problems, and at the same time creating a market for patch's compensatory services.

We can expect the spread of patch-based social services to give an impetus to the growth of the kinds of "community" schemes which have already begun to develop, some of which have very long antecedents. These include community transport, shops and bulk buying, second hand clothes stalls and exchange schemes, shared child care in "community" flats and centres, and community workshops and industry. Most if not all have developed in direct response to the increasing charges and inadequacy of mainstream public and market services and opportunities, from retailing and employment to public transport. "Community" has regrettably often become synonymous with inferior goods, jobs, training and services, frequently involving poor conditions for workers and users, less choice, insecurity and sometimes a strong smell of "welfare", with all that means in terms of paternalism and stigma. What such community schemes may actually come to represent is a return both in kind and in role to nineteenth century charitable and philanthropic provision, providing a realm of residual, generally inferior provision for the growing numbers of people penalised by the reduction of public services on which they were reliant, and unable to buy services commercially.

TAKING ACCOUNT OF SOCIAL NEED

The people we surveyed not only pointed to the problems created by the inadequacy of public services and amenities and the cuts still being made to them, but also their failure to take adequate account of social need. Thus inadequately maintained pavements are especially hazardous for old and disabled people and create a less sympathetic environment which makes it more difficult for them to live as they want. Cuts in public transport can reduce access to jobs, particularly for women if they have to manage a triple shift of paid, domestic and caring work. Several examples were cited by people of ways in which public policies and services generated or exacerbated problems that might ultimately have to be taken to social services, through their failure to recognise adequately the social element in the provision they made.

"I was waiting for a bus and I told my daughter to ask the driver to wait one minute and I was only a yard from the bus and he just said 'No' and drove off.... When I get off the bus I get nervous of those doors in the middle as once the driver drove off just before I got off. I once asked a driver if I could get off at the front and he just said 'No'." (woman in her late seventies)

"Like, these flats are nice, but as we get older, we'll find these hills beyond us, but they are still building these flats too much up the hill for people. They built some one-bedroomed flats two streets up from here." (woman in her early sixties)

"I think to help the social services or the government, if they could make more on the sea-front for visitors and local people to go and enjoy themselves. There's nowhere for people to go after a certain time. If they can get out and about they

would enjoy themselves a bit. They could provide more for people to do, like shows and do the piers up. There's no cinemas left round here. It's all bingo. There used to be lots to do — the penny arcades, the cinemas, the skating rink. Now it's all gone. I think the Council are too mean to spend money. But if they spent it, they'd get it back again."

As these comments emphasise, people's wants and needs are not a discrete subject for social services, but should be provided for and guide — if not govern — *all* policies and services. As it is, mainstream services not only neglect social need, but also discriminate against people's needs according to race, age, gender and disability. Thus the particular difficulties of Asian women needing women doctors; the problem in a multi-racial society of schooling still based on white culture, values, beliefs and history; and housing policies which intentionally or otherwise penalise black people, concentrating them in the worst accommodation. And while, for instance, the closure of post offices may meet the Post Office's criteria of increased economy and profits, it is especially damaging for old people, who face the prospect of long journeys, long queues, a deteriorating service "and the loss of what for many is a cherished weekly outing".[44]

By way of contrast, however, in Sheffield and until recently in Lothian, there has, for example, been recognition of transport as a *social* policy and the particular role of public transport in meeting social need. Experiments are also being made in Yorkshire and elsewhere to enable people in wheelchairs to use "public" transport and not have to rely on segregated services. The Greater London Council has highlighted women's particular public transport needs, for example, for access, security and cheap short journeys.

Significantly, while the patch and Pinker minority Barclay Reports have been seen as representing the opposite poles of opinion on the Barclay Committee, patch, no less than Pinker's "slimline social work",[45] can be seen to have an essentially residual role for the increasing inadequacy of other services and policies. The only difference would seem to be one of degree, with patch seeking to play a more ambitious compensatory role than Pinker would countenance.

PATCH, SUPPORT AND INDEPENDENCE

Our survey suggests that patch-based social services are unlikely to be any less marginal to the major wants and concerns expressed by our sample than traditionally orientated social services. It is not only questionable whether patch could offer them any more, but if it means, for example, a reduction in residential provision and the substitution of paid by unpaid care, it is probable that it would have less to offer. The fact that most of the needs people reported were not amenable to social services, was not, we would argue, because such needs were peripheral or exceptional, or could never be seen as suitable candidates for personal social services. Needs for social, recreational and child care provision, for example, would seem eminently suitable subjects for social services. Many major needs were involved, but they did not coincide with the brief that traditional and patch social services have constructed for themselves. There seems to be a basic mismatch between what a random sample of people saw as their wants and problems and what social services and patch have to offer.

This is not to say that social services are not engaged in some of the most traumatic and difficult problems affecting people. The problem is that their intervention, especially in contentious areas like child care, involves inequalities of power, for example, between client and department, resident and home, which means that it can be an unnecessarily negative experience, which people would prefer to avoid. It also means more generally that many people prefer to disassociate themselves from social services, as we have seen in our survey.

Social services now seem to fall between two stools. For example, in some cases the key functions home help and meals on wheels services actually serve for their recipients are providing company and social contact, which might be better met by social services offering flexible, informal and *unsegregated* opportunities for socialising. They frequently do not offer their own mainstream universalist services for particular needs, like day care for under-fives, but at the same time they make palliatory provision to meet needs arising by default of other services or policies. They provide old people's day centres and lunch clubs for want of, and rather than, general recreational amenities. They run adult training centres (ATCs) for people with mental handicaps, in the absence of proper and recognised training and job finding to which they have access. The effect of such services is often segregating, stigmatising and demeaning.

Our survey suggests that many people want their needs met through the improvement of mainstream services and policies, rather than the kind of compensatory support services patch, no less than traditional social services, aims to provide.

It has been a recurring theme in this discussion that while social services, including patch, are framed primarily in terms of care and support, most people do not seem to conceive the meeting of their needs in these terms. If independence in patch social services appears to be narrowly defined as "living in the community", rather than in "residential care", what it seemed to mean for many of the people we interviewed was having the material conditions, through adequate income, housing, social life, services and the rest, to live their day to day life without needing special support. "Care", "independence" and "prevention" all seem to have acquired specialist meanings in social services and patch different from those among the people we spoke to.

Not only did people's comments emphasise the need they felt for more public provision and resources — and public provision that took greater account of social need and was more responsive to it — they also suggested the need for a more radical reassessment of the role of social services than patch has so far involved or made possible. This problem perhaps follows from the more general failure of patch's proponents and indeed the proponents of the broader welfare pluralist position of which it is part, to locate their arguments and proposals rigorously in their political, economic, social and cultural contexts.

We are left with the question of why there seems to be such a poor fit between what people want and what social services provide. We should get some answer to this in the next chapter which looks at people's perceptions of policy formation and decision-making in social services and the influence they have over them. Ultimately, the issue of the relationship between people, their needs and the social services department hinges on the nature of the power relation between them. Issues of power have been inadequately explored in social services, but like those of gender and race, they are a crucial dimension determining the nature of social services and people's experience of and attitudes towards them.

CHAPTER NINE

Social Services, Patch and Accountability

Local Accountability

"As decentralised teams get closer to their communities local people will be increasingly involved in determining their needs and more actively involved in meeting them."
Guidelines for Decentralised Teams, East Sussex Social Services Department, 1984

PATCH AND PEOPLE'S PERCEPTIONS OF POLICY FORMATION IN SOCIAL SERVICES

The distribution of power and the process of policy formation and decision-making in social services are crucial issues raised by patch. While it begins by apparently accepting the existing operational boundaries of social services departments, through its commitment to partnership with citizens and users, patch contains within itself the possibility of these being changed. As we have seen, it is presented as a reversal of centralising and bureaucratising trends in the provision of state welfare services.[1]

> As far as the general public is concerned, the combination of the emphasis on professional expertise and large bureaucratic structures increases the gap between the services provided and the users of the services. For all the rhetoric about public participation, the citizen is typically treated as a consumer or user of services rather than as an active participant in their organisation and management.[2]

Patch is offered as being concerned with increasing the participation of grassroots workers, service users and local people. Again, as we have seen, two of its "essential principles" are: "the right of local communities to share in decision-making about service priorities and methods of provision",[3] and the adoption of "participative forms of management in patch and area teams".[4]

The minority Barclay Report on neighbourhood based social services argued that it:

> should lead to "greater participation from the community...as partners in formulating policies on service developments and also in criticising and evaluating existing services".[5]

A key measure of patch's success will be its capacity to accommodate and respond to people's demands.

Most of the people we surveyed had little knowledge of or contact with the Social Services Department. Few were or had been its clients. Perceptions of it were often based on assumptions, stereotypes, folklore, media reports and accounts of other people's experience. Very few knew of the patch reorganisation, so their ideas about local social services would often be unaffected by any of the claims made for it or the administrative changes it entailed. Nonetheless we believe their ideas and opinions about policy formation and decision-making in social services are important. We are not suggesting that their judgements are necessarily accurate or reliable. It was their *opinions* we wanted. Not only are these, like their opinions about other aspects of social services, likely to condition their expectations of and behaviour towards them, they also offer an important insight into popular feelings about the politics of this major state welfare agency.

We asked the people we surveyed what they saw as shaping social services policy in Brighton apart from central government controls and spending cuts. As might be expected a very high proportion (63) said they didn't know. The further comments some offered help explain this.

"I hate these sort of questions. I'm not a politically minded person."

"I haven't studied it."

"That's over my head. I don't give it any thought."

"I don't have enough to do with them to form an opinion."

"I don't know how to answer."

This was the highest rate of "don't knows" for any of the questions concerning social services. What was not always clear was whether people answered in this way simply because they didn't know or because they lacked the confidence to answer this kind of question. The response from people with some contact or involvement with social or other welfare state services was little different. More than half of them said they didn't know.

While we specifically asked people what they saw as shaping social services *apart* from central government cuts, 11 people gave cuts and lack of money as the main determinant of policy. In most cases it was not clear whether they meant local or central government cuts. One person said "the cuts, regarding Brighton Council", mistaking the local authority responsible for social services. Cuts were clearly seen by some people as too important to take as given, even to consider other factors affecting policy. Thus:

"The general cuts is the main thing, otherwise I don't really know. It all stems from that. It just gets whittled down. They all pass the buck."

Some people mentioned cuts in other services, health and education, which would affect the need for social services.

This again raises the question of the relationship between patch and public spending cuts. The emergence of patch and the reorganisations in East Sussex and elsewhere have coincided with large scale spending cuts in social and other state services. It has been implied that patch could offer a cheaper means of meeting need. But as Baldock has argued, we would actually expect it to cost much *more* than traditionally organised social services if it were implemented in accordance with the principles and with the small patches originally prescribed by its advocates.[6] Significantly many of the patches in East Sussex,including Hanover, are much larger than this.

As we have seen, patch is also associated with two forms of privatisation which are linked to both the ideology and quest for savings underlying Conservative government public spending cuts. First is the substitution of unpaid for paid care, and second, the increasing use of commercial rather than state services. As a Brighton social worker said in "Brighton On The Rocks":

It's very hard for us to pinpoint what the cuts are, because we've been reorganised. This has meant a whole shift in the way we're told to work, with much greater emphasis on voluntary groups doing the work, neighbourhood care and so on — which is a shift out of Social Services and out of the budget as well.... The whole drift of reorganisation is that more and more things will be done privately. They are depending on private old people's homes to take up a lot of the numbers because they're not increasing the beds in line with the rising numbers of elderly people...

They've cut five children's homes. Small group homes. They say these small homes weren't working and we're putting the money into s big children's centre and foster parents. Now foster parents are cheaper, anyway, per child. But it's hard to argue or to prove exactly that it is a cut in the service. They're saying, "It's not a cut, it's a reorganisation". We're saying, "Less money is being spent". They say, "Ah, but it's an improved service".[7]

The question we asked was one that could be answered in several ways; for example, according to what interests, institution or philosophy shaped social services policy. Only two people answered in terms of an institution — the Council. What was perhaps most interesting was how few people (8) saw *need* as determining policy.

"The demand on it by the community."

"Obviously you have a big influx of old people and they take up a lot of resources."

"I suppose it's the fact that there's far more unemployed and elderly people every year and the social services will be swamped by this."

More people (23) saw other extraneous factors or factors conflicting with need, determining policy.

"A desire to meet minimum requirements."

"What the administrators think are the needs of the people in Brighton. I don't think they know. They don't in the health service." (in which this man worked)

"...I think the Council are only interested in attacking people's living standards."

"I think they ignore a lot of what goes on..."

Only one person saw public attitudes shaping policy. Some seemed to see social services as like a pilotless ship, with nothing clearly guiding it.

"Nothing — can't see anything shaping it."

"Well not all that much I should think."

"I don't feel anything does shape it."

Thus the great majority of our sample were either apparently unacquainted with the process or determinants of social services policy formation or saw it in predominantly negative terms.

ATTITUDES TO DECISION-MAKING

We next asked them where and with whom they felt decision-making lay in the Social Services Department. Clearly there are various levels and kinds of decision-making, for example, over policy or individual cases, and the development and management of services. If in a collective, shared decision-making process, all would have a share in all decisions, in a more hierarchical, less egalitarian structure, we would expect all decisions, to some degree or other, to be influenced from above, especially since local government is based on an assumption of accountability upwards rather than downwards. We hoped from this question to get some idea of where people saw major and general decision-making located.

While the number of "don't knows" was much lower than for the previous question, it still amounted to more than a third of the sample (35). A similar picture of the reasons for people's uncertainty emerged from the comments they made.

"I haven't a clue. I suppose the social workers. I don't know the structure at all."

"I'm not really sure. I know Phillip (who visited from the Social Services Department) has meetings."

Although people were asked where they thought decision-making lay *within* the Social Services Department, the single most common response — from 18 people — was that it lay with *central* government.

"I think the local government should control it completely and not central government. They should be given more money. At present central government controls it all."

"Central government as they control the money."

"Mrs Thatcher does. She has her finger on everything."

"I think decisions are made bearing in mind an overall policy by the government."

Such comments not only reflected people's recognition of the longstanding regulatory role of central government, but also the conspicuous centralising policies of the current Conservative government.

The next most common response came from the 17 people who said "the Council" or "local government", mostly without elaboration and without distinguishing between members, officers, bureaucratic or political institution. A few others were more specific, referring to councillors, committee, leader, director and officers. Some people were concerned with where *geographically* decisions were made. Before the reorganisation of local government, Brighton social services were the responsibility of the Borough Council and run from Brighton. Since then they have come under the County, with its headquarters in Lewes, a small town very different in nature and needs from Brighton and eight miles away. This removal and centralisation of responsibilities, which has not ended with patch decentralisation, has been a cause of some concern in Brighton, as emerged in the series of discussions which we also carried out as part of this project.

Another group of eight people in the sample saw decision-making in the hands of a privileged and narrow elite. These were described not in constitutional or bureaucratic terms, but according to power and status. For example:

"It's all up to the top nobs; people who've got so much money they don't know what problems are anyway."

"People at the top."

"A couple of the big nobs..."

"The people who run it."

There were only two explicit references to decision-making being distributed through the Department and these comments were qualified and uncertain.

"I'm not sure — through people in the Department discussing it."

"I should imagine as regards individual cases possibly with the social worker concerned — hopefully, that is."

While this was a question that some people found difficult to answer, and to which responses were sometimes vague, it remains the case that only these two people seemed to see decision-making as a broad-based departmental process. Forty people saw it as either outside local control or limited to a few people in authority. Furthermore a number of people expressed their dissatisfaction with this.

"Really it's got to be the people. But it's not with them now. The Councillors, they do what they want."

"The people who use them (social services) should have the say, but at the moment local governments have the say."

"As we're told what's going to happen most of the time, it appears to come from the administrative side — people who don't know what the problems are." (Social Services Department worker)

"The patches would be the ideal areas to work out where the real needs are. It sounds quite useful in that sense. Will they go round and ask people though or get people to come to them?"

"Oh well, the head office — must be. You can't make no decision really. It's them that make it."

"OK, it's only a gut feeling, but a bureaucrat who doesn't get out to see what is required."

"It should be with the people who need the service, but at the moment, the bureaucrats."

Responses to this question have significant implications for patch based social services' aspirations to enable people to have more say in policy and services. If people — quite realistically — identify developments *away* from the participatory management of social services, like the greatly increased size of the local authority following local government reorganisation, the removal of its headquarters away from Brighton, the increasingly directive and constraining role of central government, and the existing structure of Council and committees, how are they to be persuaded that patch can somehow by-pass these changes? There is also the ambiguity of the patch reorganisation itself. While there has been a geographic decentralisation of social services teams; the six divisions established in 1974 have been reduced to two — East and West — with eight social services areas, the question remains of how far the reorganisation represents a decentralisation of power. Some fieldworkers have suggested that it has actually entailed increased centralisation and control by the directorate.[8]

The issue of conflicting trends — towards increased centralisation of power and decentralisation of services, is an important one for patch. At the same time as patch presses its claim for local autonomy, we are, for example, seeing the imposition of the Griffith idea of a general manager for the health service on Northern Ireland's social services.[9] The same tensions exist *within* patch.

PATCH AND HIERARCHY

The East Sussex reorganisation poses a question for patch which must inform any evaluation. Is there an inherent contradiction between patch based social services' commitment to decentralisation and continued reliance on hierarchical and centralised organisation? Lambert in his East Sussex patch study suggested that because:

> The trend of decentralisation is opposed by the centralising methods of organising social services... The more a department decentralises the more likely it is to be subject to strain and conflict between centre and peripheries.[10]

Didrichsen has argued that to be effective "neighbourhood work — especially where it includes a community development component — requires another reorganisation of the social services bureaucracy".[11] This ties in with the increasingly "top-down" initiation of patch. As a social worker from the London Borough of Islington's collectively working Essex Road team said:

> When it's imposed from an authoritarian distanced organisation it's a real contradiction. You cannot do community social work unless you also look at your own organisation. And that's the great discovery in Essex Road...why it's such an exceptional place. Not only did they try and work more publicly; work with local groups, get known to local groups. But they also said implicity...they came to it from their own ideological and political perspectives, saying: "We must be more collective".[12]

No less a contradiction is posed for patch by the fact that this hierarchy extends to the patch team itself. There has been an emphasis on small teams, but with a leader. This was the model informing the Barclay Report,[13] and the pattern followed in East Sussex. Significantly with the reorganisation, team leaders were renamed team *managers*. The team manager "at the interface between needs and policy" — with all the strains and conflicts of responsibility that may entail – is seen in East Sussex, as elsewhere, as occupying a "key position" in the new hierarchy.[14] The team leader or manager has become the focal point for whatever devolution of power and responsibilities takes place or is contemplated in patch. There has also been an emphasis in patch on charismatic and entrepreneurial leadership.[15] As Baldock has commented:

> Both the descriptions of actual experiments and the more ideal models in the literature all show the patch team leader as someone with a CQSW who is in charge of other people in field services. He (sic) takes note of their views, of course, but he is in charge of them and takes responsibility for the development of the team and policy.[16]

It is difficult to see how collaborative working within the team and the extension of effective control to team members, users and local people, as emphasised in patch rhetoric, can be achieved by this approach. How, for example, can team members extend greater control to citizens and users when their own powers are very limited?

A collaborative style of local management should not be confused with a collective way of working. It has been argued of some social services teams with formal leaders that they operate collectively.[17] However this raises fundamental and sometimes contentious questions about the responsibilities and roles of leader and team members, both to each other and in relation to the outside hierarchy. Members may feel they should take joint responsibility for "their" team, but at the same time they know that someone is being paid to do this job. The hierarchy may expect the leader to be their manager, while the team sees them as their representative.[18]

There are also other issues of hierarchy involved here. In his study of social services' organisational structure and occupational ideology, Hugman identified three dimensions of dominance; hierarchy, occupation and gender — which we touched on earlier. Hugman's conclusion that the culmination of these interconnected patterns of dominance was "the organisational and occupational dominance of male senior social workers"[19] seems no less true of East Sussex than of other traditional departments. Team managers in East Sussex reflect social work's occupational dominance. Most appointed were CQSW holders.[20] While there has also been an emphasis in patch writings on "flexibility of roles", with qualified social workers and other staff taking on tasks interchangeably, this has not been matched by a breaking down of job distinctions or of the inequalities in status and payment that go with them. In Normanton, for example, "social work assistants carry out the same tasks as the qualified social workers, but are paid half as much".[21] Furthermore, as we have seen in Hanover, service users traditionally given lower priority, like old people and people with disabilities, are still mainly the responsibility of ancillary staff.

Having said all this though, East Sussex Social Services may feel that they have taken important steps to challenge traditional organisational hierarchy; getting rid of separate hierarchies for field, daycare, residential and domiciliary work and reducing the number of divisions in the department. As they see it, they have created "a more streamlined management structure", with "lines of communication and accountability more simply drawn with only one route between those directly responsible for service delivery and the director".[22] Another sign of their reduction and flattening of hierarchy can be seen in the trend towards fewer areas and area officers.

This same pattern can be seen in other authorities. For example, Strathclyde SWD has abolished 19 management posts, cut out the divisional tier of its structure and replaced 32 districts with 12 larger "super districts" directly responsible to regional headquarters. As the chair of the social work committee said:

> By cutting out a layer of management and clearing the lines of communication between headquarters and districts, we should be able to improve direct services to clients.[23]

But such changes are ambiguous. East Sussex reduced its management team from 11 to six members, but lodged with them are the key functions of "determining overall policies for the department, together with priority setting and the planning of resources". The divisional management team retains local suzerainty. "Their function is to determine operational priorities and allocate resources locally, having regard to the social needs in the areas concerned."[24]

Getting rid of the middle range of hierarchy may appear to increase local independence. But is it necessarily a progressive step for those at the bottom of the organisational pyramid and on the receiving end of services? Middle level management can act as a support and buffer against pressure and control from the top, as well as reinforcing it. Everything depends on the overall distribution of power. The issue which needs to be recognised is that the degree of centralisation of power is not dependent on the exact nature of the hierarchy. Adjustments to the hierarchy may mean little so long as power continues to be concentrated at the centre. Indeed flattening the hierarchy may actually enable an increase in central control. It certainly need not be synonymous with a devolution of power. This is one of the key challenges and contradictions for patch.

PEOPLE'S SAY IN SOCIAL SERVICES

We have to restore power to patients/clients and their relatives. The curse of social work is feeling we know what consumers' experiences are.[25]

Patch and East Sussex are committed to people's involvement in social services. To gain a perspective on the task they have set themselves, it will be helpful to look first at some evidence of the level of involvement in existing departments. From what information there is, local people and users of social services, as indeed of other services, seem to have little effective say in them. The idea of user participation in the provision of social services was first given serious expression in the 1968 Seebohm Report. It talked of "community based personal social services" and "citizen participation". It recommended both individual and group participation in the provision and planning of services.[26] Its proposals for advisory bodies and the co-option of users on to the social services committee or an area based sub-committee have not however been widely implemented. One area where there have been opportunities for users to become involved has been in the management of daycare centres or as residents in that of old people's homes. Again though this appears to be uncommon and often means no more than participation in service delivery, for example, preparing meals, or in petty decision-making, like choosing the colour of furnishings.[27]

Deakin and Willmott in their study of participation in local social services in two London boroughs, found little involvement of users and local people in one of them. They reported that there was evidence of constraints in developing participation at almost every level. "...Participation at the level of planning provision of services was restricted by lack of direct access to the decision-making process at this level". While they described the commitment to participation of the other borough as "quite exceptional", "although the thinking and public statements of the authority were conducive to participation, we encountered some scepticism about implementation, at least at policy and planning levels". It was, they wrote, a pioneer in setting up a committee on participation, but this significantly was disbanded before their research began. As for councillors, in both boroughs, they wrote they were "obliged to conclude that representing the consumer voice did not seem to be a high priority for councillors at least over social services matters".[28]

They found that "the presence of parents and children at six monthly case reviews was thought by some to be little more than a sop, since the decisions still had to be taken by professionals".[29] Children and young people have been particularly powerless in their dealings with social services. For example, young people in care have little if any say in the residential provision in which they are placed or the regime it offers. They are unlikely to have any voice in its management. They are subject to petty restrictions and punishments: restrictions on when they can go out and what time they go to bed;

punishments like deductions from pocket money and not being allowed out. It is this that has led to the development of "Who Cares" groups, the National Association of Young People In Care (NAYPIC) and other agencies and groups to press for young people's rights and a greater say.

60% of clients of social services departments in the study by Sainsbury and others of clients' and social workers' perceptions in long term social work, felt that workers had acted contrary to their own expressed wishes.[30] Tyne in his study of participation in policy making and planning by families of people with mental handicaps, reported that social services departments were often quite unprepared to let parents' groups in on the processes of policy making or to use the strength of the parents movement in developing services. Often they didn't see the point of involving them. Formal arrangements for consultation and representation so far had been largely ineffectual. Many groups found their dealings with formal systems of representation like consultative committees and advisory bodies to be deeply frustrating and indeed they could often be diversionary.[31] The "major single issue" emerging from a conference in Wandsworth attended by parents, people with mental handicaps and social services' staff was "the need for more say and involvement for parents as well as for mentally handicapped people themselves in the services provided for them".[32] Oliver in his analysis of social work with disabled people has argued that "there is no relationship between the needs of disabled people and the services they receive. Rather, disabled people have their needs defined and interpreted by others." Social work interventions "have been based on inappropriate assumptions about the nature of disability".[33]

As these findings suggest, we cannot discuss people's say in social services without considering wider issues of discrimination which may inhibit it. Women, black people and members of other ethnic minorities, lesbians and gay men, like young people and people with disabilities, are particularly disadvantaged as citizens and users of social services. While some authorities and workers have sought to develop anti-discriminatory policies and practice, and the issue is beginning to be more widely acknowledged and documented, such discrimination generally seems to persist in social services departments. Stubbs, for example, in his discussion of social work and anti-racism, has argued in the context of child care that:

> Social workers are bound by statutory responsibilities and subordination to other agencies which serve to reproduce models of the "good family" which are racist, sexist and class-based. Indeed, it is because the black family is very much in the front line of these attacks that anti-racist practices must be placed at the top of the agenda within SSDs.[34]

We have already seen something of the subordinate position of women as workers in social services departments. The same is no less true of them as users of social services, of which they make up the majority, as mothers, carers, old and disabled people. Feminists have argued that social services and social work have largely perpetuated women's traditional dependent position in the family. Feminist practitioners are increasingly seeking to challenge prevailing assumptions about the role of motherhood, women's primary caring responsibilities, and expectations that they should remain in violent male dominated families, which they see as generally embodied in social services.[35]

Boaden and others in their study of participation in local services, concluded that it was "equivocal" in the personal social services.

At the level of the individual client there is a sharp inbalance between client and worker. Commitment to giving the client more say in that relationship is common as we have seen in the Seebohm Report and in the ethical code adopted by social workers. Yet at the same time, there are tendencies in the social services in quite the opposite direction... It is hard to be optimistic about client participation in such circumstances.

As they went on to say:

Dependency is perhaps the key to this area of service. Clients are obviously dependent, for service and support. The threat of losing either may be enough to limit their participation if it is critical of the department. People in local communities are also dependent: for information, for training, for skills and for other resources. They often have to seek assistance from the very department they wish to attack. Voluntary organisations too are dependent. Their close ties with government make them dependent for cash.[36]

Such analysis and research suggests a more general situation; that in relation to social services, users and citizens have little if any say in policy planning, the planning and management of provision and in decisions affecting them. We do not yet have sufficient evidence to confirm or contradict this, mainly because the issue has still to be properly placed on social services' agenda. The problem seems to be the same whether we are talking about say and involvement at the level of individual clients and their cases or of citizens and services. Service users continue to be largely powerless in residential provision and in their dealings with professionals. Their rights of access to records and to institute formal complaints, and parents' and children's rights in relation to council care all remain inadequate. Most authorities do not have schemes or arrangements for local or user management of services, and where they do, their effectiveness is often doubtful. Participation in social services seems to be mainly a matter of using volunteers or voluntary action in service delivery.[37]

PEOPLE'S POOR OPINION OF SAY IN SOCIAL SERVICES

1. For Citizens and Service Users

We have already seen that not one member of our sample felt they had even been consulted over a reorganisation of social services that was supposed to be concerned with making them closer and more responsive to people's needs. The evidence emerging from the series of discussions we also carried out as part of this project has been similar.

The views of the people we surveyed add further support to the tentative picture offered by existing research of a lack of popular say in social services. People were overwhelmingly negative when we asked them how much say they felt users and local people had. Nearly threequarters of the sample (73/74) thought they had no, very little or not enough say in the Department. Only two thought they had a "reasonable amount" or a "lot of" say. 23 said they didn't know.[38] The response was the same from the 47 people who had some contact or involvement with social and other welfare state services. While we asked people about users and local people separately, in almost all cases, neither was seen as any better off.

People's responses will have been based on at least one piece of evidence; the knowledge acquired from this survey of their own lack of involvement and consultation in the patch reorganisation. A few people either qualified their answer or felt unable to give one because of their lack of information or contact with social services. For example:

> "I'm not a good person to comment, but I'd say very little. I've never been asked anyway."

A few referred to the role of councillors.

> "The election of Councillors is the extent of their say."

> "The Councillors are very good and they get in contact and try and do things."

Most of the comments people made also emphasised a sense of powerlessness and alienation.

> "There's no campaign for that. A lot of these questions you've asked me tonight. I've never heard of."

> "None, apart from elections, except when something happens and people start writing up about it."

> "That's the point isn't it. I sit on the fence, but the feeling I get is that the amount of good comes from pressure groups, and they're not all extreme left-wing socialists and they don't get the credit."

"People that moan a lot — a lot of say. People in my situation will have no say I should think." (middle aged working class man)

"Very little unless they are a member of the local Labour Party or something."

The fact that nearly a quarter of these "local people" said they didn't know how much say local people had in the Social Services Department, may be another indication of how far removed they saw themselves from the agency.

2. Views On Workers' Say In Social Services

As might be expected a higher proportion of people (43) said they didn't know when we asked what say they felt service delivery workers had in the Department. This was the second highest proportion of "don't knows" for a question relating to social services, and the highest for any question relating to say in the social services. Two people answered "none" and 26 "very little". Ten either thought such workers had an inadequate say or that little notice would be taken of them. Thus a total of 38 people thought that grassroots workers had no, very little or not enough say.

Taken together with people's responses when asked where decision-making lay in the Social Services Department, this provides a predominant view of social services in which the workforce is largely excluded from an effective say. Again, the pattern of responses was the same for people with and without contact or involvement with social and other welfare state services.

"I don't know. We've nver really had that much contact. That social worker who came here with me said they had meetings, but whether they took any notice, I don't know. Whether their views are considered, I would really be in doubt."

"Not as much as they'd like."

"I should imagine they can argue, but I don't suppose they get very far."

"Not a lot. They have to operate the system as it is set out."

"A fair amount. Well in day to day organising, a bit, but not in overall policy making decisions."

"Very little. They do a hard job and get very little back from it."

"When I was a union member I had my say through the union, so I suppose through their union. Like now I've retired I don't have a say anymore."

At the same time, 17 people seemed to assume that grassroots workers would have a greater say in social services than the rest of us.[39] For example:

"They must have some say in it. It's agony when you sit here all bleeding day."
(social services' client)

"I think they have some say. They are democratic people."

"I should think they are listened to and about 50% of influence and advice will come from them."

"Quite a lot as they see the people."

"From what I've seen on telly, they seem to have a lot of meetings, so quite a lot."

Fourteen of the 17 people who thought workers had a lot or a reasonable amount of say in social services, thought users and local people had very little or none. Clearly they differentiated between workers and others rather than assuming a generally high level of participation. Some of the reasons they gave for thinking that grassroots workers had an appreciable say, may seem naive or optimistic. It's worth stressing though that very few references were made in this survey to apathy and the like as an explanation for people's lack of say and involvement in services, although they often figure in conventional arguments against it.

"This comes back to whether people on the ground have a say in anything. The British are apathetic. They want to get on with their garden."

"It all depends on them. There's so many who haven't got a damn clue. They've no knowledge of life or understanding."

"They don't seem to have very much say, but they don't seem to want any."

To sum up then, overall the people we interviewed offered a profile of social services that were not primarily influenced by need, where decision-making was not broad-based and in which most people, as workers, users and citizens, had little or no say.[40] As we saw earlier — and adding weight to this - less than one third of the sample thought social services had any understanding, interest or concern in the kind of issues that concerned them. This view of social services as undemocratic and unresponsive seemed to be spread quite generally through the sample. There were no appreciable differences according to sex, estimated age or length of stay in the area. People who had lived locally three years or less had similar views to those living there 10 years or more. This is of interest since short stay residents' opinions about social services may have been shaped by experience, knowledge or information from other areas, whereas those of people who had lived in the area longer might be expected to have been influenced more specifically by Brighton Social Services. There was some variation by class, with more middle class (18/26) than working class people (25/58), seeing social services as unrelated to need and giving people little or no say.

As we have seen, this prevailing view of social services was shared by the 47 people with some contact or involvement with social and other welfare state services. Thus any more knowledge of or familiarity they had with services, left them as likely as other members of the sample to see people as largely powerless and uninvolved in social services. Similarly the 24 people within that group who had experience specifically of social services as clients or from some other use of or involvement with them, expressed the same attitudes to the overall sample. The rate of "don't knows" among them in response to these four questions was close to that for the overall sample, including the question about how much say users had in social services. If the high rate of "don't knows" for two of these questions indicated the reluctance of the people we interviewed to speculate on what they felt they didn't know about, experience of and contact with social services as users and in other ways, did not seem to give people any more certainty about questions concerning where decision-making lay and what say people had in the Department.

Talking About Patch, Not Traditional Social Services

One further point needs to be made about people's comments and opinions. People were talking about *patch-based*, not traditional social services. It is important to remember that while patch has been advanced as enabling a greater say locally, the people we surveyed were speaking *after* a patch reorganisation. It clearly meant little to most of them and indeed, as we have seen, the majority did not even know about it. Their perceptions hardly reflected patch's stated commitment to participation.

WHAT SAY PEOPLE THOUGHT *THEY* HAD IN SOCIAL SERVICES

The same negative picture emerged when we asked people what influence or say in social services they felt *they* could have. While all were "local people", as we have seen, some were also present or past users, clients or workers of social services. Only three thought they could have "a reasonable amount", none "a lot" of say. 50 felt they had no say at all. Another 18 that they had very little, and one woman not enough say. A few gave personal reasons for this.

> "Not much. At my time of life it's beyond me." (retired man)

> "Nothing because I'm not interested."

Others saw themselves excluded from any say in social services unless they changed.

> "In this country if I talk from here to breakfast time, no one will listen. If they listened to us, it would be ok. They say there's no money. You can't get through."

> "None unless it is widened and ordinary people can have a say."

"As it stands now, none."

"At the moment none. If they had meetings in each area, I'm sure people could get involved a bit more."

Five people thought they would have little or no say on their own, but others took this further and felt they might have some if they were organised or linked to other people.

"Within a community, I think I could."

"On my own none. Perhaps in a group, a lot more."

"As a member of the community, I suppose I could. I don't know the area at all."

"Individually very little — less than that. But as a pressure group, a bit more."

Thus people identified the two major, sometimes overlapping and competing approaches to achieving a say in social as in other state services; through changing their structure towards their democratisation, or through putting pressure on them by collective action.

People's feelings that they had little or no say in social services seemed to be equally spread throughout the sample. The view was shared by people who had contact or involvement with welfare state services and those who had experience specifically of social services as users, clients, workers and in other ways. There was also no appreciable difference according to sex, estimated class or length of stay in the area. On the other hand people aged 60 and over seemed to be less likely to feel this (11/20) than those aged under 40 (37/53). This reflected a pattern we identified in an earlier large scale survey we made of public attitudes to participation, local government and local services, where older people were generally less critical and less demanding than other groups.[41]

Influencing Social Services

We went on to ask whether people had ever *tried* to influence the Social Services Department and what had happened. It should be said that people's expectations of how much say they have are likely to have a profound effect on what efforts they make to exert it. Not surprisingly, only five said they had ever tried to influence social services. None of them reported any success.

"I got told my ideas were stupid."

"What happened? Not a lot, nothing."

"I tried to help the next door neighbour. But people keep themselves to themselves here."

"Nothing happened."

"I ran into a brick wall."

Four of the five felt they had little or no say in the Social Services Department and perhaps not surprisingly they also had a poor opinion of it. A few people who hadn't tried offered explanatory comments.

"It's never affected me. I've never felt I've needed to."

"I wouldn't know how to go about it."

"If we want to know anything, we contact the councillors and get them to see to things."

"We've never been asked at all before you came."

PATCH AND PARTICIPATION

A community-oriented way of working implies far more accountability to family, friends, neighbours, volunteers, other local workers, both professional and manual, to say nothing of the client, and an acknowledgement by the social worker of their authority.
"Community Social Work", Neighbourhood Services Project, Dinnington[42]

We have described patch and community social work's commitment to increased say and involvement for citizens, service users and workers. The aspiration to "build partnerships" and "empower people whom traditional social services organisations too often treat as merely passive recipients of their ministrations",[43] continue to be powerful themes in their rationales and writings. What of the reality? The evidence is not available to offer an overall picture,[44] but what information we have, particularly from the major research projects that have been undertaken, is not encouraging. While as we have said one of the five major principles of patch identified in "Going Local" was "the right of local communities to share in decision-making",[45] this was not evident in any of the seven case studies discussed. At the same time a high level of staff involvement in decision-making both at patch and area levels was reported.[46] However, the editors went on to comment:

It seems that while senior managers want the benefit of local autonomy in terms of high commitment, creative work and close links with the community, they are often reluctant to give up the close central control they see as necessary for the effective running of the organisation.[47]

The Neighbourhood Services Project in Dinnington, South Yorkshire, which sought to establish "a new model of health and welfare services" revealed a corresponding conflict of view between service workers and their department over local accountability. While:

> Workers began to feel quite as much a sense of accountability to the locality and people in it as to the department, unfortunately no matching change of perspective had taken place within the rest of the department and its management.[48]

The Dinnington action-research project was committed to joint management and community involvement. This was reflected in it having a management committee which included representatives "from the community" as well as local and health authority members, officers and others. However as two of the researchers wrote in 1980, the project was imposed from the top[49] and this is generally a poor way of encouraging broader participation. Furthermore "the people who played a key part in establishing the project either had no direct control over the relevant services departments (the chief executive) or were right outside the authorities concerned (the university research team)".[50]

Nevertheless by 1984 the researchers felt they had managed to "strike root at the fieldworker level" and that while it was "not possible to be confident" there were some hopeful signs of gaining the "genuine involvement of members of the local community". At the same time though, they wrote that while the first discussion paper for the project emphasised "the involvement of members of the community" in the pattern of the new service, it proved difficult to maintain this position. Political and other constraints resulted in the project being focused "on how statutory workers should be deployed, not on how members of the community could be fully involved in the thinking, planning and execution of the project".

Including "community representatives" on the project management committee, which itself had a number of unsatisfactory features, including severely limited powers, was not successful. As the researchers wrote:

> The project has shown the futility of having community representatives in a nominal capacity on the formal management bodies without involving them where the real thinking and planning is done.

They came to see as the main hope for community participation, community representatives being involved in "those meetings which become 'learning systems', ie the fortnightly meeting of fieldworkers or the core team/research team meetings or in developments from those meetings".[51] They concluded that "despite considerable efforts the Project was substantially unsuccessful in securing lay participation".[52]

What their carefully documented case study illustrates is the way in which the overall nature and design of a project is likely to condition the degree to which broader participation is possible. It cannot be conceived of as something that can be added on to any structure regardless — whether of a research project or service delivery agency.

Normanton in West Yorkshire is probably the best known and most written about initiative in patch based social services. Yet the report of the DHSS funded research on it does not point to any increased say for users or local people.[53] The area officer has himself described how Normanton got a Home Office Voluntary Service Unit grant "under the development of local voluntary action schemes to fund a coordinating body known as the Social Care Assembly for Normanton".[54]

This body is best decribed as a local "united nations" in which any group or individual can bring local issues where initiatives can be debated and undertaken and information shared. This is an ambitious scheme which hopes to cover every aspect of community life. The only proviso is that it must remain non-sectarian and non-political. The results so far have been very encouraging.[55]

We can get some idea of its actual role from his observation of it in "Going Local" that "no decision of the (assembly) can be binding on any constituent member or individual" and that it had no executive committee.[56] Writing more recently, he described it in terms of "showing signs of bring(ing) more local people into the caring area and coordinat(ing) all those who are actually working in the field, lay or professional".[57] While described as a means of "maximising community involvement",[58] it did not have direct access to the social services department or give users or local people any say in it.[59] SCAN's organiser wrote in the project's final report:

Originally it was envisaged that SCAN would have been a means of facilitating closer bonds between formal agencies and the local people. The Town Council have resisted any involvement and indeed missed an opportunity to influence the Assembly to assist in their own concerns.[60]

It is in the area of "participative management" and workers' autonomy that the strongest and most convincing claims are made for patch.[61] Yet as Bayley and others have suggested, the extent of autonomy may have as much to do with the team being treated as or appearing to be "somewhat separate from the main work of the department", as for example was the case with Normanton and the Kent Community Care Scheme for old people, but not with Dinnington or the teams involved in the National Institute for Social Work's networks project, as with them being "community orientated" or locally based.[62]

Whether or not patch enables increased autonomy and control for workers, its aspiration to increase the say and involvement of service users and local people remains the one most difficult to achieve. Some idea of the difficulties can be gained from two helpful discussions by people implementing patch and community social work projects. Lyons and her colleagues in a field social work team, looking back on the first year's operation of a patch system, reported "the problems of making community participation a reality". While the introduction of patch had not been "a purely cosmetic exercise...the new dawn of community social work and local participation, as suggested by enthusiastic descriptions of other schemes, has not been realised".[63] Coffin and Dobson described South Birmingham Family Service Unit's efforts to work closely with people on two council estates. While discussing some of the successes the Unit had had, they concluded:

> Involving the community is not an easy task, particularly in areas of high population turnover, unemployment and poverty. It is our experience that in such areas the energies of residents are focussed on survival and that sustained commitment to both campaign and leisure groups fails when family crises recur. Low morale and lack of confidence in the potential success of community action has required persistent challenge by workers, a task made more difficult by cuts in services that have eaten away at small achievements made. A prerequisite for substantial community self help seems to be an adequate level of the necessities of life, particularly housing and income, and social workers alone cannot affect these issues.[64]

As these accounts make clear, involving users and local people in social services is demanding and time consuming. As Lyons and her colleagues observed, "It is difficult to make space to develop innovatory approaches, given continuing statutory responsibilities, particularly when the team is not fully staffed."[65] However the examples of patch and community social work that are best known and offered as examples of their potential, like Normanton and Dinnington, have tended to receive *additional* investment and resources.[66] Since patch is generally associated with *reduced* rather than increased expenditure, this may make for an unrealistic rather than helpful view of what is actually likely to be possible.

Until there are more first hand and other independent accounts of the experiences of users, workers and citizens, patch's capacity to increase local control and involvement will remain uncertain. The importance of issues of accountability and democratisation has been most clearly recognised in the Dinnington project. While it has not been able to answer some of the key questions involved, it has rightly raised them. For example, how do you resolve potential conflicts of interest between service users and other citizens? How do you deal with racism? What is the relation between local accountability to that of local elected councillors, and what do we mean by and how do we achieve local involvement that is truly "representative"? Patch advocates have generally not addressed these issues and the discussion is still at a relatively primitive stage. So far they have had little to say about how to challenge the discrimination that denies equal say and involvement to women, black and other oppressed and stigmatised people. Patch's case has also not been helped by being tied to research concentrated in areas like Dinnington and Normanton. We cannot assume that such findings can be extrapolated to deprived, multi-racial urban areas with more mobile populations, where the role of social services is most crucial and contentious.

As yet patch and its proponents seem to have had more to say about and been more concerned with changed organisation and methods of service delivery than with the redistribution of power. Geographic decentralisation does not appear to have been associated with a significant devolution of power, particularly to service users and local people. Bearing in mind the scale of the task, such limited progress on democratisation is perhaps not surprising. However this has not been made clear. Simplistic arguments and naive assumptions have persisted. If, for example, services are "more accessible" and "responsive", then — so the argument goes — increased participation and local control are likely to follow, at least to some extent. On the evidence so far though, patch seems no more likely to take us further towards increased citizen participation than the Seebohm Report's earlier rhetoric did. Indeed, where it is associated with an increased reliance on commercial provision and women's unpaid caring, the trend is likely to be in the opposite direction.

Nor have more general decentralisation schemes been associated with any real transfer of power so far. While there has been a commitment to this in authorities like Walsall and the London Boroughs of Hackney and Islington, where proposals for decentralisation have been most developed, as yet it has not been accompanied by much more than plans for advisory or consultative powers for users and local people.[67] Seabrook, celebrating Walsall's decentralisation, emphasised ways in which its neighbourhood offices gave people personal power, increasing their confidence and strength. However, as far as can be seen, no fundamental changes were made in political forms or structures to enable the widening or redistribution of political power assumed to follow from this.[68] Schemes for decentralisation have generally followed the Walsall model and been based on neighbourhood offices, although there is no reason to assume that this is the only feasible approach. So far the many questions such neighbourhood offices beg, have not been adequately explored or resolved.[69] If we look at arrangements for decentralisation in 12 local authorities surveyed in 1985, in no case had there been any devolution of executive powers or control.[70] It is difficult though to see how effective decentralisation is to be achieved so long as power continues to be concentrated largely at the centre.

PATCH AND PARTICIPATION IN EAST SUSSEX

An important voice in any system of evaluation should be that of the service user.
Director of Social Services, East Sussex, 1984.[71]

What about patch and participation in East Sussex? The Department has frequently stated its commitment to the delegation of power to patch teams, increased accountability, "partnership" and the involvement of users, local people and groups.[72] At the same time, as we have seen, the patch reorganisation was imposed from above, without local consultation. It has also been framed very much in management terms. Much of the discussion from the Department has interpreted the reorganisation in this way.[73] Jones, reviewing their account of the decentralisation, wrote of its:

stress on organisational change and managerialism, coupled with its telling silence on such a wide range of issues from community accountability, and the problems around power relations within state social work, to the manner in which patch relates to statutory obligations... "Decentralising Social Services" gives the distinct impression that patch in this case was primarily concerned with extending managerial control, of making social workers do more work and of attempting to penetrate more deeply into working class neighbourhoods.[74]

Generally users and local people have no say in, for example, the fixing of boundaries or the location of patch offices. So far as we know, there has been no transfer of power to users or local people in Hanover. We have seen little if any sign of it from our survey. In some areas forums including "local representatives" have been set up, but their powers in relation to the patch team, Department and Council are unclear and uncertain. None of the pilot projects described in East Sussex's own account of the reorganisation entailed any transfer of power, although a few involved some measure of consultation.[75]

The Department's general approach to participation for citizens and service users seems to be limited to consultation rather than more direct representation or power sharing. For example, the Director described the setting up of "specific consultation exercises with particular client groups" as one of the ways of obtaining feedback from users for the evaluation of services.

Meetings have been held with children in care to get their views of the service provided by the department and residents in homes are regularly given opportunities to discuss the way their establishments are run.[76]

The problem with such exercises is that it is difficult to know what say they actually give people. For example, could the concern of residents of a local authority old people's home about reduced staffing coupled with increased levels of infirmity among residents lead to changes in policy that entail greater expenditure? What if young people in care were opposed to the closure of a children's home? What happens to old people's views? What guarantees have they that notice will be taken of them. These are general problems with consultation exercises. Without such safeguards popular confidence in consultation deteriorates and it becomes devalued, as has most clearly been seen in its most developed case, land use planning.[77] Another of the difficulties with consultation is that it is often offered at a stage when basic plans have already been laid. Thus it tends to be a matter of responding to other people's plans and ideas rather than initiating your own.

East Sussex Social Services have laid particular stress on developing departmental policies for particular client groups. As part of this process consultation and "guideline" documents are produced. According to the Director,

> The procedure for preparing these documents itself reflects the collaborative approach the Department is seeking to develop. The departmental management team sketches out its intended policy, consults area and patch teams on its proposals, and submits the finalised proposals to the social services committee. Then follows what is often the most lengthy and complicated stage of the process when the teams engage in a wide range of consultations with local voluntary and statutory agencies on implications and implementation.[78]

Again, it is impossible to say how effective this is likely to be in practice. For instance, a consultation paper has been produced proposing the redistribution of resources from residential to "community provision", including "substitute family care, intermediate treatment and group work, for child care services. A process of consultation is planned with members and other statutory agencies, staff and trade unions",[79] but this does not appear to extend to parents, children or other interested people, groups or voluntary organisations.

Another report was prepared on "services for the mentally handicapped and their families".[80] Membership of the working party which produced it was restricted to social services officers, who were mostly managers. Sub-groups similarly were composed of social and health service officers. There was no representation from voluntary or parents' groups or of people with mental handicaps themselves. While saying that there "is thus a clear need for parental/client involvement in the planning of such services",[81] there were only three recommendations out of many developing this, and they were very limited. For example, as part of "future strategies for planning and management of services", a joint divisional/district mental handicap coordinating group was recommended "for monitoring the implementation of jointly agreed plans". However this would be made up of representatives of statutory services and only "possibly include representation of local parents groups".[82]

Ambiguities and Uncertainties in East Sussex

Many advocates of a decentralised approach would argue that its rationale should be that it produces local democracy and secures greater influence and control by local people. Whether or not this is or should be the major aim of providing services locally, the closeness of teams to their communities will inevitably mean that local people will be increasingly involved in meeting them.

Peter Dale, Staff Officer, East Sussex Social Services, 1985.[83]

While East Sussex Social Services Department appears to endorse increased citizen participation, if we look more closely at its practice and some of its statements, its commitment begins to appear more ambiguous. Thus while great emphasis is placed on the devolution of responsibilities to patch teams, there is a corresponding stress on the need for increased evaluation. As the Director put it, "to delegate authority in local government cannot be to give it away".[84] However we also begin to see that "the need for increased accountability" on which no less emphasis is laid, seems to refer primarily to greater accountability *upwards* rather than to citizens and service users. Of course the issue is not clear-cut especially since the argument for greater control is linked to that of "maintaining high standards". But while routes and mechanisms for accountability upwards are strongly developed, the same has not been the case with accountability to users and local people. For example, in the words of the Director,

If the resulting decentralised services were to operate with consistently high standards and to remain answerable to the local authority, then the system of delegation needed to be matched by a system of accountability and a set of policy guidelines to act as a reference point for the provision of services.... One of the issues most frequently raised by critics of decentralised systems of service delivery is that of monitoring and control. How can coherence and consistency be maintained if the essence of the approach is the devolution of responsibility? ....A range of methods have been introduced to monitor the performance of the department including regular reviews of computorised data on different client groups, analysis of the comparative costs of different units in the system, bed occupancy rates in homes, and the operation of a manpower planning model by the central personnel section...

About downward accountability, he was much less specific:

It may well be that the development of closer relations with other helping agencies and with local communities will provide increased feedback on views of collaborators and users alike.[85]

There are undeniable tensions between local autonomy and the maintenance of equity and agreed standards. How though do we ensure that concepts like "consistency" and "high standards" don't become euphemisms for conformity with top-down planning and closer central control? Perhaps the most interesting development in devolution in East Sussex Social Services has been the pilot schemes for local management of services for elderly people. The intention is for such schemes to become established throughout the Department in time. The political left has long argued the benefits of local or area budgets. As East Sussex's Director has said, such schemes "would give our staff money to spend at the local level in whatever way they wish".[86]

Within clear limits Area and Team Managers will be expected to make changes in the use of departmental resources and the way in which services are put together. They will be encouraged to "orchestrate" the cooperation of all relevant agencies in the patch and to break down some of the barriers that exist between services.[87]

Thus decisions about the deployment of staff and over the use of significant sums of money can now be made at team manager level. This is an important precedent in the devolution of decision-making. At the same time though, objectives include making local managers more "cost conscious in decision-making" and improving "collaborative arrangements between the statutory, voluntary and private sectors".[88] So while managers will have increased financial discretion, it is within a firm departmental policy of increased reliance on commercial and unpaid care, with the additional demand of making the most "cost-effective" decisions. In a Department tied to static or even reduced expenditure, this may well mean having to choose the cheaper option, which in narrow accounting terms means the range of unpaid, low paid and profit rather than need related services associated with current community care policies. Such local financial autonomy may actually have as much to do with extended involvement in decisions about service rationing as about improved decision-making resulting from closer contact with need. For team managers, it may be another expression of their position caught between improved knowledge of local need and responsibility to accord with departmental policies which may conflict with it. We can begin to see the possible ambiguities and contradictions of such local management schemes.

In some ways they seem to parallel the supermarket chain model of autonomy. Managers of local branches have considerable powers and responsibilities, but within closely prescribed company policy. They have some discretion to match local demand, but bear the full weight of responsibility for ensuring the viability of their outlet. Meanwhile local people and users are excluded from any say in policy or practice. While the political left has emphasised local control of budgets extending to citizens and service users, this has not been written into the East Sussex scheme, so to this extent it also does not seem to represent any increase in citizen or user control.

East Sussex's emphasis on managerialism and the market appears deep-rooted. Advertising for team managers, they have even talked of offering them "a chance to manage part of the business".[89] This overall approach raises a serious question over some of the East Sussex initiatives which at first glance might seem to be positive steps towards democratisation. We need to ask, for example, whether local management schemes aren't better seen as part of a different, market-led development. By this we mean the growing practice among commercial companies — rapidly being adopted by central government — to develop internal accountancy and profit centres. This is linked to the trend to what has been called the "core and periphery" model of market production. This involves the break-up of large factory complexes and the growth of a sub-contract and franchise economy, while retaining strong central control, with a small "core" workforce offered advantageous conditions and rewards and the rest typically on temporary contracts, working part-time, low paid, weakly organised and with poor conditions.[90] There are clear parallels in patch, with its switch to a welfare pluralist model of contracted-out services, with a greater emphasis on non-statutory and commercial provision — the latter especially offering inferior conditions to workers.[91] In the statutory services themselves, we can see other similarities, both in the extension of low paid ancillary roles for women and in the encouragement and organisation of women home workers. This goes even further than the market model, as we have seen, with women expected to work for no rather than low pay as carers.

To sum up, local management schemes, like other developments in East Sussex, may not indicate as much progress as might have been assumed or hoped for in involving citizens and users in social services' policy and practice. However, we should remember that in this the Department is certainly no worse than other areas that have "gone local" and indeed, as we have seen, more advanced than some. What does not seem to have been adequately acknowledged in East Sussex or more generally, is the scale of the issue and the size of the task in responding to it effectively. In patch, the reality of participation lags far behind the rhetoric.

PARTICIPATION IN VOLUNTARY AND COMMUNITY ORGANISATIONS

One suggestion from our survey was that there might be some correlation between people's negative views of social services and the lack of public control and involvement in them. We tried to explore this issue further by asking people about their experience of non-statutory services. Twelve of the people we interviewed said they were involved in a community group or voluntary organisation, in addition to a number of others who mentioned being involved in some other form of voluntary action. We wanted to find out from the 12 how their group or organisation was structured and decisions made and whether this was important in shaping their attitudes towards it. The organisations ranged from voluntary lunch clubs to the Campaign for Nuclear Disarmament. We were not assuming, as some advocates of welfare pluralism seem to, that voluntary organisations were necessarily better organised or preferable to statutory ones. The 1984 report of a working party on clients rights in voluntary welfare organisations urged that they pay far more attention to the rights of clients, arguing that "the time is ripe for a shift in power from provider to receiver".[92] Instead we were looking at whether there was a relationship in people's minds between feeling they had a say in an activity or agency and having positive feelings about it.

First we asked people how their group or project was organised. In all but one case this was by committee or meetings. For example:

> *"There's a committee and I'm elected on it. We decide between us how the club is run and holiday and weekend outings." (woman aged 76 talking about an old age pensioners club)*

> *"By an AGM at which local people are elected to serve on a committee." (Hanover Community Association)*

> *"A national group based in Geneva. The British Society administers itself from London. The next tier down is the county branches who make policy decisions locally. Then there's the centre which looks after the general needs of people around and makes district decisions — committees everywhere!" (British Red Cross Society)*

> *"Very well organised. The chairman is a deacon but all the other members of the committee are young people about 17 to 18. They voice the opinion of young people in the club." (Church youth club)*

> *"Group meetings." (CND)*

With two exceptions, decisions were made at meetings or through a committee.

> *"We (on the committee) all decide every Monday." (old age pensioners club)*

> *"Decisions are made at committee level re money, but other people set up classes or playgroups. People can go and set something up." (Hanover Community Association)*

"Meetings are called by leaflet and you vote." (CND)

"Through a committee. They decide where the money goes." (once a year fund-raising appeal)

"It's organised by Miss Watts." (Age Concern club)

We asked people if their project aimed to be democratic. Nine said it did, only one that it didn't.

"We try to work out what is best for the people." (pensioners club)

"They are elected annually and they are in touch with the community." (Hanover Community Association)

"Very much so." (British Red Cross Society)

"It works very well." (CND)

"Yes. If there's an outing they ask us if we'd like to go. It's for disabled people and now I'm not really disabled (anymore) so I feel a bit guilty when I go." (Age Concern lunch club)

Of course both our question and people's answers raise other questions about what is meant by *democratic*. How much say do people really have? What are their expectations? In some cases one group was providing a service for another, for example, young or old people, so we may wonder how much real say the latter actually had — especially as sometimes it was members of the first group who were telling us. However our primary concern was with the perceptions of the people we interviewed and the bearing these had on their attitudes to the agency or group in which they were involved.

We asked how the aim to be democratic actually worked out. Eight people gave positive answers, two negative ones, and two said they didn't know.

"Not very well because of the fact that only a small number of people have time to serve on the committee and put in the commitment." (Hanover Community Association)

"It's good we have outings, parties." (pensioners club)

"It works reasonably well." (British Red Cross Society)

"Very well. I think if adults were on the committee it wouldn't be so good. It's a really good thing as there is a safe place for young people between seven and ten pm." (Church youth club)

Eleven of the 12 said it was important to them that their club or organisation was organised in the way that it was. For example:

"That's my life now." (pensioners club)

"I think it is. I think one person making decisions all the time is bad." (British Red Cross Society)

"Oh yes. It's a very good club. A nice feeling of community." (Age Concern lunch club)

"Yes, it's organised very well." (Age Concern Sunday Club)

"It works very well." (CND)

Only one person felt differently.

"Not fundamentally (important). Either there could be no committee as such and it could be run by the Council and as long as what went on reflected the desires of the community, it would be OK." (Hanover Community Association)

The issue is of course that this clearly did not seem to be the case, as far as our sample was concerned, with local authority run social services.

The comments of one man who was involved in two projects — one that "looked after young mentally handicapped adults and an able-bodied and physically handicapped youth group", bring us back to some of these problems.

The youth group is an informal 'what shall we do now' sort of thing. The mental handicap organisation is more rigid and hierarchical. Getting things done the way people on the ground want them is far more difficult.

The mentally handicapped group is run by a committee which is not democratically elected. The aim isn't to be democratic. It means that in some areas all the people who have the job of implementing policy are not in favour of that policy at some time and that causes tensions. It's important to me that it's organised like that because it makes doing what I think is a good thing more difficult than is necessary."

Is there perhaps a lesson in the comments of this small group? Where people see decision-making as intended to be democratic and often actually working out as such, then they may have positive attitudes to the enterprise involved. And it is important to them how that activity or agency is organised. Thus nine of the 12 felt the aim was to be democratic and 11 that this was important. In sharp contrast, seven out of the 12 thought users, local people and they themselves had very little or no say in social services, and half had negative or mixed feelings about them.

THE DEMAND FOR MORE SAY IN SOCIAL SERVICES

A lack of say in social services becomes a problem if people feel they should have a say in them. As Campbell has reminded us, arguments that people are apathetic and don't want to get involved have come from the political left as well as the right.[93] We asked the people we surveyed what they thought about users, local people and groups, and workers having more say in the Social Services Department. While we again asked about the three separately, responses were very similar in each case. More than two thirds of the sample were unreservedly in favour of them having a greater say in the Department. This reflects other research we have carried out indicating that most people want more say in local government, including social services.[94] The deprivation of social services' users has been seen as a particular problem "limiting their capacity for participation",[98] but the proportion of those we interviewed in favour of it was similar to that of the rest of the sample. Comment after comment made the point quite clearly.

"The more people who have a say in it, the more responsive it will be."

"Users would probably realise more what services are needed so they should have a say. Local people would know better what is needed. Workers should. It would be better than two chaps touring the area and saying what was needed."

"I think users should. They know what their needs are."

"It would be a help if people could explain their needs. Social workers would appreciate the problems a bit more, so more say for them would be a good thing."

"Yes, it would be useful to know why people don't use services."

"People should. If they're local they should. They will know more about the area."

"If it's going to be a community based social services, users would have to have. Local people would learn more by doing so. Workers must do or they wouldn't know what was going on."

"Certainly. I think the valuing of priorities and sharing of resources should be done at grassroots level."

"Well they're the ones it involves. They should have a say."

Only one person was actually opposed to the idea — for local people and groups — saying, "I can't see any point in that". However he strongly supported it for service users and to a lesser extent for workers — "they're there to provide for the needs of users". On the other hand, more than four fifths of the sample gave some measure of support to workers, users and local groups and people having more say in social services.

Table 1: Breakdown of Responses to Question 23: "What do you feel about a) users; b) local people and groups; c) workers, having more say in the Social Services Department?"

Response	Number		
	Users	Local People and Groups	Workers
Strongly in favour*	24	23	19
In favour**	45	44	49
In favour with qualifications	9	11	11
Equivocal support***	8	6	6
Problems raised against it	3	3	2
Opposed to it	0	1	0
Other	4	4	4
Don't know	7	8	9
TOTAL	100	100	100

* This category included comments like "a good/very good idea", "very important".
** Including a few cases where people said groups should have *some* say in social services, since to talk of "more" implied they already had some.
*** Including comments like "I suppose so", "It sounds alright", "It may be a good idea".

The people who expressed reservations sometimes raised practical problems.

"I suppose local people should have more say, but I think someone living in a big house doesn't know what other people's needs are."

"A good idea with one reservation. The more people you have stirring the pot, the messier it gets."

"A good idea, but I suppose a lot of people aren't interested."

A few people, while they might support steps towards democratising social services, saw it as something that didn't involve them — another expression of the sense of disassociation between people and social services we have seen elsewhere in this study.

"I expect it might be alright. It doesn't affect me."

"Everyone should have a say of course. I personally have never been that type of person."

"I wouldn't have a say as I don't want to, but others should."

Others believed that such participation required skills or knowledge that not everyone would have.

"Well any who know what they're talking about, they should (have more say)."

"Not old people. They can't think. But young people can think." (old age pensioner)

"...These services are set up with an overall brief and that knowledge is not available to individuals."

"If they are old (users), they couldn't have much say." (woman in her 60s)

The challenge then for patch and community social work is to devise ways to enable and help people have a say in the social services department. There is certainly no reason why old people or any other group should be excluded from that process. Brighton, for example, has already initiated a programme of residents' committees in its homes for old people, which could be further developed. Grassroots groups are often better informed than local government departments about local needs and local circumstances, if not about local government structures and procedures, and these can be explained and made more accessible. As the Chairperson of Islington's Decentralisation Committee said when it was suggested that people would need training to participate, "Nobody required me to be trained when I was elected a Councillor". He had learned by doing the job.[96]

A SAY FOR THEMSELVES?

The discrepancy that emerged between people wanting more say for others, but not necessarily for themselves was further highlighted when we asked people directly if *they* would like more say or influence over social services. While more than two thirds had said that users, workers and local people and groups should have more say, just under half (48) wanted it for themselves, while another seven didn't know. One interpretation that is often placed on this kind of inconsistency is that it is easy for people to say they want more involvement and they will readily agree to the idea, but they are less prepared to take it on. But that still begs the question why. Can we draw other meanings from our finding — for example, that some people were not interested in such a commitment for themselves, but did support the abstract principle of community control of social services? Was it that they didn't relate the political issue of democratising social services to themselves personally, especially in view of the number who indicated that they didn't see social services as having much to do with them? Or were they offput by what they expected it to entail, for example, an endless round of meetings, committees and the like?

There is a considerable and growing rhetoric about public participation, community control and service democratisation. Putting these ideas into practice would be difficult at any time. The present political situation is particularly inauspicious for such proposals for participatory democracy. That is why it is especially important for them to be thought through carefully. It is questionable, for example, to call for people's involvement at a time of grossly reduced resources if all that involvement entails is being drawn into a divisive process of rationing, or being left with the responsibility to maintain services without the means to do so. It also makes little sense to press for "democratisation" when people do not want the services that are offered and the policy does not stem from their interests and demands. It is essential to begin with people's own perceptions and understanding of the issue.

Twenty nine of the people who said they didn't know or didn't want any more say, gave additional reasons for their views. Significantly only one person thought that more say wasn't needed — "I think the job they do is quite adequate". In all other cases, it was not that people disagreed with the principle of an increased say, but rather objected to it as far as *they* were concerned. The largest group (9) were those who didn't see it as something to do with, for, or involving them personally. For example:

"Not really. If I was involved, perhaps I would speak up about it, but not now."

"Not personally."

"I don't think I'd want to."

"Not really as it doesn't affect me."

"I think the people who are in need should have more say. Maybe one day we will be in need. I think patch will help that."

"Not in my present circumstances." (young married woman in full-time employment)

Next were seven people who felt they were unsuited or lacking in ability to take part.

"I wouldn't know what I am talking about."

"I don't know enough about it."

"I don't think a man like myself would amount to anything with those people."

"Not at my time of life. I'm just happy going to my clubs."

Five of the seven were aged 60 or more and five were women. Perhaps their lack of confidence says more about the treatment and socialisation of women and older people than about these individuals. Reviewing all the questions we asked about consultation over reorganisation and people's say and influence over the Social Services Department, we found 14 people who mentioned characteristics or the absence of skills which they saw as disqualifying them or others from having a say. They tended to be older, more likely to be women and working class than the overall sample.

Only four people gave the kind of answers that are often taken as typical of negative reactions to appeals for participation.

"Not bothered. Some things do make me annoyed, but not that."

"It would involve time and I'm fully employed. At work I have a full day's work. If the situation was different I'd probably want to."

"I'm a lazy man. I don't want to put myself out."

"Would it mean getting involved? This is a very time-consuming job. If they did a survey, I could get involved to a limited degree."

The reason four others gave was that they had never been involved in social services. One other person rejected the idea because they still saw themself as having "no say anyway".

While these kinds of reaction are often dismissed superficially as indicative of public apathy and indifference, they say much more and much else.[97] People respond according to their experience of methods and outcomes of getting involved, both of which are frequently time-consuming, unsatisfactory and unsuccessful. Our readiness to devote time to any enterprise depends on whether we expect it to be worthwhile; how far it affects us, and whether we can actually influence it. So far the picture emerging from this survey is that for most people social services do not score highly on any of these counts.

Having said that, it is still the case that almost half the people we surveyed *did* want a greater say in social services.

"I'd like to try and see what happens."

"I think I could. I've seen a lot in Brighton. I'd have a lot to say."

"I think the people who are in need should have more say. Maybe one day, we will be in need..."

"Yes, if it was done in a community."

How though did they compare with the rest of the sample? This is an important question because as has frequently been argued, people who participate tend to be unrepresentative. In fact the people we interviewed who were unreservedly in favour of service workers, users and others having more say, were typical according to length of stay, estimated age and social class. The 48 who wanted more say for themselves were atypical only in being slightly younger and including slightly more men and middle class people. They included a representative number of social services' users. Thirty nine of the 48 had wanted to be consulted over the patch reorganisation. The same proportion felt that users and local people now had very little or no say in social services. Thirty five of them thought that social services were shaped by factors other than need. Overall there were strong correlations between wanting more participation in social services and a high level of dissatisfaction with them as they were.

On the other hand, taking together people who had wanted to be consulted and wanted a greater say for themselves and others, produces a sub-group numbering a third of the sample that was *not* typical. This group, which expressed the strongest commitment to democratisation, included more men and more middle class people. More than threequarters of the group were aged under 40, compared with less than half the rest of the sample. Just over one third had lived locally for 10 years or more compared with over half the others. Again this tends to support the argument we offered earlier that the reasons for people not demanding more say may be linked with age, gender, experience and socialisation. At the same time, while those demanding a greater say in our sample were in some ways atypical, the belief that people had little or no say in social services and that the latter were undemocratic and not shaped by need, was broadly based. While we would suggest that patch schemes need to show a greater understanding of the issues involved in democratising services, our survey does not indicate that a lack of confidence or assertiveness, or other reservations, can be equated with people seeing increased participation as unnecessary. The nature of existing services, people's expectations of them, the degree of deference that has been instilled into them, and their expectations of what involvement in "having a say" is likely to mean in terms of methods, time taken and probable outcomes, all contribute to offput people, and it is these that need to be examined and changed.

MAKING PARTICIPATION WORK

It is one thing to advocate increased control by users, workers and local people in social as in other state services, quite another to make it a practical possibility. Not only is there the predictable reluctance of local and central government to relinquish any of their power. Even when there seems to be such a willingness, the problem remains that we know much more about the rhetoric of participation than about means of achieving it. Not only the prospects for people's participation need to be improved. So also do the *methods* employed if broadbased and large scale involvement is to be made possible.

So far the methods that have been used have largely been confined to the narrow range of public and formal meetings, committees, formal representation, letter writing and questionnaires. The shortcomings of these methods and the narrow and unrepresentative response that results have been well documented.[98] The lack of development of forms of involvement, which have remained largely the same for many years, offers a measure of the low commitment to wider involvement. While some attempt has been made by progressive authorities to reduce the most discriminatory effects of methods like formal public meetings by improved access for people with disabilities, signing, childcare provision or payment and translation services, they remain the main methods offered.

Personal social services are often singled out for their particularly low level of participation, lacking, for example, even the Community Health Councils of the health service or the parent governors of state schools, but *methods* have been no more developed in other public services. Furthermore this is not just a problem of public services. It extends no less to community work and community action, trade unions, and political activism and helps explain the difficulties all face engendering and maintaining large scale and broadbased involvement.

Nonetheless, if not unique, social services' low level of public involvement and accountability are particularly worrying in view of their powers to intervene in people's intimate personal lives and to abrogate fundamental human rights. So far there has been little discussion or exploration of ways of encouraging greater public involvement in their policy or practice.

What then of patch and community social work with their commitment to "community involvement"? As yet they do not seem to have gone far to address or respond to the question of how to achieve this. The long discussion there has been about participation largely seems to have passed unnoticed by the Barclay Committee, as far as we can judge from their report. Certainly they offered their own discussion of participation, but at best it appears ambiguous and an afterthought. It is clear that some members of the Committee felt a strong commitment to and understanding of the issues of clients' rights and participation, but much more uncertain that this was shared by the Committee in general.[99] The only proposals, for example, that the Barclay Report made towards increased client and local participation were "local welfare advisory committees" — recommended by the Seebohm Committee fifteen years earlier — and an "independent inspectorate". Both were limited in scope, bureaucratic, and judging from similar institutions in other policy areas, unlikely to be effective.[100] By 1985, only seven such advisory committees had been set up and despite their very limited role, they have met with opposition from local authority organisations and directors of social services.[101] The government has now created a new social services inspectorate, replacing the social work services. Its brief is to assist local authorities "to obtain value for money through the efficient and economic use of available resources".[102] In this, like the Audit Commission, it seems to take a narrow accountancy view of accountability which has little to do with increasing the say and involvement of citizens as service users, workers or local people.[103]

As we have seen the major research studies of patch and community social work have had little to say about ways of increasing people's involvement. The Social Care Assembly for Normanton (SCAN), for example, which was intended to be an open arena for local groups and people to raise and discuss issues of concern to them, may have involved people, but it afforded them no say.[104]

As we have already pointed out, patch advocates have tended to take increased community involvement for granted — as a natural consequence of localisation and greater "accessibility". These may indeed increase people's preparedness to approach social services, but that is still some way from making possible "the right of local communities to share in decision-making" promised by patch. How do we find ways of drawing more people into this essentially political process? The same shortcoming has been true of plans and provisions for general decentralisation. Although the theoretical debate has been more advanced, the methods used for consultation have been the traditional ones, while proposals for ways of involving people have either barely been developed or again been based on formal meetings and committees, with all their limitations.[105]

East Sussex Social Services have so far had little to say about *how* to involve people. While their "Guidelines for Decentralised Teams" state that they should establish a dialogue with local communities so that consumers and carers can contribute to the development of services, they do not elaborate on how this might be done.[106] Where the area programme projects reported in East Sussex's account of the patch reorganisation were concerned with involving people, it was mainly in providing a service, for example, setting up family and foster parents support groups. What the editors described as a "volunteer forum...where issues could be discussed and new ideas generated" appears to have been no more than a regular bi-monthly coordinating meeting of existing voluntary workers and organisations in the patch, with a sub-group set up to handle the budget of £300 allocated by social services. Similarly a community information campaign drew in agencies rather than unaffiliated individuals. "Local people" were "used to distribute the leaflet" that was produced. Again it was a case of drawing in people to offer a service — giving advice and information — rather than to participate in decision-making.[107] Parker, an East Sussex Social Services staff officer has argued for patch/area forums with a similar brief to school governors, involving equally patch councillors, consumers and professionals.[108] But this begs many of the questions we have already raised. How would it relate to existing local representation and policies? What powers would it actually have? Even more important here, how could local people and service users be attracted so that not just activists, affiliated individuals, consumer groups and local "leaders" were involved?

As part of what they describe as "a consumerist approach to social services", Parker and Etherington also argue for "fiscal mechanisms" as a means of increasing users' involvement in and control over services. For example, clients in association with social workers would have the chance to choose a "package of care" from either the private, non-statutory or public sector.[109] This clearly accords with patch's commitment to the pluralist supply of welfare and East Sussex's emphasis on commercial and voluntary services. It also raises all the well rehearsed issues arising from the contentious relationship between the market and social need.[110] These apply particularly to the socially and economically disadvantaged people who now make up most social services users as well as raising the threat of privatisation and casualisation for home helps and other domiciliary and care workers. It is difficult to see how such a fiscal approach whether based on vouchers, allowances or joint decisions around individual budgets could provide the safeguards to ensure an improvement in service, or effective choice for most service users, especially at a time of reduced public expenditure. Public choice has taken on particular and narrow meanings in the context of the private market. Such proposals seem more likely to result in people having to live in inadequately regulated commercial accommodation than, for example, to give women the resources to buy full-time collective child care if they want it.

One Brighton patch team which has shown an innovatory approach to involving local people has been Moulsecoomb. As well as helping to set up a locally controlled neighbourhood trust, with the help of the patch community worker and Hove-based Barefoot Video, a local action group has made its own video of the appalling housing conditions in their road. More than 100 residents came to see it and its showing has marked an important stage in the campaign to get housing improvements in the area, strengthening people's confidence and pride.[111]

At the same time, it must be said that Moulsecoomb, a large unloved council estate, like other well known examples of patch we described earlier, has been better resourced than most in East Sussex. It was a subject of special study by East Sussex's patch consultant; a pilot project for the area development programme and featured in East Sussex's patch video. It has a much higher proportion of social workers for its population than, for example, Hanover and the only full-time social services community worker in Brighton. Apart from the many other difficulties that we have identified, finding ways of involving citizens and service users is a demanding and time consuming process which requires adequate resources.

This raises again the issue of the size of patches. But perhaps the question is more one of the scale of *resources* allotted them. There have already been several patch amalgamations in East Sussex, of which Moulsecoomb has been one. At the level patches are generally staffed and resourced in the County, as for example Hanover, it is those which are larger or have a higher profile which appear more viable. Certainly they are likely to be more capable of working in a community social work way as well as undertaking conventional casework responsibilities. This raises two issues. First a continuing trend to amalgamation is a departure from decentralisation, which is the defining feature of patch. Second and more important, it may not only result in a move away from equity. It could mean that the only way in which community social work may be possible within strict financial constraints is by focussing resources on some patches, which then puts into question the capacity of the rest to serve other than a residual role.

PEOPLE'S OWN IDEAS FOR INCREASING PARTICIPATION

We wanted to find out what if any ideas the people we surveyed had about how a greater say and involvement in social services might be achieved. We asked them how they felt users, workers, local people and groups could have more say, and those who said they wanted more say themselves, how this could be achieved. Only just over a quarter said they didn't know. Just one person in answer to one of the questions felt it was not possible.

People had a wide range of proposals to make. Many of these followed conventional approaches with which they were familiar. Some might be thought naive or over-optimistic. But if they found it difficult to identify effective new methods of popular control, they certainly aren't alone. As we have seen, professionals concerned with increasing grassroots involvement in state services have not found it easy to move beyond traditional and limited forms.

Before we review people's ideas, several points are worth stressing. First, since the issue had largely never arisen as a real one for them, this was unfamiliar territory for most people. This didn't diminish the seriousness with which they approached it. People's dissatisfaction with the existing degree of grassroots control over social services and their desire for more, went hand in hand with a preparedness to put forward positive ideas of their own. Finally, we believe that people's own suggestions carry a particular weight. They may not offer the answer to how to increase citizen involvement, but they are likely to accord more with people's own wants, circumstances and ways of doing things. Perhaps even more important, inviting and then responding to local people's ideas about democratisation is itself an essential step in that process.

People's suggestions included the three main conventional methods; seeking people's views, increased access to information, and meetings. As we have seen, members of our sample generally had no experience of being canvassed for their views by the Social Services Department, and among various methods suggested were surveys.

"Surveys do put what people think over."

"A form to fill in what you think. You're allowed to vote. Why shouldn't you say what social services can do?"

"It would have to be done in the community, like asking people in these flats."

"One of the ways would be...publishing plans in the paper and asking people to write in. There is no visibility as to what is going on."

"Probably this is a good idea — asking them — but you'd need to send the questions round beforehand to give you a chance to think."

"By meetings, but they have those already. I suppose people could be invited to write if they can't get to meetings. A suggestions box perhaps at the town hall."

This table shows the frequency of people's suggestions for achieving more say in social services.

Table 2: Breakdown of Responses to Questions 24 and 63: "How do you feel this (Q24: users, workers, local people and groups; and Q63: you yourself) having more say in the Social Services Department, could be achieved?"

Method suggested	Question 24	Question 63	Total
Social services seeking people's views	17	5	22
Meetings	12	7	19
Increased information about social services	8	8	16
People getting together	10	3	13
Increased access to social services/social services involving having closer contact with people	5	5	10
Patch based social services	6	4	10
Voluntary and community groups	4	5	9
By restructuring/reform of social services/local government reform/legislative change	3	3	6
Grassroots representatives/local committees	4	1	5
Local community centre/association	3	—	3
Change of central government	3	—	3
Voting on issues	—	2	2
Local media	1	—	1
Not possible	—	1	1
Other	7	5	12
Don't know	32	9	41
TOTAL	115*	58**	173

* Total exceeds 100 because some people offered more than one way of achieving more say.
** Total higher than the 48 people who having answered YES to Question 62 ("Would you like to have more influence/say over the Social Services Department"), went on to answer this question, because some people offered more than one method.

Formal public meetings of one sort or another are almost certainly the main means used for consultation and public "participation" by government and indeed by voluntary and community organisations. For many of us, apart from the mass media, they are the closest that political events come to our personal lives, and then that may only be through hearing about them, rather than going to them.

"The only way is having meetings to put your point of view."

"Meetings, within distance of where people live, not the town hall telling you what they propose."

We saw earlier that most members of the sample knew little about social services and that some saw this lack of information as a problem. There was a strong correlation between people's felt lack of knowledge about social services and sense of their own and other people's powerlessness in relation to them. Not surprisingly, more information from and about social services was seen as a way of increasing people's say in them.

"By letting everyone know what they intend to do or can do."

"Like when you described the new system, we don't know anything about it. If it could be circulated."

"More information distributed to the community."

"...Keep people informed with simple pamphlets and that, not reams of notes."

"The most obvious thing would be that first of all more people need to be aware of the situation and what's available — a community education programme."

What limited evidence there is suggests that improving information remains a difficult task even for patch based social services. One of the expectations Lyons and others reported of team members changing to patch was "greater publicity about the role and availability" of social services. But looking back after a year, this had not been realised, instead it was "proving difficult" to alter the perceptions and role relationships of social workers and clients".[112] The two projects which aimed to improve publicity and community information, described in East Sussex's account of its reorganisation, both met with limited success. Summing up, the editors were doubtful about the use of newsletters by one as a means of meeting local needs, while the other's "open day" had few comers and very few new contacts.[113]

As we saw earlier from the example of a non-statutory community project, a high level of public knowledge about services seems to be linked with high levels of use.[114] Social services, on the other hand, are used by a minority of the population and numbers are likely to be further reduced by spending cuts. Patch however is associated with increased contact, and if such claims are borne out in the longer term, this might be both a cause and effect of greater public knowledge and awareness of social services.

"ESCATA" — THE PUBLIC FACE

East Sussex Social Services have placed a high priority on media resources. It is part of their commitment to training to enable new ways of working. In 1981 they set up their own media unit "with the aim of introducing video training to help social workers develop and improve their skills".[115] They have been a pioneer in the field, placing great weight on developing information and training packages. In 1984, ESCATA, a trading and consultancy agency, was created. Its emphasis has been on providing materials "to further training and development of social services staff and a wide range of other caring professions", undertaking "contract work with public organisations to produce training material" and "providing training consultancy, seminars and courses to other organisations".[116] East Sussex advertised one of their patch presentations, "So You're New Around Here?", a tape slide video using cartoon characters, as:

> An imaginative induction into the workings of a Patch Based Social Services Team. "Patch" the dog acts as a guide for the day to day operations of the Team Members, the range of client groups they work with, and the services they provide. The programme is ideal for new Social Services staff, voluntary organisations, and the general public.[117]

Of course the Department is producing its own version of its policy, practice and plans. In "Patchwork", a thirty minute video produced in 1985 to be used in association with trainer's notes and "Guidelines for Decentralised Teams" (£100.50 plus VAT for the package),

> Three team managers whose patches encompass different types of problems look honestly and openly at what patchwork means to them and their clients, as do members of their teams. This is the first progress report on large-scale patchwork containing invaluable lessons for anyone interested in going local.... Has it been a success or a failure? Has it solved problems or created them?[118]

The unequivocal answer given in a final voice-over is that "patchwork is a positive response to the demands of community care in the last half of the decade".[119] However, regrettably the programme does not include the views or comments of users or other local people or groups. It is also intended for professionals "actively involved in or considering decentralisation" rather than a more general audience. [120]

On the other hand, if East Sussex Social Services' commitment to citizen involvement has emerged from this study as hesitant to say the least, ESCATA has shown an increasing interest. In 1985 it produced a two part video programme, "Speaking From Experience" on "users' involvement in mental health services".[121] This was a focal part of the 1985 MIND conference "From Patients To People", whose central theme was partnership and power-sharing for users of psychiatric services. Introducing the video there, ESCATA'S training consultant pointed to the difficulties of achieving user involvement — an issue which has not yet received recognition in either departmental guidelines for decentralised teams or any other of East Sussex's published accounts of the reorganisation. According to ESCATA, the aim of the programme is:

> to strongly promote the importance of the involvement in the mental health services of people who either are using or have used these services.[122]

This faces us with the contradiction of why there seems to be such a gulf between ESCATA's interest in increased participation in psychiatric services and the Department's in its own existing social services.

So far East Sussex Social Services' video and related training and information material has not been directed towards increasing knowledge, awareness and understanding about social services among users and other local people, despite the evident need for, importance and difficulty of this task. Instead it seems to have had a less local, more commercial and promotional objective. ESCATA's materials are marketed with all the paraphernalia of current commercial techniques and sold in Britain and abroad. "Do write cheques" was the smiling invitation made at the beginning of a London launch one of us attended.[123]

Compare this with the low level of information about patch and social services among local people and service users we found both in our survey and again in 1984 when we recontacted people in our Brighton-wide group discussion project. The greater use of such resources could play a helpful part in offering information to local people and service users, keeping them in touch with developments and improving communication and contact between them and the Department.

What is not clear is why the skills that the Department has developed here have not been used more to increase public knowledge and information within the County as well as to offer services to professionals outside it. Certainly the latter is more likely to attract the widespread attention and interest East Sussex has received than the former. Meanwhile though, teams moving into their patches, for example, have relied on traditional leaflets to let users know about their work.[124]

The Department's grasp of modern methods of communication and commercial campaigning and the skill with which it has adopted and developed them, stand in some contrast with its vague and uncertain approach so far to the issue of increasing public involvement and say in its policy and services. There is also the question of how we relate the messages and technical accomplishment of its media products to some of the realities of the Department we have seen, and the issues it raises and faces: for example, a reduced home help service, understaffed council old people's homes and dearth of under-fives day care provision. East Sussex Social Services have become famous in the field for their reorganisation and consultancy and training resources. They have won an award for one of their videos. But much less known are the day to day caring services provided by their mainly women workforce. The Department's own accounts of its developments have been the predominant ones, but even these have not been widely shared with users and other local people.

OFFERING INFORMATION

We might expect the Department to concentrate its information-giving efforts where they are of most direct benefit to it and recognise that there might be a reluctance to use them where they could increase demand for already overstretched services. Thus as part of its policy of closing residential provision for children and moving to large scale fostering and adoption, it launched an intensive three months fostering campaign in the summer of 1983, including a telephone foster line and,

> "hard sell" publicity techniques to get the message across. Over 250 buses are displaying posters and a four page newspaper has been sent to 50,000 homes.[125]

As the National Council for Voluntary Organisations working party on clients' rights recommended:

> The information published by social work agencies should be written with its potential clients in mind, should avoid professional jargon, should describe the relationship the agency would hope to have with its clients, should use illustration and should be printed in appropriate languages.

> Agencies wishing to attract say, women clients and clients from ethnic minorities should employ, and ensure that clients know they employ, staff of both sexes, from a variety of backgrounds and with language skills appropriate to their potential clientele.[126]

While people involved in social services might be able to decode the following extract from a Brighton patch leaflet, would the potential users for whom it is intended?

> Most caring is done by families and community networks. We seldom get involved until these normal supports break down. We aim to become more aware of the needs and resources in our patch. This means working with

individuals, community groups, and other agencies in new and imaginative ways to improve and extend the supportive network.[127]

What is also needed to complement social services departments' own efforts, is *independent* information in accessible form that covers the whole range of rights, concerns and needs that people have regarding social services, and details the services that are available. Models for this are available in the tenants handbooks, welfare rights guides and grassroots produced tape-slide shows, leaflets and other material produced for other areas of social policy.

While such information may strengthen people's position, it does not secure their rights or ensure they have a say. Similarly, public meetings and information seeking exercises generally represent forms of consultation rather than of transferring power. As we have said, they do not offer guarantees that people's views will actually be taken into account or influence official policy. Furthermore they have many limitations, some of which we have already touched on. They are essentially passive rather than participatory in nature — particularly official surveys. Terms of reference are usually set by and their interpretation subject to the consulting authority. The individual usually has to take the initiative, for example going to the public meeting — with little expectation of anything positive coming from it. Contact with the agency is often individualised rather than people being able to develop and express shared views on a collective basis. Where this does happen, for example, with community groups, they may be dismissed as "unrepresentative" if their views are uncomfortable or conflict with the agency's. Other shortcomings in standard consultations and participation exercises contribute to their limited and partial response. People often feel uncomfortable at public meetings and lack confidence to get their points across. Meetings may also be impractical. For instance many old people, and women of all ages are often reluctant or unable to get out in the evening.[128]

"I don't know. It would be rather difficult. We can't get to their meetings. It's not the sort of thing we can do." (woman with four small children)

People showed an awareness of these sorts of problems in some of the comments they made.

"In theory by surveys, like this, and actually being listened to."

"If people would realise meetings locally were useful and made interesting."

"More discussions about what is happening and what is planned."

"They could have meetings, a cup of tea and biscuits, have a talk."

"If they do say anything their views are put aside...so people don't bother now."

A few people saw patch based social services as a possible way of increasing people's say, but significantly it was only a few.

"In the way you've said it's being reorganised."

"By this community patch I think. They'd have time to listen to an individual person. A lot of elderly people need help. I feel really sorry for them. They begin to lose a grip on things. They don't know what they're entitled to. If they could go to a community worker, it would put their minds at rest."

"I'm not sure, but something on the lines of the reorganisation you described before — getting into local areas."

"To be done in a neighbourly way — the thing they hope to bring."

"The patch system sounds an attempt."

GOING BEYOND CONSULTATION

How do we move beyond consultation towards people having a more effective say in services? Two main ways, making up more than a third of their suggestions, were mentioned by the people we interviewed — people organising and reform in government and services. Among the ideas put forward were that voluntary and community groups, including the local Community Association, could provide possible vehicles or venues. Other people advocated committees and grassroots representatives. A number just talked in terms of "getting together" — an expression perhaps of their sense of what was needed, but inability as yet to formulate a means of achieving it. The inadequacy of the community ties on which patch places such reliance was implicit in some comments.

"By people getting together and having discussions and making them (the Council) do things that should be done."

"It would only be achieved if there was a community and it was recognised by the Council..."

"They could have a few people in this area getting together and choosing a representative who could get together with other reps."

"I suppose groups from among workers in social services departments could contribute reps from workers in homes, homehelps, etc."

"Better community relations. We've only got the Hanover Community Association, but it hasn't got massive membership. I don't go. It doesn't get anything done, only a newsletter."

"Only by everybody getting together, but there's still the problem of getting through to the Council. Just because everyone's in a little group, doesn't mean the Council will listen."

"Through the (Council) Committee involved, combined with self-help groups, voluntary organisations and possibly other interested parties."

Some comments seemed to assume a different political base for social services, with local people having a direct say over them. Other people approached the issue from the local authority end, identifying changes there they saw as needed to give people a greater say.

"Restructuring it (social services) on a completely different level. There should be more participation by ordinary people. There's not the work done to involve ordinary people."

"There's no way. The only way to have influence is to pass a government act. Its no good having do-gooders."

"Don't know. It should be achieved, but I don't think it ever will be. It should be done through local government. It's no good having another watchdog or a meeting in Hanover that only 10 people will go to. Councillors should be more concerned with their electorate than party politics."

"...You'd have to open the whole system out and bring the public into the decision-making process."

"I don't believe there's much chance of achieving it through democracy or East Sussex County Council. It would have to be a fundamental change in central government who would bring about change."

"A nice left-wing labour government or local councillors. A vast change in the attitudes of local government."

"By someone being admitted in there who knows the problems, such as myself who knows about handicap." (man who looked after his disabled wife)

"By putting a more everyday person into social services, not those who have 'O' and 'A' levels."

People's ideas about how social services might be democratised perhaps beg more questions than they answer. As we said on an earlier occasion when we raised these issues with people:

Where the answers of those who had not wanted more participation often seemed to be governed by their poor opinion of it now, those who wanted more, sometimes seemed to be thinking in terms of a more abstract and idealised future where methods might matter less, given good faith and a real will for greater participation on the part of the Council. Bearing in mind the important part people's lack of trust in the local authority seems to have played in their lack of response to it, they may well have been right to think this, although it does not overcome the problem of how *effective* participation is to be obtained without means that guarantee it.[129]

The sense of many members of the sample that they had a right to a say, coexisted with an unfamiliarity with and sometimes alienation and even repugnance from politics or what they saw as political. For example:

"A form to fill in what you think. You're allowed to vote. Why shouldn't you say what social services can do?"

"It should be a commonsense thing. Politics is abhorrent when it comes to local needs. The political parties use local needs to bang their own drum. My father was called up in 1916. He was killed. I was called up in 1939. We were asked our religion but not our politics. If it was good enough for us to fight with no questions asked, why does politics come into our basic needs? It should be a commonsense thing. Really professionals should be professionals. You don't ring up a right wing tory if you have a fire. You dial 999 for the fire brigade."

"I don't know. I'm not a committee man."

"The same way as I have a say in my Union — information and ballots. People should be told. More public meetings and ask people to come. I get information as a union member so I can't see why it can't work on a community or town level. We all vote at national and local elections. They do it then on the TV. I don't think people are told or shown enough."

Such attitudes highlight the contradiction that while people may often seek to avoid "politics" and "the political" and escape into "private life", private life is itself subject to politics — as well as being political in the broader sense. Perhaps the most striking point emerging from people's proposals was the gulf between their aspirations and the practicalities of the means they suggested for realising them. It emphasises how difficult it is to make political process part of people's ordinary lives — to humanise politics — and in that sense to unite the "personal and the political". The crucial political question which continues to go unanswered is how to bridge that gap. So long as it remains, politics will continue to be an unpleasant, power-denying experience and institution for most people.

Discussion about increasing people's say in social services, we would argue, inevitably draws us to fundamental questions of political theory and philosophy as well as questions about the structural constraints on such services. Inextricable from these are the constraints such services themselves impose on their workers and the deference they draw from many users, who grateful to be getting anything, are reluctant to bite the hand that feeds them. These enormous issues have so far been ignored or sidestepped by proponents of patch and other welfare pluralist approaches to social services, as if greater say, increased accountability and more responsive services are attainable in isolation, without reference to broader political, economic, social and cultural forces.

As we have said, it is not just the ordinary people in our sample who have difficulty coming up with original and effective ways of enabling people to have a greater say in services. Attempts to democratise services are faced with the two major issues of involving more people than has traditionally been the case, and of finding ways of ensuring them effective control. These remain crucial unresolved questions.

They leave many problems in their wake. First, the typically narrow involvement there has so far been in participatory processes, makes mediation and "representation" difficult to avoid. Frequently this involves intermediate bodies between users or local people; from tenants associations and user groups to voluntary organisations and community projects. What then becomes unclear is the relation of such bodies to their wider constituencies and whose interests they actually reflect. For while they represent forms of collective action, they too are subject to the difficulties of making this broadbased and representative. Organisations of disabled people, for example, are now increasingly challenging the traditional dominance of often paternalistic agencies for disabled people which are not controlled by people with disabilities themselves. While in large part a consequence of the inadequacy of arrangements for participation, this issue of representativeness leaves a large question mark over user and grassroots organisations, making it easy to dismiss any involvement there is as untypical. This is a reactionary argument and tactic frequently used to deny or call into question any outside involvement at all. At the same time as Ouseley has argued in the case of black people:

> Decentralisation will only assume real meaning for them if they are fully involved in every aspect of its operation. If not then decentralisation will merely pass on some of the powers of the local State apparatus to known activists without changing the status quo.... Any watered-down local arrangements will be regarded with scepticism.[130]

Richardson has identified a series of such problems associated with "participation", including the uneven distribution of arrangements providing for it, the relative lack of citizen and employee participation, except indirectly for the latter through trade unions, and the very limited powers ascribed to participants, since "virtually all bodies established for the express purpose of introducing participation have only an advisory or consultative status".[131]

There is also another wider set of issues. Concern is sometimes expressed that greater grassroots involvement might lead to racist and sexist policies. This is not the place to discuss this criticism in detail, but it is worth commenting on its implicit assumption of the neutrality or at least absence of racism and sexism in existing policy, both of which have been challenged by women and members of ethnic minorities. We would suggest that broader involvement in decision-making is likely to have the opposite effect, since it would draw in just such people previously excluded or discriminated against. Rather it is the *denial* of an effective say that seems to be divisive, often setting groups against each other because of the imposition of policies over their head. Thus, for example, proposals for hostels for homeless people and people with mental handicaps generate opposition and hostility against such groups from local people denied any part in their planning. Yet evidence increasingly shows that the candidates for such institutions neither want nor need to live in them.[132] Because people have such little say in services that affect their lives, there is little or no opportunity for them to negotiate or resolve any conflicting interests there may be either between them as workers, users or local people more generally, or according to age, race, gender and other differences.

Another major question is how arrangements for increasing people's say in policy would relate to existing structures or organisations for representation. The issue arises as much for trade unions as for local government. The rhetoric of decentralisation has included devolving power to trade unions as well as "the community". Some left authorities however seem to have adopted an almost existentialist approach to decentralisation, ignoring political and social realities that have long conditioned municipal relations, as though they had been made irrelevant by this new restructuring. This has been reflected in naive and insensitive behaviour to trade unions by some of these authorities. Trade unions in turn have sometimes been characterised as playing a reactionary role in decentralisation.[133] On the other hand, it is easy to understand their caution when the political organisation inviting their proposals and involvement is also their members' employer and one with whom there is likely to be a long history of conflict. This combined with unions' traditional ways of working, helps to explain their fears of losing their right to negotiate by "participating" and drawing up their own proposals. One lesson of decentralisation is that much more than any assumed communality of interests between left Labour authorities and trade unions is needed to resolve these difficulties.[134] By way of contrast, in East Sussex, while as the Director of Social Services said, "there were good reasons to expect difficulties from the unions in negotiating the implementation of the new structures", plans generally proceeded without interruption or significant modification.[135]

Local councillors are still seen by some as sufficient means of ensuring people a say in services. As Dennis argued in 1972, provisions for "participation" often serve as a diversion and "it was only when the ordinary machinery of local councillor, MP, publicity and public discussion and so forth was utilised and 'public participation' terminated" that local people achieved any success in local planning.[136] Local authority organisations have been critical of initiatives like local welfare advisory committees for cutting across the role of elected members and confusing the democratic process.[137] But local councillors are increasingly inadequate to ensure the degree of citizen involvement that is wanted, because of their reduced numbers, increased responsibilities, reduced powers and the trend to the concentration of power in council chambers into fewer hands. Councillors have their own political affiliations and obligations which may or may not match the commitments and concerns of the majority of their constituencies or minority groups among them. It is also difficult to find a way of involving them in structures for grassroots participation without them either dominating these or creating conflicts and inconsistencies between them and existing arrangements for local government representation. The relationship of council and councillors to the rights and say of workforce, users and local people, continues to be problematic. The question of how to improve it remains open. It is very difficult to see how this can be achieved without basic changes in the present system of local representation.

WAYS AHEAD

We have discussed some of the problems and issues associated with people's increased involvement in social services. There is no doubt though that there are authorities with a genuine desire to increase users', workers' and local people's say and involvement in services.[138] If this is to bear fruit, it still needs to be coupled with more effective ways of involving people. Much more must be done to explore and develop such alternatives, but there are already examples and approaches both in statutory and non-statutory services of *how* more say and involvement can be achieved and it is worthwhile identifying some of these.

Collaborative working offers workers the promise of a greater say in policy and practice. While it may not in itself ensure users a greater involvement, it is a necessary condition if workers are to have the power to make that possible. Stevenson and Parsloe found very little collaborative working in their research on social work area teams,[139] and more recently Black and others in their comparative study of three social services teams reported a similar situation.[140] As we have seen, community social work and patch teams are generally leader based. While there are some examples in the statutory sector of collaborative working, but with people in at least nominal leader roles,[141] in non-statutory agencies, there are a range of teams where there is formal and informal collaborative and collective team working, for example, in Pensioners Link local centres, several Citizens Advice Bureaux, community work agencies like the Benwell Project and the Women's Therapy Centre.[142] These offer models and experience for statutory social services seeking to empower their workers to draw on and learn from.

A key development in increasing service users' control and confidence has been the self-advocacy movement. Originating in the United States, it is now growing in Britain, particularly in the field of mental handicap. It has inspired the setting up of student and workers councils. Among well known examples are the Senior Training Centre in Mitcham, London, the Avro Centre, Southend and Pyenest Centre in Harlow. [143] As John Fisher of Camperdown Centre in North Tyneside — which has a workers council — has said, "the whole challenge of our work is to reduce the social distances between people — sharing power and the workers council are the beginning of that".[144] Self-advocacy's development has also been associated with and assisted by citizen-advocacy, where non-handicapped advocates are linked with hand-icapped people to help represent their interests.[145] Advocacy is also being developed by other groups in other services. Local "Who Cares" groups and now the National Association of Young People In Care (NAYPIC), offer a voice for children and young people in care, on their own terms, arguing, for example, that young people in care should be allowed to attend their own case conferences and case reviews. The Hackney Multi-Ethnic Women's Health Project, as a project worker has said, aims to "defend and stand with the woman and make the woman's wishes known to the hospital, so that it's a real two-way process, not just in understanding language, but in changing what goes on in hospital if it is unacceptable to our women".[146]

Making possible the broadbased involvement of people who aren't already engaged as service users, workers or in other ways, seems to be particularly difficult. We know of few examples. It is not surprising in view of the major contribution of feminist thinking in developing new ways of organising and working, that the field of child care offers some particularly helpful insights. The Akroyd community nursery in Lewisham, for instance, provides a local catchment area based service, and employs and is managed by local people. It offers imaginative child care and has links with local schools. The community centre which is situated in the same building is very much rooted in the area and well used. The nursery management committee, when one of us attended a meeting, included a wide cross-section of people, rather than just the middle class activists and career "tenants leaders" that often predominate.[147] "The Caledonian Allstars" offers another example of local involvement. While technically a local authority grant-aided playgroup, which began as part of a women's refuge, in practice it provides all-day care for 15 children aged two and a half to five. The staff have equal pay and make collective day to day decisions. All parents are automatically members of the management committee, which is an active group, with three elected parent representatives who work closely with staff.[148]

New ways are also being found to enable people to develop their own accounts, record their own experience and put their own point of view. Community publishing has grown rapidly, particularly during the last ten years, with examples like the Centreprise Publishing Project in Hackney and QueenSpark Books in Brighton, letting people speak for .themselves. Television History Workshop, using accessible shop fronts, has produced programmes involving participants, offering people's views on making cars in Cowley and working in a City General Hospital. The Living Archive Project in Milton Keynes, in the tradition of Mass Observation, is concerned with the present as well as the past. "Local people research and relate their own history; it is then set in a form that brings it to a wider audience and becomes, again, part of local history."[149]

There are other examples of innovative ways of involving people to be found in the women's health movement, community schooling and in the women's support groups that grew out of the 1984-5 miners strike. What is interesting about the initiatives there have been in social services, is that they have not been particularly associated with patch or community social work.

SUGGESTIONS FOR CHANGE

One of the key methods proposed by the authors of "Brighton On The Rocks" for increasing people's power were more public meeting places, local recreational, sports and other amenities.[150] The people we surveyed similarly placed considerable emphasis on the lack of and need for such facilities when talking about their wants and problems. There is beginning to be recognition that leisure activities are an important, if generally neglected sphere, in which people organise — on a scale far larger than some forms of "community action" more frequently reported and discussed.[151] The same unequal distribution of opportunities for leisure as for other activities and resources is also emerging.[152] But from the unforced social contact and shared activities and experience such amenities and opportunities could make possible, could grow the "getting together" and "organising for change" on a broadbased level, that some of the people we interviewed talked about.

What this points to is the way that the nature and availability of services can affect people's involvement, just as much as people's involvement is likely to affect services. We have argued elsewhere that it is probably only through regular involvement and having an effective voice in social services that the majority of people will gain the confidence, experience and knowledge to develop their own ideas and models of policies and services to meet their needs.[153] In the meantime we can work towards increasing that involvement by building on the affiliations, interests and associations people already have, for example, with existing groups and activities, both formal and informal — from their day to day involvement in the schools their children go to, to their participation as volunteers and helpers in old people's homes, hospitals, meals on wheels and other welfare services. Moves to make services more appropriate and responsive are also likely to increase the impetus for people's involvement.[154] But people already have contributions to make now and it is important for these not to be lost. We expected that some of the people we interviewed would have ideas and suggestions to offer about what they would like to see social services doing. We wanted to explore these and give people a chance to offer their own proposals.

There is an expectation that people without a professional or occupational interest will find it difficult to do this. For example, a review of public and users' attitudes to social work and social workers prepared for the Barclay Committee, concluded:

> Another problem is that clients may have no knowledge of how alternative services might have differed from those they have received and thus are not in a position to provide an informed assessment of the service. This factor may also account, in part, for the frequently poor response from clients to requests for suggestions on how to improve the service. A more fruitful approach to client opinion appears to be controlled comparative studies where levels of satisfaction (or other criteria) for two or more different types of intervention are compared (either by allowing each client to experience more than one type of intervention or by comparing groups of clients, each group experiencing a different type of intervention)...[155]

The problem with this, of course, is that people only have a chance to choose from options they are given rather than from ones they might propose or develop themselves. What makes more sense since most of us know our needs and difficulties better than we know how they may best be met, is to take *them* rather than services as the starting point for debate, moving on, through discussion and with skilled support, to work out what services and policies might best fit them. That should be the goal, but here we had to be more modest. We began in this study by raising people's wants and needs with them. Hopefully our questions about services build on that. We recognise the limitations of any attempt to elicit their ideas for services. It runs the risk that people may not be able to think beyond existing provision — although that is a problem present policy makers and service providers themselves still have to transcend. However, our belief in asking the people we interviewed was that it was important and helpful to give them this chance to put forward whatever ideas they might have for social services. Failure to do that is likely to result in a self-fulfilling prophecy, keeping closed the doors to people's ideas and involvement.

In the event more than half the sample (55) had suggestions to make and these were not constrained by conventional social services' terms of reference. They addressed particular groups and particular issues. Most often mentioned — by a quarter of the sample — were old people and the need for more and better services for them. This may have reflected both the general concern for old people and the large number living in the area. Services for children and young people were mentioned by 12 people. Members of the sample also wanted additional provision made for people now often stigmatised or given low priority by social services, like alcoholics, people with mental illness and mental handicaps, single parents, unemployed and single people. Also mentioned were services for carers, physically disabled, poor and isolated people. There were no calls for a local social services office, more voluntary action, reliance on self-help or any of the other policies associated with patch.

People's proposals for policies and services were often imprecise, for example, "a more positive approach to elderly people living on their own", "more emphasis and resources for the unemployed and one parent families", "a better service for old people". A number simply wanted more to be done, often more of the same, for instance, more home helps and more playgroups. At a time when the emphasis from patch and welfare pluralist proponents has been on the need to reassess and reshape services, these comments offered an important reminder of the basic shortage of provision and gaps in policy felt by many people.

"More for children to do in school holidays, organised and inexpensive. Being more concerned about children. Children's homes are coming up for the axe. More done for older children, especially towards the end of and after school — unemployed teenagers."

"Again that would be more for the elderly. I think they are quite shut off. They are afraid of mugging and robbery."

"More of what they offer. More home helps, definitely."

"More for deprived children."

What was most striking about people's responses here was how many went outside the bounds of what are normally seen as social services department responsibilities. While one woman made no suggestions, saying "The things I can think of are not to do with social services", others did not let this limit them. It might be argued that in some cases this was because people were unaware of the exact province of social services. But in many others, this was clearly not so. People wanted to see more and better housing, improved policing, higher state benefits, better medical care and improved public transport. They did not see policy and services in narrow departmental terms. This echoes the issue that emerged in the last chapter, when we saw that many people's wants and needs did not fit neatly into the conventional orbit of the social services department. Much of what it did was not relevant to their key needs, while other services to which they referred had a fundamental bearing on their lives and needs.

Table 3: Breakdown of policies and provision suggested by respondents in answer to Question 20: "Are there any particular policies, services or provision you would like to see the Council's Social Services Department offering (which they may not be offering now)?"

Policy/Provision	Number
More of existing provision	15
Social/communal provision	11
Childcare provision	10
Provision for support	7
Financial/material aid	4
Housing	3
Improved public transport	3
Alcoholism services	2
Improved policing	2
Other	5
TOTAL	62*

* This figure represents the total number of references made to various policies and services, not the total of individuals making them (55).

"More financial help for old people."

"Council housing for single people."

"More liaison with the police whereby you have more cooperation with the local bobby."

"I think delivery of goods or shopping for older people. Tradesmen used to come round the streets, but now they don't."

While some people singled out specifically welfare-type provision, many mentioned mainstream broadbased services like day care provision for children meeting women's as well as children's needs, meeting places, public transport and so on. People's broad conception of *social* services was again reflected in references to policies and services to improve and enable social contacts and social life. As well as the 11 who made specific suggestions for meeting places, clubs and visitors, other proposals for services offering people support and even, for example, for improved public transport, can be seen to overlap into this domain.

"A relief to some people would be a visitor. Some old people can't get out and they never see anybody."

"A better service for old people, not just meals on wheels. I've worked in old people's homes and they need a service where they can be taken out once a week or so."

"What is the extent of their resources? It's difficult to know. I'd like to see more

trees and something to stimulate a social life, possibly more events where you can meet people."

A DIFFERENT APPROACH

To explore people's ideas and proposals further, we also asked whether they thought the social services department might have something to offer them if it had a different kind of approach, and services were provided differently. It was in response to this question that a number of people made comments about not needing social services or them "not affecting them" or being "for people like them". As we have seen 42 people seemed to see social services as for other people and not for them and only 29 thought that they had any understanding of or interest in the kind of issues and problems that concerned them. However in answer to this question 51 said they thought social services *could* have something to offer them, if they adopted a different approach and provided services differently. Significantly 18 of these 51 people were among those who did not see existing social services as for them. People's sense of distance and separation from social services seemed connected to what they saw as their actual nature and remit, rather than to some fundamental distrust, rejection or prejudice. Comments again reflected a broader view of what social services might do than is now the case. They again included making more financial assistance, having more resources, providing more social activities, information about themselves, and being more accessible. For example:

"Especially as regards divorced and unmarried mothers — like an evening out, a get-together where your children could be looked after."

"I'm not sure what that means. I suppose so if it said it would allocate more money."

"For unemployment. They could help. That could be improved."

"If they possibly circularised what services they offer, let people know, so if I had a problem, I'd know who to go to."

In addition to the ideas put forward in answer to these two questions, another 29 people spoke elsewhere in their interviews about what social services should be doing. These comments included providing more and better services for old and unemployed people, children and single parents, and support for carers. They also called for more resources for social services, better liaison with other departments, more public consultation and information, increased accessibility, more child care provision for the benefit of women and children, and the provision of meeting places and recreational facilities, more visitors and visiting, and more accommodation, particularly sheltered accommodation. There were also pleas from two people for social services to avoid sexism and the imputation of deviance and attachment of stigma to their clients.

"It's a pity that older people are on their own and not found by social services. Social services could find out they are on their own and haven't any relatives."

"There should be investigation as to the suitability of people in the administration of social services. There should be more liaison between all fields of social work, health work and social security."

"Women should be in the social services to help elderly people. A lot of older women want to talk to women."

"Teachers and doctors should liaise more with social services and an understanding be built up."

"The only thing is that I think that every elderly person should have a telephone so they can phone someone if they need to, either to get help or to talk over a problem."

To sum up, people's proposals for social services were not so much about different or innovatory ways of doing the same things as they are now doing, although a number of ideas along these lines were put forward. Instead, they suggested a much broader role and range of concerns and activities. Interestingly only one person in answer to either of the two questions we asked about people's ideas about social services, referred to patch as a way of achieving what they wanted to see.

A NEW SET OF BOUNDARIES FOR SOCIAL SERVICES?

Major questions are raised here. Could or should social services departments take on the kind of tasks mentioned by people we surveyed? At first sight their role seems to exclude providing more meeting places, recreational facilities and improved public transport. But as we have already said, social services have in some sense attempted to do this with compensatory services like community transport schemes and day centres for old people. Intermediate treatment overlaps into youth service provision and even group work may shade into adult and community education. We have questioned this approach insofar as it papers over deficiencies in mainstream services or offers separate often inferior shadow services for people they ignore or reject, and because of its own inherent limitations like segregation and stigma.

Alternatively we can think of new services and provision that people raised coming from the mainstream departments involved, for example, Transport and Recreation. An increased emphasis on criteria of social need would be essential. The transfer of responsibility for homelessness from social services to housing offered an example in the 1970s of how the limitations of a segregated approach could to some extent at least be overcome, as the movement for the educational integration of children labelled as having "special needs" does in the 1980s. Mainstream services, suitably resourced, sensitised and reorientated can also meet social need. It is not the prerogative of social services. The logic of this approach is that some at least of the functions now with social services could be integrated into other departments.

What this indicates is the need for fresh thinking about organisational boundaries closer to people's ideas about what social services might or should be. Some of the broader proposals made by members of the sample might well be brought into the social services department, for example, the provision of meeting places and a universal under fives service. On the other hand, the National Child Care Campaign, for instance, has advocated children's centres with integrated nursery provision combining the care and learning now formally divided between social services day nurseries and education department nursery schools and classes.

This discussion about people's control of and ideas for social services has brought us back to the same cruclal issue that emerged when we explored people's wants and needs — the role and function of social services. Again what is highlighted is the anomalous position of social services. Certainly people have minimal control over them and don't seem to be getting the social services they need.

We are not suggesting that the findings from one small study offer clear evidence on which to formulate or choose options for social services. That was not the aim here as we have made clear. But they do raise some important issues and questions. First does the poor fit between what many of the people we interviewed saw as major day to day needs and what social services do reflect a more general situation? Then there is the lack of clarity and logic in the present nature and functions of social services departments. Do they actually have a discrete role or competence in their present form? For us a central issue for social as for other services is the degree to which they enable their users, workers and local people to have an effective say in them. The evidence from this study as others is not encouraging. Can the fit between services and needs be improved without increasing public involvement, control and accountability? We doubt it.

Social services are in the melting pot. The continuing controversy between "specialism" and "genericism"[156] and between community social work, patch and "slimline social work" are symptomatic of this and these issues have been sharpened by the current harsh political climate. If social services commentators and academics have been searching for a changed role for social services, the comments and ideas of the people we interviewed raise even more fundamental questions. Community social work and patch have been advanced as important new ways of seeing and structuring services. However the indications from this small study at least are that they will only have value if they make possible changes in services to reflect and give priority to the wants and needs of citizens, whether as service workers, users or local people. So far there do not seem to be much grounds for optimism, judging at least from the East Sussex initiative. However, it would be mistaken to write off some of the progressive principles associated with patch, like the desire to increase people's access to and say in social services and break down barriers between workers, users and local people, because of shortcomings in the way in which it has been conceived and implemented. At the same time, as we have said elsewhere, it would be tragic if we were left with the worst result of all; the illusion for many people that a form of social services offering "democracy" and "local control" had been tried and failed.[157]

3.
INVOLVING
PEOPLE IN CHANGE

Introduction

**"In this philosophy the user is not only a client, but also a partner in
the planning and provision of services."**[1]

Social services texts and discussions are frequently frustrating. Some provide
detailed and careful descriptions, but stop short of analysis. Others offer radical
analysis and argument, but often they fail to match this with ideas for action.
Chapters of critique are followed by thin pages of rhetoric and proposals. In the last,
more speculative part of this book, we try to take a few steps towards both critique
and some practical proposals.

Chapter 10 reviews some of the unresolved issues raised by patch and
community social work. We sketch the political and economic context of patch
schemes and reflect on the different philosophies which have been used to support
them. We are then drawn back to some of the key concepts of patch; "care",
"community" and the idea of informal networks. How does "care" relate to other
concepts like need, independence and control? What of the relationship between
paid and unpaid caring? When patch speaks of informal networks in the
community, are these helping or colonising? This leads to the further question of
whether patch is, as many of its critics suggest, essentially regressive in its effects,
whatever the intentions of its initiators and practitioners. Finally, are patch and
community social work a break with existing traditions in social welfare? In whose
interests are they and can they really involve people as "a partner in the planning
and provision of services"?

The final chapter offers something different, and we hope helpful. Workers and
users of social services will recognise many of the problems we have discussed so
far in the book. What they want as well as support in understanding policy, are
insights, ideas and examples of *how to improve* the situation. We hope that the
critical frameworks we put forward both illuminate the issues and suggest
alternatives and choices. Again, we don't mean recipes for policies, but guidelines
for transforming the process of policy and practice development. So in saying that
Chapter 11 offers some practical ideas, we are not offering another policy
"blueprint" — an alternative to compete with patch and community social work.
That would contradict the central philosophy of our project: to enable people to
have the chance ot work out their own programme and policies. It is not for us or

261

any narrow band of commentators or policy makers to insist on what social services should be doing or in what relationship they should stand with other services and issues. We may have our own views, but our role should be to help people work out their own answers to these questions and to support them in doing so.

This might be seen as ducking the issue. Instead we are trying to avoid the paternalistic trap into which many social policy analysts fall. They fail to see how fundamental it is that people are enabled to participate more fully in the development and control of their *own* policies and provision. For us this is the central issue. What is crucial is exploring ideas and experience which indicate how this might be done.

CHAPTER TEN

Putting Patch into Perspective

"The central tenet of a community social work approach is that workers should be accountable not only to their organisation but also to the neighbourhoods which they serve."
Jim Dalton, Training And Development Officer, East Sussex Social Services Department[1]

Patch and community social work have raised fundamental questions about social services, even if so far they have been less successful in answering them. Rightly they have challenged traditional approaches more clearly derived from the poor law than designed to meet modern needs. They have offered the most conspicuous alternative to right-wing attacks on statutory services, although themselves bearing some uncomfortable similarities to their critiques. Because of their initiative, fresh life has been breathed into welfare's debates about itself. Workers have felt greater strength behind their desire to work more closely and equally with people, and service users have been cast in less passive terms. Patch and community social work have been concerned with some of the key issues facing social work and personal social services, including their organisational structure; the roles and relationships of users, workers, local people and other agencies; accountability; and equality of treatment and opportunity.

Patch particularly is not just concerned with decentralisation, but with change in relationships, both between statutory and other services and between social services and the provision of care. What continues to be unclear is whether some of these changes are necessarily beneficial, particularly to service workers, users, women, members of ethnic minorities and other penalised groups. Our study reinforces such reservations and doubts. We want to take up these questions by first trying to set patch and community social work in some kind of context.

Social Services In Context

In Chapter Eight we saw some of the relationships between local and national policies and developments and people's wants and needs. A strong message from this study is that people's needs and problems, like patch and community social work themselves, cannot be considered in isolation. This is not only true, for example, of the physical and mental disorder associated with unemployment and women's overburdening as carers. It extends to all aspects of our lives. Changed patterns of retailing have affected the independence of old people. The growth of satellite estates has exacerbated the difficulties and isolation of women. We live in a society where environment and attitudes are so hostile to people with disabilities that the view that the lives of babies and unborn children with disabilities should be terminated because of their appalling prospects has gained considerable acceptance.[2] The food we eat, our jobs and social class, all affect our health, the problems we face and the old age we can expect. We can do no more than raise such issues here. But they should not be ignored in any consideration of welfare. All are elements in the social construction of needs, their uneven distribution and the collective responses that are made to them.

We mentioned earlier that the relationship of personal social services with other state and welfare services was unclear and contentious. Conservative government attempts to restructure welfare have made this point even more pertinent. Both needs and patch must be considered in a context where the guiding principles of government welfare reform have been privatisation, the ending of universalism, reduced public services and expenditure. For example, these underpinned the 1985 Social Security Reviews, with their talk of "targetting on those most in need", and emphasis on private pensions, means testing, reduced and in some cases repayable benefits, a fixed sum social fund and a management board selected for their "relevant management experience of running large businesses".[3]

The people and groups most dependent on social security; old, young, unemployed, low paid, chronically sick and disabled people and those who care for them, women, single parents and members of ethnic minorities, also account for most users of social services. Reliance on social services has always been most closely associated with poverty.

Poverty defines people's lives. It governs their access to other services and amenities. Some of its consequences on health, such as homelessness, hypothermia and poor nutrition are obvious. The less evident but extensive damage was well documented in the Black Report, "Inequalities Of Health".[4]

Cuts and restructuring in other welfare services are having similarly destructive effects. Poor housing is associated with many problems, including ill-health among children, higher levels of reception into care, and anxiety and depression among women. The run-down of public housing not only means there is less suitable stock available and that repairs and maintenance have deteriorated. Nor are there sufficient resources for supportive and sheltered accommodation, or for sensitive policies for fitting aids and adaptations, so that people who want to can manage in their own homes as long as possible without needing outside assistance or making undue demands on their families.

Cuts in the Health Service mean that hospitals are having to discharge patients earlier without adequate community services to help them regain their confidence and ensure their recovery. Lengthening waiting lists result in even longer delays for hip replacement and other operations which could maintain people's independence and livelihood. Rehabilitiation services for stroke sufferers like physiotherapy are being cut reducing people's abilities and mobility. Then there are all the preventive, educational and public health measures on which there has never been enough emphasis, which are being further curtailed. Examples include efforts to improve people's diet and exercise, to provide cheaper and better public transport to reduce road accident injuries, and to control hazardous processes and substances to limit incapacitating occupational injuries and diseases.

Growing numbers of children and young people are segregated in separate schools and institutions because of the inadequacies of mainstream education. A blind child might have to attend a residential school many miles from home and most children with mental handicaps still grow up isolated from others in special schools because the resources for successful integration have not been provided.

We have only attempted the briefest of revues of government social policy in the mid 1980s. Even to attempt such a catalogue can itself be counter-productive, distancing such developments from the human misery they entail. But by ignoring them we run the greater risk of seeing patch out of perspective. Take the proposals for social security reform. We cannot be sure exactly what effect they will ultimately have, but they are important less for their detail than the intentions they indicate for the treatment of claimants and indeed users of other welfare state services. The point we want to make is that this is the climate in which personal social services must operate *now* and in which community social work and patch are being offered as a way out of many of their difficulties.

CARE AND INDEPENDENCE

Central government strategies for welfare have had two particular effects on people's lives. The first is to undermine their independence. By this we don't mean people not being able to live individualistically or "in the community", but being able to live the kind of life they want. The worsening economic situation, chronic mass unemployment and cuts in public and welfare services, all increase and exacerbate people's wants and problems. Instead of gaining new skills and opportunities, old ones are being lost. This brings us to the second effect. Rather than needs being met by mainstream public services — the founding premise of the welfare state — they are increasingly being transformed into problems requiring "care". So, for instance, getting training or a job is further away than ever for young people with mental handicaps. Instead they are to be "looked after" by their parents or in adult training centres. Single parents have their names added to stigmatic "at-risk" registers because they lack the money or support to bring up their children as they would wish or are expected to.

Let's now look more closely at these two issues of care and independence. We have observed how community *care* in particular has been offered as a means of maintaining people's independence. We would challenge the notion that the two are necessarily complementary. They may actually be more often at odds.

Consider the word "care" in social services. Frequently it serves as no more than a blanket term for whatever departments do. So we have *day care, care services, care worker* and reception into *care*. This usage does more than add a label. It also changes the sense, giving it idiosyncratic meanings far removed from people's day to day definitions. There are connotations of storage, control, passivity and keeping people occupied. So instead of the positive values that are placed on *careful* work or *caring* relationships, it is these passive meanings — looking after, minding, a caretaker role — that are more often attached to welfare.

Prevailing norms place little value on caring. This is apparent not only from the penny-pinching way in which "community care" policies have been developed, but also the poor conditions and pay for paid carers in health and welfare agencies and the low priority and under-development of many caring services. It is not surprising that women carry out the greater part of caring given their concentration in the worst rewarded employment and the low value placed on their traditional caring role, whatever the right-wing rhetoric about women, home and family.

But all this has more fundamental origins. It reflects the low status state and market attach to those people seen as the *objects* of care. This is unlikely to change so long as they are valued primarily in narrow economic terms which write off people who are old, chronically sick and disabled, people with mental illness and mental handicaps, and indeed children, as "unproductive", a "burden" and not part of the creation of "real wealth".

The important question here, particularly for social services, is whether, within such a framework and with such meanings now attached to "care", it could provide the basis for an adequate response to people's needs.

Perhaps even more important is whether it is this kind of response people want. Judging from what people said to us, this is doubtful. The people we interviewed largely defined their needs in terms of mainstream public policies and services rather than of care and support — except at the level of personal relationships — and certainly not in terms of social services' care.

When we compare this with the arguments of radical groups of people with disabilities, we find a rejection of the notion of care — at least in the sense it is now offered by social services. Instead ideas of *independence* have been at the forefront of thinking and action. We have raised elsewhere the deficiencies of the concept of care when set against ideas of independence and collective living.[5] What we find radical disability groups arguing assumes a redefinition of the debate. Although their demands include the need for "support", this is no longer framed as being "cared for" or "looked after". And disability is not seen merely as a misfortune. For example, the Union Of The Physically Impaired Against Segregation have defined disability as:

> The disadvantage or restriction of ability caused by a contemporary social organisation which takes little or no account of people who have physical impairment, and thus excludes them from participation in the mainstream of social activities.... Physical disability is therefore a particular form of social oppression.[6]

Such a redefinition underpins demands for equal participation by the growing Independent Living Movement. As Davies of the Derbyshire Coalition of Disabled People has argued:

> Our aim (is) full participation and equality for all disabled people... Disabled people are the *only* people who can translate this aim into reality.... It is still overwhelmingly the case that we are starved of access to basic information; have difficulty obtaining well designed housing; are often denied appropriate aids and equipment; are extremely lucky if we have flexible and comprehensive sources of secure personal assistance; are largely excluded from public transport; and still hold a dream of a barrier free built environment.[7]

There is a clear contrast between this and conceiving of people in terms of care and inviting assumptions of their dependence. Moreover, caring is increasingly being stereotyped as responsibility for heavily dependent people. Not only does this neglect the wide variety of relationships and responsibilities included under its heading. It also misrepresents the position of people "cared for" and glosses over the social and political location of the causes of disability and dependence emphasised by UPIAS, Davies and others. Cuts and restructuring in social and other public services are polarising people into carers and dependants, attacking the interests of both.

What we are saying is that more and more needs are being created and exacerbated and then reframed in terms of care by such policies, to be placed at the door of social services. It is important that these two effects are recognised as interlinked and part of a wider move. At the same time even more needs are coming the way of departments because of "community care" policies to discharge people from psychiatric and mental handicap hospitals and as a result of the growing number of very old people in the population. But if social services are facing growing responsibilities as more of us are made candidates for care, they have been subjected to the same central government constraints as other services. Put these developments together and we begin to see the emergence of an overall philosophy for the public sector which implies a radically changed role for statutory social services. Instead of being service providers, they are to become "enabling authorities" mainly concerned with contracting out services to commercial businesses and voluntary agencies, and left with only vestigial "policing" and regulatory roles.

Social services workers, particularly social workers, know only too well what it is like to be left trying to deal with problems whose causes and solutions lie elsewhere, and of then being blamed if anything goes wrong — especially in the case of child care tragedies. We are not suggesting that there is not a role for "care" in social services — although the meaning we would hope to see is not the passive custodial one we have described — but rather that this role must be carefully considered in relation to wider policies and pressures if social services are to avoid being pushed into a palliatory poor law role.

To sum up then, the effect of these policies and developments is to increase the demand for care while reducing the capacity of social and health services to provide it. They involve a massive switch from public services to private care — both in the sense of commercial provision, and on an even larger and more exploitative scale, the unpaid labour of women. Ironically, the closure of public sector residential provision has been justified in the name of "community care" — with all the obligations it imposes on women, yet it has also been the occasion for an enormous expansion in commercial homes and hostels.

On the positive side, however, some attempts have been made to put "community care" in the wider context we have discussed of policies and needs. The 1985 House of Commons Social Services Select Committee's report argued that genuine community care policies would only be achieved through a real increase in expenditure.[8] Renee Short, who chaired the Committee, has argued that:

> If community care is to work, you have to have good housing conditions, psychiatric care and a complete rejigging of the social security system.[9]

The National Union of Public Employees has proposed an alternative approach to turn "community neglect into community care" which recognises the need "not only for resources, but carefully constructed policies and strategies. As well as pressing for the development of suitable statutory services to enable people with particular needs to live independently as they would wish, it argues the need to extend and sensitise mainstream services like housing; to design services that are anti-discriminatory; tackle problems collectively; provide maximum support to people "choosing to do the caring themselves", and to decentralise decision-making and involve workers and users in the planning and delivery of services.[10]

Just as we have seen how people's independence can be undermined by government policies, so other initiatives show how it can be fostered and extended. Examples of this include flexible employment schemes for women with disabilities; support units for elderly people, intended to offer assistance and opportunities on their own terms; and repair and improvement projects for elderly owner occupiers to enable them to stay in their own home.[11]

Developing different notions of support, independence and care, like those we have been considering, we can begin to examine current patch and community care initiatives and challenge their rhetoric. Are people coming out of institutions, or are they being shifted from one kind of institution to another? Are unpaid carers and the people they have cared for getting the choices and support they want from the services and resources being offered? Do social services policies foster self-determination, or are they drifting or being pushed even further into a marginal role?

CARE AND CASH

We have pointed to one way in which care needs to be reassessed. Another is in relation to money. Having a paid job is a key value in our society. We are also taught the importance of helping others. However put caring and money together and there often seems to be a conflict. Instead of trying to resolve this, the tendency — particularly by the political right — has been to trade on it, extolling the merits of unpaid altruism, while keeping silent over the fact that women habitually do much more giving than receiving and that philanthropy unsupported by an independent income is liable to exploitation.

"Care" in our ordinary lives has connotations of love and affection as well as support. We see no inherent reason why this cannot also be the case with collective public services. It has long been true of many relationships between home helps, care assistants and their clients. Yet there is still a tendency to see loving or caring relationships as qualified or precluded by the payment that goes with employment. Slipman, for example, has suggested:

> Professional, paid workers are invaluable, but they cannot offer the space for human warmth and friendship which our society needs if it is to find civilised solutions to its problems and re-build the base to its communities.

Significantly, she raised this argument when proposing a Social Democratic Party "national community volunteer service scheme" as one of the "urgent solutions" to deal with "the crisis of care" she sees the increasing numbers of old people creating.[12]

Titmuss, in his discussion of blood donation, suggested that selling that service for money impaired the gift.[13] The same is sometimes suggested of caring. Unpaid caring is seen as somehow better or more virtuous and unalloyed than paid services. It is easy to see this as a relic from pre-industrial times when social obligations were more clearly demarcated, even if not necessarily maintained. Just how exploitative this usually unstated argument can be — that it is wrong to expect to be paid for helping others and that vocation is its own reward, nurses and other care workers know to their cost.[14] We have already also seen how unsupported unpaid caring jeopardises the very love and affection that is advanced as its unique advantage. Usually the only model envisaged for such emotionally inspired care is the two or three generational family. As Finch has observed, this denies the "possibility of non-heterosexual relationships, of close relationships without a sexual component, and of women's experience of sisterhood", and the warmth and attachment that can equally go with them.[15] Another of the ironies of the shift away from state employment to "community care", of course, has been the expansion in provision for *profit* it has generated at the same time as exhorting the "voluntary ideal" and an increase in women's unpaid labour at home.

While often discussed in isolation, the issue of paying people is hardly one that applies solely or particularly to care and social services. The same argument can equally apply to the provision of other goods and services. Yet we would not expect the tinker, tailor or candlestick maker to work for low or no pay because they offered a "public" service. Caring does not somehow exist outside wider economic realities, although there seems to be a reluctance to acknowledge its relation with them. We live in a wage based economy where most people work for a living or have to rely on benefits whose inferior levels follow from wage rates.

Paid caring always involves a *social* as well as an economic relationship. We need to look afresh at the relationship between paid carers and the recipients of such services, just as we need to consider that between paid and unpaid carers. As we see it, citizens contribute to the state so that people can be employed on proper terms to provide services collectively. This is as reciprocal and altruistic as Titmuss's gift relationship. Such a model of collective payment for collective services can be consistent with the independence of both service workers and users. It is far preferable to the state seeking to harness the unpaid labour of often exploited people and groups. Only through the provision of such alternative paid services will women have an effective choice between being carers or not, and having adequate and appropriate support if they are. Countering sexism is more likely to be an achievable goal in organised formal services than in the home — especially in the shorter term. None of this runs counter to the longer term objective of providing adequate income maintenance, mainstream policies and services following from people's needs and demands. It will only be through this and from equal access to employment that potential carers and candidates for care, will secure their rights and preferred way of living, and tensions between their different interests resolved.

PATCH, WELFARE AND WORK

The conception of caring as paid or unpaid work leads us to another issue. There are now growing arguments for a guaranteed income for all. The idea is for a "social dividend", not linked to the labour market, but allowing everyone the freedom to choose whether they want to be employed.[16] There is no doubt that such thinking has followed from the harsh blow dealt to conventional economic wisdoms by recession, mass unemployment, the collapse of traditional manufacturing and emergence of new technology. Doubts about these proposals usually focus on the problem of securing a high enough basic income in a market based economy. We have a more fundamental criticism, which is to ask whether such schemes have confused a decline in employment with a decline in *work*. It is one thing to observe changes in the pattern of paid employment and quite another to claim as some writers have done, that there won't be enough "work" to go round, or that we must "say goodbye to the working class".[17] Few women caught in the treadmill of housework, cooking and caring are likely to recognise the picture being painted.

It all depends on what we mean by work. As Braverman pointed out, pressing clothing in a factory is recorded as manufacturing, while doing essentially the same job in a cleaning plant is part of service industry.[18] As we can see, if this or a host of other tasks is done as part of "informal caring", the work disappears from economic statistics altogether. The point is not to "create" such work, but to see what needs to be done — and what is already being done as unpaid home-work with especially damaging effects for women as carers and workers — as an ideal candidate for expanding paid employment. Such human service activities would be a welcome successor to the often dehumanising conditions of manufacture and give people a real choice between working for pay or not. Significantly, arguments for the "leisure society", "social dividend" and the like, have traditionally come from white employed men, while not surprisingly those demanding greater access to employment, including women and people with physical and mental handicaps, have been among those worst discriminated against by the labour market. What is clear is that those needs and wants which welfare could and should address are not separate from or in conflict with wider economic goals. We need to consider social policy — and personal social services particularly — much more as a growing source and enabler of employment, rather than as an alternative to it.

CARE AND CONTROL

Last we want to say something about "care" when it is linked to "control". In social services work, the two are often run together. Social services workers will point out that they don't create this ambiguity. The terms are part of the legal framework within which they work. It means that on one occasion their powers and duties will support someone's rights — to housing for instance — and on another they may be taking rights away — conspicuously those of parents with their children. Nevertheless, it is worth asking what it does to the concept of care when, for example, "in care" signifies a technical and legal status for a young person. When words become a formula run off in one breath, the meanings themselves are easily fused and confused.

How then do patch and community social work tackle this dual responsibility for care and control? Many claims have been made for them, but perhaps the keenest demand they can expect to face is whether they offer ways forward in safeguarding the rights and needs of children and their families. To some extent they have ducked the issue by focussing on work seen as less contentious, such as that with old people. Even here though, there are statutory powers involving compulsion and the rights of clients, especially in relation to residential homes. Unfortunately these issues have not been properly recognised and discussed within the debate on patch.

On the other hand, for both old people and families and children, the advocates of community social work have stressed its *preventive* approach. Their idea is that a more supportive and helpful intervention at an earlier stage in people's problems will head off many of the emergencies which involve compulsion. Social services workers will then intervene far less often in a crisis. Or if they do, because they know the people and their circumstances, their action won't be clumsy or precipitate.

We are not implying that patch and community social work deny a place for social control in social services. For instance, the Barclay Committee saw a continuing need for "social policing".[19] Practitioners in patch teams are only too aware that of all the "policing" functions, the most worrying — for workers and for the public generally — concerns child abuse. Despite a fall in the number of documented cases of serious injury or death to a child caused by a parent or guardian, the tragedies of 1984 and 1985 again spotlighted this issue.

There is some reason for optimism here. A longitudinal study of children in care in North Battersea, for example, showed positive results after a reorganisation to neighbourhood working. There was more decisive planning and a stronger sense among social workers of being able to carry out their work with families and children sensitively and effectively.[20] This is a welcome change which could lead to important improvements over past practice.

However, workers who expect patch and community social work to offer answers to all the problems we have raised are likely to be disappointed. Despite their potential, there remain several serious difficulties.

A practical obstacle is whether a patch approach will even be tried when it comes to "statutory" cases. In Normanton, for example, almost all cases involving elderly and disabled people were dealt with by patch workers — who included social work assistants and care workers — in their own patch. At the same time it was social workers who took on most of the family and child care work, and this was allocated across patch boundaries.[21] So sadly, the most controversial cases, where a new approach is particularly needed, were those where basic patch principles were set aside.

But there are more fundamental issues. In child abuse, just as with many other problems, there are wider pressures which patch cannot conjure away. The North Battersea study did not explore the interaction between family breakdown and child abuse, and the ever worsening conditions faced by local black and white working class families. So while it showed a reduction in the number of children in care in the area, what was not clear was what struggles such parents and their children *generally* were having to face. We are not condoning the battering of a child because an area suffers from economic decline and political reaction. What we are saying is that these public issues and people's private troubles come together in a destructive way. Patch's advocates, like the majority members of the Barclay Committee, have given inadequate attention to the relationship of social and economic conditions and individual behaviour seen as needing "policing".

Until such external constraints on people are reduced and unless social services have adequate support services of their own, whether they are "community orientated" or not, they are likely to be under continued pressure to maintain essentially social control roles, both supervising parents and providing education and training to keep them — particularly mothers — in conformity with prevailing models of parenting. What is at issue here is the relation between policies pushing people towards family breakdown and child abuse, and individualised responses focussed on the families affected — the two often interacting with each other in a stigmatic and destructive way. Any impact the preventive policies of patch might have are likely to be swallowed up by the intensifying hardships people now face.

Patch's advocates have also yet to look adequately at another issue; the extent to which social control must be based on consent and accountability. East Sussex Social Services has asked:

Is there a conflict between developing the trust and acceptance of a community and yet at the same time taking its children into care?[22]

We would suggest that this misses the point. Service users are likely to be ambivalent about the idea of an approachable neighbourhood worker. Anyone with both control and confidant functions will not find them sitting together easily. And although many of the demands for control will come from outside, it will also be neighbours, relatives and friends who insist that social services "do something" about an isolated old person or a child where abuse is suspected.

The crucial issue here is whether the "community" has any real say in the department's dealings with its members. Social services control functions are certain to be contentious. The real question is whether they are felt as invasive and alienating. We think they will be as long as control is not *shared* with workers, users and local people.

This is particularly important for patch and community social work because of their concern to draw in and orchestrate the involvement of other people and agencies in providing care. It is difficult to see how their desire to "harness" and develop informal care, community and voluntary organisations can escape becoming colonialistic so long as service users, workers and local people involved have no effective say in it. We'd stress again the disturbing issues raised by the idea of male dominated and predominantly white social services seeking to "tap" the informal and voluntary action of women, black people and members of other ethnic minorities. Gordon has argued of community policing that if it does not entail any greater control of the police by the public then it does not represent a break from old and new fashions in reactive policing, but rather complements them.[23] The same point applies to patch and community social work. Without such citizen accountability, it is not clear how they will differ qualitatively from traditional social services.[24]

COMMUNITY VERSUS CLIENT?

In this chapter we have focussed so far on the concept of "care". What of the associated idea of "community"? In the thinking of patch and community social work, doesn't this offer at least the possibility of moving away from the individualising traditional services? Earlier in the book, we charted the inadequacies — particularly the gender bias — of patch's conception of community. We want to return to this briefly before suggesting an alternative approach.

As we've seen, patch and community social work emphasise that their "target" for social services' care is different to their predecessors'. Patch advocates contrast what they see as the dominant "client-centred" philosophy with their own "community-centred" model, which has as its starting point "recognition of the central importance of informal systems of care and the need to devise ways of interweaving statutory services with such systems to create the best joint contribution of the two".[25] However, they use the term "client-centred" in a very particular way: to mean helping individuals with insufficient personal and other resources to cope.[26]

We would argue that social services departments have never been client or user centred in the sense of being based on their wants and needs. That was a view shared by many of the people we spoke to. The mistake often seems to be to assume that work with "the community" is somehow better or more "progressive", while service to individuals has to be traditional, bureaucratic and consensual. As Leonard has argued in his discussion of radical social work practice:

A simplistic notion has developed that social work with individuals and families must operate within a framework of acceptance of the status quo, while community work is essentially equated with radical action for social change. Many radical critics while acknowledging that community-work activities can be as oppressive as any form of individual work, fall into the trap of assuming there can be no radical individual practice outside the provision of information about welfare rights, and that radical action must be centred on collectivities of various kinds. To accept such an assumption is to accept the dominant definitions of social work with individuals and families which centre on the goals of adjustment and resocialisation, rather than confronting such definitions and struggling to change them.[27]

Baldock in his critical consideration of patch, developed this point,

Although there is nothing intrinsically incompatible between patch organisation and casework practice, there is a distinct tendency in "patch" literature to denigrate casework as an activity.... Good casework is not only an essential service for certain vulnerable individuals. It is also the most radical element in current social work practice.... The need...is for a breakthrough to discover the real needs that casework can meet and its radical potential in its practical realisation of the common humanity of worker and client behind the masks of their state determined roles.... When clients evaluate social work or talk about the sort of social work they would like to see their perspectives often have much more in common with those of the best of the casework theorists than with those of the enthusiasts for "patch".[28]

It is ironic that as the political left has begun to rediscover the importance of "the personal" and communality through the influence of the women's movement, the liberal rhetoric of social services seems to be casting off both in favour of "community".

"COMMUNITY" AND THE REDEFINITION OF NETWORKS

The importance of "community" for patch and community social work arises from their emphasis on "community networks" and informal care. There is a strong flavour of nineteenth century nostalgia here. Two examples help us to begin recasting these issues in current terms.

Mackenzie's study of gender and environment, which we referred to earlier, leads to a very different view of networks than the one offered by patch proponents. Instead of focussing on them as a means of maintaining women's caring roles, she showed their relationship with women's liberation and equal opportunities, making the connection between women's networks and women's organisation. Mackenzie found that the extension of women's dual role in the home and labour market "motivated the development of a series of new organisational networks in the area of fertility control, child-birth, childcare and wage work, which were shown to be combining domestic-community and employment concerns".

More and more, the maintenance of the greater control women had over their "biological" and interpersonal family life called for the collective use of "social" facilities through which this control was made available. For some women, the maintenance of this control became a political priority, calling for an active defence and simultaneous critique of facilities. For some women, it also called for a growing range of alternative networks, to educate women in the use, defence and critique of these facilities, to simultaneously defend themselves against medical "dangers" and "inadequacies", and to provide alternatives which met their widening knowledge and needs. The provision of some control called for developing new networks to assure more and new forms of control. While most of the women I spoke to were not involved in political action around these issues almost all (the local women I interviewed) had opinions on and situated themselves with reference to various aspects of the activists' explicit critiques.[29]

The emerging networks Mackenzie described, like women's health, lesbian and peace groups, child care campaigns and women's centres, contrast with the kind of traditional domestic/care orientated ones patch has sought to mobilise or resuscitate. Indeed much of the opposition to increased unpaid caring responsibilities has come from women involved in these newer networks. Similarly networks have been developed among black, gay, elderly, disabled and other groups of people, which are concerned with countering prevailing views, prejudices and expectations of them, as well as offering alternative support services.

Earlier we referred to SCAN, the "Social Care Assembly for Normanton" and saw how it had been unable to offer local people the effective say in services originally envisaged. SCAN, however, found a new role during the 1984-1985 coalminers' strike. Its objectives had always included encouraging voluntary and informal networks, but this took on a new meaning during the dispute. "Community" was a word much heard through the year long strike. But this was no longer the traditional white male dominated "community" strongly associated with pit towns and villages — which interestingly have figured conspicuously as the location of much patch and community social work research. Instead it was a community where women took on new and equal roles — where close support came from other areas and other countries; and new links were forged with black people, members of other ethnic minorities, and gay people.

SCAN became the home of the local Miners' Support Group and offered it considerable support. According to SCAN's researchers, while the Support Group's primary task was of course to relieve hardship, this relationship led to other gains — in community activity in the town; in increased self-confidence and experience in organising among group members; and a greater knowledge among them of a whole range of local needs and issues.

> The Support Group has been the focus of a wider community involvement and has offered a new dimension to self-help and support in the town... SCAN has proved to be an ideal local forum to support the immediate concerns of the Miners' Support Group in Normanton.[30]

Sadly, having found a role, SCAN lost its funding. It became useful in a way that could not have been envisaged and may not have been intended when it was funded by the Home Office. Again it shows that community and networks can have other meanings than those associated with patch.

PATCH, STATE WELFARE AND PERSONAL RELATIONSHIPS

If informal networks cannot be equated with informal care, it remains the case that patch represents a different model of state social services, and one which at least acknowledges such networks. At the same time it entails a *shift away* from statutory to informal, voluntary and commercial services — especially in authorities like East Sussex. We may accept patch's criticisms of traditional social services departments as over-centralised, bureaucratic and crisis-orientated. But the question is why, cost cutting and ideological arguments aside, these have been seen as a reason for *turning away* from state services, like residential and domiciliary care, rather than *improving* them if necessary? After all, we know that other suppliers of services have their own problems and shortcomings; for example, the duplication and uneven distribution of voluntary organisations, and the poor quality control of commercial provision.

We have argued that there are particularly strong practical and ideological arguments against increased reliance on informal care — especially those relating to women's rights and equal opportunities. Yet informal care has been seen by many of patch and community social work's advocates as the major and ideal means of providing services. Judging from our study, people largely want to get their "care and support" informally, but as they recognise, this is not always possible or desirable for demographic, occupational, personal or other reasons. These contradictions raise a serious question about patch's strategy. Perhaps the answer is neither to restructure informal networks to "make them work" or to try and build formal services on their foundations, as patch has sought to do. Instead because people cannot always get the help and support they want informally, why not restructure statutory services to give them the qualities people value in personal relationships? Why not aim for informality, affection, accessibility and so on, while rejecting those characteristics that are regressive and discriminatory? Thus informal care and support would help serve as a *model* rather than a method of providing social services.

In our survey, two people described situations where the distinction between formal and informal support was apparently blurred by the overlap between neighbour and professional roles.

"The old lady across the road came to me and asked — as I'm a nurse — if I would be willing to come everyday or evening to see her husband who has bronchitis. She didn't want 'official' help but just informal help from 'within the community'. Quite a lot of people down the street are like that. My sister is a legal adviser and in her street the same thing happens. People pop in and want informal advice. Of course it's a very difficult position for both of us. We've full time jobs and can't possibly take on the problems of the street. But I do feel there is a need for a less official kind of help."

"The young woman who used to live in this house was a district nurse. She used to get all kinds of people from the neighbourhood knocking on her door asking for help at all hours."

These examples are interesting first because they show people needing help quite prepared to approach others for it. This contrasted with the reservations expressed in the survey about seeking or receiving formal or informal support. Second, and crucially, both were cases where a specific, recognised skill was involved and where its practitioners were personally known. Of course we are not advocating such an arrangement as a basis for services. It would be unworkable, overburdening and unacceptable. But it does offer insights for the organisation and operation of social services along the lines we suggest.

AMBIGUITIES AND OVERLAPS: PATCH AND THE WELFARE POLITICS OF THE RIGHT

We have talked about the restructuring of welfare by the right and clearly this has fundamental implications for patch and community social work. But what is also apparent are striking similarities between the two. Each, for instance, is concerned with a changed role for statutory services, the pluralist supply of welfare and an increased reliance on unpaid and voluntary services. In 1984 the Secretary of State for Social Services echoed patch advocates in arguing the importance of a local dimension to social services departments, saying that "services should be closely related to the neighbourhoods whose innate resources departments are seeking to mobilise and support".[31] His predecessor was a strong supporter of patch before taking on the brief of curtailing local political control through ratecapping and the abolition of the Greater London Council and metropolitan authorities.[32] Welfare pluralism has also been strongly associated with the Social Democratic Party, with its rightward shift, growing commitment to social market economic theory and talk of minimal "essential safety net" welfare.[33]

What can we make of this apparent overlap between patch and right-wing welfare ideology? Is there a qualitative difference between the two, or are the critics of community social work justified in seeing it as a smokescreen for cuts and reactionary policy? What quickly becomes apparent on close examination of patch and in discussion with its practitioners, is that quite different philosophies are attached to the same stated principles — which may help explain its wide political appeal. This is not only true from one authority to another, but at different levels within the same one. So while a council may adopt patch as part of a right-wing cost-cutting strategy, or indeed as a left-wing attempt to enlist popular support, social services workers meanwhile may see it as a means of making possible a better service for their clients and constituency.

Whatever the intentions of politicians or senior officers, some workers do report closer contact and better understanding with service users and other agencies, as well as a sense of increased accessibility and local involvement.[34] Such divergent aims, however, are likely to cause problems, particularly for practitioners. It is they who will have to face the strains of ensuring an adequate service with inadequate resources, or of mitigating the worst effects of reduced staffing and services.

This still leaves us and practitioners with an unanswered question. What is the essential thrust of a "community-orientated" policy? Is it in some way inherently progressive, or are workers only able to make some gains offsetting other basic deficiencies? There is no simple answer, particularly because, as we have stressed, patch and community social work are implemented in many different forms. Certainly we would argue that they are flawed by reliance on women's unpaid labour. There are also undoubted ambiguities. These are reflected in some of the tensions in patch; between the centre and decentralised teams; between enabling and orchestrating local involvement; between departmental constraints and local demands; and between the role of team manager as agent of the department and advocate for local needs. Patch highlights rather than overcomes the problems of local allegiance and departmental constraints that have always faced state workers.

The difference between patch as implemented and right wing Conservative welfare may turn out to be one of degree — if that. At the same time, the gains practitioners claim should not be minimised or ignored. But we can expect an increasing convergence between community social work and right wing philosophy in a harsh political climate, making it more and more difficult for workers to respond to local needs as they would wish.

SOCIAL SERVICES, THE MARKET AND THE NEW CONSUMERISM

Let's now turn to another development which highlights ambiguities in welfare politics. The emergence of arguments for patch, community social work and the pluralist supply of welfare has not resulted in a major expansion of voluntary agencies. The burden of informal care may have grown, but it was already being carried on a massive scale. What we have seen though, has been a great increase in commercial activity, both through the privatisation of welfare services and the growth of commercial provision. This has signalled a new interest in "consumerism" in social services. It is particularly significant that we find the idea of increasing citizens' and users' say and involvement couched in this market vocabulary. Thus according to its advocates, "we must work towards state policies that build on the strengths of a consumerist approach".[35] Such arguments about welfare reflect a wider political interest in consumerism, notably from the SDP, where individual credits, dividends and profit sharing are seen as a key route to increased consumer rights and social ownership.[36]

The market, however, has always produced its own idiosyncratic and many would say inegalitarian version of "public choice". Is the idea of consumerism likely to help advance the rights and say of citizens and service users, or does it merely reflect the market's increasing hold on social services? Why conceive of users of social services as "consumers" at all? It seems even less helpful than the euphemistic "client". Williams in his discussion of the choices that face our society has pointed out powerfully the defects of this passive and individualising figure — the consumer — whose needs are manipulated rather than met by the market.[37]

One argument, of course, is that private sector provision will be self-regulating, since its customers can switch their purchases and allegiance. This ignores the history of regulation in the commercial field. Products and services largely maintain safety and standards only so far as their makers and providers are compelled by state legislation and regulation. We can see this, for example, with car seat belts, lead in petrol and system-built housing — and such controls are not always adequate. The rights and say of users and workers are essentially subordinate to the key interests of owners and large stockholders.

Furthermore, commitment to the private sector often goes hand in hand with opposition to restrictions on it. How will statutory services maintain adequate control as their own provision dwindles and they become increasingly dependent on commercial services? Will a situation of unequal rights develop with users of statutory services having better safeguards and conditions than those in private provision? Whatever its limitations statutory provision is ultimately accountable to the elected authority. Commercial services are responsible to their shareholders. As for people having an increased choice, the relative share of the different suppliers of services is unlikely to be determined by people's preferences unmediated by economic considerations. What real option, for example, would people be offered by vouchers to choose between state psychiatric or mental handicap hospital or commercial provision, if the latter is inadequately regulated; or by tickets for respite care if spending cuts mean there is not enough to meet their needs?

One answer offered is that pressure would come from the consumer movement. Why not frame citizens' rights as consumers' rights, especially as people will be asked to pay directly for what they get? The difficulty here is that while the consumer movement has grown greatly in western market economies since the 1950s, it has met with limited success. In Britain there has been no discernible trend to improved rights, say or choice for producers or users of commercial goods and services. Instead we can see moves in the opposite direction, for instance, in the expansion of car-orientated retailing; the increased use of food additives; and the drastically reduced scope of Wages Councils. Should we hope for anything better in the social services? Perhaps we can expect less. The consumer movement has been most effective at the upper end of the market, but in economic terms, social services operate nearer the bottom.

Despite this, the view is increasingly put forward that the market has something to teach us about improving rights and choice in social services.[38] Laming, for example, looking to America, found private welfare agencies dominating service provision, while the planning agencies had little control or influence. Market forces, he concluded, "produce neither an efficient system nor relief for the tax-payer". Nonetheless, he still favoured a welfare pluralist approach for Britain, seeing it offer increased accountability and choice for the consumer. But why would a British version ensure "the guarantees against exploitation" and "assurances of minimal standards" the U.S. experience taught him were essential?[39] It seems highly questionable, especially since U.S. citizens have a range of legal and constitutional rights lacking here and states have a stronger tradition as regulatory bodies than British local authorities. To our knowledge, none of the welfare pluralists in Britain have come anywhere near arguing, for example, for such bodies as Massachusetts' "Office For Children". This state funded review agency was set up with direct elections, its own budget, paid staff and a legal framework giving local people substantial powers of inspection. The elected citizens' boards were encouraged to lobby officials and legislators, with legal powers to recommend the withdrawal of funding and cancellation of contracts for children's services.[40]

The prospects for anything resembling this in Britain seem poor, given the Government's response to initiatives such as those of the Greater London Council, funding a wide range of anti-discriminatory, locally controlled voluntary and community organisations — the equivalent of the U.S. non-profit private sector. Contracting out services looks far less likely to mean this kind of model, than the expansion of commercial provision with inadequate mechanisms for regulation and review which we are already seeing.

Perhaps the biggest difficulty in responding to consumerism is that it has many different strands, ranging from right-wing populism to left-wing libertarianism.[41] Questioning it, we can appear to be opposing free market forces; individual freedom to choose; or even the development of consumer protection. On the other hand, there may be more specific reasons for the case for citizens' rights and involvement in social services to be reframed in the economistic terms of consumerism. It may reflect increased recognition of the need for protection as people's vulnerability grows with the rising tide of privatisation. Alternatively it may serve as a way of disguising the damaging effects of privatisation. Given this ambiguity, it is all too easy to fall into the trap of advocating "consumers'" rights but succeeding only in sugaring the pill of reduced rights that privatisation actually brings. Rather than challenging it, we end up easing its passage and offering a rationalisation for it.

We can make more sense of consumerism if we start with a yardstick that respects users and providers of welfare services as citizens who should participate in the shaping and control of those services. The private market takes us no nearer this goal. However unsatisfactory the present statutory system, there can be no justification for adopting another which has always shown the greatest difficulties in reconciling the demands of need and those of profit. Arguments that the commercial sector offers better rights and redress than the public sector are as unsupported by evidence as assumptions of its greater efficiency.

The issues, as we have repeatedly argued, are about power; about participation and democratising services. It may be that one of the reasons for the appeal of consumerism, is its ability to depoliticise: to distance problems from their structural relations. Instead it emphasises deficiencies in relations between people as producers and consumers, rather than questioning their economic origins and the way people's wants and needs are turned into commodities.

CLIENTS' STRENGTHS OR PATCH'S WEAKNESS?

Patch and community social work place an emphasis on the capacities as well as difficulties of social services users. It is a welcome departure. We only have to recall that the British Association of Social Workers entitled a 1980 report on users' rights "Clients Are Fellow Citizens", as if making a remarkable discovery, to appreciate how ingrained patronising and condescending attitudes still are in welfare. Not only is this humiliating and degrading. It also misrepresents people's abilities and perpetuates their powerlessness. There must be recognition of people's worth and competence if they are to be enabled to take their own initiatives and achieve what they are capable of. So far, for example, it has more often been the limited expectations of agencies and families, rather than any inherent incapacities of their own, that have restricted the opportunities and attainments of people with mental handicaps. But there is an ambiguity to community social work's stress on users' and communities' "strengths". Rather than reflecting the recognition of their rights and abilities in the sense we have outlined, patch often seems to mean assessing their potential to provide unpaid or low paid care and support.[42] Thus people's "weaknesses" are where the department has to intervene; their "strengths", code for things it is thought they can do for the department or to relieve the department of further demands. Of course, we agree that people's own caring should be valued. But that is not the same as seeing it as a resource to be harnessed and extended.

IN WHOSE INTERESTS?

This brings us back to a recurring question. For whom do patch and community social work offer a solution? To whose benefit are they? Generally the impetus for them has not come from the service users, fieldworkers, local people and groups for whom the most gains have been claimed. On the other hand, they clearly help meet the needs of the academics, authorities and departments who have pressed their case, seeking or forced to find ways of meeting needs with reduced budgets. The development of patch and community social work has filled a vacuum. We can see at least part of the explanation for their successful rise in the confused role of social services departments and their uncertain relationship with needs and other services — just as this helps explain the effectiveness of right wing attacks on welfare.

Glennerster, in a critical consideration of community care, has suggested that the changing balance of demands on social services departments may challenge the rhetoric and rationales of patch and community social work. How, he has asked, will they maintain their community-centred and preventive approach in the face of the "qualitatively new burden on their resources" of growing numbers of frail elderly people and people with handicaps living outside hospitals, as well as statutory duties to regulate the rapidly expanding private sector?[43] We have already discussed the wide range of aims attached to patch and community social work. Whose interests they actually serve is likely to depend on where control lies. So far, as we have seen, efforts to extend control have lagged far behind attempts to extend responsibility. Meanwhile, the criteria by which they are judged and the definitions of success will not be those of their users, but of politicians and senior officers.

PATCH AS A POLICY

This study has raised some uncomfortable questions about patch and community social work. We certainly don't see that as reason to write off either of them. They have helped open up rather than close the kind of issues people raised in our research. However, as is often the case in social policy, epitaphs are now being written for decentralisation, too late to be helpful and just when managers and fieldworkers are faced with all the problems of implementation.[44] One aim of this study was to encourage discussion about this new initiative in social services and whether it matched people's needs more closely. We recognise that there is no uniformity about patch in theory or practice, but it does seem to have gains to offer. Localisation is likely to play a part in improving services, so long as equity can be achieved. We may live in a global village, but most of us are tied to place, whether by home or job. We are more likely to be mobile over time than from day to day. Patch promises services on a human scale that do not penalise people with limited mobility or without cars.

Decentralisation: A New Approach?

However, more fundamental questions about decentralisation need to be raised. Patch's advocates have not only offered it as a means of making services local, but closely associated it with a devolution of power. One of the strongest appeals of such decentralisation is that it allows people to build from their own local demands and solutions, freed from institutionalised ideology and aims from the centre, while rejecting inequity and discrimination. The reality of patch, however, is difficult to reconcile with such ambitious aims. This is especially true as patch and indeed more general decentralisation schemes are increasingly introduced from the top-down, with corresponding aims, ideologies and interests attached to them.

The diversity of these rationales and aspirations is itself significant; from increasing organisational efficiency and responsiveness and developing people's "political awareness", to gaining public support for Labour local authorities against central government, popular empowerment and "creating a new set of (socialist) social relations".[45] Left-wing populist schemes for decentralisation, for example, may no more follow from public preferences than their right wing equivalents. Decentralisation thus becomes just another local or indeed central government policy instead of a new approach to politics and policy development.[46] Whether such top-down schemes are consistent with the values and goals of patch is open to question, but any arrangements for decentralisation that remain subject to strong central control seem at least ambiguous and at worst no more than a rejigging of that control — as unfortunately appears to be the case in East Sussex.

New Policy Or Old Process?

Our examination of patch and community social work points to three particularly important issues. First, how far do they enable bottom-up accountability and extend public control and involvement? Second, do they help equalise the rights and opportunities of people facing discrimination? Finally, how do they relate to the perpetuation and resolution of human needs through other policies and wider social structure?

These issues are far from unique to patch, even if they are highlighted by it. They are crucial to any new approach to social services, and indeed to all public policies. But clearly numerous question marks hang over patch and community social work's performance in these key areas. The findings of the most detailed study so far of community-based services, the Dinnington action-research project — which really only explored the first two of these issues — are not encouraging.[47]

But it is not that we want to pursue now, so much as question the essential approach to policy development that patch and community social work reflect. Ultimately it is this which constrains them. They represent a valid attempt to reshuffle practice and provision within existing departmental and conceptual boundaries. We have, however, seen some of the problems of trying to do that, particularly in the comments of the people we interviewed. Patch social services did not seem to relate closely to the key needs they expressed. These overlapped into wider spheres of public policy — although they were still often unmet. Schemes for more general decentralisation at least offer the possibility of breaking down and redrawing departmental divisions, even if that is not their main concern. But there is a more basic issue here.

Patch and community social work have been offered as packages for improving the provision of social services. They have, however, been offered as answers without much clarity about what the original question was. Was it simply: how do we provide cheaper services and shift some of the responsibility away from the state, as cynics have suggested? Or are they concerned, as their advocates argue, with how best to relate services to people's needs, and work out the role of social services departments in relation to other interventions and collective action? Certainly, they have changed the relationship between people's needs and social services by trying to place greater weight on informal and other services. Whether this has improved the fit with need is more questionable — although as we have said, patch and community social work have doubtless brought some of their own benefits. This takes us to what we see as the central question.

Instead of starting with patch — or any other policy— surely it makes more sense to begin with needs. Then the form and function of services could follow from the needs they are intended to meet, instead of, as is now often the case, those needs having to fit in with what is provided. It is true that the recipes offered by patch are different from its predecessors'; more group and project work instead of casework. But they remain recipes from outside. If service users are now offered a self-help or support group rather than counselling, their part in this change of strategy is likely to be as limited as before. How though can we work out what services are required unless we first know what people want? The point we are making is that patch and community social work would only make sense as a *response* to people's needs, not as a panacea for them.

PATCH'S CONTRADICTORY PRINCIPLES

There is a real dilemma here for patch and community social work, because their proponents have expressed a *dual* commitment: to increased public involvement in social services in service delivery; and in the planning and control of policy and services. But are the two necessarily consistent? If people were given a greater say, would they opt for an increased emphasis and reliance on informal care and voluntary aid, as predicated by patch? The indications from our study are that they would not, but instead want alternative services. This question has not been properly put to the test, because attempts to give people a say in patch social services have fallen so far behind efforts to increase their involvement in providing services. If more progress is made to involve people in the development of social services, we may well see a major conflict emerging between two central principles of patch and community social work; those of *self-help* and *self-management*. This issue arises from including principles of policy alongside principles of political *process* in the patch package. Once people have the opportunity to influence policy development, there is no reason why they should adhere to a set of externally determined criteria to which they were not party.

THE PRIORITY OF PUBLIC INVOLVEMENT

Commentators and policy makers frequently insist that they are not offering "blueprints" and that their words should not be taken as "tablets of stone" — indeed these cliches are now firmly established in social service vocabulary. But this often seems to have less to do with a reluctance to offer prescriptions than with an inability to explain them in detail.[48]

The dominant tradition in personal social services as in British social policy generally has been prescriptive. This is as true of fabian and marxist analyses as of utilitarian and thatcherite ones. In spite of their participatory aspirations, patch and community social work have so far failed to break this mould.[49]

Instead of enabling a developmental process that involves people and makes it possible for them to ask their own questions, patch offers *its* answer. What sense does it make to start with a policy and then try and establish how well — or badly — it works? Yet that has been a consistent model for each new intitiative in social services policy, including patch and community social work.

This is where we part company with patch and why we see ourselves less as its critics — since it may have much to offer — than as patch agnostics. We take a different starting point. The development of any policy or provision should begin by finding from people what they want. Then it starts to be possible to work out what is needed. It seems sad, for example, that after five years action-research, the Dinnington Project could only conclude that "there was no clear evidence that it provided a more satisfactory service for users and carers".[50] How can we begin to establish what the needs are other than by first involving the people experiencing them? As we have seen in our project, this immediately puts the discussion in a broader context, pulling us away from existing conceptual and policy frameworks and drawing in all the wider issues of socio-economic structure, social relations and public policy. In our view, and we believe this study adds weight to it, any social policy initiative that does not start with the involvement of the people for whom it is intended, is likely to be as problematic as the policy it replaces. Constructing a policy like patch as the first step, and then imposing it from above as a participatory initiative, is a contradiction in terms.

FINDING WAYS FORWARD

We have placed weight on the fact that many of the people we interviewed knew little or nothing about social services and patch. It may be argued that this is neither remarkable nor inappropriate. Why should people be familiar with services most would not expect to use? But as we have contended, their lack of knowledge says something about the present nature of social services, as well perhaps as about people's unfamiliarity with and exclusion from public and political life more generally. It is crucial for patch and community social work that people don't see them as marginal. Both rely on their involvement in service delivery. If patch perceives people as a resource and is concerned to mobilise them, then surely they need to know about it, if they are to respond? People's involvement is not only necessary to meet patch's needs. More to the point, many people themselves want their say.

Of late there does seem to have been an increased awareness among conventional commentators of the importance of users' and local people's perspectives and involvement.[51] A new round of rhetoric for involvement, however, is rarely accompanied by much help towards *how* that can be achieved. The time has passed when recognising the need for an increased say for users, workers and local people was sufficient. Now we are faced with the task of making it a reality.

CHAPTER ELEVEN

Our Welfare: A Framework For Citizen Involvement

"Dialogue with consumers is fundamental to patch"

Director of Social Services, East Sussex[1]

INTRODUCTION

Making it possible for people to develop their own plans, policies and services is a massive undertaking. It entails an entirely different approach to social services. But the size of the overall task should not deter people from attempting at least some part of it. Nor should it be allowed to act as an excuse for inertia by authorities. Change can be achieved at different levels and to different degrees. There can be short and long term goals; small and large scale objectives. It may be embarked upon if community social work or patch based working is contemplated, has already been implemented, or if there is just a desire in a department or among some of its workers to improve the fit between service and users. While large scale change demands recognition of structural constraints and perhaps a fundamental shift in them, smaller changes are possible even with the restrictions on funding and policy now imposed by central government. There are changes that can be made in individual teams and departmental practice *now* — changes which have in some cases already been attempted. Increasing people's say in social services is not an all or nothing affair. Every small step taken is likely to have disproportionately helpful effects in building up trust, improving understanding and improving services — not least because of the poverty of such efforts in the past.

There is no ready-made model of how to involve people. We certainly wouldn't pretend to provide one and it is also unlikely to be what is needed. We have already pointed to some helpful examples of how people may be able to increase their say and involvement and there are undoubtedly others. But we still await a well worked out philosophy and practice. Much more thought and discussion needs to be devoted to this. What we can offer though are some sketches of how things might be. These have grown out of our own and other people's experience in social and other services and in community action. They are principles and processes that we have found helpful.

It may or may not be appropriate to talk of feminist ways of organising. What is certain is that the women's liberation movement has played a crucial part in raising the whole issue of how we organise and work together, changing thinking and practice. Our discussion is deeply indebted to feminist insights and scholarship.

We appreciate that much of what follows may be familiar to some readers already involved in such approaches themselves. Our apologies to them in advance; we aren't trying to teach our grandparents how to suck eggs! But we have seen much re-inventing of the wheel in efforts to involve people in social services and community work. The same difficulties are encountered without knowledge of how to deal with them and the same mistakes made time and time again. There may be little new to say, but there are innumerable unheeded lessons and much ignored or unreported experience. Patch and community social work provide poignant examples of this themselves. They often seem to be offered as if the experience of more than 20 years of community work was not there either to be acknowledged or learned from.

While we offer these proposals and ideas in the context of patch and community social work, they certainly don't only apply to them. They have a much wider relevance — to social and other public services more generally, to community work and community action, planning and general decentralisation schemes — wherever, indeed, there is a desire to increase people's say and involvement.

In our experience, both from this project and from training and discussions, the two major concerns of workers involved in a patch or community social work approach are developing team working and fostering relationships in their local neighbourhood. Both have tended to be neglected in the past, but they are of interlocking importance for involving people. Our discussion should be helpful for both. We see as the starting point the need to open up the debate on patch and community social work — the underlying aim of this book.

As we have seen, the debate has so far been a narrow one. In this it has been typical of social services more generally. The dominant voices have been those of white male academics and managers. Service users have not been involved. Most service workers and voluntary and community organisations have had little or no part to play in the initiation and discussion of the new policies.

If patch is to be a community orientated initiative in any real sense, it is essential that the debate is made more open. This doesn't only mean involving people in general debates about patch, but also drawing them into discussions about their *own* local social services. Conspicuously, neither seemed to be happening with the people we interviewed in Brighton. It is important that it does, both because people have a right to a voice in services that affect them, and because of the value of their insights and experience. Policy makers and academics must stop just talking to themselves. It is increasingly frustrating to read glowing accounts of patch and community social work schemes by their advocates and initiators, and tantalising to wonder what the people they are writing about would have to say — given the chance.[2]

PLAN OF THE CHAPTER

However many steps we take, we need to be clear of the direction in which we are going. "Participation" is conspicious for its pitfalls and ambiguities. It can be as powerful a means of preventing people's effective involvement as of making it possible. We've tried to offer some pointers and criteria to help people who want to enable citizen involvement and accountability pursue that goal. We don't offer them as a complete or definitive list. We'd be very grateful if people would feed back to us their own experience, any criticisms they may have and other ideas they have found helpful. We don't see our tentative proposals as a programme to follow precisely, but rather as a primer to help and prompt their own questions, decisions and ways of working.

This final chapter contains comments and ideas which are intended to be acted on. We start with a closer look at how people's accounts and views can become part of the policy process, comparing the standard approaches used with the dialogic one we have proposed. The second section deals with the need for new forums, and asks a number of questions, including who sets agendas, and whether involvement is sometimes best served by having separate forums for the agency and for people outside. In the final section, we begin to raise a number of specific issues about how involvement could be carried out. Each of these fits into the overall framework, although it may also be helpful to treat this section as a checklist for enabling citizen-involvement in services.

*   *   *   *

PART 1: NEEDS ASSESSMENT AND BEYOND

How can people be drawn in? In chapter 10 we argued that ways must be found of shaping services to meet people's needs. As we have also pointed out, this aim has frequently been interpreted to mean no more than that needs should simply be measured and assessed by social service agencies.

CONVENTIONAL APPROACHES

We have discussed the limitations of "consultation" and some of the methods used. The other main approach adopted has been "needs assessment". The

Barclay Committee, for example, saw this as one of the constituents of "social care planning", which together with face to face contact with clients made up "the two interlocking tasks of social workers".[3] In East Sussex, it is one of the seven elements which make up the Authority's "new approach" to decentralisation,[4] and formed the basis for two of the Department's area development programme projects.[5]

Some doubts and questions about needs assessment were raised earlier. Before going on to suggest alternatives, it may be helpful to set out our criticisms in detail. One starting point is the "Guide to the Assessment of Community Needs and Resources" produced by the National Institute for Social Work in 1975 and regularly reprinted and widely used since.[6] Its aims are:

> To strengthen the ability of area teams to assess the needs and resources of their communities and thus to prepare viable local plans for future service provision ... With adequate information about needs and knowledge of available resources, services may be planned in a more rational and comprehensive fashion.[7]

As well as improved planning, needs assessment is seen to offer other advantages. There can be better liaison with other statutory and voluntary agencies; more familiarity with local people and their problems; better knowledge of the local area, and information sharing. The guide proposes that all these can also be used to provide data to gain extra resources.[8] These have continued to be the main aims attached to needs assessment as it has become one of the basic "tools" used in patch and community social work.

The sources and methods for assessing needs and resources described by NISW have also become the standard ones, used in East Sussex and elsewhere. They include the collection of data on the area and its population from census and other local and national sources. Agency caseload and referral data are used, as is information from workers in other local statutory and voluntary agencies, and from local people. An assessment will look at the level and pattern of service provision in an area, and other resources and amenities, including "caring resources" provided by family and neighbourhood networks.[9] As well as collecting and collating existing data, the NISW guide recommends needs surveys and other more "qualititative" and informal methods of getting information — often from local people.[10]

Gathering information in this way is essentially an intelligence exercise. Not surprisingly, it raises concerns about people's privacy and civil rights. Pinker made this point forcefully in his minority Barclay Report, condemning the collection and storage of information without proper safeguards; perhaps without even the knowledge of the person concerned.[11]

Corporate management and "community involvement" were the rationale given for this information gathering in the NISW guide. However, by the time of the Barclay Report, as Pinker pointed out, the aims had altered to fostering a sense of community and helping to detect needs at an early stage.[12] It is difficult to see how the blanket collection of some of the information suggested would accord with any of these aims, or indeed how it could ever be justified, for example: Electricity Board warrants for disconnection of supply; notices to quit and evictions by court order of council tenants; decrees of divorce; juveniles cautioned by the police; families accepted under county council rent guarantee schemes, and prosecutions for truancy.[13]

Some of the methods advocated by the guide appear dubious as well as more than a little curious. For instance:

> There is a great variety of contexts in which the needs investigator can learn about the attitudes and opinions of locals... Much thought must be given to such approaches because the investigator runs the risk of making people so defensive or self-conscious that very little useful information is obtained. There are a number of devices that can be used to create a situation where the investigator can more naturally draw people into conversation about the locality. These include the use of a street map. If the investigator carries a map, and looks lost or puzzled, people will usually offer to help him (sic) and he can use this opportunity to extend the conversation to community needs...[14]

This might be laughable if it wasn't also disturbing. There is no indication of how local people or service users would have any control over the collection or use of such information and no apparent recognition of the need for such control.[15] The Barclay Committee, for instance, envisaged that it would be the social work team who, having assessed the levels of social needs, would decide on priorities and appropriate service provision, both for individual clients and client groups.[16]

Overall then, this kind of needs assessment is likely to be a one-sided affair, in which "the community" has little if any say. Its aims are set by social services, which initiates the exercise. It decides the indicators of "need" employed — like the census data on which East Sussex has placed considerable reliance. An assessment is as much concerned with "tapping resources" as identifying need. That is to say, the "needs" being met can become those of social services departments concerned to deflect the pressures of demands on *themselves*.

From all this it is difficult to see how community involvement would be fostered in the sense of any transfer of power to users or local people, giving them a say in the shaping of services. Needs assessment might actually reinforce rather than reverse the dominance of departments. It might have the effect of redistributing power and resources *within* a department. For example, an aim of the NISW guide was to increase social workers' participation in forming policy — which was felt to have been weakened.[17]

But this does not seem to extend beyond the boundaries of the department to local people and service users.

One of the East Sussex needs assessment projects we referred to earlier seemed to be aimed at extending participation. According to the team, the goal was "to work with the community to achieve collective tasks".[18] Yet the project itself was decided by the team and they designed and analysed the survey questionnaire. The Department fixed the timetable, which excluded community involvement even further. As the team explained, the Department "required regular short-term feedback on progress to social services colleagues, but the community steadfastly refused to move quickly enough for the team to do this as planned — we were governed by deadlines but they were not".[19]

As we argue later, this issue of time is a crucial one. Again, to quote the same project:

Sometimes the team were concerned that their pace was too hot, and that the project was becoming "ours" rather than the community's. Indeed some initial antipathy when the findings about isolation were fed back was attributed to a failure to keep in step with community partners.[20]

Although results were fed back to local agencies and individuals the team were in touch with, again it was the team alone who decided what action to take. This accorded with East Sussex Guidelines which set out that teams rather than local people or service users should determine priorities, assess needs and match resources to them.[21]

Another East Sussex team assessed the needs of old people. They wanted to find out "how they saw the situation" and share the results with them. Once again it seems that what came out of the exercise followed closely what that team originally proposed. Before making a survey, they thought a "drop-in centre" was needed for old people. After the survey, this became a "social club".[22]

To summarise, while needs assessment draws on people's views, in practice this seems only to inform and complement social services' existing perceptions and policies. Clearly this is a step out of the department's own cocoon. But it certainly is not any kind of partnership or involvement, as has sometimes been suggested.

BEYOND NEEDS ASSESSMENT TO DIALOGUE

Through local teams decentralised organisations should establish a dialogue with local communities so that the consumers of services and the carers can contribute to the development of services which are responsive to their needs.

"Guidelines For Decentralised Teams", East Sussex Social Services Department, 1984

Social services have in general been less concerned with matching services to people's needs than with arguments about which kind of agency and agency structure will best "go out to the community" and interpret "their" needs. The debate among writers on social services work has reflected this preoccupation.[23] Needs assessment in the form we have discussed it has also followed the same path. The agency or needs investigator, is seen as the central and active participant; users and local people are survey "respondents" who provide the data that is turned into the professionals' knowledge.[24]

If we are to go beyond this and involve other points of view as partners in a full sense, then we are looking for something other than more and improved needs assessments. How can people be more fully involved in the process of initiating, planning and eventually running the services they want to see? Clearly a non-participatory model of information gathering is hardly a good starting point for the kind of *dialogue* we advocate between people and social services.

Yet East Sussex and its Director have expressed commitment to such dialogue. Evaluating one of the needs assessment exercises, the team manager wrote:

The team has enthusiastically entered into a dialogue with this part of the patch and two-way communication is firmly established.[25]

But dialogue, like partnership, means more than seeking people's views and hearing what they say. Nor is it just offering people the chance to fit into agency agendas. We see it crucially as a two-way *continuing* process, rather than the one-sided, one-off "snapshots" that needs assessments tend to mean. This is consistent with patch and community social work philosophy. One of their principles is to seek to move service users on from expectations of individual relations with social services. The other side of this coin is to support people to get together in groups and collectivities to put their point of view and negotiate with social services departments.

We suggest in this book that people need the opportunity to develop their own accounts and judgements of existing services and what they want, as a basis for eventual decision-making. This in turn requires an exchange with greater equality and a mutually agreed process of talking and listening based on trust and understanding. In the case of a large institution like social services, with its regulatory powers, this is more easily said than done!

What we are proposing will require skills, experience and safeguards. It first of all demands that agencies themselves give up, or can be pressed into giving up, their reluctance to consider such a dialogue. But we are not so utopian as to believe that after this, everything will fall into place. We recognise the inherent difficulties involved.

People trying to develop such dialogues in other situations have encountered many problems: ensuring the rights of individuals; working through differences in language; finding common agendas; matching timescales; bridging differences in class, culture and power, as well as finding ways of overcoming rather than reinforcing inequalities attached to race and gender.

We would not propose such an agenda for social service workers, users and local people, if we had not met or heard of individual staff who try to build these sorts of relationships with services users, or if we were not convinced of the wish of many people to take part in such a dialogue.

Nevertheless, agencies and teams with this commitment face substantial difficulties which should not be glossed over with rhetoric or rose-tinted accounts of easy successes. In many ways this is uncharted territory. How do you make possible a dialogue which has a degree of equality, trust and shared agendas?

Teams trying to extend involvement are exposed to all these contradictions. So are service users and local people on the receiving end. People in a position to give power can also take it away. What equality can there be between a voluntary or community organisation and statutory social services if the former is dependent on the latter for funding? Agencies which seek wider involvement may manipulate people, inadvertently or otherwise, especially people who are inexperienced in working in such situations with others — as will often be the case. Another problem arises when a team has built its own common judgements about a range of issues. This is unlikely to be so for many local people and service users. Will the team be able to admit and listen to views that challenge the consensus it has achieved?

This raises the risk of incorporation, with the more powerful views of agency and workers outweighing others. It can also be divisive, with some users and local people allying themselves with the agency interest and point of view for the gains it can offer, while others are excluded or marginalised because their perspective or ways of working are not consistent with the agency's.

These are far from theoretical issues. Nor are we being overly pessimistic. We are describing well known if inadequately explored and reported problems in community work and community action.

UTOPIAN IDEAS OR PRACTICAL PROPOSALS?

Efforts to involve people not only face numerous obstacles, they also draw criticism from many quarters. It is still frequently argued that such ideas are utopian, impractical, naive, or even a diversion from efforts to bring about more fundamental change or to get on with the day to day job. The very fact that people are not now involved is put forward as a rationale for why things could not be different. "How would people know what to have?" "What would you do — just ask them what they want?" "How could it possibly fit into realistic time scales?" "Wouldn't you just be raising false expectations?" "People don't really want to get involved." These kinds of criticisms increasingly don't hold. More and more they look like excuses for an unwillingness or inability to go beyond rhetoric and begin the hard work of building wider involvement.

It will be hard to achieve. Dialogue and involvement cannot be taken for granted, and it isn't merely a question of asking people what they want. What is certain is that the claims made for patch and community social work won't be realised without the effort being made. On the other hand, we are not arguing for something completely new to be attempted. Although there is substantial pioneering still to do, some experience has been gained and advances made in various fields, from which we can learn.

Sometimes attracting people's involvement is not a problem. For example, many people are often drawn into crisis single issue campaigns closely affecting their lives. But it is after this that things can go wrong, restricting their involvement. We want to stress the importance of distinguishing methods of getting people together to start with, and ways of enabling that involvement once they have become engaged so that they can work and learn together. What are needed are forms or means both for attracting people's involvement and for realising and sustaining it.

There is also another point. People may see what we advocate as something already under way. Aren't teams and workers involved in daily discussions with individuals and groups? Isn't this an inherent part of their existing work? Many social services workers may insist that in at least part of their work they strive to put into effect the kind of approaches we recommend. In that case, the problem has two parts; to recognise and support work of this kind, and to extend it overall so that it can grow into the sort of dialogue we outline.

GIVING PRIORITY TO PEOPLE'S OWN ACCOUNTS

Throughout this book, we have stressed the priority we attach to people's own accounts of their wants and circumstances. This has been a guiding principle of both the overall project and this study within it. Beginning with people's own definitions and viewpoints is what good social service workers do in their daily practice. We suggest that this should also be seen as the basis for the development of policy and services. This makes particular sense given the changed orientation of patch and community social work from the individual to their milieu. The most progressive recent policies and services have either come directly from the people concerned — for example, lesbian lines and gay switchboards, rape crisis centres and the independent living movement — or from listening to what people want, as has been the case, for instance, with normalisation, self-advocacy and integrated education for children with special needs.

We have already touched on ways of enabling such discussion. Much experience has been gained elsewhere. Group work, assertion training, women's groups, black consciousness raising and health groups each provide insights and guidelines here. Conversations with people on their own and discussion groups may be helpful. Both have their own particular pressures and constraints which may permit or debar people from saying certain things.[26] We found that even in our interviews, people's thoughts about social services seemed to develop simply because they had an opportunity, perhaps for the first time, to focus on the issue. In our group discussions, as well as this happening, there were the additional effects of the interactions and dynamics of the group. Not only could individual views develop and change, from sharing information, experience and ideas, but so might those of the group. Other techniques have also been used, for example, video-recording interviews with individuals who have then agreed to come together to see the tape and talk about it. More ambitiously people's views can be put together as video programmes and these used as a basis for group or wider discussion. All these approaches give people the chance to formulate, reflect on, develop and exchange their views. What they may previously have seen as private feelings, experiences and troubles, they find are common, shared concerns.

What emerges is the complexity and changeability of people's perceptions and accounts. Cornwell in her discussion of health and illness in East London found that the people she interviewed gave different answers to the same questions at different times. Instead of dismissing this, she sought to make sense of it. She concluded that public accounts reproduced prevailing public assumptions — the socially acceptable point of view — while private accounts derived from personal experience and emerged when the threat of social judgement receded. The nature of the interaction between people and interviewer/expert — the degree of equality between them — seemed to determine which was presented.[27] Similarly a group of middle class women we spoke with in Brighton, gave the initial impression that loss of independence and lack of collective child care were not issues for them. But they went on to discuss among themselves the way their lives and careers had been restricted by marriage and children. All this emphasises the need to move away from static, opinion poll approaches to people's wants and views. As we said before, just asking people what they want is as likely to distort as to enable them to express their feelings and experiences.

CITIZEN RESEARCH

We've referred before to citizen or "participatory" research as a description of the approach we advocate. A brief sketch may be useful, especially as the word "research" may seem removed from the notion of involving users and local people. It is used here in the sense of a *critical investigation*. Most important, the investigation and the critique belong not ot the "experts" or "professionals", but to people as citizens.

This kind of research differs fundamentally from conventional needs assessment exercises, and indeed from research more generally, in its emphasis on empowerment and popular control. Hall has provided a useful summary of what participative research tries to achieve. His description also makes it clear why and how it fits the argument we have put forward.

> Participatory research is most commonly described as an integrated activity that combines social investigation, educational work and action.

It seeks to involve people in the workplace or community in the control of the entire process of the research. It aims to benefit them by strengthening their awareness of their own abilities and resources. The "researcher" in such a model includes both the outsiders with specialised training "who must be committed participants and learners in a process that leads to action rather than detachment" — and the community and workplace people involved themselves.[28]

The creation of "popular knowledge" is a key goal here. Again, to quote Hall:

> For many participatory research is a process by which the "raw" and sometimes unformed — or, at least, unexpressed — knowledge of ordinary people is brought out into the open and incorporated into a connectable whole through discussion, analysis and the "reflected" knowledge gained with or without allied intellectuals...[29]

The value of research is to be judged

> not in terms of static description but...of the ability of the researcher to feed back the research work into a form of practice with the population with whom (s)he is working.[30]

Participatory research is both based on a process of dialogue and seeks to enable it. It is this approach we have sought to follow in our project. The survey we have reported was not undertaken so that a book might add to some specialist "body of knowledge". The process of carrying out the survey and of feeding back the results — in this book and in shorter pamphlet form — is aimed at opening up discussion among and between people in Brighton, and hopefully elsewhere, about social services. As we explained earlier when describing our approach to this study, besides the local survey, our main method has been a process of group discussions involving over 50 groups in Brighton. Some came together for the project; others already existed. People taking part included social services users, workers and local people. Discussions involved many different viewpoints and issues: being a woman with small children, living in an old people's home, having a mental illness, being a single parent, bereaved, or involved in a voluntary project.

We are not suggesting this is the only possible model, or that we solved the problems of involving people in what was, after all, a very limited project, working with minimal resources. But we believe that other attempts to work participatively will share our main concerns. First, to enable people whose views have not generally been sought or listened to on these issues to have a chance to express, exchange and develop them. Second, to develop as democratic a process of discussion and research as possible, which aims to ensure participants the maximum feasible involvement in and control over the process and its outcome. We have tried to do this so far by tape-recording discussions with people's agreement, returning transcripts for comment, and meeting with people again to update and discuss their contributions.

This kind of participatory approach is being developed in a variety of different ways and contexts, quite often by people who might not recognise what they do as "research". We have come across the explicit use of a participatory research model, for instance, to explore ideologies of community work in a dialogue with community workers; to work with council tenants to discover what if any facilities they wanted on their estate after a short-term voluntary project came to an end, and how they could control them; and to work with a collectively managed welfare team to describe and understand how they run.

The same principles and ideas are at work in many other situations. For example, a group of parents of under-fives getting together, with outside support, to work out what child care services are wanted in their area; designing and carrying out the research themselves and being paid to do it. Similarly, members of an unfunded community group learning how to represent themselves and campaign over planning public inquiries, and getting the information and evidence to fight their own case.

As we have seen in this study, people do have views and ideas about social services. Because these have usually been kept at arm's length, they are often restricted to individual thoughts, private conversations or informal discussions. Generally they do not get on to the agendas of wider or more influential debates.

We have described ways in which people could move beyond personal discussion to become part of a public debate and, by interacting with it, their views and ideas develop and gain greater equality with those of professionals and policy makers. Until this begins to happen, their views of social services will continue to be hampered by low expectations, deference, uncertainty and lack of confidence. At the same time, much of what we "know" of these views is itself based on research approaches which may distort it. The kind of dialogic approach we advocate is concerned both with equipping and supporting people to engage in debate, as well as giving priority to their involvement in such a process.

FROM PERSONAL EXPERIENCE TO PUBLIC ISSUES

We see the process from people putting together their own accounts to forming agendas and judgements about what they want and what to do as a continuing one. Ideas develop, opinions change. Personal opinions inform and give rise to collective views. Through a process of discussion, learning and negotiation, personal positions and needs grow into group judgements and demands. Our experience is that such discussions are best framed initially in terms of people's perceptions of their own circumstances, wants and needs, and not in terms of services. The latter can unnecessarily and unhelpfully limit their thinking to existing services they know of. People are far more likely to know their own needs than what services would best fit them. They may be unaware of the options available, although equally, they may hear about interesting initiatives elsewhere, with which their own department and its workers are unfamiliar.

What comes next is the process of working out how their needs might then be translated into policies or services that can meet them. This is one of the areas where skilled support is important. Seeking to involve people in service and policy development and management does not take away the need for independent skills as is sometimes suggested, but it does call for a changed relationship between those with such skills to offer and the people with whom they work.

A supportive rather than directive role is needed. This and other kinds of assistance are crucial through all the stages of public involvement if people are to gain the necessary confidence, information, and abilities to make the contribution they want to. Different people need different degrees and kinds of support. Some may be used to working in such situations. More may not. Flexibility and sensitivity are crucial. One form of support that is always likely to be valuable is expert advice, for example, about local and central government procedures, structure and regulations, social services department legislation and responsibilities, or the detail of available forms of provision. But at least as important, if less often recognised, is the need for support and guidance for people trying to work together, possibly for the first time in such a formal setting, perhaps as service users, or in a mixed group also including service workers, local people and groups.

Rules and structures are needed if individuals, especially those who are less experienced and conventionally articulate, or who face institutional discrimination, are to be able to express their feelings and arguments with as much weight as anybody else. Gibson, for example, described a planning meeting where each of the officials and professionals present:

was labelled so that residents knew who did what. The rule was that if you wore a label you couldn't speak until you were spoken to by a resident. This kept the initiative where it belonged — with the residents.[31]

Such rules and structures should be supportive of participants' own forms, language and ideas. They have to ensure they have time and space for themselves if and when they want it.

Support can sometimes blur into direction. The distinction between the two is not always clear and it is important to be conscious of this danger. It is easy to guide inexperienced hands unintentionally. Social workers, for example, sometimes underestimate their considerable powers, both statutory and personal, over users because of their own limited control over their agency. Residents in a tenants group where we live were deferential to the local authority community development workers who intervened in our housing problem. While they may have seen themselves as radical activists, tenants still acquiesced to them as council officials. For this reason we think it is important to have consultants and supporters who are independent of the agency or organisation seeking to involve people. And even those who are primarily employed because of some technical or social services' skill or experience, should have an understanding of the collaborative working and organisational issues we have raised.

FROM CITIZEN AGENDAS TO PUBLIC POLICY

The final stage in the process of public involvement we have outlined is converting people's agendas, judgements and demands into agency decisions and action. This can be the most difficult and daunting part of the process. This is not only because of any eventual unwillingness of the agency actually to do what people want, but also because it is at this point that the different often conflicting cultures, structures and ways of working of citizen and state come into closest contact. The prevailing pattern is for decisions to be made from above to be implemented from below. Decision-making also tends to be seen as the end of the story, just as getting married is in popular romantic fiction. In fact it is very much the beginning, especially now in times of retrenchment and financial constraints. The East Sussex patch reorganisation itself offers a pertinent example. The formal decision to "go local" was made in 1981, but the actual process of implementation has been going on ever since, with frequent delays, hiccups and modifications. Indeed, we have observed a number of patch reorganisations where surprisingly little attention seems to have been paid to the ramifications for staff, training, premises, resources and organisation at the time the key decision is made.

The model of policy development we have outlined is significantly different, since the process of initiation, discussion and the forming of judgements extends to the level of implementation and the practicalities and responsibilities of realising policies and services. The emphasis is much more on people at all levels, outside as well as within the agency, discussing and thinking through the *whole* process of policy development. Thus by the time some consensus is achieved and a decision might be made, they will have a much clearer idea of what they intend and how they will achieve and implement it. There is much less stress on the often rather artificial notion of decision-making that informs and indeed frequently confuses and obscures most conventional policy development.

Problems may not arise in attempting this new participatory approach if the issue is a very local one or one involving very limited resources — for example, the expenditure of a small sum allocated for "community use". But if it has wider ramifications, concerns a significant change in policy or provision, or issues of workers' or users' rights, then difficulties can be expected. Then too, the whole issue of the relationship between efforts to enable broadbased involvement and existing arrangements for local representation and decision-making arise. Put like this, the issue may seem obvious. But what is clear, for example, is the surprise shown by many well-intentioned local councillors when they realise that their decentralisation initiatives have implications for their *own* position as elected members. "Where does that leave us?" they ask. This tension must be understood and faced if "community involvement" is really to progress.

SUMMARY

Effective dialogue between agency, users, workers and local people is not just a means of developing appropriate services, but of making services democratic. Services that are structured, planned and run democratically will reflect and change in accordance with people's own definitions of their needs and demands.

We have said that efforts to involve people should be a collaborative process containing three interlocking elements which bring together both learning and action. These are:

1. The expression and development of people's own individual and collective perspectives and accounts, building shared meanings.[32]

2. The forming of their agendas and judgements about what to do.

3. Agency action and decision-making based on these.

We would stress that this is a process rather than a set of rigid procedures. Nor are the three elements separate from each other. It will also be apparent that this involves the construction of new kinds of open forums. This is the issue we turn to next.

* * * *

PART 2: CREATING OPEN FORUMS

The idea of partnership implies a high level of honesty and *openness*. "Partners" have to trust each other and speak their minds — about plans and information, about their views and feelings. They need to know whether or not they agree. Just as clear is that creating a space where people feel able to speak freely, often depends on having barriers to outsiders. We can see this, for instance, when a group of black women feel able to "open" up to each other, partly because they can exclude anyone who isn't a black woman.

There are tensions here which don't disappear when an agency adopts the aim of "partnership" with users and local people. Nevertheless, we suggest that to be effective this change of policy must carry a very substantial degree of openness. Perhaps the simplest solution is to reverse the normal assumption and ensure that things should be open unless there are good reasons against it. Otherwise there will be major difficulties. For example, the problem with most efforts to involve people is the failure to tell them the whole story. The sense of let-down that follows is likely to leave a worse situation between agency and people than there was before.

Are staff inside the agency prepared for the openness this demands? Have people thought about the reality of more transparent relationships, and how far this may challenge existing links between elected members and officers; or among the different parts of an authority or department? Take, for instance, a departmental culture which stifles criticism and dissent.[33] If this persists it is likely to undermine the process of open dialogue with users and local people.

Another way of putting this is to say that workers need to be candid about their agendas with each other as a condition of being clear to people outside. The decision for involvement might come at agency, team or sub-team level. There must be clarity among those involved about what exactly is being offered or negotiated. This isn't a matter of leaving the responsibility — or passing the blame — to another level in the hierarchy. At whatever level the decision is made, the politicians and staff concerned must be prepared to accept responsibility for their own views and obligations.

There is unlikely to be a consensus at departmental level. There may not be even at team level, because of competing interests, points of view and aims. But if there cannot be debate leading to agreement about the extent of involvement or the obligations that have been accepted, then both the people asked to participate and eventually the team itself are likely to suffer. What will almost certainly ensue are confusion misrepresentation and distrust.

This emphasises the importance of improving communication within departments. That begins with personal practice and extends to policy and service development. How open are we as workers with each other and in individual dialogues with clients? How open are our departmental assessments and records? Social services departments have been notoriously fragmented, and one of the major positive aims of patch has been to break down divisional divides. But there is still much to be done in most departments, for example, to develop dialogue between field, day and residential care workers, who frequently remain isolated and alienated from each other.

We don't ask that all conflicts be settled or reconciled before the involvement of outsiders can begin. But differences within an authority or department may intrude into or compromise any project to involve people. They should either be negotiated in advance, or if irreconcilable, recognised as a possible reason for postponing or abandoning the exercise, or placed on the agenda for proper negotiation by *all* participants.

AGENDAS

We have used the word "agenda" to mean the different aims and reasons people have for entering a process of involvement. This is not simply a metaphor for an implicit list of things that the different parties might want to come out of it. It also refers to the fact that agencies and their workers don't operate in a policy vacuum. They will have their own reasons for trying to involve people. In a completely literal sense, any initiative aimed at involving people will be constrained. There will be a number of "items" that are not open to negotiation or manoeuvre. For example, social services departments have to follow the policies of the majority party. They have statutory responsibilities, although it is worth saying that these are subject to wide interpretation. Some items *ought* to be included. Anti-discrimination should be on any agenda. At the same time it is important that people aren't presented with the social services department's terms of reference — for example, its way of doing things, as if these were the only ones. Instead they should be encouraged to look beyond them.

As we have said, there may also be conflict and disagreement within the agency. Agendas may be at the level of an authority or department talking about involving people and responding to what they want in its overall operation[34] or of a patch team who want local people to participate in deciding how a small budget they've been allocated should be spent. It is important that workers are clear among themselves, and to users and local people, where the initiative is coming from, and if there are internal disagreements about the agenda. There are many impetuses for such initiatives. They may arise from something specific, like the commitment of a particular team or the appointment of a new manager, or alternatively from a new departmental policy. Initiatives in one part of a department may or may not be taken up elsewhere. We saw how in East Sussex efforts to involve people arose from the Department's new area development training programme.

We are not saying that a team or department can or should leave its own agendas out of wider negotiations. Nor are we suggesting that they must do whatever members of the public tell them to. But there are inherent conflicts and contradictions in an agency bringing its own predetermined agendas into any process of involving people. It is essential that differences between the agency's agendas and those of users and local people are acknowledged. And the key point for us is that agencies and workers must recognise and tell people what the limits are. They must be open about how far their agendas are fixed, and how far negotiable. Only then are agendas truly open to challenge by people, and conflict and negotiation can be overt rather than hidden. It is one thing for an agency to feel that the process should have a focus — child care, for example — although this may not be what people outside would choose. It is quite another for the agency to go into a process, supposedly of public involvement, when it has determined on a particular child care policy in advance, for instance, support for playgroups rather than day nurseries.

This is not an isolated argument, but one that clearly emerges if we look at the issues in a wider context. Parenti, for example, in his study of power and pluralism "viewed from the bottom", argued that:

> One of the most important aspects of power is not to prevail in a struggle but to predetermine the agenda of struggle — to determine whether certain questions ever reach the competition stage.[35]

Gaventa, discussing power and powerlessness, saw another level to the problem:

> Not only might A exercise power over B by prevailing in the resolution of key issues or by preventing B from effectively raising those issues, but also through affecting B's conceptions of the issues altogether.[36]

AVOIDING A STAGE ARMY

One particular sort of hidden agenda requires further comment. There is a temptation for authorities, departments, teams and workers to seek to enlist public involvement in support of their own policies and plans rather than to enable popularly based ones. For example, councillors have often looked to community groups to strengthen their position in the council chamber. Fieldworkers with little power of their own, trying to advance their own progressive policies and practice in the face of obstruction or inertia from their departments, understandably turn for support to service users, local people and groups. We are not suggesting they should not. We would want to draw a distinction though between this kind of campaigning, and a strategy which is concerned with broadbased democratic policies and services.

In the same way, decentralisation has been adopted by some left Labour local authorities like Hackney as a way of raising people's political awareness. But if what this actually means is "educating" the local electorate to support council policies against central government, it may be both patronising and populist. Instead of people's involvement becoming the basis of council policy, they may actually only be being invited to endorse it.

It is crucial that citizens are not just seen as foul weather friends to be called upon in times of crisis. The question is will local councils' and departments' interest in "community control" wane if and when the political climate improves and their independence and resources are restored? If it does and no ways can be found to renew their commitment, then any public confidence that has grown in local government is likely to be replaced by cynicism and anger.

We want to state this very clearly. Participation does not mean tagging people's involvement on to an already decided agenda, with little or no negotiation or modification possible. The result will at best be tokenism, and at worst incorporation. Using service users and local people to legitimate the agency's own policies, or as a stick to beat the agency, trade unions, or grassroots workers, is unlikely to advance their effective involvement. It is more likely to reduce them to the role of stage army.

These criticisms are not confined to local authorities and their officers. For example, the same problem is especially common in community work and community action. A pattern in community work is still often for a group of paid workers or community activists to work out their own programme or idea. Only then do they seek wider support by enlisting other people. But the proposed idea is presented as something that has come from service users and local people and is *"theirs"*. This is plainly not the same as first finding out what people want and then working with them to achieve it.

In community work as in local authorities, there are two reasons why this often happens. First there is a poor fit between popular process and that of conventional policy funding and development. Second there can seem to be a conflict between achieving objectives and involving people in the process. What may be forgotten is that the objective isn't just setting up the playgroup or establishing the community building, but getting the policies and reforms that people want. This can only be achieved with their involvement. We know of many examples where projects have materialised in the name of local tenants or services users who had little effective say in their development at any stage. In one case, for example, community workers succeeded in setting up a community association when what most tenants had actually wanted was to leave the estate. But this was not placed on the project's agenda.

COMMON OR SEPARATE FORUMS?

It follows from our argument that in some situations there may be so many constraints that effective involvement is unlikely to be possible. It is essential to analyse each situation to see what if any room for manoeuvre there actually is. If the policy or service, time scale and resources are all fixed, what is there for people to be involved in — beyond minutiae? As we have stressed, the actual position and all its ramifications should be communicated to the people who might become involved. It is for them to decide if the effort and possible gains justify taking a particular risk. But they need all the information that is available to make this decision to the best of their ability. There will be many occasions when immovable agendas debar effective involvement and decide people against seeking it. But there will be others where open negotiation and bargaining may be appropriate and necessary between people within and outside the department.

Just as there are some issues which an agency will not put up for negotiation, and internal forums it will want to retain for discussion of policies, so, as we suggested, the same will be true for many people and groups who may not want to develop their own accounts and perspectives under the aegis of social services. They may prefer to do so independently, and come together after achieving some solidarity and agreement. Such a relationship with an agency need not be combative. It could actually reduce the risks and fears of co-option and strengthen the possibility of a more egalitarian partnership. Social services could facilitate this by funding people to get together in this way — without strings. It is also likely to increase the possibility of initiatives for involvement coming from outside the agency. Knowledge that the department would welcome it, could itself encourage such initiatives.

Similarly, many social services workers may only want to get involved in negotiations with their department through their trade unions. Unions, particularly NALGO have been criticised for their response to decentralisation proposals in some Labour local authorities. Here the rhetoric and practical politics of participation come face to face. But at least part of the responsibility belongs to local councils who approached the issue in the traditional way of public participation exercises. They expected workers to respond to their often unclear proposals without offering them commitments. This did not accord with trade union ways of working and inevitably raised their suspicions and distrust. Significantly, when the London Borough of Islington's Chair of Decentralisation addressed around 50 workplace meetings, it was with the Union's proviso that he was to answer questions not canvass opinions. Authorities should offer information instead of expecting workers' views to be given unconditionally.[37]

Social services' workers who opt for involvement through their trade unions, may find themselves in the ambiguous position of seeking users' and local people's participation on other, less satisfactory terms. Even workers with little say in their agency do have the support and protection of their unions. Service users and local people at most may only have the help of small community groups and associations. It is important to consider ways in which workers can overcome possible dilemmas posed by being expected to involve people on potentially unequal and inferior terms.

We recognise that what we have argued could be described differently. Discussions about community work and community action tend to classify community involvement according to two alternative models; consensual and adversarial. *Consensus* involves the search for common interests and agreement — often excluding the realities of conflict. *Adversarial* models stress the conflict of interests. But in discussing shared or separate forums, we are not suggesting such a simplified typology.

As we accept, a focus on consensus may lead to co-option. On the other hand, the adversarial approach frequently contains elements of hidden agreement and negotiation that make it more complex and colluding than first appears. An example of this is the "radical" community group or project which is actually closer in culture and experience to the authority with which it is in conflict than to its nominal constituency. Polarising approaches as either attacking the council or trying to work from within, is neither helpful nor accurate.

The kind of dialogic politics we are advocating would challenge and move beyond this. Dialogue may start from within an agency, or from people getting together outside. But either admits of both conflict *and* cooperation. Participants collaborating with agency initiatives would do so within a framework of rights and rules. People developing their own discussion and demands could expect to enter into dialogue with a department without sacrificing their independence. Citizens may be engaged in discussion with the authority at one point and then step back to discuss their own plans and position at another.

This relates to another issue. It is frequently assumed that the three key interests on which we have focussed in this project; service workers, users and local people, are essentially antagonistic. This is offered as a strong argument against the possibility of increased participation. Service users are frequently presented as stigmatised by and distanced from other local people. Inherent conflicts are seen between service users and workers. There is some truth in this view and we don't assume a false consensus between these groups. However, not only does it underestimate the extent to which such roles are interchangeable: today's worker may be yesterday's local resident and tomorrow's old person receiving domiciliary services. It also overlooks the extent to which such polarisation is itself the product of existing marginalised services, and an argument *for* their democratisation rather than against it.

This leads to a further point. In developing schemes or structures for involving people in services, it is important to guard against perpetuating such artifical divisions. Thus drawing users and local people into forums created by the local state, which can then become part of its apparatus confronting workers and their unions, is unlikely to be helpful.[38] Local authorities have tried to enlist the aid of the public to support them. It is likely to be more feasible and more productive to develop joint forums and alliances between workers, users and local people. We already have examples of such collaboration, for example, between tenants associations and trade unions over estate repairs and maintenance, and claimants and social security staff over cuts in welfare benefits services. Such forums would not replace or conflict with those of individual groups like service users, but offer additional opportunities to develop dialogue between them.

PARTICIPATION FOR BETTER NOT WORSE

There is another vital issue to be considered if we are concerned with public involvement that is to the benefit of participants. It cannot be assumed that people want to be involved at any cost, or on any terms, or even on every issue. It is questionable, for example, whether people would want to participate in the running and decision-making of a service which they saw as basically unjust, inadequate and unsuitable, like, for instance, the present supplementary benefits system.

Participation may not be an imposition in principle, but it is frequently reduced to one in practice. Given central government cuts in public resources, increased public involvement and control may be a very mixed blessing. With severely reduced expenditure, people are likely to have more responsibility than power. They may be put in the invidious position of being involved in rationing decisions and trying to maintain services without adequate resources. Public involvement in the management and control of services, could become as burdensome and unacceptable as women's increased involvement in the provision of services as unpaid and low paid carers.

Such citizen involvement seems like an extension of the patch approach to decentralisation which devolves increasing responsibilities to neighbourhood teams while overall resources available to them decline. At a time of unprecedented cuts, it is important to guard against people's involvement in social services mainly resulting in them being drawn into divisive decision-making, with increasingly fraught responsibilities offloaded on to them. All the same, people could still play an important part in ensuring that remaining resources were matched more closely with need, as well as being able to strengthen their position to press for more.

DISCUSSION

Again, we will briefly restate some of the main points, and ask some questions. It will be clear that we advocate as open an agenda as possible. We mean "open" in two senses: that what is already on it is spelled out plainly and honestly to people; and that the development of the agenda is as mutual a process as possible — the beginning of the dialogue we have discussed. There are tensions between these two meanings. They shouldn't be fudged. A commitment to open agendas may limit the scale or range of issues that can be brought into public debate — at least initially. But it is much more likely to result in effective involvement.

Openness is as important for the *forms* of participation as for its objectives. The methods of involvement will affect who becomes involved and thus the outcome of involvement. Service workers may gravitate to a conventional model they are familiar with, for example, of meetings leading to a formal committee or steering group. But what ideas have possible participants got? How would they like to get together; through groups they are already involved in, or perhaps by setting up a new ad-hoc grouping? This needs to be an early item on the agenda.

If distrust colours many people's reluctance to get involved, the willingness of others is often accompanied by a hopefulness and political innocence that is a fragile but precious contribution. It is vital not to make promises that cannot be kept. It is essential to minimise hidden agendas.

We are not suggesting that agencies are likely to be deliberately dishonest. But there can be a problem of people not being kept fully informed of all that's going on or is likely to happen. This can often be because the agency or individuals concerned assume that people know something because they do. This happened to us as tenants. After the Council tried to compel the landlord to carry out repairs, he sold the block to escape his obligations. "It's a common tactic", the community worker then told us tenants. But he hadn't mentioned it before and had we all known, we might have approached the issue in a different way.

Knowledge is power and a crucial part of the openness we are talking about concerns access to information. This can include information about how the agency works, about helpful service initiatives elsewhere or indeed successful ways of involving people. It raises the whole question of how we acquire and share knowledge and information. Much of it comes from formal and informal discussion. But there is also the recorded information of the printed page and electronic media. We have seen in this study how little most people knew about social services. Blaming this on "public ignorance" is tautological and takes us nowhere. Departments are tied to their own ways of thinking and information tends to be organised accordingly. We have to break out of this. Greater *accessibility* is what is needed. Much more work needs to be done to find ways of improving the storage and exchange of such information, both within agencies and among their constituencies.

Some pioneering work is already being done. Finding space and mood for specialist reading is a problem for many service workers and even less likely as a day to day activity for the rest of us. We need to develop better ways of presenting information to make it more appropriate and responsive in form, language and content to meet people's different class, cultural and other expectations and demands. One of the successes of the community action and welfare rights movement of the 1970s was the accessible information they disseminated about specific issues like how tenants could get their housing repairs done or trace what company owned what assets in their neighbour-hood. Information and discussion about social services has to be brought off the library shelves into the public domain. The more citizens know about social services, the more they will be able to negotiate and manage them — instead of vice versa.

* * * *

PART 3: SOME PRACTICALITIES OF PUBLIC INVOLVEMENT

Let's now assume that a public agency has made the decision to embark on a process of public involvement — or had it made for it. How in practice would we envisage an effective outcome being achieved? We have encountered many people working in departments which have either switched to patch and community social work or are contemplating doing so, who have received little support or guidance in how to work in the new "community-orientated" way. It is also sad to witness the representatives of agencies, very often with genuine commitment to the idea, announce that the "consumer" view is now being heard, when in fact they have failed to provide the means to enable it to happen.[39]

On the other hand, we recognise that there will inevitably be problems and shortcomings in any attempt to involve and empower people, however carefully the process is set up. We have found it far better to recognise the difficulties and constraints at the start than to learn them by bitter experience. The reality will always fall short of the aspiration. That is no reason for abandoning the effort or for not getting involved, but it does emphasise the need to do all that's possible. It is only when efforts to involve people are taken out of the realm of rhetoric and the extraordinary, and grounded in a thorough appreciation of reality, that they are likely to succeed. There are steps that can be taken to minimise the difficulties.

Having discussed some general guidelines, we now take up a number of more detailed points, offering our suggestions. The topics covered are listed next. They are not intended to be comprehensive, nor the last word on each point. We will have succeeded in our aim if people find our comments and observations sparking off their own.

1. *Involving People From The Start.* A suggestion that we should start as we mean to go on.

2. *Making Commitments.* Agencies must be prepared to act on the results of public involvement.

3. *Modest Aspirations.* A plea for small beginnings.

4. *Developing Skills And Learning Together.* Participation entails education.

5. *Resource Implications.* Agencies will need to make space and time for the new approaches, as well as finding money and other resources to tackle new work and maintain the old.

6. *Rights And Safeguards.* Equality in participation and services.

7. *Self-Help And Self-Management.* The two should go together.

8. *Participation And Power.* Can we overcome inequalities and achieve a partnership between citizens and services?

1. INVOLVING PEOPLE FROM THE START

Public participation has long raised uncomfortable questions about who it is for and why it is initiated. This has generally been because the initiative has not come from those whose involvement is sought and the objectives and benefits have frequently been ambiguous — to say the least. The fact that the initiative comes from an agency rather than its constitutency, however, should not be seen as an argument against it. The natural expectation of most of us is not to be involved in public policies and services. Britain does not have a strong tradition of participative democracy. We should therefore not be surprised or offput if initiatives for public involvement are not broadbased.

For these reasons, and for the others we have raised before, it is essential that any attempt to involve people is as carefully thought out as possible from the beginning, and seeks that involvement at the earliest possible stage. Both points are crucial. We must not let our enthusiasm for the principle stop us asking some basic questions — however much this may feel like pouring cold water on the idea. Why do we want to get involvement? Do we really want to have it? Do we recognise it means a loss of power? Have we that power to give away?

We place such a strong emphasis on starting as you mean to go on because once the process has begun, it becomes increasingly difficult either to stop it or to put it right. It develops its own momentum, dynamics and direction. The balance of power, interests and sub-groupings will all be significantly shaped by its initial design.

The longer the delay before people are drawn in, the more likely it is that the agendas of those initiating the exercise will become established and predominate. Also in our experience, the less likely people will be to have a sense of the project being their's and wanting to become involved. Why should they want to get involved in something that probably is somebody else's property? Broadbased involvement is more difficult to engender the longer it is left.

Clearly, there are issues of aims, resources, constraints and timescales which need to be communicated openly and honestly to people from the very beginning so that they know as soon as possible what they are letting themselves in for. Only then can they make a rational decision. The agency and its workers must negotiate, agree and clarify the key issues involved.

Suppose a team or even agency does not have all the information they need? Circumstances also change. In both cases let that be known. People can then take it into account. In our experience, people do understand these realities. What they don't understand and are less willing to tolerate, is only hearing about them later on when it may be too late to get out or take the action they want to. Similarly, they can cope with uncertainty, but are less forgiving of false optimism. The same principle applies to changes that become necessary once a project is underway. Users and local people involved must be told as fully and as soon as possible.

Where an agency has not been open, people who have got involved may feel themselves in an invidious position. They are reluctant to throw away work done and possible gains by withdrawing. Yet they may be unhappy and uncomfortable with a process and structure which they don't feel belongs to or respects them; over which they have inadequate influence, and which works more and more against the explicit aims for which it was set up.

We have seen the results of many such exercises, from self-help groups set up by social workers, to campaigns initiated by community activists. While there may be practical outcomes to be written about or reported, the process that has produced them has been one of narrowing involvement. What emerges often has little to do with the original stated aims, explicit commitments made by agencies, or what is known of people's wishes.

2. MAKING COMMITMENTS

One issue which should be thought through from the beginning is the importance of explicit undertakings from agencies to adhere to the outcomes of public involvement. Such guarantees are important at whatever level citizens are involved with a department, whether it is members of a patch team working with a local group, or a large-scale initiative involving politicians and senior officers. Social services have made increasing use of casework "contracts" with clients in recent years, although what obligations these impose on departments and what redress users actually have, remains unclear. Mutually binding contracts, however, might offer citizens and community groups a helpful model for negotiations with social services.

There's another point to emphasise. Commitments should not be seen as something to be sought or gained during the process of involvement. They must be there from the start if people's participation is to be warranted. Even when they have been made, there may be a struggle to ensure they are honoured. Without them, those people who stay involved and do not withdraw in frustration and regret, can expect a long drawn out struggle with ever-diminishing returns. Why should people want to get involved and spend precious time and effort without any guarantees that notice will be taken of them? Moreover, why should a department be reluctant to reassure them with firm commitments if it is genuinely prepared to act in accordance with what they want?

We do not think it is appropriate to see the first stages of bringing people together to develop their accounts and demands, as a means of exerting public pressure to influence agency action and decision-making and to achieve such commitments. It is likely to lead to the confusion of a dialogic approach with traditional combative community action. Such a strategy offers people the worst of all worlds: a high likelihood of wasted effort; dangers of incorporation, and further disenchantment.

The decision to invite dialogue must be seen as imposing large obligations on the agency and its workers if it is to have any meaning. It carries an implicit promise that people have a part to play; their contribution is valued; notice will be taken of it, and that it will affect affairs. This promise if not honoured will reinforce strong traditions of distrust and suspicion. On the other hand, the fulfillment of commitments is likely to have a disproportionately positive effect in people's minds.

To sum up, our experience of efforts to involve people in participatory projects and exercises, has convinced us that it is both questionable and unwise to embark upon the initial stages of the process without a real capacity and commitment on the part of the agency to act in accordance with what people want — although as we said before, this might limit the scale of objectives.

3. MODEST ASPIRATIONS

We want to emphasise again the importance of small beginnings, whether or not the hope is to go on to something bigger. As must now be clear, there are many obstacles to effective public participation. Some goals may seem humble, for example, enabling service users and local people to decide on the allocation of a small sum of money available, or users of day centre provision to have a real say in its regime. But if accomplished, these represent major gains and achievements and will be widely seen as such. Small scale initiatives are much more attainable, especially now when resources are few and constraints unprecedented. They are also less likely to whip up the right-wing ideological opposition that gets levelled at any attempt to extend local democracy or develop popular policies — from the GLC's Fares Fair scheme to Walsall's neighbourhood offices initiative.

"Think small" would be our watchword for projects and participation. The presentation of patch and community social work has tended to encourage over-optimistic and unrealistc hopes and expectations. As a result, it is easy for practitioners to become jaundiced and disillusioned. It is important that they can offer others realistic expectations and equally maintain realistic expectations of themselves.

Public participation is always likely to take longer and demand more skills and resources than we expect. There seems to be a tendency though, to aim for more visible and ambitious objectives. Modest proposals may be more effective, but they are less likely to bring status and prestige to departments or individual teams and workers — and this points to another potential conflict of interest between agency and public. The large scale decentralisation schemes initiated by impoverished Labour local authorities typify this. Are they the organisational equivalents of the grandiose municipal buildings that serve as monuments to the vanity of victorian city fathers? They suggest the same preoccupation with bricks and mortar and inability to plan on a personal and appropriate scale. Starting small means we can build on existing relations with people, existing collectivities and affiliations. It gives us time and does not railroad people into the relentless timetables of large project planning.

Small scale projects are much more likely to match people's initial expectations and abilities, and provide a base from which to develop. Large scale initiatives fly in the face of the massive political and economic constraints that govern our institutions and lives. Starting small gives us a chance to develop our capacity to challenge such obstacles. People can keep pace and stay in control with a series of small steps. Large leaps are excluding and alienating. It is easy to build on small successes, difficult to overcome large failures.

4. DEVELOPING SKILLS AND LEARNING TOGETHER

Meeting workers from many patch teams, we have talked to few who have been given sufficient training to enable them to work in the new ways now expected of them. East Sussex has been unusual in devoting major resources and priority to community social work training. As will already be clear the approach to social services we propose which takes patch's rhetoric of community involvement as the crucial starting point for planning and provision, puts a high premium on developing new skills. Training is needed for all the participants involved to equip them for this different, sometimes difficult approach to planning, policy development and service provision. This includes politicians and the social services department hierarchy and managers, as well as fieldworkers, service users, local people, groups and other agencies. It is especially important for service workers, for it is they who will be trying to initiate and enable such involvement in their agencies. Many new skills are needed, especially learning to work in supportive rather than directive ways, with groups of people in addition to individuals, and in association with other workers as well as individually. Yet so far the need for such training has hardly been recognised. But this is not just true of new initiatives in social services. It might be expected to be well advanced in the fields of community work and community action, but they have generally shown the same low level of awareness of the need to develop public involvement and skills to enable it.

The starting point for any participatory approach to social services must be the development of skills. The whole model of public involvement we have proposed is one of learning and confidence building: finding out what people want and enabling them to develop the services to meet their needs. Most important it is concerned with learning to work in a collaborative rather than individualistic or hierarchial way.

Most if not all of us will need help if we are to play an effective part in a process of public involvement. Many of the arguments suggesting that service users particularly are incapable of becoming involved, rest on an expectation that they would be attempting it unassisted. This is an invitation to fail. Training and the acquisition of skills should not be a pre-condition of involvement — as they often are implicitly now. Instead, they should be seen as an inherent part of the continuing process of involvement.

For example, one of us, as a claimant, has been involved in a project for claimants intended as "a model for involving the consumer". While an expert on the detail of social security was employed as a consultant, there wasn't a similar recognition on the part of the project's initiators of the need to draw in skills to help the group — which was relatively inexperienced — learn to work together, develop their confidence and abilities to make their own decisions and carry them out — resulting in predictable difficulties.[40] This example also emphasises the more general need for independent advice and training for people involved in such participatory projects.

Patch and community social work most often encourage people to organise and form groups for voluntary and mutual aid and support. But there is no reason why groups set up for one reason can't develop to do other things if participants wish. Cope family groups, for example, which are active in East Sussex and elsewhere, effectively make the point. Their primary concern is providing opportunities for members to relax, make friends and gain social skills. But at the same time they offer a model of how previously inexperienced people can get together as an effective group.[41] The methods and process they use and the skills and solidarity they impart could provide a basis for people to become involved in the running of social services departments as well as the meeting of their own needs.

This points to a tension which we have already touched on and which has ramifications for the approach to participation we have offered. As a group gets together and builds its skills and solidarity, the possibility then arises, intentionally or otherwise, of it excluding others. What may be a friendly and supportive group to its members, can appear a clique to outsiders. From our experience, when newcomers have come to such a group, there need be no difficulty in their joining and adding their contribution, so long as crucially there are shared agendas and commitments. But if groups are excluding, our framework would suggest two possible responses. The first is to invite a skilled outsider to review with members what is happening and to see if change is possible. Second is to ensure that opportunities and resources are provided for newcomers to establish other forums so that they can develop their skill and strengths and be in a position to collaborate on equal terms with peer groups, agency and others.

While stressing the importance of offering participants support and training, we would not want this to be seen as suggesting that they are incapable of involving and organising themselves. Just as we would challenge arguments that people are generally unwilling to become involved, so we would reject those that they are unable to. As we have seen, Hoggett and Bishop in their study of the neglected area of the social organisation of leisure have offered important evidence of people's capacity to organise their own activities *on their own terms*.[42] People do get involved, but not necessarily in the spheres of activity on which attention has most often been focussed. In the case of local politics and services, we can see much of the explanation for people's non-participation in these institutions' own culture and characteristics. That is why we place particular weight in this context on developing people's skills and offering them support.

At the same time, skills are not only needed to enable people to become involved in such initiatives, they are also necessary for those seeking to involve them. As well as developing technical abilities, for example, how to understand how legislation or local government work, carry out our own research or produce our own reports, we also need to learn how to work together. It is not something that can be taken for granted. Research has shown the general lack of collaboration in social services teams.[43] It will require even more skill and support to make it possible between departments and the outside world.

The process of learning should itself be a collaborative one. As the educationalist Paulo Freire argued, workers and users should be seen as co-learners and the contribution of both valued.[44] Learning and teaching are not discrete tasks demanding separate roles, but overlapping activities.[45] Local people can help patch workers understand their needs and experience while in turn gaining some of their skills and knowledge. If the goal is for patch workers to work as a team, then it makes sense for them to learn together. Learning should not be seen as something restricted to formal situations. It is inextricable from people's practice, and runs through their day to day work. It can be enhanced by opportunities for informal contact, conversation and exchange, as well as more structured occasions and experiences.

The kind of training we have in mind should also not be confused with teaching people how to fit into the agency's existing conceptual, cultural and procedural frameworks. Instead it should be concerned with finding ways of enabling them to work and communicate that suit them.

We have already commented on the fine line there can sometimes be between support and direction, and this applies very much to training, where the aim should be to help people equip themselves with the skills and resources to develop their own independence, judgements and decisions. We see this extending to assertion training and consciousness raising to resist attempts to dominate and manipulate participants. Service workers face this problem as much as other people. They can have just as difficult a relationship with their agency as service users.

Collaborative team working and the search for closer relations with local people make it especially important to equip people to work in anti-racist and anti-sexist ways, as well as to work towards explicitly anti-discriminatory objectives. In other words, the process is as important as the goal. Discriminatory behaviour is pervasive and insidious. If we seem to be labouring a well-worn point, it is one that hasn't been adequately acknowledged in community social work and which still confronts even the most progressive agencies. Typical examples from our experience are the worker who gives information about a meeting to discuss the effects of government policy on black people only to a black member of the group, or who makes it an embarassing issue for the woman who needs to claim child care expenses if she is to come to a meeting, saying, "Well, I've always managed to sort something out and get by".

5. RESOURCE IMPLICATIONS

Making Spaces

Workers and agencies seeking wider participation should first see what forums and groupings already exist. What other attempts are already being made to involve people? It is important to build on the collectivities we already have. At the same time, many of the situations and institutions that traditionally existed for people to get together, both formally and informally, have declined in numbers or significance, from the church to cafes, cinemas, dance halls and bingo. A number of the people we interviewed felt there was a lack of meeting places. So it may often be helpful to support the setting up of new forums and meeting places where people can begin to get together.

Initially teams will want to sound out and negotiate with local spokespersons and community "representatives" like committee members of community groups, voluntary organisations and tenants and residents associations. But it is essential to go beyond such formal groups and intermediaries to the many people who aren't actively affiliated in this way. This can raise fundamental questions for social services workers who may then seem to be questioning the legitimacy of such local leaders and organisations. The difficult task that faces them if they want to go beyond the activists already involved — who can always be dismissed by their authorities and opponents as unrepresentative, and indeed may very well be so — is to find ways, in concert with them, of involving people in a more broadbased way. They must steer a sensitive course between initiating yet another round of meetings or another local group, and leaving people in isolation who are not involved in existing organisations or activities. This is the first and perhaps biggest job confronting community orientated services, but starting small, developing dialogue and extending networks as we have suggested, it can be done.

Equally it is important that social services engage with rather than *expropriate* available networks and resources. Community centres, for instance, can easily slip into becoming welfare institutions that mainly house a cluster of social services facilities, for example, old people's lunch clubs, local surgeries and chiropody sessions, instead of also being people's own independent social clubs as was orginally intended. Social services must be explicit about their interest in such resources, negotiating with local people and groups to place it on their agenda.

Then there are the actual forms of involvement. Some people steer clear of formal public meetings because they are embarassed or afraid of making fools of themselves. They feel that "people like me don't go to meetings". They are almost certainly right as it becomes a self-fulfilling prophecy. Their views are more and more likely to be in a minority and they are increasingly discouraged from going. Others find informal settings just as awkward and difficult, especially among people they don't know.[46]

Different people prefer different methods of involvement. There is no one right way. The same applies to service workers. For example, some may be able to relate comfortably and spontaneously to service users and local people in informal settings like cafes, pubs or clubs, while for others it would be artificial and intrusive. What is at issue is finding ways of communicating with and relating to each other both within and beyond the boundaries of social services that are consistent with our participatory goals and which suit our personal preferences, politics and experience.

There is no ideal way, but all forms of mediation, whether by people or media, can put obstacles in the way of involvement. Face to face contact is more likely to inform and engage people than any number of leaflets and newsletters. Where people meet is also important. Better their own or at least neutral territory. The social services department, even the patch office, may have its own unwelcome connotations. The guiding question should always be how people see and feel about a method of coming together; its form, the place, and so on.

What is important is that people's involvement is something they value rather than experience as onerous, an imposition, or with suspicion. Their perceptions and responses are likely to depend on both the purposes of such involvement and what it actually entails. We have often heard workers complain that local people say they want something but just aren't prepared to come along to meetings to do anything about it. Perhaps that means they aren't really interested and the ideas should be forgotten. Or perhaps the methods of involvement employed should no longer be taken for granted, but instead *different* ones attempted. Critics are right to say that most people won't want to get involved if it means interminable meetings, procedures and formalities. Their failure has been not to look beyond these for more appropriate forms and methods. For citizen involvement to be a positive and desired activity — *and why shouldn't it be* — it must be on people's *own* terms — and that includes means as well as ends.

Making Time

Participatory democracy takes time. It is symptomatic of the under-development of the issue that there is an inadequate appreciation of just how much time is needed to involve people; establishing relationships, building on existing collectivities, developing new ones and helping people to work together. If patch teams are to do this in an effective rather than superficial or tokenistic way, then they must be assured a realistic proportion and length of time. Our experience is that this is likely to be much more than might be expected. It is also likely to entail additional staff and other resources, though it is difficult to see where these will come from in a period of ever-reduced supply. The rationale of community social work may be that traditional day to day "reactive" responsibilities will wither away as practitioners work with "the community" rather than clients. If we are ever to find out whether this is the case, workers must first be given sufficient time to develop their work in this different way.

This contrasts sharply with our knowledge of a number of teams working patch schemes — and not just in East Sussex. While they may now be supposed to work in a "community-orientated" way, they are also expected to fulfil existing casework and statutory responsibilities. Patch workers frequently complain that they are expected to do their project and other community-based work *in addition* to all the other tasks they have done. They may well then meet with the criticism from their departments that they have remained wedded to a casework approach instead of shifting their emphasis to community social work. But heaven help the team or worker committed to community-based working if something goes wrong with a statutory case.

Some patch based workers ask "are we supposed to go to evening meetings with community groups and local people on top of all our present work?". Others explain how they negotiate with each other so that, for instance, one has a third of her time freed for project work by three colleagues dividing up her former reponsibilities among them. Workload management schemes are also advanced as a means of dealing with such difficulties. However, putting aside questions of how work is quantified, weighted and negotiated, however helpful such schemes may be, if there is more work to do, without additional resources it ultimately means greater workloads for staff.

Emphasising the time taken may appear to endorse traditional arguments against participation on the grounds that it is inefficient. However, we question whether hierarchial decision-making is actually any faster. More important we must reconsider what we mean by "efficient" if we are to compare like with like. It is only by involving people effectively in policy development and service provision that they can really get what they want. There are no short cuts to this. The alternative is to impose policies and services on them. There is little reason to think this can match people's needs and much evidence to show that it doesn't. Certainly, excluding people from involvement is likely to take more time as it generates further problems of alienation, distrust and discord.

A symptom of this problem and another source of tension between citizen and service is likely to be departmental pressure for results. Social services departments will want something to show for the time spent on their new way of working and practitioners will be expected to provide it. But what if the team discovers that local people don't want to engage in the initiatve on offer, or get involved on the available terms? The right result might be for a project not to go ahead. Then at one level there might be little to show for months of work, although at another, it might mean closer relations and better understanding between service and citizens. Teams must have the freedom to make such choices and departments develop the sensitivity and understanding to allow them it.

A general issue here is that local authority timescales usually bear little relation to personal ones. They are either inordinately long, demanding a length of commitment many people are unwilling or unable to sustain, or tied to financial and administrative deadlines that may ill-accord with people's and groups' own deliberations and developments. We have stressed that achieving broadbased involvement takes time, but this is unlikely to fit the constraints of council timetables — unless they are changed.

The time taken to be democratic is not a reason for pessimism. What is, however, are the lost opportunities there have already been to make a start. It is now 18 years since the Seebohm Report argued for the "maximum community participation" in social services and four years since the Barclay Committee made the same plea.[47] Yet so far little progress has been made.

Resources

One of the contentious issues of patch and community social work is whether they save money as their advocates suggest. Whatever the case may be, there is no doubt that *public involvement* properly enabled cannot be done on the cheap, but will have considerable cost implications. This is not only because of the additional time and staff resources needed. Many of the skills required may also have to be bought in — at least initially — because the approach is radically different. A social services research department may have great experience in carrying out surveys, for example, but not of assisting people to make their own. They may have little familiarity with or understanding of the kind of dialogic and interactive research approach we have described.

We have stressed the value of independent consultants helping people to work collaboratively. There are also important issues of payment for participation. As anyone who has ever been involved — as we frequently have — in a management or other committee where everybody else seems to be paid for being there as part of their employment, we also need to consider the option — for people who want it — of *payment* for participation. Why shouldn't service users, local people and groups be paid for work they do and skills they bring and acquire, developing their own accounts, carrying out their own research, pulling together their own demands? The idea of their involvement being voluntary may fit a paternalistic model of letting them put their views, but not one of a partnership aspiring to equality. Here the "voluntary ideal" appears especially one-sided. Their skills and involvement are no less crucial than those of agency workers involved. Payment also offers another way of getting departmental resources directly to the area and its citizens, instead of mainly being spent on intermediaries.

The range of resources and expenditure that effective public involvement in social services will entail, including places to meet, publicity, secretarial and other support, training, payment and the recruitment of new and outside skills, is likely to be considerable. The first step is for this to be properly appreciated by departments and budgetted for. To this must be added the cost of the policies and provisions that people may actually want to pursue. It cannot be assumed that this will be the same as for traditionally developed programmes.

It is important for people's involvement to be based on clear terms of reference that balance need with available resources. However, while resources are finite, they are never fixed. This brings us back to the issue of whether gaining such resources should be a task for people who have become involved or whether that involvement should only be initiated after resources have been made available. It may be a difficult choice to make and one that is also constrained by the way in which local authorities tend to work. If resources have been allocated prior to people's involvement, then other agendas may also have been set which may need to be changed. It may be difficult for people to free themselves of the strings attached. On the other hand, if the responsibility is left to participants, getting money may become a diversion that occupies much of their time. It may also undermine people's preparedness to get involved. Clearly it is essential that the terms of involvement are made clear to potential participants and that departments declare what efforts they will make to secure central government or other funding if it is needed. We believe though that a department should commit resources rather than leave it to people to try and wrest them from it. It is another of the commitments we would argue departments need to make to the idea of "community involvement" if it is to be embarked upon in good faith and with a likelihood of success.

The East Sussex Experience

East Sussex Social Services' own area development programme highlights some of the issues and constraints we have been discussing. The programme was intended to support "patch teams in the development of new approaches"[48]. It offered those involved specific time to develop, review and carry out their projects, additional resources in some cases, and the support and skills of a divisonal consultancy group and outside consultant. There was clearly a recognition of the need for time, skills and resources for project development. Nonetheless the authors of East Sussex's own account of the programme identified as one of two main problems "workload pressures" it created, with teams still "expected to make space for the projects without cutting back on essential work".[49]

It is also evident from the East Sussex book that some teams' aims were still unrealistically ambitious. The team trying to carry out an "assessment of community needs and resources", for example, relied on school students given a modicum of training to carry out a sensitive survey, which as they concluded, "led to some poor quality interviews". They were also hampered by not being able to carry out a pilot survey "because of time constraints". Like us, workers involved in establishing a family support group concluded that "if progress was to happen at all it was likely to be slow, erratic and not capable of being rushed". They identified the problem that the departmental "pressures of the area development programme tended to blind us to the need for change to occur at the pace of group members rather than in response to external demands". Another team decided to set up a family aide scheme on their patch. This was the only one of the projects "which depended entirely on the recruitment of additional staff", and as the authors acknowledged "at a time of financial constraint much of the team's energy was consumed by securing the funding for the staff".[50]

We should remember that these difficulties with time, training and resources, still occured in an exercise where the Department showed both an understanding of and attempt to get to grips with them. This adds further weight to the view that efforts to involve service users and local people that are most likely to succeed are those that start on a small scale.

6. RIGHTS AND SAFEGUARDS

Inherent in the whole process of public participation is the importance of rights and safeguards for people who get involved. This applies through every phase and demands fundamental change in local departments. Issues of rights and safeguards are still far from resolved even at the level of individual client's complaints. As Huntingford has asked:

"How can social work agencies belittle the efforts of other agencies, such as the frequent scorn with which police complaints procedures are greeted (because there is no independent scrutiny), while there exists not even rudimentary internal review procedures in most social work agencies?".[51]

Effective public involvement is more a flexible process than a set of procedures and rules. The question of rights raises this issue again. The problem with rights is that they always tend to be more substantial on paper than in reality — as women, members of ethnic minorities, employees and people with disabilities all know to their cost. People have "rights" to welfare benefits which they are reluctant to take up; rights to legal representation of which they don't avail themselves. Claimants have had rights of appeal in the social security system but speaking from experience, this can be more humiliating than rewarding. Social services' clients may gain the right of access to their files or to be present at reviews or meetings that concern them, but important information or discussion may then be held elsewhere.

On the other hand, people without formal rights may, for example, be well equipped to understand the working of a social services department and to deal with it, if workers keep them well informed and support them in their negotiations with it. Thus because of the sensitivity of workers, problems may not arise, and if they do, people know how to respond to them effectively. Such an approach rests on openness, trust, a sense of equality and a good flow of information from workers to users.

We are not saying that such informal arrangements offer sufficient safeguards or that formal rights, with or without the force of law, are necessarily inadequate. The point we want to make is that such rights are not only manipulable, but also tend to be *procedural* in a way which makes it difficult for many people to negotiate them. Procedures can be used to trap, exclude or disable. Informality on the other hand, may also actually mean "the tyranny of structurelessness", where power is hidden, with some people refusing to own the power they exercise and others prevented from fixing responsiblity.[52] What is needed — especially in the highly political arena of public involvement in state services — is some kind of synthesis of the two which offers the advantages of an open and flexible process as well as the final protection and appeal of formalised principles and rights.

As we have said, people do not always take up their nominal rights, even when there is a desire to ensure they have an effective say. Offered the opportunity to read and amend transcripts of their comments to give them control over any statement of their views, they may not want to do so. They may not respond to invitations to meet with managers whose "doors are always open". When this happens, those initiating the exercise should reconsider the methods they use, rather than assume that people don't want the rights offered. If a process doesn't work, it is not an argument for scrapping safeguards, but for finding better ones. Instead of interpreting such a lack of response as apathy or a surrender of control, we need to ask whether participation is being offered on people's own terms or ones that are alien and difficult. Structures and forums are needed that enable engagement with social services on equal terms and with equal rights — both at the level of people's personal use of, and collective involvement in services.

Equal Rights

All projects for public involvement must have explicitly anti-racist, anti-sexist and other anti-discriminatory goals if they are to ensure the rights of people and groups discriminated against. The *process* of public involvement should share the same allegiance to equal opportunities. This demands a commitment to explore and develop structures, methods and practices which are not excluding or marginalising, but which instead aim to reach and involve such people. Training and support should be provided for all involved, including officers, managers and politicians, to enable them to pursue such policies and practice. Such an anti-discriminatory approach should also not be seen as restricted to the point of public involvement. It has wider ramifications for the overall structure and operation of the authority and its services.[53]

For us the starting point for equal rights is equal access to public involvement — and that as we have seen is far from being achieved. This brings us back yet again to the issue of "community". How do you develop "community involvement" when no clear community exists? Talk of "handing power to the community" or developing dialogue with it implies a homogeneity and consensus that don't exist and ignores class, race and gender divisions that clearly do. There are also the differences within these groupings, for example, between and within ethnic minorities — less often talked about, but no less important. There are likely to be as many conflicts and divisions outside the agency as between it and outsiders. The purpose of public involvement is to attempt to negotiate and resolve such differences, not deny them. What can make it particularly difficult is the differential access to involvement associated with them.

The issue of equal rights offers a firm reminder that involving people is not a neutral technical exercise, where consultants' games and new skills alone will overcome difficulties and get us working together. Some people may never be able to cooperate — for personal or political reasons, or because of prejudice and unequal power. How ultimately, for instance, do we overcome extreme racism except with the rule of law and measures of self-defence? We have to recognise such realities and reject naive notions of communality.

It's also important to remember how the stage management of public participation and the many obstacles in its way, have encouraged the emergence of "community leaders" rather than broadbased involvement. Participation has served as a career ladder to political, personal and professional power as much as a means of citizen empowerment. The hegemony of career activism has to be challenged and undermined if wider involvement is to be possible. Otherwise as Ouseley has argued of decentralisation, it will merely mean "passing on some of the powers of the local state apparatus to known activists without changing the status quo".[54]

7. SELF-HELP AND SELF-MANAGEMENT

Much of the effort towards public involvement in community-orientated social services has focussed on setting up schemes and projects in which local people and service users play a key part as service providers. These include self-help and support groups, good neighbour and educational schemes. It is essential that such projects are enabled to become independent of social services as soon as possible — if not from the beginning. By independent, we do not mean the withdrawal of social services' skills and support — which is often what departments seem to take this to mean — but rather that the project is run *by* the people and area for whom it is intended.

This is the traditional model of effective self-help groups, like Alcoholics Anonymous, but it has become blurred as social services and large voluntary organisations have increasingly initiated such groups rather than them being self-generated. Self-management, we believe, is the only way voluntary and community projects can escape problems of co-option and colonialisation, with all the issues of gender and racial bias that may arise given the prevailing nature of present social services. Such schemes should only grow out of people's own demands and judgements and not, as has frequently been the case with patch and community social work, from social services' intervention. Social services can play a helpful part in testing demand, but certainly not in creating it.

Departments often want self-help groups to be available on a long term basis as an outlet for regular referrals to complement their own dwindling resources. People involved in such groups, on the other hand, may see them as much more informal and ephemeral, offering a personal rather than an agency service. They and social services may have quite different agendas and such groups and projects need to be in a position to negotiate and safeguard their own. Self-help without self-management is a recipe for disaster.

There are fundamental objections to schemes which rely on women's low paid or unpaid labour and which may be provided in place of properly paid services. But so long as such schemes are contemplated, it is essential for there to be an awareness of the gender issues involved to inform decisions about whether to go ahead with them at all, and if they are to be implemented, to minimise risks of sexism and unequal opportunities. It is especially important that such schemes are self-run because of the particular responsibilities they place on participants, and the safeguards such autonomy offers them against exploitation.

This still leaves the issue of how such projects are to achieve effective self-management. The problems remain formidable.[55] An additional difficulty frequently facing self-help projects, like many voluntary organisations, is the option of time-consuming fund-raising or financial dependence on statutory services.

THE IMPORTANCE OF COLLABORATIVE WORKING

Collaborative working is part of patch and community social work rhetoric. We believe it is fundamental to participative practice and citizen involvement. It is a key issue, both inside the agency — with team working — and in its wider relations outside.

Let's begin with collaborative team working, which research has shown to be conspicuously lacking in social services departments. It has tended to be treated lightly — as another bandwaggon to be jumped on or attacked. If we want to pursue it seriously though, it is likely to take us on a journey into the very politics of work. We don't claim special knowledge or experience in this field. It is not an issue we can develop adequately. However, there are some questions we do want to raise that may point readers in helpful directions.[56]

First though, we should remember that there are still several different *kinds* of teams, even excluding specialist ones, operating in social services, including patch and community social work based departments. As well as traditional social work teams, there are social services teams, including home helps, occupational therapists, day care workers and others, and multi-disciplinary teams, where agencies work together and occupational groups are also included from other departments, notably health.

Many of the disputes about community social work specifically and social work more generally, have focussed on the idea of "specialist" and "generic" working. The Barclay majority report and its neighbourhood-based minority report, both seemed to opt for generalist workers in teams, either dividing their time equally between social care planning and counselling, or acting as undifferentiated patch workers. Pinker, on the other hand, in his "alternative view" emphasised the importance of specialism.

Let's look at these two models more carefully. Specialism is based on a division of labour; genericism on an assumption of everybody doing everything. There are inherent problems with both.

Dividing tasks up not only leads to their segregation as the private province of individuals, but also to formal and informal hierarchies — of power, status and reward. Interestingly, this is what actually seems to be happening in many patch teams with increased numbers of social work aides and other ancillary staff.

On the other hand, genericism runs the risk of riding roughshod over particular skills required to meet individual needs. It also ignores the differences in people's orientation, abilities, interests and experience, and is as likely to undermine their existing skills as enable them to develop new ones.

We see collaborative working as a third way which offers an alternative to the present polarisation between specialist and generic practice. Tensions invariably arise from people's different skills and preferences. You can remove external obstacles like hierarchies, but not human differences. Specialism attempts to separate and institutionalise them; genericism to mix them up. The model of collaborative working we have in mind recognises these tensions. There are different tasks to be done. Some of us will be better at or more interested in some than others. But it doesn't try and abolish this by pretending such distinctions don't exist and trying to submerge them. Instead it asks people to deal with them together as a work group, while questioning status and power differences they have been tied to.

Collaborative working tries to unite people's different activities and abilities through dialogue and an overall shared philosophy and values, both towards the agency's function and its users. To this extent, we agree with Pinker's conclusion that "there is no irreconcilable conflict between the notion of a generic team — as distinct from a generic worker — and that of specialist practice".[57] However, we see a team less as an aggregation of its members' individual and different skills than as a co-learning, co-working group, whose members' various abilities and preferences are related, developed and synthesised by both a process and a philosophy of collaboration and participation. We don't see collaborative team working "eroding workers' autonomy" as Bowl and others have, but rather complementing it and giving it the added strength of collectivity.[58]

There are four other issues of collaborative working we want to touch on — specifically as they relate to community social work and patch working.

1. The Importance Of Collaborative Working In Extending The Power of Workers

Their lack of power in their departments has frequently been commented on, and the people we interviewed shared this view. Patch places much emphasis on "participatory management", just as it stresses more general participation by "the community". The two are closely related. But how can workers share power with people if they don't have it themselves? How can they invite users and local people to get involved in discussion, when in East Sussex, for example, workers have had to hide behind anonymity or the safety of having left the Department to express critical views?[59] Collaborative team working not only offers workers the promise of greater solidarity and mutual support, but also a counterweight to the power of higher management.

2. Leadership In Patch Teams And Changing Staff Roles

Both these issues have already cropped up in this study. Here patch seems to put obstacles in the way of team working. The position of team leader or team manager has increasingly emerged as the key role in community-orientated social services. It stands at the crucial meeting point between agency and "community". The growing emphasis and responsibilities that have been attached to this role have major ramifications for those occupying it — since it is likely to be highly stressed and demanding more support than may yet have been recognised. We have also raised the question of how such formal leader/management roles are reconciled with the idea of *collaborative* team working. Patch and community social work may have effectively developed their own new occupational and managerial hierarchy of home helps, patch workers, social work aides, social workers and team leaders, rather than moved closer to a structure consistent with collaboration. Even where this ancillary-based model has not been pursued, for example, in some London boroughs, they may still entail a hierarchy — between social workers and unpaid carers. The contradictions between the aspirations and the organisational model have yet to be adequately addressed, but the prospects are not encouraging. Many workers are asked to change their ways of working without necessary changes being made to the structures in which they must operate. While there has been an early emphasis on the administrative reorganisation of grassroots workers, so that often they find themselves arbitrarily relocated without adequate understanding or back-up, the same has much less often been the case for management. Few departments have reorganised as radically as East Sussex. For example, many which claim to have moved to patch or community social work retain the old unhelpful administrative divisions between fieldwork, day and residential care. Making changes at this level has profound implications for management, which it has frequently resisted.

It is worth stressing that what we are talking about are changed relationships among workers and beween them and service users and local people. A move to collaborative and participative working should have radical implications for staff roles. The reorientation of social services through increased citizen involvement is likely to place different demands on both the agency and its workers, with ramifications for the work they do and the division of labour. Many existing social service roles would need to be reconsidered. Already in some authorities there is talk of traditional divisions between staff by function being replaced, for example, by teams of staff designated as community support workers devising with individual old people an appropriate mixture of help.[60]

This raises a related issue. As we have seen, patch and community social work have emphasised the capacity of academically and professionally unqualified local people to take on responsibilities and acquire skills it was hitherto often assumed they couldn't handle. Regrettably this has generally not been matched with corresponding improvements in the wages and conditions of the women workers predominantly involved, who have merely been given more demanding jobs without any breaking down of professional and status boundaries. However, it does point to another important way in which local people can become involved and develop the skills to do so — by *working* for social services. Human service agencies are potentially a major source of new and socially-useful employment for the future. Such job creation would not only be a positive way of getting resources directly back to people who need them in the form of properly paid and trained work, but also offer an effective basis for regular involvement and learning within departments, with the added potential of unionisation.

3. Networks And The Size Of Teams

There seem to be two common fantasies associated with going patch. First is an extraordinary optimism that once teams are outposted and "in the community", everything will get better. Second is an unreasoning fear that when they are in their patch office, like a beleagured garrison, workers will be overrun by a greatly increased "bombardment" from clients. Like most fantasies, there is some truth in both. More people probably will turn to social services when they are local — at least initially. Outposted workers are likely to be in closer contact with their neighbourhood. People's fears have much to do with the small size of many patch teams — especially of teams organised along artificial hierarchies as patch teams often are — so that some workers like home helps, day care and residential staff, aren't necesarily included as members of the team at all.

There is a concern that patch teams may not be large enough to include the whole range of skills and resources needed. Certainly it is larger teams which seem most able to develop the project and group work associated with patch.

However this may merely be because they have the numbers to take on these tasks as well as conventional responsibilities.

But we would question such a numerical conception of teams. Patch teams should not be seen in isolation as separate, self-contained entities. It is neither possible nor desirable for them to be such. No less important than collaborative relations within the team are collaborative relations *outside*, beginning with other teams. Each team should be seen as part of a working and learning network. Closer communication is another of the issues addressed by collaborative working. While patch is associated with genericism and generic teams, it frequently coexists in practice with a plethora of specialist teams and groupings; for example, fostering and adoption, intermediate treatment, under-fives, and teenage fostering. In many reorganisations day care and residential workers are still separate from field workers. It is important that networks between such areas and workers are encouraged and facilitated. Similarly management schemes and structures need to be revised to ensure better communication and collaboration.

An associated issue facing teams trying to work collaboratively is that of overlapping chains of command, with, for example, members of a team like clerks, specialist social workers or occupational therapists, responsible to other outside hierarchies or individuals. This can cause conflicts of loyalty and create problems for collaborative team working. But there is no reason why it should paralyse it.

Again it is helpful to see the issue in terms of networks rather than as a special question in itself. Where the networks involved seem negative, the team can use its strength — and the power of a strong team should not be under-estimated — to improve understanding, and if need be, to restrain or challenge them and get support from other positive networks. It can put its resources both into supporting its own members and attempting to change the external constraint upon them. It is equally important to encourage links between people with specialist roles in teams and with their colleagues outside, so that they can develop and share their learning and skills and not feel isolated. This seems to be a particular issue for occupational therapists, clerical and home care workers.

Workers have sometimes seen patch decentralisation as a means of dividing and weakening them. Some managements may be reluctant to support the development of internal networks which enable opportunites for contact and exchange, because they see them as a threat to their own authority. Then are they serious about patch's promise of partnership and participation? Such internal links are one of the starting point for wider collaborative networks with citizens and other agencies. Freeing ourselves of hierarchical relations of status and power in our work is inextricably linked with getting rid of hierarchical views of others, whether they are service users, local people or non-statutory workers.

4. Collaboration Between Social Services And The Wider World

If the partnership between statutory and other services and carers so frequently talked about in patch and community social work is to be fulfilled, there must be a new equality between participants.

People and groups are still likely to be dealing with hierarchical organisations where power is unequally distributed and this will limit what can be achieved. But there is no reason why at the point of people's involvement and over the issues in which they are involved, more egalitarian and collaborative working should not be possible. We should also remember that it is not only statutory organisations which are hierarchical and not just formal hierarchies where power is unequally spread. The practice and process of community work and community action have typically reflected the bias and discriminations of larger society. Instead of denying them, we need to find structures and ways of working to counter the "heavy votes", "founder member syndrome" and other expressions of personal hierarchy so that everybody can make their contribution without prejudice. The process of collaborative working has the important advantage of handling many of the difficulties that getting involved presents. For example, the cost of being more assertive can frequently be more conflict, bringing with it greater personal stress. This is true for service workers, users and local people. The solidarity and support of others that can come from working collaboratively provides perhaps the most effective way of coping with this.

8. PARTICIPATION AND POWER

It is essential to accept that any attempt to devolve power or hand over control demands a preparedness to take *risks*. Things may not go as intended or expected. People may not do what the agency or team had in mind. The department and its workers will in one sense at least be weakening their own position — although other greater strengths may result from alliances with citizens and organisations outside.

Of all the constraints acting on and against people's involvement in social services, the most fundamental and pervasive are inequalities of power. These apply between the agency and all involved, including workers, as well as among and between the different participants. While this may seem self-evident, it has been conspicuously underplayed in discussions of partnership and participation in patch and community social work.

Power is at the heart of the discussion. Yet debates about welfare, particularly about personal social services, have still to be adequately related to political thinking and theories of power. It is not a task we can attempt here. But we can stress its importance. Understanding issues of power will make us more aware of our potential for change, as well as helping us understand and question the limitations we face.

With patch, the nature of the organisation and its intervention may change, but the distribution of power remains essentially the same. This has many expressions beyond the longstanding unequal and paternalistic relations between clients and social workers. For example, patch workers tell of their departments persistently looking over their shoulder, pressing them for results, instead of giving them the trust and space to pursue a participatory way of working. Other more subtle pressures force people to conform to the agency's own framework and terms of reference. A familiar example in the fields of community work and community action especially is where people are rushed into making project applications that will get funding because they fit existing official priorities and criteria, rather than being helped to challenge these and work out what *they* actually want. Similarly people are encourged to write reports in the expected manner rather than to develop their own ways and forms of expressing themselves.

We have talked about increasing people's personal power through training and confidence building. We have also stressed the need for processes and structures that increase and equalise people's access to *political* power in personal social services. There is sometimes a tendency to confuse the two as if increased personal power automatically leads to greater political power.[61] The lesson we have learned is that both are essential if people are to be effectively empowered in statutory and other services.

There is also a third kind of power conspicuous in social services — *professional* power. We have tried to draw a distinction between differences in skills, interests and orientation, and differential statuses and reward attached to them. We have also pointed to the need to reconsider professional roles if the changed relations among and between service workers and users envisaged by patch and community social work are to be realised. The existing occupational hierarchy in social services departments finds many expressions, from the overall professional dominance of social work, to, for example, the different weights attached to the views of home helps and social workers. The inequalities of power it embodies and the problems of deference and paternalism it leads to, represent serious obstacles to collaboration and dialogue between service workers, users and local people. So far the trend has been to seek to extend professionalisation. Any commitment to participation must cause us to question this.

Power in social services departments, however, is not monolithic. It is possible to gain commitments from politicians and hierarchy to create areas of opportunity for public involvement. It may be difficult if not impossible for citizens to challenge departmental authority in some spheres at personal or local level. But once the issue of power is articulated and made explicit, it begins to be possible to see where there is room for manoeuvre and challenge — and to take advantage of it.

There are sufficient ambiguities and differences of interest to offer people hope. But what must also not be forgotten is that people's *own* power as service users, workers and local inhabitants, is not fixed. The essential argument of this discussion is that it is possible for that power to grow if people are enabled and given access to develop their own accounts, skills, judgement and collectivity. What is important is for those committed to these goals, particularly within social services and other official agencies, to be able to pursue them more effectively than has so far generally been the case.

CONCLUSION

We believe that any attempt to give people an effective say in services will ultimately demand significant changes in local political and administrative structures. It clearly also has massive ramifications for the relation between local and central state. It raises the whole enormous issue of democracy and can't be squeezed into a small separate pigeonhole of "patch" or "community social work". However small the step intended, it represents a quantum political leap. No wonder that isolated arguments for community involvement are so appealing and so deceiving. They at once imply it is possible to alter the relation of citizen and state, while changing virtually nothing. Perhaps this is why in 20 or so years of "public participation" there has been so much said and so little achieved. Equally, it is not surprising that earnest attempts to increase public control, like those of some left Labour local authority decentralisation schemes, have run into such difficulties. We certainly wouldn't argue for increasing people's involvement without an awareness of the major political and structural issues involved.

It is essential for the issue of participation to be given the high priority on public agendas it demands — especially on those of local authorities arguing for greater public involvement. It must be recognised as a crucial question of local democracy, and no longer glossed over with the easy verbiage of "community involvement and control". Having said all this though, we still believe there is room for manoeuvre at team and local level. It is that space these guidelines hope to make the most of. Our experience cautions us against assumptions of predetermined structures and monolithic institutions — except perhaps as intimations of inaction and grand theorising!

The advocates of patch have challenged and reconceived the relation between people's needs and the role of social services. They have perhaps done this more powerfully in print than in practice. Patch and community social work speak to some deeply held hopes of many social services workers who want to involve users and local people and work more closely and equally with them, seeing more responsive and accountable services as the only way forward. We share this commitment to the democratisation of services. Patch and community social work's grasp may not be as great as their reach. But they have offered an important starting point for discussion. We have tried here to extend and open that up. They have also argued for "community" rather than "client" orientated services, although we have suggested that social services are still neither. What we believe is needed are *citizen*-based services. Beginning modestly by involving people in this discussion, we may at last arrive at the *public* services they want.

Research Method

The kind of questionnaire we used in the survey, with a high proportion of open-ended questions, and the method of interviewing, recording all people's additional comments, followed the approach which we first used in a large scale survey of local attitudes to planning, participation and social need in North Battersea.[1]

While the duration of interviews in Hanover varied from 20 minutes to as long as one and a half hours and more, on average they lasted about 45 minutes.

People's responses to open-ended questions were recorded verbatim as far as possible and only categorised later. The one exception to this was where they were asked to describe their income according to one of several given categories, or if they wished, offer their own description which was then placed in an "other" category. So, for example, when we asked people what they knew about local authority social services, we tabulated their comments in the following way.

Breakdown of Responses to Question 6: "What Do You Know About What (Council) Social Services Do?"

Response	Number
Nothing	35
Very little	29
Quite a lot/A reasonable amount	7
A lot	0
Description offered of what social services do	29
TOTAL	100

The category "very little" included comments like "not much", "virtually nothing", "very little", "not a lot", while that of "quite a lot/a reasonable amount", included responses like "something", "fair amount" and "a rough idea".

The Patch and the Surveyed Sub-Area

Using data from the 1981 census, we were able to compare the population in the sub-area of Hanover patch we sampled with the overall patch population. This was done for both areas by adding together appropriate census enumeration districts and parts of districts — the basic building blocks of the census. Each enumeration district contains about 200 households.

The survey area and patch populations matched each other very closely and sometimes were identical according to a wide range of characteristics. There were no significnat differences between them. These characteristics included breakdowns for: sex, age structure, tenure and social class; economic position (economically active or inactive); sex/marital status breakdown of the economic position of all residents; the economic position of married and independent women with dependent children; housing conditions according to tenure, and for households with dependent children; the proportion of pensioners living on their own and their housing conditions; and people's access to cars.[2]

Our Sample And The Patch Population

To try and avoid any problem of the sample being skewed through inaccuracies in the electoral roll or its failure to reflect change and mobility in the population, where a person included for interview no longer lived at the stated address or in the survey area, then we substituted another person currently living there, preferably of the same sex. In all this occurred in 19 cases, including 10 of the 100 people actually interviewed. While they may not have matched the characteristics of those originally identified for inclusion in the sample, although they did correspond according to sex, this adjustment will have ensuřed that the sample reflected the current population, which we believed to be important, in view of the known mobility locally.

In five cases, the person selected for interview opted to be interviewed with someone else in their household, mostly a partner and in one case their sister. These were more or less joint interviews, but they were only counted as one respondent in quantifying results, except where comparisons according to gender were involved, where both participants were included in the total to avoid any distortion.

The socio-economic categories we constructed were based on criteria of present, past or usual employment, accent, home decor and other such soft criteria and cues which we ordinarily employ in allotting ourselves and other people to social class roles. This categorisation is soft and potentially idiosyncratic and should be treated with reserve, but it does offer the possiblity of some interesting and helpful insights and coincides closely with census social class distribution for the area, although this was differently based.

The following tables afford comparison between our sample and the patch population along a range of key criteria.

TABLE 1: Breakdown by Age and Sex

Sample: Breakdown by sex and estimated age

Age	men	women	total
18-29	11	20	31
30-39	15	7	22
40-49	6	10	16
50-59	4	7	11
60-70	5	11	16
70+	—	4	4
Total	41	59	100

Sample: Breakdown by sex where people wanted to be interviewed with partner or other person:

men	women	total
44	61	105

Patch Population[3]

	%					
Age	Men		Women		Total	
Total	47	(6248)	53	(6945)	100	(13192)
Under 5	6		5		5	
5-15	12		9		10	
16-29	26		22		24	
30-39	15		12		13	
40-49	9		8		9	
50-59	10		10		10	
60-69	11		14		13	
70-74	6		8		7	
75-79	3		6		5	
80-84	2		4		3	
85+	1		2		2	
Total %	100		100		100	

TABLE 2: Breakdown by Social Class

Sample: Breakdown by Estimated Social Class

Category	Number
A (middle class)	26
B (intermediate)	16
C (working class)	58
Total	100

Patch Population [4]

Social Class	%	
I	3)	23
II	20)	
III (non-manual)	16 - 16	
III (manual)	36)	
IV	15)	56
V	5)	
Armed forces and inadequately described	5	
Total	100	

These two tables are not directly comparable. The social class breakdown offered by the 1981 census 10% sample is a "classification of jobs", which excludes people who are retired and is based on "economically active heads of households". However it does suggest some similarities to our breakdown.

TABLE 3: Breakdown According to Housing Tenure

Tenure	Sample		Patch Population [5]
	Number/%		%
Owner occupation	56	(60)**	59
Council	16	(18)	21
Housing association	1	(1)	1
Rented with business	2	(2)	1
By virtue of employment	—	—	—
Private rented	13	(14)	17
Other	12*	(5)	—
Total	100	100	100

* This includes 11 people staying with or subletting from family or friends. It includes four cases where the tenure of parents was not known.
** These totals include seven of the 11 people previously mentioned, staying with or paying parents etc, where tenure was known and categorised accordingly.

Single Parents

In addition to the married women with dependent children, our sample included two lone women parents (but no lone male parents), both with under-fives; one in part-time employment and the other "economically inactive". This corresponded to the proportions in the patch population.[6] We used this categorisation to enable comparison with census data for the patch. Significantly though, women's subjective definitions of themselves sometimes varied from such external ones. One woman who was married, for example, preferred to think of herself as single, while another mother who was unmarried but living with a partner, said she did not see herself as a single parent. Similarly while we have had to use such categories for comparability, we do not accept census definitions of "housewives" as "economically inactive". Instead we see their labour contributing significantly to the overall economy.

TABLE 4: Breakdown According to Economic Position
Sample

Economic position	Total persons	Male total	Male SWD	M	Female total	Female SWD	M
All persons 18+	100	41	19	22	59	20	39
Total econ active	68	38	18	20	30	12	18
Total working	58	31	16	15	27	10	17
Working F/time	47	29	15	14	18	8	10
Working P/time	11	2	1	1	9	2	7
Seeking work	8	5	2	3	3	2	1
Temporarily sick	2	2	—	2	—	—	—
Total econ inactive	32	3	1	2	29	8	21
Permanently sick	—	—	—	—	—	—	—
Retired	18	3	1	2	15*	6	9
Student	—	—	—	—	—	—	—
Other inactive	—	—	—	—	—	—	—
Community domestic work**	14	—	—	—	14	2	12

* This was based on women who had reached retirement age and may have included some who had not been in paid employment.
** The census category "other inactive" included people of "independent means" and "housewives". We have taken such women out of this category and included them in that of "community domestic work".
SWD = single, widowed or divorced; M = married.

Patch Population[7]
Sample

Economic position	Total persons	% total	Male SWD	M	Female total	Female SWD	M
All persons 16+	10993	46	20	27	54	27	27
Total econ active	57	34	14	20	24	11	13
Total working	51	29	11	18	22	10	12
Working F/time	42	28	11	17	14	8	6
Working P/time	9	2	1*	1*	8	2	6
Seeking work	5	4	2	2	1	1	*
Temporarily sick	1	*	*	*	*	*	*
Total econ inactive	42	13	6	7	30	16	14
Permanently sick	2	1	*	1*	1*	1*	*
Retired	19	9	3	6	10	7	3
Student	4	2	2	*	2	2	*
Other inactive**	18	*	*	*	18	6	11

* Less than 1%
** Including women engaged in community domestic work, classified as "housewives".

Reaching Local Residents

The mobility in the population and the trend to owner-occupation was further reflected in the relatively large number of empty houses of which a number were being renovated for sale. The overall turnover among all those we interviewed and tried to contact on the basis of the 1982 electoral roll, including people who had moved or died or who were about to or planned to move, was 21 percent. At least three recalls were made in cases where people could not be contacted, sometimes as many as 10, at all times of the day and evening and at weekends as well as on weekdays.

TABLE 5: Breakdown by Gender of People in Full and Part-time Employment

	Sample (number)		Patch population (%)[8]	
Employment status	men	women	men	women
Full-time employment	29	18	95	62
Part-time employment	2	9	5	38
Total	31	27	100	100

Percentage of patch population in employment[9]
Men   63
Women   41

TABLE 6: Breakdown of Employment of Married Women with Children
Sample

In household with:	Total married women	Married women econ active	married women in employment		
			Total	Full-time	Part-time
No child aged 0-15	22	11	10	7	3
Child(ren) 0-4 with or without any 5-15	10	3	3	1	2
Child(ren) aged 5-15 only	7	4	4	2	2

Patch Population[10]

In household with:	Total married women	Married women econ active	married women in employment		
			Total	Full-time	Part-time
No child aged 0-15	1733	810	788	433	355
Chid(ren) 0-4 with or without any 5-15	497	123	122	25	97
Child(ren) aged 5-15 only	493	324	319	88	230

There were 11 cases where people could not be interviewed because they were ill or incapacitated at home. In all cases where people were included as "incapacitated", it was on the basis of *their* decision rather than ours. They not only included two elderly people who said they were "too old" and "not up to it", but also three people who were deaf or hard of hearing, one for example, saying "I get embarrassed and confused because I can't hear", and a very old man who said he was "very deaf and wouldn't be able to do it properly". It would be helpful in such cases if the interviewer had signing or fingerspelling skills, so that people would not feel excluded or that they had to exclude themselves.

The Pattern of Refusals

When approaching people, the interviewer explained that the survey was part of an independent, Brighton-wide study of local people's needs and the services available to help them, stressing that interviews were informal, anonymous and confidential. After being interviewed, people were told they would be kept in touch with the findings of the survey and any subsequent developments.

We were able to attempt some comparisons between refusals and those who could not take part in the survey and the sample actually interviewed according to criteria of sex and estimated age and social class.[11]

TABLE 7: Breakdown of Responses and Non-Responses in Sample Survey

Category*	Number
Interviews completed	100
Address vacant**	12
Premises in different, non-residential use	2
Selected person dead***	2
No trace of address	1
Selected person not contacted	15
Selected person in hospital during survey period	1
Selected person refused interview	62
Refusal on behalf of selected person by someone else in household	1
Selected person ill	6
Selected person incapacitated	5
TOTAL	207

* Categorisation based on that employed by Social and Community Planning Research, Interviewers' Manual.
** Including at least one person said by neighbours to be dead.
*** Where no replacement was possible.

TABLE 8: Breakdown by sex of people interviewed compared with those contacted but not interviewed

Category	Men	Women	Total
Interviewed sample	41	59	100
People contacted but not interviewed	31	42	73
Refusals	26	36	62
Total	98	137	235

TABLE 9: Breakdown by estimated social class of people interviewed compared with those contacted but not interviewed

	Estimated Social Class				
Category	A	B	C	Not Known	Total
Interviewed sample	26	16	58	—	100
People contacted but not interviewed	8	3	60	2	73
Refusals	8	3	49	2	62
Total	42	22	167	4	235

While the proportion of women and men was the same for those interviewed and those not, people categorised as working class, and as middle aged and older, were over-represented among those not interviewed, compared with the interviewed sample. For example, people aged less than 40 accounted for more than half of those interviewed but just under a quarter of refusals. The relatively high proportion of older and incapacitated people inflated the numbers of those who were contacted but could not be interviewed. Our North Battersea research indicated that middle-aged and older people tended to be more conservative and less demanding than other groups.[12] If the findings from the present survey reflect a slight skewing of the interviewed sample in age and social class terms, with an under-representation of middle aged and older people (which helps explain the higher percentage in the sample than in the patch population fitting the category of "economically active" — 68 percent compared with 57 percent), then this may be compensated for by the absence of the more demanding under-18 year olds. Furthermore, any such skewing of the interviewed sample away from older working class and towards young middle class people, also reflects the continuing trend in the area due to gentrification to a younger, middle class population.

TABLE 10: Breakdown by estimated age of people interviewed compared with those contacted but not interviewed

| Category | Estimated Age | | | | |
	18-39	40-59	60 and over	Not known	Total
Interviewed sample	53	27	20	—	100
People contacted but not interviewed	15	31	26	1	73
Refusals	15	29	17	1	62
Total	83	87	63	2	235

Implications Of Refusals

Why were older people less likely to take part in such a survey? Most of the people who didn't want to be interviewed, either volunteered or were asked why. The range of reasons they gave were similar to those we enountered in our earlier study of public attitudes to planning, participation and social need.[13]

TABLE 11: Breakdown of reasons given by people for refusing to take part in the survey

| Category | Number | |
	Middle-aged and older people	All
Not interested/too busy	19	26
Concern about confidentiality	2	2
Serious problem of ill-health in the household	2	3
Not an issue or problem that applies to them	3	4
Not wishing to be involved in such an exercise	3	3
Not qualified to take part	2	4
Such surveys seen as pointless	1	2
Other	3	4
Not known	11	14
Total	46	62

Nearly half either said they were not interested or too busy, and while in some cases being "busy" really did seem to be the reason for people not participating, in others it seemed to be the low priority they attached to such an activity. This is likely to be related to people's justifiably low expectations of the use and effectiveness of such surveys. For instance:

"I've done these surveys before. It's silly, a waste of time."

As well as the reasons for refusals which we have already discussed in Chapter 3, some people had other reservations about surveys, doubting, for example, whether they would really be guaranteed confidentiality and not liking to be interviewed.

"I'm sorry dear, but I don't believe it will be confidential. I'm not saying I don't believe you, but I've worked with the police for 19 years and I know what goes on. You never know where it goes."

"I don't like to be interviewed. I was interviewed on Radio Brighton and I didn't like it."

"If it's not official, I don't want to know."

Others had their own particular reasons, like the two women with seriously ill husbands and the mother with a premature baby; the recent arrivals who felt they weren't competent or qualified to talk about local issues, and the woman who said her husband "didn't want her answering questions". Particularly interesting, however, were those, mostly middle aged and older people, who didn't want to be involved or didn't feel they were involved in such issues.

APPENDIX II

The Interview Schedule

INTRODUCTION

The interviewer introduces herself and the project explaining that it is independent and the survey based on a random sample. People's participation is voluntary, anything they say will be treated in the strictest confidence and no names mentioned.

1. Could I begin by asking you how long you have lived round here?

2. What do you feel about living round here?

3. Do you have any experience of the Council's Social Services (Department)? (Make sure distinction is clear between SSD and social security, and SSD and voluntary organistions. NB SSD currently based in Princes Street)   YES/NO/DK* *detail***

4. Have you ever used them for anything?   YES/NO/DK *detail*

5. Did you get any help from them?   YES/NO/DK *detail*

6. What do you know about what (Council) Social Services do?   *detail*

7. What do you think of (Council) Social Services?   *detail*

8. Do you know that the Council Social Services Department has been reorganised to what is called a "patch" system?   YES/NO/DK *detail*

9. *IF YES TO QUESTION 8:*   (preferably month and year)
   a) when did you first hear about the reorganisation?   *detail*
   b) How did you first hear about it?   *detail*
   c) What do you know about the reorganisation?   *detail*

10. Have you ever been consulted or your views sought about the reorganisation?   *YES/NO/DK detail*

11. Would you like to have been consulted about the reorganisation?   YES/NO/DK *detail*

12. I'd like to ask you your views on some of the main ideas associated with the reorganisation:

KEY: *DK = Don't Know; **The interviewer listens to and answers people's comments and questions and records them verbatim as far as possible.

344

a) What do you feel about having (social services) teams based in local offices? YES/NO/DK *detail*

b) What do you feel about an increased emphasis and reliance on voluntary organisations and volunteers? *detail*

c) What do you feel about an increased emphasis on "informal helping networks" — that is, people looking after each other? *detail*

d) What do you feel about Social Services working more closely with voluntary, community and self-help groups? *detail*

13. What are your feelings about such a patch reorganisation generally? *detail*

14. Did you know that the Social Services Department in this patch — Hanover — is planning to set up a "neighbourhood care scheme" for old people, hopefully beginning next October? *detail*

15. How would you describe your own needs? (Prompt if necessary: ie things you want/lack; your day to day circumstances, problems and difficulties) *detail*

16. What particular problems or difficulties do you feel people like you (Prompt if necessary: in your situation/with comparable circumstances, for example, having small children, being old etc) face in Brighton? *detail*

17. What does it mean for you when people talk about a place being a "community"? *detail*

18. Do you feel it is a "community" round here? YES/NO/DK *detail*

19. What sort of area makes up your "community" or neighbourhood for you? (establish which — community, or neighbourhood, or both, they are referring to) *detail*

20. Are there any particular policies, services or provision you would like to see the Council's Social Services Department offering (which they may not be offering now)? YES/NO/DK *detail*

21. Would you like to have closer contact with Social Services? YES/NO/DK *detail*

22. How much say do you feel:
a) users
b) local people
have in the Social Services Department? *detail*

23. What do you feel about:
a) users
b) local people and groups
c) workers
having more say in the Social Services Department? *detail*

24. How do you think this (users, workers, local people and groups having more say in the Social Services Department) could be achieved? *detail*

25. Do you think the Council's Social Services Department has:
    a) any understanding of the kind of issues and problems that   YES/NO/DK *detail*
    concern you? or
    b) any interest or concern in them?   YES/NO/DK *detail*

26. Do you think Council's Social Services might have something, or   YES/NO/DK *detail*
    more to offer you if they had a different kind of approach and
    services were provided differently?

27. Are you in paid employment?   YES/NO/DK

28. *IF YES TO QUESTION 27:*
    Full or part-time?

29. What is your occupation? (present, past, retired/unemployed.
    This includes unpaid occupations like housewife/husband)

30. Do you receive state benefits? (Prompt if necessary: for example,   YES/NO/DK *detail*
    state pension, sickness benefit, unemployment benefit, family
    income supplement, supplementary benefit or pension; other (eg
    attendance allowance, mobility allowance, etc)

31. How would you describe your income?
    a) comfortable
    b) adequate
    c) inadequte
    d) difficult to manage
    e) other

32. Sex of respondent.

33. Estimated age of respondent. (Record estimated age for
    categorisation later)

34. Do you have children living with you?   YES/NO/DK
    a) total number of children
    b) number of under-5s
    c) number of school age
    d) number over school age

35. Do you also look after other relatives: YES/NO/DK
    a) at home   *detail*
    b) elsewhere   *detail*

36. Would you describe yourself as single? (Prompt if necessary: YES/NO/DK *detail*
    including widow(er) etc)

37. *FOR THOSE LOOKING AFTER CHILDREN:*
    Do you have a partner to look after the children with, or are you a   *detail*
    single parent?

38. *FOR WOMEN WITH CHILDREN:*
    Is child care a problem for you?
        YES/NO/DK *detail*

39. *FOR WOMEN WITH CHILDREN — NOT IN PAID WORK:*
Is child care a problem for you, preventing you having a job?   YES/NO/DK *detail*

40. Housing tenure:
a) owner occupier
b) private tenant
c) council tenant
d) housing association
e) other: specify

41. Are there any larger issues or trends that you see as affecting your   YES/NO/DK *detail*
own needs and situation?

42. Do you see any other policies — local or national — creating or   YES/NO/DK *detail*
making worse the problems you face?

43. Apart from central government controls and cuts in spending,   *detail*
what do you see as shaping social services' policy in Brighton?

44. Where and with whom do you feel decision making lies in the   *detail*
Social Services Department?

45. How much say do you feel workers on the ground/grassroots   *detail*
workers have in the Social Services Department? (Prompt if
necessary: for example, home helps, social workers, workers in
homes and day centres etc)

46. Social services and social workers talk a lot about "care" and   *detail*
"support". Could you tell me what these two words mean for you
personally?

47. In your own life, speaking for yourself, where do you get care and
support from? (Prompt if necessary: for example, in day to day life
and over special situations or problems; informal and formal
help, for instance from: *detail*
friends
peer group
family (of origin or marriage/partnership)
neighbours
lover/husband/wife/partner
community organisations
voluntary organisations
Social Services Department
church
other — specify.)

48. Do you get the kind of care and support you want?   YES/NO/DK *detail*

48a. Do you get as much care and support as you would like?   YES/NO/DK *detail*

49. Do you see any obstacles in the way of caring and being cared for   YES/NO/DK *detail*
as you prefer:
a) for yourself?
b) for people more generally?

50. Do you feel women are expected to do most of the caring and   YES/NO/DK *detail*
    supporting in our society?

51. Do you think views like that about women being expected to do   YES/NO/DK *detail*
    do most of the caring and supporting are built into the Social
    Services Department?

52. Are you at present in contact with Council Social Services? (NB   YES/NO/DK *detail*
    home helps are a SSD services. Note if respondents are unaware
    of this)   (Prompt if necessary: what
                                                                      kind of worker involved/
                                                                      help offered; over what
                                                                      issue)

53. Are you involved in any community group or voluntary   YES/NO/DK *detail*
    organisation? (Specify whether as a user — eg of an Age Concern
    club and/or active member)

54. How is it organised? (Prompt if necessary: ie informally, with a   *detail*
    formal hierarchy, with group meetings, collectively working)

55. How are decisions made? (Prompt if necessary: ie through a   *detail*
    committee, by vote, through everyone's participation)

56. Is the aim to be democratic?   YES/NO/DK *detail*

57. How does this work out?   *detail*

58. Is it important to you that it is organised and decisions are made YES/NO/DK *detail*
    the way they are?

59. What influence over or say in the Social Services Department do   *detail*
    you feel you can have?

60. Have you ever tried to influence it?   YES/NO/DK *detail*

61. *IF YES TO QUESTION 60:*
    What happened?   *detail*

62. Would you like to have more influence/say over the Social
    Services Department?   YES/NO/DK *detail*

63. How do you feel this (having more say in the Social Services
    Department) could be achieved?   *detail*

64. Are there any other issues you would like to raise yourself?   *detail*

Thank you very much for your help. As I have said, the aim of this project is to try and improve the
match between the needs and problems people have and what Social Services can do to help and
resolve them. We are anxious to keep people who have helped us in this survey informed of what
happens and shall be trying to do that.

NOTES AND REFERENCES

INTRODUCTION

1. C Jones, in a review of East Sussex's own account of its patch reorganisation: *A Tricky Patch?*, Youth And Policy, No 14, Autumn 1985, pp 22-23, p 23.
2. See, C Glendinning, *Unshared Care: Parents and their disabled children*, Routledge, 1983, pp 6-8. There have been relatively few studies of public perceptions of local authority social services (G Craig, *Studies Of Knowledge, Opinions And Expressed Needs Of Social Work Consumers And The Public*, produced for the Barclay Committee, NISW, 1982. This lists 14 studies of general public views over the period 1961-81.). Studies of public and users' views have tended to focus particularly on social work and social workers (G Craig, *Review Of Studies Of The Public And Users' Attitudes, Opinions And Expressed Needs With Respect To Social Work And Social Workers*, produced for the Barclay Committee, NISW, 1982). We know little or nothing about what service users, local people and groups feel about "going local" and what it might mean for them. So far only two patch teams have been the subject of systematic evaluation. The DHSS funded research project by R Hadley and M McGrath on the Normanton (Wakefield) patch system included a sub-study of "users' knowledge and perceptions of social services and satisfaction with these services", but no study of non-users' or public perceptions of patch (See, R Hadley and M McGrath, *When Social Services Are Local: The Normanton experience*, National Institute Social Services Library No 48, George Allen and Unwin, 1984.). The research on the neighbourhood services project in Dinnington, Rotherham, by M Bayley and others included a user study and a non-user study, but the latter was confined to elderly people aged 70-80 and their "principal carers" (See, M Bayley and others, *Neighbourhood Services Project Dinnington*, Working Papers 1-12, Department of Sociological Studies, University of Sheffield, 1981-85.).

CHAPTER ONE

1. Cited in R Lambert, Untitled thesis on patch, presented in part fulfilment of MSW Degree, Sussex University, 1982, p 1.
2. R Hadley and M McGrath, *Patch Based Social Services Teams*, Community Care, 11 October 1979, pp 16-18.
3. R Hadley and M McGrath, (eds), *Patch Based Social Services Teams*, Bulletin No 1, Jan 1980, and Bulletin No 2, December 1980, Department of Social Administration, University of Lancaster.
4. R Hadley and M McGrath, (eds), *Going Local: Neighbourhood social services*, NCVO Occasional Paper One, Bedford Square Press, 1980.
   Several of the schemes described in *Going Local* began in the early 1970s and at least one in 1970, the same year as the Social Services Act which led to the setting up of social services departments.
   As Lambert wrote ((1) op cit, p 1) "Thus patch can be seen as a feature of the post-Seebohm

social services department, rather than a later reaction to it as its more recent advocates have suggested."

What Lambert described as patch's "more rapid and widely publicised phase of development which began in 1979" coincided with the intervention of Hadley and the election of a Conservative government. Lambert traced this phase in patch's development which crucially involved Hadley's initial DHSS funded research on the patch scheme in Normanton, South Yorkshire, initiated by the Area Officer, Mike Cooper. ((1) op cit, p 2).

5. S Latto and C Rowlings, *Evidence to the Barclay Committee*, 1981. The researchers advised caution in the interpretation of these figures because it was not always clear if the authorities replying to their questionnaire had fully understood their definition of a patch team. 218 or about 18 percent of the 1,586 area teams on which they obtained information were said to be organised on patch lines.

6. *Social Workers: Their role and tasks*, (The Barclay Report), Bedford Square Press, 1982, p 207, Paras 13.33-13.34.

7. R Hadley and M Cooper, *Letting A Hundred Patches Bloom*, Community Care, 24 May 1984, p 10.

8. R Hadley and M Cooper, *Patch Based Social Services Teams*, Bulletin No 3, Department of Social Administration, University of Lancaster, 1984.

9. See for example, O Stevenson, *Specialisation In Social Service Teams*, George Allen and Unwin, 1981.

10. See, for example, T Philpot, (ed), *A New Direction For Social Work: The Barclay Report and its Implications*, Community Care, 1982; and R A Pinker, *An Alternative View*, Appendix B, (6) op cit.

11. (6) op cit, p 207, Para 13.33.

12. (8) op cit, p 2.

13. R Hadley and S Hatch, *Social Welfare And The Failure Of The State: Centralised social services and participatory alternatives*, George Allen and Unwin, 1981, p 152.

14. (4) op cit, p 96.

15. (4) op cit, p 10.

16. (4) op cit, p 96.

17. (6) op cit, pp 226-229.

18. (4) op cit, p 10.

19. M Cooper, *The Normanton Patch System*, in L Smith and D Jones, (eds), *Deprivation, Participation And Community Action*, Routledge, 1981, p 172.

20. (8) op cit, p 2.

21. (4) op cit, p 10.

22. J Joslin, *Essex Road Team — A community based team adopts a patch system*, in (4) op cit, p 69.

23. (4) op cit, p 11.

24. (19) op cit, p 171.

25. (8) op cit, p 4.

26. (4) op cit, p 10.

27. K Young, *Changing Social Services In East Sussex*, Local Government Studies, March/April 1982, p 22.

28. R Hadley, *Tapping Experience*, Community Care, 31 March 1983, p 19.

29. *Social Services Policy And Objectives*, agreed by Social Services Committee and confirmed by East Sussex County Council, December 1977.

30. M Henwood, *There's No Substitute For Good "League" Placings*, Community Care, 28 November 1985, pp 10-11.

31. K Young and R Hadley, *Managing To Go Patch*, Community Care, 29 September 1983, p 18. However, as the Department reported in *Decentralising Social Services*, (R Hadley, P Dale and P Sills, *Decentralising Social Services: A model for change*, Bedford Square Press/NCVO, 1984, p 14), three main types of resources were excluded from this and not managed by team managers; the Department's children and family centres, intermediate treatment and hospital social work services.

32. Information pack for job applicants: 2, *The Structure*, East Sussex Social Services Department, 1985.

33. A Whitehouse, *A Community Safety Valve*, Community Care, 19 August 1982, pp 18-19.

34. *Review Of Departmental Structure*, Social Services Department, East Sussex County Council, mimeographed, September 1980, pp 3-4.

35. (27) op cit, p 19.

36. (7) op cit.

37. (27) op cit, p 22.
38. Ken Young in his foreword to R Hadley, P Dale and P Sills, (31) op cit. See this book also for their own more detailed account of the restructuring.
39. (27) op cit, p 19.
40. (31) op cit, p 19.
41. *Patch Teams Offices Search Ends*, Community Care, 4 July 1985, p 7.
42. For example in (27) op cit, p 22.
43. For example, P Dale, Staff Officer, East Sussex Social Services Department, reporting on the reorganisation in (8) op cit, p 43.
44. (32) and (41) op cit.
45. Brighton Voice, No 82, November 1981, p 6.
46. Quoted in (33) op cit, p 20.
47. QueenSpark Rates Book Group, *Brighton On The Rocks: Monetarism and the local state*, QueenSpark New Series 1, 1983, pp 47-48.
48. (6) op cit, p 207, Para 13.33.
49. R Hadley, *The Philosophy Of Patch Work And Its Implementation*, in I Sinclair and D N Thomas, (eds), *Perspectives On Patch*, National Institute for Social Work, Paper No 14, NISW, 1983, p 6.

CHAPTER TWO

1. *Urban Programme, Evidence Of Social Need*, East Sussex County Council, Social Services Department, 1983.
2. (1) op cit, p 3.
3. *Unemployment By Constituency*, male unemployment from the 1981 Census, Research Note No 98, House of Commons Library Research Division, 1982, p 7.
4. Brighton Voice, No 94, May 1983.
5. Manpower Services Commission statistics 1982-1984, Brighton Job Centre. The rate of registered unemployment for Brighton since 1981 is not available in percentage terms.
   For background information about Brighton and Hanover, see also, T Browne and A Fielding, *Maps By Computer: The 1981 census atlas of Brighton and Hove*, Info Press, 1986; and T Browne and A Fielding, *The Brighton And Hove Census Atlas*, Working Papers 1-3, First results, population, housing, employment, Geography Laboratory, University of Sussex, 1985.
6. B Clare and C Kedward, *The Needs Of Young People: Report of a survey in Brighton*, Brighton Council for Voluntary Service, NCVO, 1982.
7. Moulsecoomb, for example, has the only full-time social services department community worker in Brighton attached to it, while Whitehawk had a sub-office long before the rest of Brighton went patch.
8. A Tomlinson, *The Illusion Of Community: Cultural values and the meaning of leisure in a gentrifying neighbourhood*, in A Tomlinson, (ed), *Leisure And Popular Culture*, Brighton Polytechnic Chelsea School of Human Movement, 1983, pp 68-88, p 76.
9. (1) op cit, p 2.
10. Calculation from Brighton Corporation Borough Treasurer's Reports, 1970-71, 1979-80.
11. *Racism In Brighton*, Community Information Bulletin, No 30, Brighton Council for Voluntary Service, Sept-Oct 1984, pp 10-11.
12. P Dale, in *Patch Based Social Services Teams*, Bulletin No 3, R Hadley and M Cooper, (eds), Department of Social Administration, University of Lancaster, 1984, p 43.
13. Quoted in 'County Councils Gazette', March 1982, p 421.
14. *The Idea Of Major Change By Casework Alone Seems Indefensible*, interview with Roger Hadley, Social Work Today, 27 August 1984, pp 16-19, p 19.
15. K Young and R Hadley, *Managing To Go Patch*, Community Care, 29 September 1983, p 19.
16. *Census Small Area Statistics For Hanover Patch*, SPME Unit, Social Services Department, East Sussex County Council, 1983.
17. For example, R Hadley, *The Philosophy Of Patchwork And Its Implementation*, in I Sinclair and D N Thomas, (eds), *Perspectives On Patch*, NISW Paper No 14, 1983, p 5.
18. (12) op cit, p 43.
19. *Going Patch In Brighton*, East Sussex Social Services Department, December 1981, p (1).

20. *Central Area, Brighton, Children In Care Statistics*, East Sussex Social Services Department, July 1983 and 1984.

CHAPTER THREE

1. For a more detailed account of the research project, see: S Croft and P Beresford, *Patch And Participation: The case for citizen research*, Research and Practice Monograph, Social Work Today, 17 August 1984, pp 18-24.
2. Cited in I Taylor, P Walter, J Young, *Critical Criminology In Britain: Review and prospects*, Routledge, 1975, pp 26-27.
3. See, for example, M Fisher, (ed), *Speaking Of Clients*, Community Care Social Services Monographs, University of Sheffield Joint Unit for Social Services Research, 1983.
4. S Croft and P Beresford, *Soapbox*, Social Work Today, 21 October 1985, p 46.
5. Personal Communication, 21 October 1985.
6. A Oakley, *Interviewing Women: A contradiction in terms*, in H Roberts, (ed), *Doing Feminist Research*, Routledge, 1981, pp 30-61, p 58.
7. Personal accounts like those, for example, included in *Brighton On The Rocks*, (QueenSpark Rates Book Group 1983) however much they reflect our experience, can always be dismissed as idiosyncratic and atypical and the basis by which they are selected, challenged and rejected.
8. a) D Sheridan, *The Mass-Observation Records 1937-49: A guide for researchers*, The Tom Harrison Mass-Observation Archive, University of Sussex 1981.
   b) Personal Communication, D Sheridan, 27 September 1982.
   c) S Winchester and J Tucker, *Ordinary People*, Sunday Times, 15 August 1982.
   d) A Calder and D Sheridan, (eds), *Speak For Yourself: A mass-observation anthology*, Jonathan Cape, 1984.
9. (8c) op cit.
10. C Jameson, *Who Needs Polls?*, New Statesman, 6 February 1981, pp 13-14, p 13.
11. (6) op cit. In a few cases where there might be a risk of breaching people's confidentiality, details have been changed, but not in a way that would affect the meaning of what they said.
12. 1982 Electoral Roll, Qualifying date 10 October 1981.
13. B Clare and C Kedward, *The Needs Of Young People: Report of a survey in Brighton*, Brighton Council for Voluntary Service, National Council for Voluntary Organisations, 1982.
14. We calculated our response rate in accordance with the guidelines set out in the Social and Community Planning Research (SCPR) *Interviewers' Manual*, excluding "deadwood", namely empty premises, premises in different, non-residential use, and where an addressee was not traced and an (unsubstitutable) individual had died.
15. It compared, for example, with a 10 percent refusal rate in our large scale North Battersea sample survey, covering similar issues and with the same main interviewer.
16. Like, for example, the person we interviewed who said "I thought you were going to be a bit more nosey, but you haven't been".

CHAPTER FOUR

1. R Hadley and M McGrath, (eds), *Going Local: Neighbourhood social services*, NCVO Occasional Paper One, Bedford Square Press, 1980, p 96.
2. For example, recent ESRC funded research *A Study Of Ambivalence In Public Opinion About State Welfare*, P Taylor-Gooby, Kent University; J Le Grand, *The Strategy Of Equality: Redistribution and the social services*, George Allen and Unwin, 1982.
3. *Local Government Financial Statistics, England and Wales*, 1981/2, Department of the Environment, Welsh Office, HMSO, 1983, Table A. Percentage of total expenditure was nine per cent for "law, order and protective services", compared with over seven per cent for personal social services.
4. (3) op cit.

5. *Brighton On The Rocks: Monetarism and the local state*, QueenSpark Rates Book Group, QueenSpark New Series 1, 1983, p 90.
6. This confusion appears to be far-reaching. When, for example, BBC Television News featured as a main item the publication of a new report on the social security system, they headlined it a "new report on social services"; BBC TV 9 pm news, 29 August 1984.
7. See Research Method Appendix for details of how people's comments were categorised.
8. S Weir, *What Do People Think About Social Workers?*, First national survey of public attitudes towards social workers, commissioned by New Society and the Barclay Committee on Social Work, New Society, 7 May 1981, pp 216-218.
9. Research on public opinion surveys has shown people's preparedness to offer opinions on issues they know nothing about. See, for example, G F Bishop and others, Public Opinion Quarterly, Vol 44, No 2, p 198, 1980. The researchers questioned a total of 1,849 residents of Cincinnati, Ohio about a totally fictitious issue, "The Repeal Of The 1975 Public Affairs Act". One third offered opinions on the Act, a similar proportion encountered in other survey experiments. The authors concluded however that the respondents who gave an opinion were more likely to be black, less educated, less interested in politics and less trusting of government. Those lowest on trust were inclined to agree with the idea of repealing the act. Indeed the authors ventured to suggest that the phoney question was in fact measuring something very real — positive and negative feelings towards government.
10. P Taylor-Gooby, *Public Opinion*, letter, New Society, 21 March 1985, p 456; and *Public Opinion, Ideology And State Welfare*, Routledge, 1985. Our findings are also echoed in studies cited by D Thomas, *The Turning Tide Of Public Opinion*, New Society, 14 March 1985, pp 397-400, p 399.
11. For example, J Joslin, *Essex Road Team - A Community Based Team Adopts A Patch System*, in (1) op cit.
12. *Brighton Social Services*, Programme One, BBC Radio Brighton, producer Jennifer Bowen, 22 February 1982.
13. For example, a pamphlet produced by the London Borough of Wandsworth, where we live, says of what social services do:
    "Thousands of people receive help in many ways such as meals on wheels, home helps, day centres, special equipment for the handicapped, homes for the elderly, child minders, day nursery places, special advice and help for the blind and deaf and advice to hospital patients and relatives."
    This was further qualified by the additional caveat that "the public demand more than we can supply so some facilities may be full and have a waiting list" (from *How Can Social Workers Help?*, London Borough of Wandsworth, 1982.). Again this is hardly indicative of a universalistic service available for all of us. One of the services of which that might appear,to be true, day nurseries, has been severely cut and its clientele is confined to council defined "priority one" cases.
14. *Report Of The Committee On Local Authority And Allied Personal Social Services*, (The Seebohm Report) CMND 3703, HMS0, 1968.
15. L Knight, *If In Doubt Blame The Social Worker*, Cosmopolitan, December 1985, pp 74-81, p 76.
16. L Eaton, *Bringing Balm To Bradford*, Social Work Today, 24 June 1985, pp 15-17, p 17.
17. (12) op cit. Conditions are now different in Hanover with the move to a patch office, but this description is one that will feel familiar to workers and users of social services in many parts of the country.
18. (8) op cit, p 218.
19. This is true both of their own and other services. R Cohen and M Tarpey, *"The Trouble With Take-up: A report of work with social services to increase take-up of Social Security Benefits"*, Action Research Project, Islington People's Rights, 1982, described an attempt to increase the take-up of social security benefits among people coming to a social services team.
20. J Boucherat, *The Southdown Project Survey*, The Southdown Project/Children's Society, 1984; B Holman, *Feedback*, Community Care, 14 February 1985, p 11.

CHAPTER FIVE

1. K Young, *Changing Social Services In East Sussex*, Local Government Studies, March/April 1982, p 21.

2. *Brighton Social Services*, Programme One, BBC Radio Brighton, producer, Jennifer Bowen, 22 February 1982.
3. K Young, Director of Social Services, East Sussex, speaking at the Annual General Meeting of Hove Council for Voluntary Service, 22 April 1982.
4. *Going Patch In Brighton*, East Sussex Social Services Department, December 1981, p 1.
5. R Pinker, *An Alternative View*, Appendix B, *Social Workers: Their role and tasks*, (The Barclay Report), Bedford Square Press, 1982, pp 236-262; N Leighton, *Patch In Perspective*, Community Care, 15 October 1981, pp 18-19.
6. R Hadley, *Tapping Experience*, Community Care, 31 March 1983, p 19.
7. R Hadley and M Cooper, *Letting A Hundred Patches Bloom*, Community Care, 24 May 1984, p 10.
8. We made an earlier survey study of a local government planning participation exercise (*A Say In The Future*, Battersea Community Action, 1978), which may cast some light on this. In that case there had been considerable publicity, but again only a minority of local people (39%) knew about it. While there were particular practical deficiencies in the Council's publicity, we concluded it was something more than that which accounted for people's unawareness of the exercise, writing at the time that:

"While people said that they did not know about the participation exercise, what may actually have been the case was that they weren't interested in what they saw and didn't remember reading or hearing about it. Living in a world where people are bombarded with trivial and irrelevant information, we need to know much more about the way they filter and sort information according to the importance they attach to it, before we can come to any clear conclusion about the Council's attempt to publicise participation. In this case was it simply that people didn't think it worth absorbing or remembering?". (p 40).

The answer indicated by the research was the latter, because of the suspicion and distrust of, and alienation from the local authority felt by many people. In the present case, the marginality of social services for most people would offer a similar explanation for them ignoring or screening out information about their reorganisation.
9. R Hadley and M McGrath, (eds), *Going Local: Neighbourhood social services*, Occasional Paper One, NCVO, Bedford Square Press, 1980, p 10.
10. R Hadley and M McGrath, *When Social Services Are Local: The Normanton experience*, National Institute Social Services Library No 48, George Allen and Unwin, 1984, p 13.
11. *Social Workers: Their role and tasks*, (The Barclay Report), Bedford Square Press, 1982, P 229.
12. (1) op cit, p 220.
13. *People And Planning: Report of the committee on public participation in planning*, (The Skeffington Report), Department of the Environment, Scottish Development Department, Welsh Office, HMSO, 1969, p 1. This formative government publication on public participation defined it "as the act of sharing in the formulation of policies and proposals". See also, N Dennis, *Public Participation And Planners' Blight*, Faber and Faber, 1972, pp 220-221.

At present public participation in most if not all spheres of policy does not allow for a true partnership between public and policy makers at the formative stage. Instead, it is (at best) a matter of the public or users of services being asked their opinions after the authority has laid the basis of its plan. The choice is already made. As one man said to us in our London study of public participation, "They only ask for objections to *their* plans".

Significantly, it is at the level of objections that what local participation there has been in the East Sussex Social Services reorganisation has taken place. There have been local objections to the siting of several patch offices. For example, as a result of objections from local people after the site of the Queens Park office had been decided on by the Department, certain minor changes have been made to improve local privacy and provide more car parking.
14. (9) op cit.
15. From an interview with Roger Hadley, Social Work Today, 27 August 1984, p 17; (7) op cit.
16. S Croft and P Beresford, *Making Our Own Plans: Going local or popular planning*, Chartist, Feb/April, 1983.
17. D Nicholas, *Neighbourhood Offices: The Walsall experience*, Wandsworth Community Publications, 1981, p 8.
18. East Sussex's Director of Social Services has made the point himself. See K Young and R Hadley, *Managing To Go Patch*, Community Care, 29 September 1983, p 20.
19. (10) op cit, p 13.
20. S Hatch, *Outside The State: Voluntary organisations in three English towns*, Croom Helm, London, 1980, p 119 and following.
21. (11) op cit, p 220.

22. For example, P Abrams, *Social Change, Social Networks And Neighbourhood Care*, Social Work Service, No 22, DHSS, January 1981, pp 14 and 23.

23. S Weir, *What Do People Think About Social Workers?*, First national survey of public attitudes towards social workers, New Society, 7 May 1981, p 217.

24. R Hadley and M Cooper, *Patch Based Social Services Teams*, Bulletin No 3, Department of Social Administration, University of Lancaster, 1984, p 4.

25. There was no consultation with local people over the setting of patch boundaries generally. The consultation that took place was *within* the Department between the planning section and operational staff at area and team manager level. Personal Communication, East Sussex Social Services Department, 22 August 1984.

26. See P Gordon, *Community Policing: Towards the local police state*, Critical Social Policy 10, Summer 1984, pp 38-58. This discusses police intervention and involvement in the allocation of grants to local voluntary and community groups.

27. (10) op cit, p 15.

28. This status has since been discontinued in patch teams.

29. *Hanover Neighbourhood Care, Six-Monthly Report, October 1982-April 1983*, Brighton Council for Voluntary Service, April 1983, p 1.

30. (29) op cit, p 2.

31. *Be A Friend, Help A Neighbour*, leaflet, Tarner Neighbourhood Care Scheme, 1982.

32. (29) op cit, p 2.

33. (29) op cit, p 3.

34. For example, a project brief prepared by the Lewes Town patch in 1982 as part of the Department's "Area Development Programme", was concerned with "Publicity And The Patch Team", and sought to increase local knowledge and involvement. A wide range of methods were initially considered and then a survey suggested, but this was felt to be too large a task. The team instead held an open day and produced a monthly newsletter as well as information about local resources and developments for people in the patch and particular groups like old people. However this represents a major demand on their own resources and at the time of writing despite their commitment, it has not been possible to produce the newsletter for nine months.

35. See for example (a) Report of the Director of Social Services: *Elderly People In East Sussex*, East Sussex County Council, Social Services Committee, 11 December 1981, Agenda item 9; and (b) RG Borley, SM Taylor and CR West, *Balance Of Care — A User's View Of A New Approach To Joint Strategic Planning*, Omega, The International Journal of Management Science, Vol 9, No 5, 1981, pp 493-499.

36. (35(a)) op cit.

37. (35(a)) op cit.

38. *Home Help Spending*, The Guardian, 17 October 1985; M Henwood, *There's No Substitute For Good 'League' Placings*, Community Care, 28 November 1985, pp 10-11. It may be argued that it may no longer make sense to judge the quality of care in the community on the basis of an indicator such as home help provision, bearing in mind the expansion of innovative community care schemes. But as Henwood has pointed out, so far there has generally been a lack of monitoring of such schemes and they are better seen as a complement to rather than a substitute for statutory services.

The DHSS no longer issues normative guidelines of minimum service provision in such areas as home helps, meals on wheels or residential care. It is likely however that even its minimum guidelines of 12 home helps per 1,000 population recommended in 1977 is no longer adequate because of the "ageing" of the elderly population since then, with growing numbers of people aged over 75 and especially over 85.

39. (35(a)) op cit, appendix (c), NUPE response to Social Services Committee paper *Elderly People In East Sussex* and the Director of Social Services' summary of the response to consultation on it.

40. A series of such projects form the basis of the book about the patch reorganisation in East Sussex: R Hadley, P Sills and P Dale, *Decentralising Social Services: A model for change*, Bedford Square Press, 1984.

41. K Lyons and others, *Our Crowd*, Social Work Today, 13 December 1983, p 43.

42. (24) op cit, p 43.

43. (18) op cit, pp 19-20.

44. See, for example, *Family Finders Centre Set Up*, Community Care, 10 January 1985; *Helpers Sought For Play Schemes*, Community Care, 1 August 1985; *Family Scheme*, Community Care, 15 November 1984; *Club Celebrates*, Community Care, 6 December 1984.

45. The joint funded IDCS, Intensive Domiciliary Care Service, was intended to meet the needs of people requiring a higher degree of home care to maintain them in the community. It was initially controlled centrally and has since been devolved to patch level. At the time of writing, 850 hours of the service were available for all Brighton. For a social worker's comments about the conditions of workers in this scheme, see Brighton On The Rocks, op cit, p 47. The scheme has also been criticised by the National Union of Public Employees as under-resourced. See (39) op cit.

46. Brighton Evening Argus, 9 November 1982.

47. Brighton Evening Argus, 29 October 1982.

48. (46) op cit.

49. (29) op cit, p 2.

50. Brighton Evening Argus, advertisement, 5 August 1982.

51. (50) op cit. This has been slightly increased since.

52. (29) op cit, p 4. Although £600 a year was originally budgetted for running costs, only £400 was now available.

53. (29) op cit, p 3.

54. (29) op cit, p 3.

55. (29) op cit, p3. See also R Hedley and A Norman, Home Help: Key issues in service provision, Centre for Policy Studies in Ageing, 1982; and Home Helps: Working party report, National Union of Public Employees, 1983, for a breakdown of the work done by home helps.

56. Personal Communication, Helen Kahn, Brighton Council for Voluntary Service, 22 February 1983.

57. Personal Communication, Helen Kahn, Brighton Council for Voluntary Service, 26 July 1983.

58. Personal Communication, Helen Kahn, Brighton Council for Voluntary Service, 6 July 1984. See also Praise For The Caring Samaritan, Brighton Evening Argus, 19 November 1985.

59. Brighton Evening Argus (58) op cit.

60. (2) op cit, Programme 5, 22 March 1982.

61. Significantly in 1985 in pay negotiations, national employers attempted to divide home helps into those performing a "caring role" and those not, limiting the proposed pay rise to the former. The trade union negotiator argued that the employers' proposals were unworkable: "All home helps mix personal care with their domestic duties and it would be totally impractical to try and categorise home helps into two groups. Demarcation problems would be inevitable and the service would be inflexible and unworkable". We can see the same difficulty in distinguishing between the role of home helps and the work neighbourhood care scheme volunteers could be expected to do. The national employers of home helps, "LACSAB", said that the "caring role" would be defined as carrying out physical duties in the care of the sick, and "social duties" of helping with shopping and recreation and maintaining contact with families. (See S Hardingham, Two Types Of Home Helps Plan Slated, Community Care, 11 April 1985, p 4) Such "caring" duties have never reflected the overall role of home helps. They not only overlap with the "social role" referred to, but also the role of community health workers.

62. (39) op cit.

63. Report Of The Joint Working Group On The Home Help Service, DHSS Northern Ireland, 1985. For a critique of the report, see R Rowthorn, Scrapping The Home Help Service, NUPE, Belfast, 1985.

64. See, for example, M Dexter and W Harbert, The Home Help Service, Tavistock Publications, 1983; D Clode, Home Helps: The glove cast down, Social Work Today, 10 December 1984, p 7.

65. See Disquiet On The Home Front, leader, Community Care, 11 April 1985, p 1.

66. Growing Old In Brighton: A Development Group exercise in Brighton 1977-79, DHSS, Social Work Service Development Group and Social Work Service Southern Region, East Sussex County Council Social Services Department, HMSO, 1980.

67. Census Small Area Statistics For Hanover Patch, SPME Unit, East Sussex Social Services Department, p 1, Table B, 1983.

68. (66) op cit, pp 5-6.

69. (66) op cit, pp 72-111.

70. R Hadley and S Hatch, Social Welfare And The Failure Of The State: Centralised social services and participatory alternatives, George Allen and Unwin, 1981, p 154.

71. Personal Communication, Helen Kahn, Brighton Council for Voluntary Service, 6 July 1984.

72. See J Cowan, People Cope: Family groups in action, Cope, 1982; also pamphlets produced by Cope; Family Groups And The Under Fives: A social services initiative, Family Groups, and Children And Families: Shared needs. In Hanover, at the time of writing, the patch team was hoping to focus the project on the Milner Kingswood flats, whose residents have particular problems. So

far recruits for the project's "group leaders", while from within the patch, have tended to be middle class.
73. (11) op cit; Appendix A, *A Case For Neighbourhood-Based Social Work And Social Services*, pp 219-235.
74. This is the prevailing picture which emerged from the Brighton-wide group discussions we held.

CHAPTER SIX

1. R Williams, *Key Words: A vocabulary of culture and society*, Fontana Paperbacks, 1983, p 76. One of the problems with patch is that it is not always clear in which sense it is being used. This ambiguity sometimes seems to serve — intentionally or otherwise — to gain support where it might not otherwise be forthcoming. It is part of the wider issue of patch's liberal rhetoric sometimes obscuring a reactionary reality.
2. *Social Workers: Their role and tasks*, (The Barclay Report), Bedford Square Press, 1982, *A Case For Neighbourhood-Based Social Work And Social Services*, Appendix A, p 234.
3. R Hadley and M McGrath, *Going Local: Neighbourhood social services*, NCVO Occasional Paper One, Bedford Square Press, 1980, p 96.
4. (3) op cit, p 96.
5. Reflected, for example, by the publication in 1984 of; P Willmott and D Thomas, *Community In Social Policy*, Policy Studies Institute, which argued for "a study commission on community" like the Study Commission on the Family set up in 1978.
6. P Baldock, *Patch Systems: A Radical Change For The Better?*, in I Sinclair and D N Thomas, (eds), *Perspectives On Patch*, Paper No 14, NISW, 1983, p 40.
7. (2) op cit, p 220.
8. (2) op cit, p 219 and following.
9. J Finch and D Groves, *Community Care And The Family: A case for equal opportunities?*, Journal of Social Policy, Vol 9, pp 486-511, p 494.
10. (6) op cit, p 40.
11. (2) op cit, p 220.
12. (2) op cit, p 219.
13. (2) op cit, p 220.
14. (9) op cit, p 495.
15. For example, P Abrams, *Community Care: Some research problems and priorities*, Policy and Politics, 6 February 1977, pp 125-151.
16. E Wilson, *Women In The "Community" And The "Family"*, in A Walker, (ed), *Community Care: The family, the state and social policy*, Blackwell/Martin Robertson, 1982, p 55.
17. J Finch, *Community Care: Developing non-sexist alternatives*, Critical Social Policy, Issue 9, Spring 1984, pp 6-18, pp 11-12.
18. (17) op cit; and, J Finch, *A Response To Robert Harris, "End Points And Starting Points"*, Critical Social Policy, Issue 12, Spring 1985, 123-126.
19. Easy access to local shopping, which is lacking for most of the elderly residents of Hanover, can have a significant bearing on the capacity of old people to continue to maintain themselves. See, for example, A Kar and C Newbery, *"I Wouldn't Have Gone To The Welfare": A study of outreach work in Spitalfields*, London Borough of Tower Hamlets, Social Services Department, October 1973. This reported (p 7) that the proximity of a market actually "enabled some of the older residents ... who felt deeply attached to the neighbourhood ... to continue shopping for themselves (who) could not have managed long walks laden with heavy shopping baskets". Another study enlarged on this point, offering an important explanation for the failure to give it adequate recognition:
> "One important reason why shopping provision is under-researched and undervalued may be that shopping as an activity is usually done by women and — like most things that women normally do — society devalues it. At the same time, changes in local shopping patterns — particularly the closure of shops — affect women more than men. Mothers with young children, or older women (two thirds of pensioners are women) are relatively immobile and

unable to move further afield to compensate for deteriorating shopping provision in their neighbourhood".

(*From Blacksmiths To White Elephants: Benwell's changing shops*, Benwell Community Project, Newcastle-Upon-Tyne, 1979, p 4)

20. A Tomlinson, *The Illusion Of Community: Cultural values and the meaning of leisure in a gentrifying neighbourhood*, in *Leisure And Popular Cultural Forms*, A Tomlinson, (ed), Brighton Polytechnic, Chelsea School of Human Movement, 1983, pp v, 66-68.

21. The extent of mobility becomes even more apparent if we look at the refusals and people who could not be contacted in the survey. The population from which the sample was drawn came from the Electoral Register finalised in October 1981. Of the 33 cases where people could not be contacted, 16 residents at least were known to have moved or died. There were nine refusals where the sample person had moved and refusal was by their replacement — in four cases because they had just arrived days or a few weeks earlier. Two more refusals were from people about to move.

 We can get an additional idea of the rapidity of turnover and its recent nature from the fact that four of those surveyed had only lived in the area for six weeks or less, while another six of those interviewed were about to or planning to leave. Of the interviewed sample, there were eight cases where the named person had left and a new resident interviewed instead, as well as two where the original interviewee had moved and a relation in the same house was interviewed instead.

22. (20) op cit, pp 75-76

23. Of 23 working class people aged under 40, 14 had lived in the area 10 or more years; 18, six or more years, whereas 14 of the 23 middle class people in that age range had lived locally for three years or less, 20 for five years or less, and five, one year or less.

24. One third of the sample had unreservedly positive feelings about living in the area and also felt it was a community locally, compared with nine who expressed negative views about living locally and did not think it was a community. Thus there was a stronger link between liking the area and thinking it was a community than between disliking it and thinking it was not.

25. (20) op cit, pp 80,86.

26. (20) op cit, p 75.

27. S D Mackenzie, *Gender And Environment: The reproduction of labour in post-war Brighton*, Phd thesis, University of Sussex, 1983, pp 174,178.

28. (20) op cit, p 77.

29. (27) op cit, pp 148, 178.

30. Most of those (35/43) who felt it wasn't a community locally, reiterated this when we asked them this question.

31. K Young and R Hadley, *Planning, Evaluation And Control*, Community Care, 8 November 1984, p 21.

32. (2) op cit, p 230; and, A Whitehouse, *It Is Still The Same Sharing And Caring*, Community Care, 1 December 1983, pp 26-29.

33. (3) op cit, p 13.

34. R Hadley and M Cooper, (eds), *Patch Based Social Services Teams*, Bulletin No 3, Department of Social Administration, University of Lancaster, 1984, p 2.

35. Some interesting insights on this issue come from China. (See: *The Heart of the Dragon, Caring*, Channel Four Television, 6 February 1984.) There neighbourhoods consisting of about 2,000 people have "neighbourhood committees". These committees consist of retired women, one social worker and a chairperson. Their responsibilities for looking after local people extend to finding ways to make work for unemployed people, neighbourhood security, fire precautions and combatting delinquency. Their size comes much closer to the scale of neigbourhood referred to by some of our sample than to patch.

36. R Hadley, *Retrenchment Or Participation: A choice for the social services in developed countries*, in S K Sharma, (ed), *The Dynamics Of Development: An international perspective*, Vol 11, Concept Publishing Company, Delhi, 1978, p 524.

37. (27) op cit, p 148.

38. These three women, one of whom sadly died a few months after recording this discussion, all eventually moved back into the Hanover area. These extracts from their discussion were edited with their agreement.

39. (27) op cit, p 148.

40. Brighton Evening Argus, 9 November 1982.

41. (20) op cit, pp 68-75.

CHAPTER SEVEN

1. Official concern with the potential "burden of dependency" resulting from an ageing population in a worsening economic climate, was first made clear by the 1978 DHSS discussion document on old people, *A Happier Old Age* (HMSO). As Means has said, (R Means, *Decentralisation And The Personal Social Services*, in R Hambleton and P Hoggett, (eds), *The Politics Of Decentralisation: Theory and practice of a radical local government initiative*, Working Paper 46, School For Advanced Urban Studies, University of Bristol, 1985, p 88) "*A Happier Old Age*" made it clear that the DHSS was determined to control pressure on domiciliary services and residential care and this was to be carried out through an extension of family and community support".

2. For example, D Anderson, M Hewitt, *Careless Talk*, The Guardian, 20 October 1982, p 9.

3. M Davies, *The Essential Social Worker — A guide to positive practice*, Heinemann Educational Books, Community Care Practice Handbooks, 1981, pp 12-13, 212-213. A revised second edition of this book was published in 1985. These statements about care were no longer included, but they were not replaced by other definitions of care. The vagueness and lack of clarity about care was if anything increased.

4. (3) op cit, p 209 (first edition); p 236 (second edition) 1985.

5. I Illich, *Vernacular Values*, Co-Evolution Quarterly, Whole Earth Catalog, California, USA, No 26, Summer 1980, pp 22-49, p 41.

6. J Finch, *Community Care: Developing non-sexist alternatives*, Critical Social Policy, Issue 9, Spring 1984, pp 6-18, p 13.

7. H Graham, *Caring: A labour of love*, in J Finch and D Groves, (eds), *A Labour Of Love: Women, work and caring*, Routledge, 1983.

8. C Ungerson, *Women and Caring: Skills, tasks and taboos*, in E Gamarnikov, D Morgan, J Purvis and D Taylorson, (eds), *The Public And The Private*, Heinemann, 1983.

9. They are typical, for example, of North Battersea where we live, undermining social relations and existing informal networks. A study of children and young people in care in North Battersea, for example, found that most families with children in care said that they had little or no informal support to turn to. P Beresford and S Taylor, *In Care In North Battersea*, draft report, North Battersea Research Group, 1979.

10. G C Wenger, *The Supportive Network: Coping with old age*, National Institute Social Services Library No 46, George Allen and Unwin, 1984. Wenger's study while arriving at this conclusion, was not designed to indicate the extent of unmet need, of how adequate the help supplied actually was, to assess the "quality or meaningfulness" of contacts with family, friends or neighbours, or to establish what kind of support people would actually *prefer*. Nor did it seriously challenge the argument that the brunt of unpaid caring is carried out by women within the family.

11. P Phillimore, *Families Speaking: A study of fifty-one families' views of social work"*, Family Service Units, 1981, p 69.

12. H Sharron, *A Stitch in Time ...*, Social Work Today, Vol 13, No 18, 12 January 1982, p 9.

13. P Sheridan, *Southsea: Developing a patch system in the inner city*, in R Hadley and M McGrath, (eds), *Going Local: Neighbourhood social services*, NCVO Occasional Paper 1, Bedford Square Press/NCVO, 1980, pp 55-66, pp 61-62.

14. Appendix A, *Social Workers: Their role and tasks*, (The Barclay Report), Bedford Square Press, 1982, p 222.

15. N Politt, *The Paradox Of Alderson*, letter, The Guardian, 2 October 1981.

16. P Gordon, *Community Policing: Towards the local police state*, Critical Social Policy, Issue 10, Summer 1984, pp 38-58, p 39.

17. For a discussion of this and comparison of community social work with community policing, see P Beresford and S Croft, "*A Person Rather Than A Policeman": The implications of community policing*, Community Care, 31 October 1985, pp 15-17.

18. *Social Workers: Their role and tasks*, (The Barclay Report) Bedford Square Press, 1982, pp 254-5.

19. R Lambert, Untitled MSW thesis on patch, University of Sussex, 1982, p 27.

20. P Beresford, *The Relieving Officer: Poor law personified*, New Society, 6 November 1969, pp 721-3.

21. (18) op cit, p 256.

22. See a) *Caring For The Elderly And Handicapped: Community care policies and women's lives*, Equal Opportunities Commission, 1982, p 2; b) M Bayley, *Mental Handicap And Community Care*, Routledge, 1983; c) C Glendinning, *Unshared Care: Parents and their disabled children*, Routledge,

1983; d) D Wilkin, *Caring For The Mentally Handicapped Child*, Croom Helm, 1979.

23. *The Experience Of Caring For Elderly And Handicapped Dependants*, Equal Opportunities Commission, 1980, p 7.

24. (22a) op cit, p 14.

25. Cited in (22a) op cit, p 14.

26. D Piachaud, *Round About Fifty Hours A Week*, Child Poverty Action Group, 1984.

27. R Hadley and S Hatch, *The Welfare State Has Fallen Into What Might Be Called A Dependency Trap*, The Guardian, 16 September 1981.

28. (18) op cit, p 235.

29. R Hadley and M McGrath, *When Social Services Are Local: The Normanton experience*, National Institute Social Services Library No 48, George Allen and Unwin, 1984, p 17.

30. M Bayley, R Seyd, A Tennant, *Summary Of Main Findings And Recommendations To The Department Of Health And Social Security*, Neighbourhood Services Project Dinnington, Department of Sociological Studies, University of Sheffield, 1985, p 5.

31. P Abrams, S Abrams, R Humphrey, R Snaith, *Action For Care: A review of good neighbour schemes in England*, Volunteer Centre, 1981.

32. I Sinclair, D Crosbie, P O'Connor, L Stanforth, A Vickery, *Networks Project: A study of informal care, services and social work for elderly clients living alone*, extract from the main unpublished report, National Institute for Social Work Research Unit, 1984, p 136.

33. The Guardian, 17 February 1982, p 1. See, for example the proposal of the Cabinet Family Policy Group "to encourage family in the widest sense — to reassume responsibilities taken on by the state, for example, responsibilities for ... unemployed sixteen year olds". This is also reflected in the government's desire to restrict young people's access to bed and breakfast accommodation and to withdraw supplementary benefit from young people under the age of 19.

34. Cited in, *Health Or Human Rights? — A happier old age ...*, pamphlet, Barefoot Video, 1985, p 4.

35. (23) op cit, p 23.

36. See, for example: a) H Graham, *Women, Health And The Family*, Wheatsheaf Books, 1984; b) *Behind Closed Doors*, Equal Opportunities Commission, 1981; c) M Henwood and M Wicks, *The Forgotten Army: Family care and elderly people*, Family Studies Policy Centre Briefing Paper, Family Studies Policy Centre, 1984; d) *Time To Be Me*, DHSS Social Work Service Development Group video, East Sussex Consultancy and Training Agency, 1984; e) L Rimmer and S Benton, *The Treadmill of Caring*, New Statesman, 14 May 1982, pp 8-9; f) B Rogerson, *Time To Ease The Burden*, Community Care, 22 August 1985, pp 22-23; g) S Baldwin, *The Cost Of Caring*, Routledge, 1985; h) CJ Gilleard, H Belford, E Gilliard, JE Whittick and K Gledhill, *Emotional Distress Amongst The Supporters Of The Elderly Mentally Infirm*, British Journal of Psychiatry, vol 145, no 8, 1984, pp 172-177. Significantly the researchers in this study found that whatever support community services or other members of the family gave to carers, these did not seem to affect the level of distress they experienced - pointing to the inherent stresses of being a primary carer. For first hand accounts of caring, see, for example, N Murray, *"I used to long to go away by myself for a few days"*, Community Care, 1 August 1985, pp 20-22; A Briggs and J Oliver, (eds), *Caring — Experiences of looking after disabled relatives*, Routledge, 1985; *Women As Carers Conference: Breaking down the barriers — a report back on the Women as Carers Conference organized by the GLC Women's Committee*, GLC, 1986.

37. *Going Local* (13) op cit, pp 6-7.

38. It is for example lacking in both (29) op cit, and R Hadley, P Dale and P Sills, *Decentralising Social Services: A model for change*, Bedford Square Press, 1985 — the discussions of patch in Normanton and East Sussex.

39. R Kanter, *Women And the Structure of Organisations*, pp 34-37; and L Lofland, *The "Thereness" of Women* pp 144-170, in M Millman and R Kanter, (eds), *Another Voice: Feminist perspectives on social life and social science*, Anchor, New York, 1975.

40. S Edgell and V Duke, *Gender and Social Policy: The impact of public expenditure cuts and reactions to them*, Journal of Social Policy, 12: 3, July 1983, pp 357-378.

41. This can be seen to be one of the problems of the account of the East Sussex reorganisation contained in R Hadley, P Dale and P Sills, (38) op cit.

42. M Willis, *An Investigation Of The Causes And Effects Of Factory Redundancies On Men And Women: A study of the positions of men and women in relation to work*, Unpublished MA thesis, University of York, 1982.

All four of these studies are relatively small scale, but they are all based either on in-depth interviews or discussions with participants.

43. S D Mackenzie, *Gender and Environment: The reproduction of labour in post-war Brighton*, Unpublished Phd thesis, University of Sussex, 1983.
44. F Henwood, *Employment, Unemployment And Housework: An empirical study of the experiences of women and men in and out of formal employment*, Unpublished M Sc thesis, University of Sussex, 1983.
45. K Swirsky, *The Effects Of Involuntary Unemployment On Women*, Unpublished MSW thesis, University of Sussex, 1983.
46. L Rimmer and S Benton, *The Treadmill Of Caring*, New Statesman, 14 May 1982, pp 8-9, p 9.
47. M Nissell and L Bonnerjea, *Family Care For The Handicapped Elderly: Who pays?*, Policy Studies Institute, 1982. They estimated that the earnings lost by women who gave up work to care, were around £4,500 a year (at 1980 prices) and for those who reduced their paid employment, around £1,900.
    The Invalid Care Allowance is the only benefit available to meet carers' costs. It is not available to married or "cohabiting" women, who form the vast majority of carers, and it is also limited to carers between the ages of 16 and 60 (or 65 for men). At the time of writing the Advocate General of the European Court has advised that this breaches EEC equality rules, and judgement is awaited.
48. J Martin and C Roberts, *Women And Employment*, OPCS, Department of Employment, HMSO, 1984; J Finch and D Groves, *Community Care And The Family: A case for equal opportunities?* Journal of Social Policy, 9, 4, 1980, pp 487-511, p 505; (42) op cit, pp 20, 32.
49. K Price, *Women's Employment And Unemployment In The Current Recession: Facts or Ms information?*, Built Environment, Vol 10, No 1, 1984, pp 53-60, p 53.
50. (43) op cit, p 188.
51. (44) op cit, p 59.
52. (43) op cit, p 211.
53. (42) op cit, p 103.
54. (43) op cit, p 265.
55. J Martin and C Roberts, (48) op cit; (42) op cit.
56. R Davies, *Women And Work*, Hutchinson, 1975.
57. J Coussins and A Coote, *The Family In The Firing Line: A discussion document on family policy*, National Council for Civil Liberties and Child Poverty Action Group publication, 1981, p 8.
58. The Guardian, 17 February 1983, p 1.
59. Judging from advance comments of the Secretary of State and leaks in the media. The publication of this review has been long delayed. At the time of writing, we were informed by the DHSS press office that they could not say when it would be published.
60. Trades Union Congress (TUC), *Working Women*, TUC, 1983.
61. M Mason, R Stanton and M Willis, *The Office Question*, Lewis Cohen Urban Studies Centre, 1985, pp 9-11. See also U Huws, *New Technology And Women's Employment: Case studies from West Yorkshire*, Equal Opportunities Commission, 1984.
62. (49) op cit, p 55. The women Mackenzie spoke to ((43) op cit, p 210), in Brighton, said that "many of the casual "little jobs you can pick up here and there" were disappearing ... Part-time jobs for clerical, health and educational staff were now impossible to find". Thus women were being forced into the position of either having to work full-time, when they didn't want to, or leaving paid employment altogether.
63. (60) op cit.
64. (42) op cit, p 42.
65. For example, in the London Borough of Haringey, 90% of people using home helps are women; 69% of people receiving meals on wheels are women and 75% of people in old people's homes are women. See: L Loach, *Local Government: What have women got to lose?*, Spare Rib, No 151, February 1985, p 20.
66. (43) op cit, p 188.
67. (43) op cit, p 211.
68. J Oliver, Director of the Association of Carers, quoted in the Guardian, 10 December 1984.
69. J Black, R Bowl, D Burns, C Critcher, G Grant, R Stockford, *Social Work In Context: A comparative study of three social services teams*, Tavistock, 1983, p 107.
70. (42) op cit, pp 90, 92. (45) op cit, p 67.
71. (49) op cit, p 59.
72. (42) op cit, p 91. (45) op cit, p 74.
73. (42) op cit, p 91.
74. (42) op cit, p 92.
75. Man aged eighty two quoted by Willis (42) op cit, p 93.

76. See, for example, *Housing For Ethnic Elders*, Age Concern, 1984; G Evans, *The Quality Of Life*, the concern of the Standing Conference of Ethnic Minority Senior Citizens (SCEMSC) with the quality of life of all ethnic minority older people in London and elsewhere, Spare Rib, Issue 154, May 1985, p 19; N Murray, *The Central Issue Is Racism*, Community Care, 28 February 1985, pp 19-20; H Sharron, *Meeting The Ethnic Challenge*, Social Work Today, 6 August 1984, pp 9-11; *It's Our Right: Problems of ethnic minorities in social security*, conference, Greater London Council Welfare Benefits Resources Network, 7 February 1986. According to the Fourth Annual Report of the Commission For Racial Equality (1985), the personal social services are still often ethnocentric and inappropriate for members of ethnic minorities and more needs to be done to change them. See J Cooper, *Do Better*, Community Care, 29 August 1985, p 11.

77. See, for example, *Chance Or Choice: Community care and women as carers*, GLC Women's Committee/Health Panel Publication, 1984; A Walker, *The Care Gap: How can local authorities meet the needs of the elderly?*, Local Government Information Unit, 1985.

78. An Equal Opportunities Commission study (A Charlesworth, D Wilkin and A Durie, *Carers and Services: A comparison of men and women caring for dependent elderly people*, EOC, 1984), has shown that women who are looking after elderly disabled relatives at home actually get *less* help from social services than do men in the same position.

79. J Finch and D Groves, (48) op cit, p 487.

80. (27) op cit.

81. M Henwood, *The Cost Time Bomb Under Forgotten Army*, Community Care, 16 August 1984, p 10.

82. (81) op cit.

83. Quoted in A Walker, (ed), *Community Care*, Blackwell/Robertson, 1982, p 34.

84. Published by HMSO.

85. (18) op cit. para 13.68, p 216.

86. J Finch, *A Response to Robert Harris, "End Points and Starting Points"*, Critical Social Policy, Issue 12, Spring 1985, pp 123-126, p 125.

87. As for example Harris does: R Harris, *End Points and Starting Points: Some critical remarks on Janet Finch, "Community Care: developing non-sexist alternatives"*, Critical Social Policy, Issue 12, Spring 1985, pp 115-122.

88. (49) op cit, p 60.

89. L McKee, *Wives And The Recession*, Paper presented to the Central Birmingham Health Education Department Conference, *Unemployment And Its Effects On The Family*, 1983; L Morris, *Renegotiation Of The Domestic Division Of Labour In The Context Of Male Redundancy*, Paper presented to the British Sociological Association Annual Conference, 1983.

90. H Land, *Parity Begins At Home: Women's and men's work in the home and its effects on their paid employment*, Equal Opportunities Commission/Social Science Research Council, 1981, p 21.

91. J Martin and C Roberts, (48) op cit.

92. (90) op cit, p 24.

93. See S Dex and C Phillipson, *Older Women In The Labour Market: A review of current trends*, Critical Social Policy, Issue 15, Spring 1986, pp 79-83.

94. (90) op cit, p 24.

95. Two studies of neighbourhood care schemes both show that the volunteer helpers recruited are mainly women. See P Abrams, S Abrams, R Humphrey and R Snaith, *Creating Care In The Neighbourhood*, D Leat, (ed), Advance, 1986; *Survey Of Neighbourhood Care Schemes In London*, Neighbourhood Care Action Programme, reported in Network Exchange, NCAP, December 1985, p 6.

96. This seems to be the case, for example, with "Cope" groups, like those being set up in East Sussex. Land (90) op cit, pp 18-19, described the same emphasis in the community care policy of the Court Committee on child health services. This was committed to reorientating care "wherever possible from hospital to home". While there was recognition of the need for more nursing support in the community, much of its discussion centred on the need to give parents advice and education rather than practical support.

97. R Kanter, (40) op cit.

98. R G Walton, *Women In Social Work*, Routledge, 1975, p 238.

99. See D Howe, *The Segregation Of Women And Their Work In The Personal Social Services*, Critical Social Policy, Issue 15, Spring 1986, pp 21-35.

100. R P Hugman, *The Relationship Between Organisation Structure and Occupational Ideology In Social Services Departments*, Unpublished Phd thesis, University of Lancaster, 1984, pp 557, 565, 569.

101. In this it seems to be continuing the longstanding trend for home helps to be overworked and underpaid. For example Goldsberg and Connelly (EM Goldsberg and N Connelly, *Reviewing*

Services For the Old, Community Care, 6 December 1978), commented on the high proportion of home helps who reported they did jobs for service users outside hours — unpaid.

102. M Cooper, J Mooring and J Scott, *Neighbourhood Work In A Social Services Department*, Wakefield Social Services Department, 1975, p 9.

103. (6) op cit, p 10.

104. (6) op cit, p 10.

105. P West, R Illsley and H Kelman, *Public Preferences For The Care Of Dependency Groups*, Social Science and Medicine, Vol 18, No 4, 1984, pp 287-295.

106. *Harris Research Centre Survey Of British Attitudes*, published in the Observer Colour Magazine, 7 October 1984, pp 79-82.

107. H Graham, (36) op cit. Similarly Hadley and McGrath ((29) op cit, p 151) found that the families of local patch "wardens" — who were women — were drawn into helping and supporting them in their work.

108. From an advertisement to recruit team managers, *What It Means To Be A Team Manager In East Sussex*, East Sussex Social Services Department, Community Care, 7 March 1985.

109. *The Private Cost*, Community Care, Leader, 24 January 1985, p 1.

110. Government White Paper, *Expenditure Plans 1984/6-1987/8*, presented to Parliament January 1985.

111. House of Commons, Social Services Committee, *Fourth Report*, 1983-84.

112. *A Happier Old Age*, (1) op cit.

113. B Lewis, Director of Social Services, Oldham, *Who Goes Where*, Association of Directors of Social Services 1985, quoted in *Incarcerating The Elderly*, New Society, 4 October 1985, p 31. Similar findings of differences between residents of local authority and private homes were reported by A Tibbenham, *Private Care Of Elderly People: Facts and fiction*, Community Care, 15 August 1985, pp 19-21. A Study by J Pearce, *Lives In The Balance*, commissioned by the North Lincolnshire health authority, 1985, one of the first detailed assessments of government community care policy, was critical of the way long term psychiatric patients were being transferred "to the community". The lodgings where patients stayed on release were "becoming mini-institutions, and placed considerable responsibility on unqualified landlords". See report in The Guardian, 20 August 1985.

114. Quoted in Community Care, 24 January 1985, p 4.

115. (109) op cit.

116. *Paying In Private*, Leader, Community Care, 15 November 1984, p 1.

117. See, for example, W Shaw, *Registered Homes Act (1984) — Off Target*, Community Care, 25 April 1985, pp 18-21.

118. A Tibbenham (113) op cit.

119. See, for example, A Tibbenham (113) op cit; A recent Which survey (March 1985) revealed a lack of amenities and privacy in many private and voluntary old people's homes; *Cashing In On Care*, SCAT/NUPE publications, 1985, pp 8-15. It is also important to remember that the range of conditions in the private sector is also reflected in the range of charges and it is provision at the lower end of the scale of price and conditions that is available to the majority of old people reliant on state benefits. T Weaver, D Willcocks, L Kellaher, *The Business Of Care: A study of care in private residential homes for old people*, Centre For Environmental And Social Studies in Ageing, Polytechnic of North London, 1985.

120. See, for example, A Tibbenham (113) op cit; SCAT/NUPE (119) op cit; T Weaver and others (119) op cit.

121. Quoted in (34) op cit, p 1.

122. Cited in (34) op cit, p 4. They identified 49 private rest homes in one square mile of Hove. There are some 8,000 private beds provided by registered rest homes in East Sussex (reported in *Health Or Human Rights? A happier old age* ..., video, Barefoot Video, Channel 4 TV, 18 September 1985.)

123. (34) op cit, p 2.

124. Video (122) op cit; (34) op cit, pp 4,6; *Who Cares And How Much?*, produced by Brunswick Community Association Video Group, 1984; *Now We Are Older*, produced by Brunswick Community Association Video Group, 1985; *A Happier Old Age?*, Health Service Staff and Barefoot Video Co-production, 1985.

125. Interviewed in video (122) op cit.

126. R Sherrott, *Fifty Volunteers*; and D Leat, *Explaining Volunteering: A sociological perspective*, in S Hatch, (ed), *Volunteers: Patterns, meanings and motives*, The Volunteer Centre, 1983.

127. Personal communication, H Jackson, Home Office Research and Planning Unit, 19 December

1985; I Mocroft, Volunteer Centre, 20 December 1985.

128. Swirsky in her study of the effects of involuntary unemployment on women ((45 op cit), found that some of the women she interviewed had engaged in voluntary work. This had been a source of satisfaction and social contact, but it offered no substitute for the financial independence and personal autonomy which they felt were reduced by unemployment.

129. Brighton Evening Argus, 29 October 1982.

130. S Humble, *Voluntary Action In The 1980s: A summary of the findings of a national survey*, The Volunteer Centre, 1982, pp 5, 13. 1,886 people were interviewed in this study.

131. *Hanover Neighbourhood Care: Six monthly report*, Brighton Council for Voluntary Service, March 1983, pp 3, 4.

132. (131) op cit, p 4.

133. P and S Beresford, *A Say In The Future: Planning, participation and meeting social need*, Battersea Community Action, 1978. The strong message from this North Battersea study of participation was that most people did not want to get involved in such activities.

134. R Hadley and M McGrath, (eds), (13) op cit, p 1.

135. These ideas run through *Going Local*, for example, (13) op cit.

136. For example, Hadley speaking at the first of a series of three seminars *Beyond Welfare Pluralism: The future of voluntary effort*, Manchester Council for Voluntary Service/Manchester University, Department of Social Administration, April 27 1983.

137. See the discussion on colonisation in: P Abrams, (edited by M Bulmer), *Realities Of Neighbourhood Care: The interactions between statutory, voluntary and informal social care*, Policy And Politics, vol 12, no 4, 1984, pp 413-429, pp 421 and following.

138. J Didrichsen, *Dilemmas of Neighbourhood Work: A social workers viewpoint*, Social Work Service, No 31, 1982, pp 31-35.

139. M E David, *Motherhood And Social Policy — A matter of education?*, Critical Social Policy, Issue 12, Spring 1985, pp 28-43, pp 30-31.

140. For example, at the Race and Caring workshop of the GLC Women's Committee Conference, *Women As Carers*, 22 September 1985. See, *Women As Carers*, Conference report (36) op cit.

141. W Harbert, (ed), *Community-based Social Care: The Avon experience*, NCVO, Occasional Paper no 4, 1983, as described in publisher's list.

142. M Davies (3) op cit, (second edition), p 241.

143. *Working In The Community: Questions raised by the Barclay Report*, a paper produced for the AGM of the London Voluntary Service Council, 27 October 1982, by a small consultation group convened by the Volunteers Advisory Service of the LCVS.

144. K Young, *Changing Social Services In East Sussex*, Local Government Studies, March/April 1982, pp 18-22, pp 18, 22.

145. (143) op cit.

146. *The Future Of Voluntary Organisations*, (The Wolfenden Report), Croom Helm, 1977.

147. D Leat, G Smolka, G Unell, *Voluntary And Statutory Collaboration: Rhetoric or reality?* Bedford Square Press, 1981.

148. J Bishop, *Local Practice Scrutinised*, Voluntary Action, Autumn, 1981.

149. (131) op cit, p 4.

150. (69) op cit, p 82.

151. R Hadley, P Dale and P Sills, (38) op cit, p 4.

152. D Crousaz, C Davies, A Weston, *Towards Participation — A study of self-management in a neighbourhood community centre*, DHSS Statistics and Research Division Research Report No 3, HMSO, 1978, p 50.

153. O Stevenson, *Support For Informal Carers*, letter, Community Care, 7 April 1983, pp 8-9.

154. R Hadley, *The Philosophy Of Patchwork And Its Implementation*, in I Sinclair, D N Thomas, (eds), *Perspectives On Patch*, NISW Paper No 14, 1983, pp 4-8, p 5.

155. R Hadley and M McGrath, *Patch Based Social Services*, Community Care, 11 October 1979, pp 16-17, p 16.

156. (29) op cit, p 11.

157. R Hadley and M McGrath, (eds), (13) op cit, pp 10-11.

158. R Hadley and M McGrath, (eds), (13) op cit, pp 97, 101.

159. R Hadley and M Cooper, *Patch Based Social Services Teams*; Bulletin No 3, Department of Social Administration, University of Lancaster, 1984, p 43.

160. *Supporting The Informal Carers: Fifty Styles of Caring; models of practice for planners and practitioners*, Social Work Service Development Group Project Report, DHSS, 1984, p 5.

161. (160) op cit. p 1.

162. (160) op cit. The practical help offered was thus largely provided by volunteers or low paid ancillaries as home aides or care attendants, often for only a short time or for limited hours. Only two examples were described that were different to this; one providing home adaptations for people with disabilities — an unremarkable and longstanding role of social services departments; the other a special baby liaison visitor scheme, in which community based nurses provided support to such babies and families during the early days at home.

Of the remaining schemes, five offered training, education or advice, and one was commercial and available only to those who could pay.

In the few cases where the gender of supporters was given, they were almost entirely women. Other wages mentioned were £1.78 per hour for care attendants in a scheme for carers of sick people and people with disabilities.

163. *Time To Be Me*, Video, (36) op cit.
164. (160) op cit, p 58.
165. A I Roith, *A Survey Of Parental Attitudes*, Journal of Mental Subnormality, 1963.
166. (163) op cit.
167. (81) op cit.
168. (160) op cit, p 6.
169. A Tinker, *Staying At Home: Helping elderly people*, Department of Environment, HMSO, 1985.
170. R Hadley, P Dale and P Sills, (38) op cit. The other schemes were concerned with needs assessment, information giving, establishing a volunteer forum and integrating services for old people.
171. East Sussex has also been selected as one of three authorities funded under the government's "Helping The Community To Care" policy, a follow-up to its "supporting the carers" initiative. East Sussex's Director of Social Services, who was a member of the special development group of the DHSS examining this issue, made the successful application. Under this programme, the government is making available £600,000 spread over three years to the voluntary sector in East Sussex. It is to be used to develop and fund existing and proposed schemes for carers from both groups of carers themselves and voluntary organisations. After their successful bid, a consortium was set up and a coordinator appointed. The SSD is paying his salary, but there is no commitment for it to continue funding for any of the schemes or projects that might be grant-aided after the initial funding expires. The project — *Care For The Carers — East Sussex —* is still at a formative stage having officially come into existence at the beginning of 1986. The intention is to use half the money allocated for direct grants, a small amount for central administration and the rest for research and development, employing one full, and two part-time development workers. (Personal communication, Director, Age Concern East Sussex, 31 January 1986; P Endersby, Coordinator, Care For The Carers East Sussex, 5 February 1986)

Bearing in mind the very limited amount of money involved, it is difficult to see how the kind of schemes that could be supported could be other than along the lines of those described in the DHSS report (160) op cit, based on self-help, unpaid and low paid work for women.

172. (7) op cit. Also see Programme 3 in the series *Mothers And Daughters*, Channel 4 TV, reshown 31 March 1984, in which the actress Sheila Hancock spoke very positively about the chance to care for and nurse her mother through her fatal illness, referring to it as a privilege and a way of repaying her for all she had done for her, and through which she hoped she had achieved a greater closeness with her.

173. (86) op cit, p 125.
174. *Who Cares For The Carers*, Equal Opportunities Commission, 1982, pp 21-29. See Also, J Finch and D Groves, (eds), (7) op cit.
175. P Henderson and P Taylor, *Voluntarism — A Practitioner View*, Association of Community Workers, 1982, p 12.
176. J Finch, (6) op cit, p 13.
177. See S Croft, *Women, Caring And The Recasting Of Need - A Feminist Reappraisal*, Critical Social Policy, Issue 16, Summer 1986.

The first task of the development officer of the *Care For The Carers — East Sussex* project is to make a three months long appraisal of local needs. Judging from our experience this would be scant time to attempt to work out with carers themselves what their needs were and how they wanted them met, rather than rely on the interpretations of voluntary organisations and groups. The Consortium responsible for the project includes national, regional and county-wide representatives of voluntary organisations (themselves all full-time paid employees at the time of writing) as well as the Director of Social Services and his health authority equivalent. (Personal communication (171) op cit.)

178. *Time To Be Me*, Video, (36) op cit.

CHAPTER EIGHT

1. See, for example, A Forder, *Concepts In Social Administration: A framework for analysis*, Routledge, 1974, pp 39-57.
2. See, for example, L Doyal and I Gough, *A Theory Of Human Needs*, Critical Social Policy, Issue 10, Summer 1984, pp 6-38; D Clifford, *Concept Formation In Radical Theories Of Need: A comment on Doyal and Gough's "A Theory Of Human Needs"*, Critical Social Policy, Issue 11, Winter 1984, pp 147-150.
3. R Pinker, *Social Work Is Casework*, in T Philpot, (ed), *A New Direction For Social Work: The Barclay Report and its implications*, Community Care/IPC Business Press, 1982, p 68.
4. D Smith (Centre for Crime, Youth and Community, University of Lancaster), *Social Work Must Be Specific*, letter to Community Care, 31 July 1980.
5. D Behan, *Accepting The Ambiguities*, letter to Community Care, 3 March 1983, p 10.
6. This reflects the findings of Edgell and Duke (S Edgell and V Duke, *The Perceived Impact Of The Spending Cuts In Britain 1980/1 To 1983/4: Social class, life cycle and sectoral location influences*, Paper prepared for seminar on *Production, Welfare And Mass Behaviour In Urban Politics*, Copenhagen, May 9-11, 1985.
7. There may also have been other people receiving housing benefit, but we did not ask specifically about this.
8. Respondents were asked whether they would describe their income as a) comfortable, b) adequate, c) inadequate, d) difficult, or e) other; and responses were categorised accordingly. There were 17 "other" comments, eight fell within the "inadequate" or "difficult to manage" categories; seven in the "comfortable" or "adequate" categories, and two were "don't knows".
9. There was one single woman with a daughter in her 20s at university.
10. I (SC) advised her to contact Social Services for help. She was clearly not very well herself and shaky on her feet. She is now apparently receiving a home help.
11. See, for example, A Briggs and J Oliver, *Caring: Experiences of looking after disabled relatives*, Routledge, 1985.
12. *1981 Census Small Area Statistics For The Hanover Patch*, Table G, East Sussex Social Services Department, SPME Unit.
13. QueenSpark Rates Book Group, *Brighton On The Rocks: Monetarism and the local state*, QueenSpark New Series 1, 1983, pp 123-6.
14. (13) op cit, pp 122-123.
15. See *Unemployment And The Social Services*, Municipal Review and AMA News, No 647, June 1984, p 41, reporting the commencement by the Association of Metropolitan Authorities of "important research aimed at clarifying some of the implications of unemployment for social services authorities". For its findings, see S Balloch, C Hume, B Jones and P Westland, *Caring For Unemployed People: A study of the impact of unemployment on demand for personal social services*, Bedford Square Press/NCVO, 1985; N Murray, *The Politics Of Uselessness*, Community Care, 3 November 1983, pp 18-20.
16. See N Murray, *Unemployment: From dole queue to day centre*, Community Care, 24 October 1984, pp 13-15; G Fimister, *Digging Deeper Into Their Pockets*, Social Work Today, 22 October 1984, pp 16-18; S Etherington, *Handing Out A Crumb Of Comfort*, Social Work Today, 15 October 1984, pp 14-15.
17. Quoted in Community Care, 3 November 1983, p 5.
18. *Social Workers: Their role and tasks*, (The Barclay Report), R Pinker *An Alternative View*, Appendix B, Bedford Square Press, 1982, p 237.
19. B Jordan, *Social Work: Back to the Poor Law?*, New Society, 6 May 1982, p 209.
20. In a set of visual display panels, *Patch Working — What does it mean: The Principles*, ESCATA, East Sussex Social Services, 1984. Thus "Locally based teams serving the social services needs of an identifiable community or patch".
21. (3) op cit, p 68.
22. R Hadley and M McGrath, (eds), *Going Local: Neighbourhood social services*, NCVO Occasional Paper 1, Bedford Square Press, 1980, p 96.
23. R Hadley and M McGrath, *When Social Services Are Local: The Normanton experience*, National Institute Social Services Library No 48, George Allen and Unwin, 1984, pp 35-36; 257-259. Similarly key gains emerging from information supplied by patch schemes over the country in 1984 included "much better knowledge of the community and community groups", "quicker response to referrals" and "closer identification by staff with the area". See R Hadley and M

Cooper, *Letting A Hundred Patches Bloom*, Community Care, 24 May 1984, p 10.

24. K Lyons and others, *Our Crowd*, Social Work Today, 13 December 1983, pp 16-18, pp 16-17.

25. R Hadley and M Cooper, (eds), *Patch Based Social Services Teams*, Bulletin No 3, Department of Social Administration, University of Lancaster, 1984, p 7.

26. For example, in Wandsworth in 1978, when the new Conservative Council sacked the Community Development Team which was attached to the Chief Executive's Office and had been directly involved in campaigns against Council practices and policies, significantly they did offer its workers redeployment as "community social workers", but they turned this down.

27. M Cooper and J Denne, *A Problem Of Coordination*, Community Care, 31 March 1983, pp 16-18.

28. (18) op cit, pp 255-6.

29. Exactly the same "preventive" argument has been offered for community policing, but it is equally incapable of doing anything about the underlying issues of poverty, racism, disaffiliation and deteriorating services. The 1985 disturbances called its rationale into particular question. See, P Beresford and S Croft, '*A Person Rather Than A Policeman': The implications of community policing*, Community Care, 31 October 1985, pp 15-17.

30. *Brighton Social Services*, BBC Radio Brighton, Programme Two, 1 March 1982; Hanover social workers describe the problems and process of non-accidental injury cases and admission into care.

31. See *Policy Change Puts Emphasis On Families*, Community Care, 14 February 1985, p 6.

32. R Hodgkin, H Penn, J Streather, J Tunstill, *The Case For Prevention*, Community Care, 13 October 1983, pp 31-32, p 31.

33. (27) op cit, p 18.

34. G Dalley, *Ideologies of Care: A feminist contribution to the debate*, Critical Social Policy, Issue 8, Autumn 1983, pp 72-81; J Finch *A Response To Robert Harris, "End Points And Starting Points"*, Critical Social Policy, Issue 12, Spring 1985, pp 123-126; P Beresford and S Croft, *Living Together: A redefinition of group care services* in T Philpot, (ed), *Group Care Practice: The challenge of the next decade*, Community Care/Business Press International, 1984, pp 99-105.

35. (22) op cit, p 101.

36. See *Care In The Community: A consultative document on moving resources for care in England*, DHSS, 1981; T Whitehead, *Rowing Together*, Community Care, 9 August 1984, p 11, which discusses developments in Brighton for integrated services for elderly mentally ill people.

37. According to the deputy leader of St Helens (speaking at *Community Social Work — Action And Reaction*, conference, Lancashire Polytechnic, 24 November 1985) ideally leisure, education, housing and social services departments could all have been combined, "but this wasn't politically feasible". In the event the combination of housing and social services has been contentious. See, for example, *St Helens Suspended Director Speaks Out*, Social Work Today, 30 January 1986, p 3.

38. Manifesto of Walsall Labour Party, 1980.

39. Quoted in D Nicholas, *Neighbourhood Offices — The Walsall Experience*, Wandsworth Community Publications, 1981, p 4.

40. (39) op cit, *Range Of Functions To Be Performed By Neighbourhood Offices*, p 7; J Seabrook, *The Idea Of Neighbourhood: What local politics should be about*, Pluto, 1984; J David, *Walsall And Decentralisation*, Critical Social Policy, Issue 7, Summer 1983, pp 75-79. Walsall's plans for the decentralisation of social services, environmental health, leisure and education were halted when Labour lost control of the Council in the 1982 local elections. However, "towards the end of 1984, some 35 members of the social services staff, designated "community care officers", were transferred into the neighbourhood offices"; R Hambleton and P Hoggett, (eds), *The Politics Of Decentralisation: Theory and practice of a radical local government initiative*, School For Advanced Urban Studies, University of Bristol, 1985, Annex 1, p 3.

41. P Hoggett, C Fudge and S Lawrence, *Decentralisation In Local Government: The Hackney experience; A research report from the School for Advanced Urban Studies, (University of Bristol) to the London Borough of Hackney*, August 1983; p 14. According to Drucker (P Drucker, *People And Performance*, Heinemann, 1977, p 355, a "zero-based budget", "assumes that each project or activity must justify again any expenditure (above zero) for each new year even if the project or activity was justified previously".

42. P Hoggett, S Lawrence and C Fudge, *The Politics Of Decentralisation In Hackney*, in R Hambleton and P Hoggett, (eds), (40) op cit, pp 62-79.

43. For example: R Moseley, *Learning Decentralisation*, London Community Work Service Newsletter, May 1983, pp 6-7; N Murray, *Decentralisation Is Here To Stay*, Community Care, 7 April 1984, pp 12-13; R Shield, *Decentralisation And Socialism*, Chartist, June/August 1982, pp

10-14; R Shield, *The Socialist Case For "Going Local"*, Chartist, November/January 1983, p 21; S Croft and P Beresford, *Making Our Own Plans*, Chartist, February/April 1983, pp 26-27; K McDonnell, *Which Way To Decentralisation*, Chartist, May/June 1983; Islington Labour Party Working Group on Decentralisation, *Decentralising Social Services In Islington, Discussion Paper*, 1983; D Blunkett and G Green *Building From The Bottom: The Sheffield experience*, Fabian Tract 491, Fabian Society, 1983; C Fudge, *Decentralisation: Socialism goes local?*, in M Boddy and C Fudge, (eds), *Local Socialism?*, Macmillan, 1984.

44. N Murray, *Why Pensioners Need Their Post Offices*, Community Care, 11 April 1985, p 8; *PO Closures Rouse Sleeping Giant*, report of a conference organised by the Castlemilk Elderly Forum in Glasgow as part of a campaign to reverse national policy on post office closure, Community Care, 15 November 1984, p 4.

45. R Pinker, *Slimline Social Work*, New Society, 13 December 1979, pp 595-596.

CHAPTER NINE

1. For example in, R Hadley and M McGrath, (eds), *Going Local: Neighbourhood social services*, NCVO Occasional Paper 1, Bedford Square Press, 1980, p 1 and following.
2. (1) op cit, pp 3-4.
3. (1) op cit, p 10.
4. (1) op cit, p 96.
5. *Social Workers: Their role and tasks*, (The Barclay Report), Bedford Square Press, 1982, p229.
6. P Baldock, *Patch System: A radical change for the better?*, in I Sinclair, DN Thomas, (eds), *Perspectives On Patch*, NISW Paper No 14, 1983, p 39.
7. Quoted in, QueenSpark Rates Book Group, *Brighton On The Rocks: Monetarism and the local state*, QueenSpark new series 1, 1983, p 46.
8. See for example letters from past and present East Sussex workers in Community Care, 10 January 1985, 14 February 1985 and 28 February 1985.
9. T Philpot, *Puppets On A String*, Community Care, 21 February 1985, pp 12-15.
10. R Lambert, Untitled MSW thesis on Patch, summary, University of Sussex, 1982.
11. J Didrichsen, *Dilemmas Of Neighbourhood Work: A social worker's viewpoint*, Social Work Service, 31, 1982, p 35.
12. Quoted in: A Stanton, *Collective Working In The Personal Social Services: A study with nine agencies*, MSc thesis (unpublished), Cranfield Institute of Technology, 1983, p 64.
13. (5) op cit, p 132 and following.
14. R Hadley, P Dale and P Sills, *Decentralising Social Services: A model for change*, Bedford Square Press, 1984, p 24; K Young and R Hadley, *In The Front Line*, Community Care, 15 November 1984, pp 21-22, p 21.
15. See for example, R Hadley and M McGrath, *When Social Services Are Local: The Normanton experience*, George Allen and Unwin, 1984, pp 207, 260-261.
16. For example, R Hadley and S Hatch, *Social Welfare And The Failure Of The State: Centralised social services and participatory alternatives*. George Allen and Unwin, 1981. Writing of Normanton, they said, "Much necessarily depends on the political skills and commitment of the area officer. If he moves elsewhere the future of the system may well be in jeopardy" (p 156). See also G Jones, *Nature Makes No Leaps* in (1) op cit, p 16 and following — an account of a similar leader-inspired approach to patch and the patch team.
17. See J Joslin, *Essex Road Team — A Community Based Team Adopts a Patch System*, in (1) op cit, pp 63-70, p 65; B Bennett, *The Sub Office: A team approach to local authority fieldwork practice* in M Brake and R Bailey, (eds), *Radical Social Work and Practice*, Edward Arnold, 1980, pp 155-181, p 175.
18. There are examples in voluntary organisations of team members overcoming some of these problems by pooling and equalising their wages. A Stanton's current research on collective teams, Cranfield Institute of Technology, strongly suggests that while collaborative working within a formal hierarchy is feasible, there are severe tensions both for the formal leaders and team members.
19. R P Hugman, *The Relationship Between Organisational Structure And Occupational Ideology In Social Services Departments*, Unpublished Phd thesis, University of Lancaster, 1984. Hugman

did not identify another key dimension of dominance — race.

20. R Hadley, P Dale, P Sills, (14) op cit, p 15.
21. H Sharron, *A Stitch In Time*, Social Work Today, 12 January 1982, pp 7-9, p 9.
22. R Hadley, P Dale, P Sills, (14) op cit, p 13.
23. Quoted in *Restyled Districts: 19 posts to go*, Social Work Today, 24 June 1985, p 5.
24. *East Sussex Social Services Information For Job Applicants; 2: East Sussex Social Services — the structure*, East Sussex Social Services Department, 1985. The Strathclyde reorganisation also abandoned the divisional tier in favour of a strengthened headquarters, creating a number of new senior management posts. See Community Care, 19 September 1985, p 4.
25. D Brandon, Social Work Today, 13 August 1981, p 9.
26. *Report Of The "Committee On Local Authority And Allied Personal Social Services"*, (The Seebohm Report), HMSO, 1968.
27. For example, see A Richardson, *Participation*, Routledge, 1983, pp 39-40.
28. R Deakin and P Willmott, *Participation In Local Social Services: An exploratory study*, Studies in Participation 1, Personal Social Services Council, 1979.
29. (28) op cit, p 15.
30. E Sainsbury, S Nixon and D Phillips, *Social Work In Focus: Clients' and social workers' perceptions in long-term social work*, Routledge, 1982, p 21.
31. A Tyne, *Participation by Families Of Mentally Handicapped People In Policy Making And Planning*, Personal Social Services Council, 1978. A similar finding about the ineffectiveness of formal machinery for participation for people with disabilities was reported in: C Low, G Rose, B Cranshaw, *Participation In Services For The Handicapped: Two contrasting models*, Studies in Participation 2, Personal Social Services Council, 1979.
32. *Working Together*, Report of Wandsworth Participation Steering Group For Mentally Handicapped People, 1979, p 1.
33. M Oliver, *Social Work With Disabled People*, Practical Social Work Series, British Association of Social Workers, MacMillan, pp 124,130.
34. P Stubbs, *The Employment Of Black Social Workers: From "ethnic sensitivity" to anti-racism?*, Critical Social Policy, Issue 12, Spring 1985, pp 6-27, p 25; H Sharron, *Meeting The Ethnic Challenge*, Social Work Today, 6 August 1984, pp 9-11; J Griffiths *Study Of Social Service Provision To Ethnic Minority Groups*, Derbyshire County Council, 1984; N Murray, *The Central Issue Is Racism*, Community Care, 28 February 1985, pp 19-20.

    Statutory obligations can be redefined. See, for example, *Racial Attacks And Harassment — A social services response*, internal paper by the team leader, Beckton Team, Social Services Department, London Borough of Newham, 1985. This argued that racism should be seen as a legitimate concern of the social services department, which "in some cases would attain the priority of other At Risk cases such as those of Child Abuse and the vulnerable elderly. Under Section S71 of the Race Relations Act, 1976, Newham Council has a duty to work to eliminate racial discrimination and to promote good relations between persons of different racial groups. The fulfilment of the statutory duties require an appropriate response by Newham Social Services which addresses itself to the dual tasks of providing support for victims of racial attacks and attempting to prevent further attacks from happening. This would clearly need a reprioritising of this work compared with other work."

    It went on to give suggestions how "greater emphasis could be placed on working in the field of racial harassment by the Social Work Service Department, recognising the current procedures which are in use".
35. See, for example, L Dominelli, *Violence: A family affair*, Community Care, March 21 1981, pp 17-19; ME David, *Motherhood And Social Policy — A matter of education?*, Critical Social Policy, Issue 12, Spring 1985, pp 28-43.
36. N Boaden, M Goldsmith, W Hampton, P Stringer, *Public Participation In Local Services*, Longman, 1982, pp 146-147.
37. See, for example, (28) and (36) op cit.
38. For details of the way such comments were categorised, see the Research Method Appendix. Three people's responses about "users" were included in an "other" category as were those of four people about "local people". Some of these also expressed the view that users and local people had very little or no say.
39. These were the 16 people who thought workers would have "a reasonable amount of say" and one who thought they would have "a lot".
40. We made a breakdown of people's responses according to whether they saw social services as consistent (positive) or inconsistent (negative) with criteria of need; having broadbased

decision-making, and enabling users, workers and local people to have a say in them. More than half the sample thought that social services did not accord with two or more of these criteria; a quarter with three or more. Less than one fifth thought social services were consistent with even one of them. Perhaps not surprisingly, there was also a relationship between negative attitudes to social services and seeing them as inconsistent with these criteria. Thus two thirds of people making negative comments about social services (24/36) also gave two or more negative responses to these criteria, suggesting that people also tended to be dissatisfied with social services they saw as narrowly based and unrelated to need.

41. P and S Beresford, *A Say In The Future: Planning, participation and meeting social need*, Battersea Community Action, 1978.
42. R Seyd, A Tennant, M Bayley and P Parker, *Community Social Work*, Paper No 8, Neighbourhood Services Project, Dinnington, Department of Sociological Studies, University of Sheffield, 1984.
43. R Hadley and M Cooper, (eds), *Patch Based Social Services Teams*, Bulletin No 3, Department of Social Administration, University of Lancaster, 1984, p 7.
44. (43) op cit, offers details of patch schemes throughout the country collated from questionnaires returned by teams. Regrettably it does not offer information on this.
45. (1) op cit, p 10.
46. (1) op cit, p 98.
47. (1) op cit, p 102.
48. (42) op cit, p 110.
49. M Bayley and P Parker, *Dinnington: An experiment in health and welfare cooperation*, in (1) op cit, p 79.
50. M Bayley, P Parker, R Seyd, A Tennant, *Successes And Failures In Developing Joint Management*, Neighbourhood Services Project Dinnington, Paper No 4, Department of Sociological Studies, University of Sheffield, 1984, p 193.
51. (50) op cit, pp 191-194.
52. M Bayley, R Seyd, A Tennant, *Summary Of Main Findings And Recommendations To The Department Of Health And Social Security*, Neighbourhood Services Project Dinnington, Department of Sociological Studies, University of Sheffield, 1985, p 7.
53. (15) op cit.
54. M Cooper, *Community Social Work*, in B Jordan and N Parton, (eds), *The Political Dimensions Of Social Work*, Blackwell, 1983, p 161.
55. M Cooper, *Putting Philosophy Into Practice*, in I Sinclair, DN Thomas, (eds), (6) op cit, pp 9-15, p 10.
56. M Cooper, *Normanton: Interweaving social work and the community*, in (1) op cit, pp 29-40, p 40.
57. (54) op cit, p 161.
58. (55) op cit, p 10.
59. See I Cole, E Butterworth, First and Second Research Reports on *The Social Care Assembly For Normanton*, Department of Social Administration and Social Work, University of York, 1983 and 1984.
60. M Loveland, *Organiser's Final Report*, SCAN, February 1985, p 7.
61. See, for example, (15) op cit, p 252; and R Hadley and M McGrath, *The Normanton Experience*, Community Care, pp 23-24, p 24.
62. (42) op cit, pp 110-112.
63. K Lyons, A Bolger, P Hale, R Schaedel, L Williamson, S Thomson, *Our Crowd*, Social Work Today, 13 December 1983, pp 16-18.
64. G Coffin and P Dobson, *Finding Our Hidden Strengths*, Social Work Today, 12 November 1984, pp 16-18, p 18.
65. (63) op cit, p 18.
66. For example, in Normanton, the Home Office funding for the SCAN project, and in Dinningon, the additional "action" resources from the action-research project.
67. Decentralisation is a continuing process, so our comments are tied to the time we are writing. For example Manchester is embarking on a major decentralisation programme based on 51 neighbourhood offices.

Islington is probably the local authority where the implementation of plans for decentralisation is most advanced. But the extent to which there will be any effective devolution of power to service users and local people remains unclear. Significantly, at the beginning of 1986, there were already 15 neighbourhood offices open and nine more due by the middle of the year. But formal arrangements for any redistribution of power were still unresolved, nearly four years after the Council came to power with a manifesto commitment to decentralise. In 1984 it published a paper for consultation in which the local committees originally envisaged as having a management role were now conceived much more in advisory terms. (*Setting Up Advisory Councils In Decentralised Neighbourhood Areas, A paper for consultation*, London Borough of Islington, June 1984). In October 1985 another consultation document was produced for discussion at a local conference. (*Neighbourhood Forums: Issues for Conference, A consultative document*, Policy And Partnership Committee. See also a report of the conference, *Neighbourhood Forums — What Future?*, Decentralisation Unit, London Borough of Islington.

This formed the basis for the report to go to Council, after some modification from the conference and with some amendments by the Decentralisation Sub-Committee and Policy and Partnership Committee. (See *Guidelines For The Establishment Of Neighbourhood Forums*, Appendix A, Policy and Partnership Committee, 11 February 1986). This report seemed to go further than the 1984 consultation document. Neighbourhood forums would, for example, have a say in a very small local budget (£2,000), the £1 million borough-wide environmental improvement budget and the chance to "make bids" for other monies. They would have "a major role in maintaining, improving, and monitoring the quality and quantity of the services being provided in the neighbourhood (whether through the Neighbourhood Office or otherwise)". However, the relationship of any powers they might have with the existing council structure and the rights and responsibilities of workers remained uncertain. While, for example, having "the power to effectively control decisions delegated to the Neighbourhood Office", "If Officers are not able to accept a particular recommendation they will refer the matter for decision to the appropriate Council Committe or Senior Officer ... The limits of decision making delegated to the Forums will be determined by the Council."

The draft "public guidelines" for neighbourhood forums (*Have A Say On Your Neighbourhood*; neighbourhood forums: public guidelines, second draft, Islington Council Decentralisation Co-ordination Unit, 1986) introduces them as no more than an "opportunity (for local people) to meet regularly, discuss and make recommendations on issues that concern them". (p (ii))

Thus as we write, the extent and practicalities of any devolution of power in Islington continue to be unclear. Certainly, however, the trend does seem to be towards a dilution of devolution since the original commitment to decentralisaton and democratisation was made. (See, for example, *Decentralising Social Services In Islington, discussion paper*, Labour Party Working Goup on Decentralisation, September 1983; *Power Down Below: Decentralisation of services in Islington — a discussion paper arguing for a clear socialist commitment to local democracy*, Labour Party Working Group On Decentralisation, January 1984.

While Hackney's plans for comprehensive decentralisation may have been "discredited as an 'across the borough' grand political initiative" (P Hoggett, S Lawrence and C Fudge, (eds), *The Politics Of Decentralisation: Theory and practice of a radical local government initiative*, Working Paper 46, SAUS, University of Bristol, 1985, p 76.), its original Redprint 1 remains interesting because of its apparent recognition of issues which have generally either not been adequately acknowledged or have been whittled away in implementation. As Hoggett, Lawrence and Fudge have said, summing it up (pp 74-5 op cit):

"Briefly it envisaged the decentralisation *and* reorganisation of services into at least 20 ward-based neighbourhood offices. A Neighbourhood Committee with executive and financial powers, involving local councillors and community groups with reserved places for representation from particular sections of the community, would exist alongside each neighbourhood office. Service Committees would not be disbanded but would lose their executive powers and assume a monitoring and advisory role vis a vis neighbourhood committees. The Policy and Resources Committee would retain executive powers and would have final responsibility for maintaining borough-wide controls and standards.

The first Redprint envisaged largely self-managed neighbourhood offices directly accountable to local neighbourhood committees. Hierarchical line-management structures would be rejected, senior managerial and professional staff assuming a support and consultancy function rather than a management control function. In other words the first Redprint was arguing for a radical measure of devolved control both within the bureaucracy itself and between the bureaucracy and the recipients of its services."

68. J Seabrook, *The Idea Of Neighbourhood: What local politics should be about*, Pluto Press, 1984.
69. For example, questions of cost for the bricks and mortar — especially at a time of financial cuts; of creating another tier of "mini town halls", and an extended bureaucratic and professional elite, albeit locally rather than centrally based. Neighbourhood offices may offer the advocates

of general decentralisation the comfort of achievement in bricks and mortar — there certainly has been progress in establishing them — but this certainly does not necessarily go hand in hand with extending local and user control, which as we have seen is still at a much more preliminary and fugitive stage.

70. *Decentralisation: Who's doing what?*, Community Care, 18 April 1985, p 19.

71. K Young and R Hadley, *Planning, Evaluation And Control*, Community Care, 8 November 1984, pp 21-22, p 21.

72. For example, K Young, *Changing Social Services In East Sussex*, Local Government Studies, March/April 1982, pp 18-22; *Guidelines For Decentralised Teams*, ESCATA, East Sussex Social Services Department, 1984; K Young and R Hadley, (14) op cit; R Hadley, P Dale, P Sills, (14) op cit, Foreword by K Young; K Young and R Hadley, *Managing To Go Patch*, Community Care, 29 September 1983, pp 18-20.

73. See, for example, K Young and R Hadley, *Managing To Go Patch*, Community Care, 29 September 1983, pp 18-20; K Young, *Changing Social Services In East Sussex*, Local Government Studies, March/April 1982, pp 19-22. Both these articles were included in the information pack sent to job applicants by East Sussex Social Services. See also, K Young and R Hadley, *Planning, Evaluation And Control*, Community Care, 8 November 1984, pp 21-22.

   This emphasis is also reflected in other activities of the Department. East Sussex Social Services in association with the Institute of Local Government Studies, (INLOGOV), University of Birmingham, has developed "management development programmes", video assisted "management development packages for health and social services", and conferences on management. For example, *Managing For An Uncertain Future?*, 30-31 October 1985, including *Achieving Value For Money: The manager's role*, John Banham, controller, Audit Commission; and guest speaker, Mike Brearley, "former captain of England", *The Art Of Captaincy*,

74. C. Jones, *A Tricky Patch*, Youth And Policy, Autumn, 1985, pp 22-23.

75. R Hadley, P Dale, P Sills, (14) op cit.

76. (71) op cit, p 22. Two methods to encourage consumer evaluation in East Sussex were mentioned. First was good publicity about services. As we have seen, this does not seem to have been effective from the experience of our sample. "A second approach to public involvement, has been a natural consequence of the development of joint initiatives at patch level with the local community. Working together, with voluntary groups, for example, or a publicity campaign or in setting up a volunteer network, opens the teams to the views of the local community, as does the encouragement of closer relations between a residential home and the people living in the neighbourhood." However, exposure to local and service users' views and closer local contact with provision certainly need not mean any increased say in departmental policy or practice, even if it may result in the department or patch team being able to base its decisions on different or additional information. Decision-making will remain where it is.

77. See, for example, the attitudes of people in our study (41) op cit.

78. (71) op cit, p 22.

79. *Policy Change Puts Emphasis On Families*, Community Care, 14 February 1985, p 6.

80. *Report Of The Working Group On Services For The Mentally Handicapped And Their Families In The West Division*, East Sussex Social Services, undated.

81. (80) op cit, p 4.

82. (80) op cit, p 6. The two other recommendations were that "Parents and local (special) schools should be involved in the planning, setting up and running of alternative family placement schemes", (p 145) and that all day care services assessment conferences should include trainees/residential staff and/or parents (p 78).

83. P Dale, *Trainer's Notes*, for *Patchwork*, video, ESCATA, East Sussex Social Services Department, 1985.

84. (71) op cit, p 21.

85. K Young and R Hadley (1983) (72) op cit.

86. Quoted in Community Care, 3 November 1983, p 5.

87. From *Director's Report To Social Services Committee*, East Sussex County Council, 24 February 1984.

88. (87) op cit.

89. *What It Means To Be A Team Manager In East Sussex*, job advertisement for team managers, East Sussex Social Services Department, Community Care, 7 March 1985.

90. See, for example, R Murray, *Benetton Britain: The new economic order*, Marxism Today,

November 1985, pp 28-32; *The Future Of Work; Part 2: What Kind Of Work*, Society Today supplement, New Society, 8 November 1985.

91. And indeed offer even less likelihood of a choice or say for their users. As Barefoot Video pointed out (*Health Or Human Rights?, A happier old age ...*, pamphlet, 1985), elderly people in Brighton and Hove were not consulted about the closure of long stay hospital beds and wards, reductions in community based services or their increasing placement in commercial old people's and nursing homes.

92. *Clients' Rights: Report of an NCVO Working Party*, Bedford Square Press, 1984, p 84.

93. B Campbell, *Wigan Pier And Beyond*, New Statesman, 16/23 December 1983, pp 23-24, p 23.

94. (41) op cit; P Beresford and S Croft, *"It's Not Much Of A Prospect": First findings from a study of young people, participation and powerlessness*, Community Care, 10 September 1981, pp 18-20, p 19.

95. For example, (28) op cit, p 21.

96. Discussion day on neighbourhood offices, London Borough of Islington, 16 April 1983.

97. They also closely reflect the reasons people gave in our large scale study of participation (41) op cit, for not wanting a greater say in local decisions. Almost half (49%) of those who answered in this way gave as their reason feeling too old, being too busy, not suitably qualified, or the belief that there was no point since it would be ineffective.

98. See the *Interim Research Papers* published by the Linked Research Project into Public Participation in Structure Planning, Department of Extra-Mural Studies, University of Sheffield, 1975-78.

99. P Beresford, *Including The Public*, review article, Social Work Today, 19 October 1982, p 14.

100. See P Beresford, *A Service For Clients*, in T Philpot, (ed), *A New Direction For Social Work?: The Barclay Report and its implications*, Community Care/IPC Business Press, 1982, pp 49-62.

101. See report and comments on this research by the Association of Directors of Social Services, Community Care, 28 March 1985, pp 1,2; Social Work Today, 25 March 1985, p 4. The Association of County Councils and Association of Metropolitan Authorities also raised objections to such committees.

102. See *An Inspector Calls*, Social Work Today, 1 April 1985, pp 10-11; E Harbridge, *Social Services Inspectorate: Has the leopard changed its spots?*, Community Care, 16 January 1986, pp 15-17.

103. See, for example, *Managing Social Services For the Elderly More Effectively*, HMSO, 1985; A Fry, *Huge Variations In Cost Of Same Services*, three "value for money" reports on social services prepared for the audit inspectorate by management consultants, Community Care 7 July 1983, pp 4-5; *Commission And Omission*, leader, Community Care, 28 February 1985, p 1; A Fry, *Audit Report: "Banham's boys must do better"*, Community Care, 7 March 1985, p 3.

104. We take up the subsequent history of SCAN in the next chapter.

105. Islington, as we have said, is probably the authority that is most advanced in implementing its proposals for comprehensive decentralisation, but the basic issue of overcoming the problems of involving people in such formal bodies as neighbourhood forums do not seem to have been worked through, although there does seem to be recognition of the issue. For example, reserving places for people and groups who face particular discrimination, as they suggest in their guidelines for neighbourhood forums doesn't resolve the issue of how to enable that involvement to be as broadbased as possible. There is also a particular problem because of the desire of the authority to set up forums "as quickly as possible". Trying to achieve broadbased involvement quickly is a contradiction in terms, judging from decades of experience in community action. Key workers in neighbourhood offices, like neighbourhood officers themselves, community workers and welfare rights workers may have a reponsibility to draw in people's involvement written into their job descriptions. But this still requires the development of particular skills which cannot be taken for granted. This labour intensive activity must also be placed in the context of other demands on their time, which is likely to be overstretched in a period of restricted resources. There are also potential conflicts of interest here which need to be worked through. There is likely to be an understandable reluctance on the part of at least some workers to devolve power to service users and local people, if it comes from their own already limited stock of control.

106. *Guidelines For Decentralised Teams* (72) op cit.

107. R Hadley, P Dale, P Sills, (14) op cit, pp 78-93.

108. C Parker, *Lessons School Bosses Can Teach*, Social Work Today, 17 December 1984, pp 12-13.

109. S Etherington and C Parker, *Time To Get Street Wise*, Social Work Today, 13 May 1985, pp 13-14.

110. See, for example, P Beresford and S Croft, *Welfare Pluralism: The new face of fabianism*, Critical Social Policy, Issue 9, Spring 1984, pp 19-39.

111. See, for example, N Khan, *Showdown*, New Statesman, 8 March 1985, p 36.

112. (63) op cit, pp 16, 18.
113. R Hadley, P Dale, P Sills, (14) op cit, pp 93, 105. While "it has been claimed that the Normanton Patch system will increase the knowledge that the population has of the local social services ((15) op cit, p 254) Hadley and McGrath's recent research study did not explore this issue and offers no data on it. Similarly, the Dinnington Neighbourhood Services Project did not explore people's knowledge of social services. What it was concerned with was "whether people saw formal and informal care as an integrated package", Personal Communication, M Bayley, Director, 10 May 1985.
114. B Holman, Feed Back, Community Care, 14 February 1985, p 11; J Boucherat, The Southdown Project Survey, Southdown Project, Children's Society, 1984.
115. A Whitehouse, In The Picture, Community Care, 8 November 1984, pp 12-14.
116. Video Assisted Learning Materials, Training, Consultancy, Publications, the ESCATA catalogue, 1984.
117. Media Unit Catalogue and Price List 1983, East Sussex Social Services Department, 1983.
118. New Release Notes for Patchwork video, ESCATA, East Sussex Social Services Department, 1985.
119. Patchwork video, ESCATA, East Sussex Social Services Department, 1985. The ESCATA catalogue (116) op cit, also reported a programme Decentralisation, giving "an informed and balanced view of the process of decentralisation in East Sussex Social Services Department, available in December 1985".
120. (118) op cit.
121. Speaking From Experience: The user's involvement in mental health services, video, ESCATA, East Sussex Social Services Department, 1985.
122. Speaking From Experience, promotional pamphlet, ESCATA, East Sussex Social Services Department, 1985.
123. Presentation of video assisted training materials, London, 5 March 1985. For further information about ESCATA, see also, J Stroud, When Taking A Gamble Pays Off, Social Work Today, 20 May 1985, pp 20-22. Its turnover for its second year "is predicted to approach £1m".
124. See, for example, (43) op cit, pp 46-47. Meanwhile in April 1986, ESCATA announced that it was "going alone" as an independent trading company.
125. Community Care, 30 June 1983, p 7.
126. (92) op cit, pp 21-4, 85.
127. Social Services In The Seven Dials Area of Brighton, "leaflet produced by the Social Services Department for local users to explain the work of the patch team", reproduced in (43) op cit, pp 45-47.
128. See, for example, (41) op cit, pp 36-61.
129. (41) op cit, pp 77-78.
130. H Ouseley, "Treating Them All The Same" — Decentralising institutionalised racism, Going Local?: Newsletter of the Decentralisation Research and Information Centre, No 2, Polytechnic of Central London, April 1985, pp 8-9, p 9.
131. (27) op cit, pp 45-49.
132. See, for example, P Beresford, Hostile Reception, New Society, 22 September 1977, p 600-601; P Beresford, Resettlement Policy, New Society, 9 October 1980, pp 68-69.
133. (68) op cit.
134. See, for example, E Pilkington, Looking For New Friends, New Statesman, 5 April 1985, pp 8-9.
135. K Young and R Hadley (1983), (72) op cit, p 19.
136. N Dennis, Public Participation And Planners' Blight, Faber and Faber, 1972, pp 213-280.
137. (101) op cit.
138. See, for example, M Coleman, Why We Must Involve The Public, Local Government Chronicle, 2 September 1983, p 955; and A Crine, Accountability In Action, Community Care, 3 February 1983, p 5.
139. O Stevenson and P Parsloe, Social Service Teams: The practioners' view, HMSO, 1978, p 308; P Parsloe, Social Services Area Teams, Allen and Unwin, 1981.
140. J Black, R Bowl, D Burns, C Critcher, D Grant, D Stockford, Social Work In Context: A comparative study of three social services teams, Tavistock, 1983, pp 212, 221.
141. J Joslin, (17) op cit; B Bennett, (17) op cit.
142. A Stanton, Collective Working In The Personal Social Services: A study with nine agencies, (unpublished) MSc thesis, Cranfield Institute of Technology, Department of Social Policy, 1983.
143. See P Williams and B Shoultz, We Can Speak For Ourselves, Human Horizons Series, Souvenir Press, 1982. We have tried when referring to examples of involvement to restrict ourselves to those which are either directly known to us or to people we are associated with, or which have

received careful independent reporting. Such initiatives are dynamic, not static. They have their good and difficult times. They change. Another issue in making sense of participatory projects is that undertandably when they are described, particularly by their initiators, there is sometimes a tendency for them to be seen through rose-tinted spectacles. We are not suggesting that the examples we offer have "got it all right", but they do show ways forward for involving and empowering people.

144. D Brandon, *Drifting Away From The Mainstream*, Social Work Today, 13 August 1984, pp 14-15, p 15.
145. (143) op cit, p 191.
146. J Cornwell and P Gordon, (eds), *An Experiment In Advocacy: The Hackney Women's Health Project*, King's Fund Centre, 1985; A Karpf, *The Hospital Pain Killers*, The Guardian, 13 March 1985; B Sang and B O'Brien, *Advocacy: The UK and American Experiences*, King's Fund Centre, 1985.
147. See Akroyd Under Fives Group *Annual Reports*, Akroyd Community Centre, 1983 onwards.
148. (141) op cit, p 8.
149. N Khan, *Roots*, New Statesman, 3 May 1985, p 38.
150. (7) op cit, p 180.
151. See, for example, J Bishop and P Hoggett, *Leisure Beyond The "Individual Consumer"*, Report on leisure research, School of Advanced Urban Studies, University of Bristol, 1984.
152. See, for example, *Being Together: Southwark women talking about leisure*, London Borough of Southwark's Women's Equality Unit, 1984.
153. See, for example, (41) op cit.
154. See, for example, P Beresford and S Croft *Democratising Social Services*, paper presented at 1982 Labour Coordinating Committee *Beyond Welfare Conference*, Battersea Community Action, 1982.
155. G Craig, *Review Of Studies Of The Public And Users' Attitudes, Opinions And Expressed Needs With Respect To Social Work And Social Workers*, produced for the Barclay Committee, NISW, 1982, pp 16-17.
156. See, for example, O Stevenson, *Specialisation In Social Service Teams*, George Allen and Unwin, 1981.
157. P Beresford, *Patch In Perspective: Decentralising and democratising social services*, discussion paper, Battersea Community Action, 1984, introduction.

PART THREE INTRODUCTION

1. R Hadley and M McGrath, *When Social Services Are Local: The Normanton experience*, George Allen and Unwin, 1984, p 15.

CHAPTER TEN

1. J Dalton (now General Manager ESCATA), in *Patching The Community Together*, Community Care, 6 May 1982, pp 20-21, p 21.
2. See, A Shearer, *Everybody's Ethics: The future of handicapped babies*, Campaign for People with Mental Handicaps (CMH), 1984.
3. Green Paper, *Reform Of Social Security*, Cmnd 9517; *Programme For Change*, Cmnd 9518; and *Background Papers*, Cmnd 9519, HMSO, 1985.
   The effect of such proposals if implemented would be greatly to increase people's social and economic insecurity. They particularly penalise and discriminate against women and members of ethnic minorities. The two thirds of people with disabilities living in or on the margins of poverty would be made increasingly dependent on others or at risk of institutionalisation because of the drastic drop in their living standard.
   See, for example, *The Claimant Speaks*, Community Care, 27 June, 1985, pp 22-23, for the views

of some claimants themselves; J Lister, *Burying Beveridge*, Community Care, 11 July 1985, pp 19-21; L Lennard and I McMaster, *The Disabling Effect Of The Green Paper*, Community Care, 20 June 1985, pp 14-15; M Tarpey, *Review: Information On The Social Security Reviews*, Issue 6, produced for the London Advice Services Alliance by the Community Information Project, Bethnal Green Library, June 1985; *Ethnic Minorities And The Social Security Reviews*, Conference, London Advice Services Alliance, 26 June 1985; *It's Our Right: Problems of ethnic minorities in social security*, Conference, GLC/CCS Welfare Benefits Resource Network, 7 February 1986.

4. P Townsend and N Davidson, (eds), *Inequalities In Health Working Group Report*, Sir Douglas Black (chairman), (The Black Report), Penguin, 1982.

5. P Beresford and S Croft, *Living Together: A redefinition of group care services*, in T Philpot, (ed), *Group Care Practice: The challenge of the next decade*, Business Press International, 1984, pp 99-105.

6. UPIAS and Disability Alliance, *Fundamental Principles Of Disability*, 1975, p 14.

7. K Davies, *The Politics Of Independent Living: Keeping the movement radical*, in The Bulletin (on social policy), No 16, Winter 1985, pp 45-52, p 46.

8. Second Report of the Commons Social Services Committee: *Community Care*, HMSO, 1985. Whether "community care" is cheaper than traditional policies depends very much on how it is interpreted and what is provided. Certainly providing appropriate and adequate services in "the community" is unlikely to be a cheaper, and indeed may be a more expensive option — if judged only in narrow financial terms. See, for example, J Cooper, *Care In The Community By NHS Is Not Cheaper*, Community Care, 5 September 1985, p 12.

9. Speaking at the World Federation For Mental Health Conference, reported in, Community Care, 1 August 1985, p 5.

10. *Cashing In On Care*, NUPE/SCAT publication, 1985, pp 27-28.

11. See, J Campling, *Flexi Ideas*, Community Care, 6 December 1984, p 13; R Macdonald, H Qureshi and A Walker, *Sheffield Shows The Way: Elderly Persons Support Units*, Community Care, 18 October 1984, pp 28-30; R Wheeler, *Don't Move: We've got you covered*, The Institute of Housing and Age Concern, 1985.

12. S Slipman, *The Cost Of Caring*, The Guardian, 10 January 1986. A member of the SDP National Committee, she chaired the group which produced the report, *A National Community Volunteer Service Scheme*, an SDP policy document, 1986. A recent study clearly contradicts her argument. P Abrams, S Abrams, R Humphrey and R Snaith, *Creating Care In The Neighbourhood*, (ed) D Leat, Advance, 1986, found that "payment does not prevent caring relationships being formed between helper and clients".

13. RM Titmuss, *The Gift Relationship: From human blood to social policy*, George Allen and Unwin, 1970. Significantly where blood is paid for, it is the poorest people who most conspicuously supply it.

14. As Oliver has argued against "the myth that we do not support our elderly, disabled and dying" (J Oliver, *Who Cares?*, New Society, 23 May 1985, p 295), "precisely the same proportion of dependent people are cared for in institutions today as were in 1900 — 5 per cent. When one considers the vast increase in the numbers of dependent people it is apparent that we now care *more* for the disabled, dying and frail than has ever been the case in the past."

15. J Finch, *A Reponse To Robert Harris: "End Points And Starting Points"*, Critical Social Policy, Issue 12, Spring 1985, pp 123-126, p 124.

16. ·See, for example, H Salmon, *Unemployment: The two nations*, Association of Community Workers, 1984; B Jordan, *The State: Authority and autonomy*, Blackwell, 1985.

17. A Gorz, *Farewell To The Working Class*, Pluto Press, 1982.

18. H Braverman, *Labour And Monopoly Capital*, Monthly Review Press, New York, 1974, p 361.

19. *Social Workers: Their role and tasks*, (The Barclay Report), Bedford Square Press, 1982, para 3.58, p 47.

20. P Beresford and others, *In Care In North Battersea*, University of Surrey, 1986.

21. R Hadley and M McGrath, *When Social Services Are Local: The Normanton experience*, George Allen and Unwin, 1984. This reported that the bulk of the work social workers took on concerned family problems (41%) or financial problems (30%). Any formal referrals with statutory implications, such as delinquency or those involving family relationships, were normally allocated to a social worker. Qualified social workers dealt with more than half of family/children cases and only 4% of those involving care of elderly and disabled people. This perpetuation of traditional social work priorities was also reflected in the cases dealt with by patch workers. Care workers dealt with 6% of family/children cases and 36% of care of elderly and disabled people. Three quarters of their work concerned the physical care of elderly and

physically disabled people. They dealt with very few formal referrals. (see pp 86-88, 104-106.)
22. P Dale, *Trainer's Notes*, for *Patchwork* video, ESCATA, East Sussex Social Services Department, 1985.
23. P Gordon, *Community Policing: Towards the local police state?*, Critical Social Policy, Issue 10, Summer 1984, pp 39-58.
24. See, P Beresford and S Croft, *"A Person Rather Than A Policeman": The implications of community policing*, Community Care, 31 October 1985, pp 15-17.
25. (21) op cit, p 12; also see pp 8-15.
26. (21) op cit, p 8.
27. P Leonard, *A Paradigm For Radical Practice*, in R Bailey and M Brake, (eds), *Radical Social Work*, Edward Arnold, 1975, pp 46-61, p 50.
28. P Baldock, *Patch Systems: A radical change for the better?*, in I Sinclair and DN Thomas, (eds), *Perspectives On Patch*, NISW Paper No 14, 1983, pp 38-45, p 44.
29. SD Mackenzie, *Gender And Environment: The reproduction of labour in post-war Brighton*, unpublished Phd thesis, University of Sussex, 1983, Abstract and p 297.
30. I Cole and E Butterworth, *The Second Research Report: The Social Care Assembly for Normanton*, Department of Social Administration and Social Work, University of York, July 1984, pp 43-44.
31. Norman Fowler in a speech announcing the government review of the personal social services, Social Services Conference, September 1984.
32. Patrick Jenkin, formerly Secretary of State for Social Services and then Secretary of State for the Environment.
33. See, M Rutherford, *It's Dr Owen's Party Now*, Financial Times, 16 September 1983; W Rodgers, lecture to the Tawney Society, 16 May 1985, critical of the growing enthusiasm in the leadership of the SDP for a social market economic theory.
34. As, for example, has happened in Wandsworth where we live. See (20) op cit.
35. S Etherington and C Parker, *Time To Get Street-Wise*, Social Work Today, 13 May 1985, pp 13-14, p 14.
36. See, *Open Forum: Wider share ownership*, SDP, August 1985; N Bosanquet, *Services For Mentally Handicapped People In Britain 1968-82: A case study in the mixed economy of welfare*, paper for the Social Administration Association Conference 1983; and N Bosanquet, *Choose Or We Lose*, The Guardian, 27 July 1983, p 11.
37. R Williams, *Towards 2000*, Pelican, 1985, pp 27-29.
38. See, for example, the comments of Jef Smith, Director of Social Services in the London Borough of Ealing and member of the NCVO working party on clients' rights, *Give Consumers More Choice Urges Director*, Community Care, 20/27 December 1984, p 5. He argued that "We need to deliberately build in more choice. If you buy oranges in Kingston Market you can feel the oranges and I'd like to see choice in social services".
39. H Laming, *Lessons From America*, Policy Studies Institute, 1985; H Laming, *Striking It Richer Than Texan oil*, The Guardian, 11 June 1985.
40. Set up by Massachusetts State Statute, 1972. See also, *Children's Advocacy*, neighbourhood action guide, Massachusetts Office for Children, 1979.
41. *Socialists In Consumers' Clothing*, leader, Social Work Today, 17 December 1984, p 2.
42. It is used in East Sussex and elsewhere in this sense. See, for example, R Hadley, P Dale and P Sills, *Decentralising Social Services: A model for change*, Bedford Square Press, 1984, pp 4, 56; *Getting To Know The Neighbourhood*, in *Guidelines For Decentralised Teams*, ESCATA, East Sussex Social Services Department, 1984; R Hadley and M McGrath, *Going Local: Neighbourhood Social Services*, NCVO Occasional Paper One, Bedford Square Press, 1980, p 99. The idea is also explicit in the Barclay Report, (19) op cit, for example, p 199.
43. H Glennerster, *The Wilting Flowers Of Community Care*, Community Care, 12 September 1985, pp 19-20.
44. See, for example, N Deakin, *The Fashionable Choice*, Community Care, 18 April 1985, pp 12-14.
45. See, for example, (44) op cit, p 13; *"Future Labour Government Won't Give Up Powers"*, Claim, Community Care, 2 May 1985, p 5; J Mcdonnell, *Decentralisation And The New Social Relations*, Going Local?, No 1, Decentralisaton Research and Information Centre, Polytechnic of Central London, December 1984, p 1.
46. Current critiques of the "new urban left's" "local socialism", suggest that they have placed too much trust on the local state, neglecting its power. (See, for example, L Trinder, review of J Gyford, *The Politics Of Local Socialism*, Critical Social Policy, Issue 15, Spring 1986, pp 122-123.) Such criticisms fail to take account of the extent to which members of the new urban left have themselves become part of the local state having sought and gained political and bureaucratic

advancement within it, and more important failed to change the power structure. Indeed it is this that has so far been the key shortcoming of left-wing efforts at decentralisation.

47. M Bayley, R Seyd, A Tennant, *Summary Of Main Findings And Recommendations To The Department Of Health And Social Security*, Neighbourhood Services Project Dinnington, Department of Sociological Studies, University of Sheffield, 1985, pp 6, 8.

48. For example, both expressions are used by an East Sussex spokesperson in, R Hadley and M Cooper, (eds), *Patch Based Social Services Teams*: Bulletin No 3, Department of Social Administration, University of Lancaster, 1984, p 43.

49. This prescriptive approach also extends to the general decentralisation schemes that have emerged from the political left. The key issue of reconciling increased public involvement with their existing ideology and interests, is one that does not seem to have been resolved. Gyford, for example, in his discussion of local socialism (J Gyford, *The Politics Of Local Socialism*, George Allen and Unwin, 1985), raises the question as it concerns the left — if you set out to involve people more in local politics, devolving power, will the result necessarily be socialist? He identifies the Labour Party activist as the vital component to ensure that the answer is yes. We may not all share his trust that left-wing activists are the only true custodians of "socialism". Indeed, for us, a key problem of socialism which helps account for its marginality and perpetual fragmentation, is its effective exclusion of most people from active involvement, especially those most discriminated against in the wider society, and the dominance of structures and process favouring a narrow elitist activism. For us socialist thinking and policies *begin* with the broadbased involvement of citizens, rather than being jeopardised by it. This contradiction between traditional left "preceptoralism" and democratic involvement, facing the relatively small number of politicians and associated activists behind left decentralisation policies, may be one of the causes of the lack of commitment and ambivalence towards neighbourhood decentralisation that is now increasingly being argued. (See, for example, K Beuret and G Stoker, *The Labour Party And Neighbourhood Decentralisation: Flirtation or commitment?*, forthcoming.)

50. (47) op cit, p 7.

51. S Croft and P Beresford, *Soapbox*, Social Work Today, 21 October 1985, p 46.

CHAPTER ELEVEN

1. In a letter *Fundamental To Patch*, Social Work Today, 22 October 1984, p 3.

2. See, for example, M Simmons, *Becoming Part Of The Network*, Community Care, 8 August 1985, pp 23-25, is an example typical of the genre. For instance:

   I have been accepted into the social network by being known more intimately by the clients than I have ever been before. Sharing feelings about all sorts of things, my home life, politics, my family. The most touching closeness has come through my present pregnancy. Being pregnant in itself seemed to break down barriers as some people obviously thought social workers above such things, such comments as "I never thought you had it in you" and "What have you been doing" were amusing. (p 25)

3. *Social Workers: Their role and tasks*, (The Barclay Report), Bedford Square Press, 1982, p 33.

4. Outlined in its, *Guidelines For Decentralised Teams*, ESCATA, East Sussex Social Services Department, 1984.

5. See, R Hadley, P Dale and P Sills, *Decentralising Social Services: A model for change*, Bedford Square Press, 1984, pp 65-67. There was also an added emphasis on team development and a "community-based approach".

6. Voluntary agencies have been urged to follow essentially the same approach to needs and evaluation. See, for example, R Hedley, *Measuring Success: A guide to evaluation for voluntary and community groups*, Advance, 1985.

7. A Glampson, T Scott, DN Thomas, *A Guide To The Assessment Of Community Needs And Resources*, National Institute For Social Work, fifth printing, 1982.

8. (7) op cit, pp 6-7.

9. (7) op cit, p 9 and following; and (4) op cit.

10. (7) op cit. East Sussex follows the framework suggested by the NISW guide closely and offers it as recommended reading for patch teams. See (4) op cit, sections on "Setting objectives",

"Getting to know the neighbourhood", and "Assessing community needs and resources".

11. (3) op cit, pp 254-5. See also P Beresford and S Croft, 'A Person Rather Than A Policeman': Community policing and community social work, Community Care, 31 October 1985, pp 15-17.

12. (3) op cit, p 255.

13. (7) op cit, pp 29-32.

14. (7) op cit, pp 76-77.

15. For a discussion of similar issues and dilemmas arising when Mass Observation was used by the Ministry of Information in the second world war, see, N Hibbin, I Was A Mass Observer, New Statesman, 31 May 1985, pp34-35.

16. (3) op cit, p 133.

17. (7) op cit, pp 2-7.

18. (5) op cit, p 70.

19. (5) op cit, p 70.

20. (5) op cit, p 70.

21. (4) op cit. See section on "Assessing community needs and resources".

22. (5) op cit, pp 73-75.

23. For example, J Black, R Bowl, D Burns, C Critcher, G Grant, D Stockford, Social Work In Context: A comparative study of three social services teams, Tavistock, 1983.

24. A Stanton, Participatory research on collective working with Newcastle Family Service Unit, forthcoming.

25. (5) op cit, p 70.

26. Personal communication, Jocelyn Cornwell, 15 May 1985.

27. J Cornwell, Hard Earned Lives: Accounts of health and illness from East London, Tavistock, 1984. See also A Karpf's review of her book, New Statesman, 22 March 1985, p 29. These issues of inequalities of power within research which seeks people's accounts have also been raised and helpfully discussed by feminist writers like Oakley. See, for example, A Oakley, Interviewing Women: A contradiction in terms, in H Roberts, (ed), Doing Feminist Research, Routledge, pp 30-61, p 58.

28. BJ Hall, Participatory Research, Popular Knowledge And Power: A personal reflection, Convergence, vol 7 No 1, USA, 1981.

29. (28) op cit.

30. I Taylor, P Walton, J Young, Critical Criminology In Britain: Review and prospects, Routledge, 1975, pp 26-27.

31. T Gibson, People Power: Community and work groups in action, Penguin, 1979, p 119.

32. See, for example Rowbotham's discussion of building shared meanings and consciousness moving in: S Rowbotham, Problems Of Organisation And Strategy, in Dreams And Dilemmas, Virago, 1983, pp 65-67, pp 67-68.

> You are doing explicitly what you did implicitly in little pockets of female defensiveness before.... You are not only learning a new picture of how things are together, you are creating your own very important strength. You are trusting other women. You are consciousness moving (p 68).

33. C Satyamurti, Occupational Survival: The case of the local authority social worker, Blackwell, 1981.

34. N Murray, 'We're Trying To Run A People-centred Authority', Community Care, 13 June 1985, pp 20-22.

35. M Parenti, Power And Pluralism: A view from the bottom, Journal of Politics, 32, USA, 1970, pp 501-530.

36. J Gaventa, Power And Powerlessness: Quiescence and rebellion in an Appalachian valley, Clarendon Press, 1980, p 12.

37. See, E Pilkington, Looking For New Friends, New Statesman, 5 April 1985, pp 8-9; and D Thomas, Tortoise In The Works, New Society, 7 June 1985, pp 365-366.

38. For example, this appears a potential problem with the London Borough of Islington's proposals for neighbourhood forums. See Guidelines For The Establishment Of Neighbourhood Forums, Agenda Item Appendix "A", Policy and Partnership Committee, London Borough of Islington, 11 February 1986, pp 9-10 and para 12.13.

39. See, for example, A Rae, For, Not Of, Community Care, 11 July 1985, p 11. This described the setting up of the GLC's London Consortium On Disability, "to provide a forum for the genuine voice of disabled people in London's affairs", and the GLC's inability to understand "the crucially important difference between organisations for and of disabled people".

40. See Statement Of Disassociation, GLC Claimants Commission First Report July 1985, GLC, pp 22-23.

41. Cope *Annual Report, 1984-85*; Cope Conference, *Community Partnerships: Problems and priorities*, 16 October 1985; P Beresford, *Responses to Partnership*, paper given at 1985 Cope Conference.
42. P Hoggett and J Bishop, *The Social Organisation Of Leisure: A Study of groups in their voluntary sector context*, Sports Council and ESRC, 1985; and *Organising Around Enthusiasms: Patterns of mutual aid in leisure*, Comedia, 1986.
43. O Stevenson and P Parsloe, *Social Service Teams: The practitioner's view*, HMSO, 1978.
44. P Freire, *Pedagogy Of The Oppressed*, Penguin, 1972.
45. See P Beresford and M Richardson, *Deschooling Social Work*, Battersea Community Action, 1979.
46. See, for example, JJ Mansbridge, *Beyond Adversary Democracy*, University of Chicago, USA, 1983, p 70 and following. It can equally be the case for people among those they *do* know.
47. *Report Of The Committee On Local Authority And Allied Personal Social Services*, Cmnd 3703, HMSO, 1968; and (3) op cit.
48. (5) op cit, p 23.
49. P Dale, R Hadley and P Sills, *Training For Decentralisation: East Sussex Social Services' experience*, Training Newsletter, Sept/Oct 1985. p 7.
50. (5) op cit, pp 68-69, 116, 115, 101.
51. T Huntingford, "Soapbox", Social Work Today, 30 September 1985, p 54.
52. See J Freeman (Also known as Joreen), *The Tyranny Of Structurelessness*, Dark Star, 1982; and C Levine, *The Tyranny of Tyranny*, Dark Star, 1983. The issue is not that hidden power is a characteristic confined to less formal organisation and structures (with Freeman's argument being misread to suggest that "too much informality leads to undemocratic practices and the emergence of elites"), but that unless the problem is recognised and resolved, hidden power is likely to be present in them, just as it is in formal organisations.
53. H Ouseley, *"Treating Them All The Same": Decentralising institutional racism*, Going Local?, Newsletter of the Decentralisation Research and Information Centre, No 2, April 1985, pp 8-9.
54. (53) op cit, p 9.
55. See, for example, *The Management Committees Issue*, Management Development Unit Bulleting, NCVO, No 5, June 1985; and putting this in context, R Williams, *Towards 2,000*, Pelican, 1985, pp 38, 42.
56. See particularly the work of A Stanton on collectively working teams, for example, (24), op cit.
57. R Pinker, *Against The Flow*, Community Care, 18 April 1985, pp 20-22, p 22.
58. (23) op cit, p 212.
59. See letters in Community Care, 10 January 1985, 14 February 1985, and 28 February 1985.
60. A Walker, for example, discusses developments in Sheffield; see *From Charring to Caring*, The Guardian, 2 October 1985, and *The Care Gap: How can local authorities meet the needs of the elderly?*, Local Government Information Unit, 1985.
61. See, for example, J Seabrook, *The Idea of Neighbourhood: What local politics should be about*, Pluto, 1984.

APPENDIX 1: RESEARCH METHOD

1. P and S Beresford, *A Say In The Future: Planning, participation and meeting social need*, Battersea Community Action, 1978. People's responses were written on blank paper rather than pre-printed questionnaires, allowing as much space as they needed for their comments.
2. *1981 Census Small Area Statistics For The Hanover Patch*, and for the *Survey Area For The Hanover Patch*. Figures for social class came from 10 percent sample data — a classification of jobs. East Sussex Social Services,, SPME Unit.
3. From Table B 1981 Census Small Area Statistics For Hanover Patch, (2) op cit.
4. From Table 52, *1981 Census Small Area Statistics For Hanover Patch*, 10 percent sample, (2) op cit.
5. From Table 10, *1981 Census Small Area Statistics For Hanover Patch*, (2) op cit.
6. Table F, *1981 Census Small Area Statistics For Hanover Patch*, (2) op cit.
7. Based on Table D, *1981 Census Small Area Statistics For Hanover Patch*, (2) op cit.
8. From Table D, (7) op cit.
9. From Table D, (7) op cit.
10. Table E, *1981 Census Small Area Statistics For Hanover Patch*, (2) op cit.

11. In the case of those people not interviewed, age classification was again based on the estimate of the interviewer. Social class was estimated according to accent, appearance, home decor — as seen through the front door — and in some cases there was sufficient conversation to establish people's occupational status.
12. (1) op cit, p 74 and following.
13. (1) op cit, p 14.

FURTHER READING

Readers who want to can pursue some of the topics we have raised through this list of books and articles. It is not intended to be comprehensive, but to open up areas we've covered and their controversies. We have grouped material accordingly. We'd refer readers who want a more detailed bibliography to our **Notes and References**

Patch In East Sussex

R Hadley, P Dale and P Sills, *Decentralising Social Services: A model for change*, Bedford Square Press, 1984.

QuéenSpark Rates Book Group, *Brighton On The Rocks: Monetarism and the local state*, QueenSpark New Series 1, 1983.

Patch And Community Social Work

Social Workers: Their role and tasks, (The Barclay Report), Bedford Square Press, 1982.

R Hadley and M McGrath, *When Social Services Are Local: The Normanton experience*, National Institute Social Services Library No. 48, George Allen and Unwin, 1984.

M Bayley, P Parker, R Seyd, K Simons and A Tennant, *Neighbourhood Services Project Dinnington*, Working Papers 1-12, Department of Sociological Studies, University of Sheffield, 1981-5.

P Beresford, *Patch In Perspective: Decentralising and democratising social services*, Battersea Community Action, 1984.

New Approaches To Research

S Croft and P Beresford, *Patch And Participation: The case for citizen research*, Social Work Today, 17 September 1984, pp 18-24.

H Roberts, (ed), *Doing Feminist Research*, Routledge, 1981.

P Reason and J Rowan, (eds), *Human Inquiry: A source book of new paradigm research*, John Wiley, 1981.

Women and Caring

J Finch and D Groves, *Community Care And The Family: A case for equal opportunities?*, Journal of Social Policy, Vol 9, 1980, pp 486-511

J Finch and D Groves, (eds), *A Labour Of Love: Women, work and caring*, Routledge, 1983.

Women As Carers Conference: Breaking down the barriers — a report back on the Women as Carers Conference organised by the GLC Women's Committee, GLC, 1986.

Strategies For Social Welfare

R Hadley and S Hatch, *Social Welfare And The Failure Of The State: Centralised social services and participatory alternatives*, George Allen and Unwin, 1981.

P Beresford and S Croft, *Welfare Pluralism: The new face of fabianism*, Critical Social Policy, Issue 9, Spring 1984, pp 19-39.

D Whitfield, *Making It Public: The case against privatisation*, Pluto, 1982.

P Stubbs, *The Employment Of Black Social Workers: From "ethnic sensitivity" to "anti-racism"?*, Critical Social Policy, Issue 12, Spring 1985, pp 6-27.

H Sharron, *Meeting The Ethnic Challenge*, Social Work Today, 6 August 1984, pp 9-11.

S Croft and P Beresford, *Towards A Social Strategy*, discussion paper, Battersea Community Action, 1983.

Decentralisation

R Hambleton and P Hoggett, (eds), *The Politics Of Decentralisation: Theory and practice of a radical local government initiative*, Working Paper 46, School for Advanced Urban Studies, University of Bristol, 1985.

J Gyford, *The Politics Of Local Socialism*, George Allen and Unwin, 1985.

H Ouseley, *"Treating Them All The Same" — Decentralising institutionalised racism*, Going Local?: Newsletter of the Decentralisation Research and Information Centre, No 2, Polytechnic of Central London, April 1985, pp 8-9.

S Croft and P Beresford, *Making Our Own Plans*, Chartist, February/April 1983, pp 26-27.

Participation

A Richardson, *Participation*, Concepts in Social Policy One, Routledge, 1983.

N Boaden, M Goldsmith, W Hampton and P Stringer, *Public Participation In Local Services*, Longman, 1982.

A Stanton, *Windows On Collective Working: Questions and themes*, Department of Social Policy, Cranfield Institute of Technology, 1984.

P Beresford, *Public Participation And The Redefinition Of Social Policy*, in C Jones and J Stevenson, (eds), *The Year Book Of Social Policy In Britain 1980-81*,

Routledge, 1982, pp 20-41.

P Williams and B Shoultz, *We Can Speak For Ourselves: Self-advocacy by mentally handicapped people*, Human Horizons Series, Souvenir Press, 1982.